Video Production Handbook

MIDLOTHIAN
PUBLIC LIBRARY

Video Production Handbook
Third edition

Gerald Millerson

Focal Press

OXFORD AMSTERDAM BOSTON LONDON NEW YORK PARIS
SAN DIEGO SAN FRANCISCO SINGAPORE SYDNEY TOKYO

Focal Press
An imprint of Elsevier Science
Linacre House, Jordan Hill, Oxford OX2 8DP
225 Wildwood Avenue, Woburn, MA 01801-2041

First published 1987
Reprinted 1988, 1989
Second edition 1992
Reprinted 1993 (twice), 1994, 1995 (twice), 1998, 1999, 2000
Third edition 2001
Reprinted 2002

British Library Cataloguing in Publication Data
Millerson, Gerald
    Video production handbook. – 3rd ed.
    1. Video recordings   2. Video recordings – Production and
    direction
    I. Title
    778.5'9

Library of Congress Cataloguing in Publication Data
Millerson, Gerald.
    Video production handbook/Gerald Millerson. – 3rd ed.
    p. cm.
    ISBN 0-240-51597-8 (alk. paper)
    1. Video tape recorders and recording.   2. Video recordings –
    Production and direction.
    I. Title.
    TK6655.V5 M55
    778.59–dc21   2001018933

ISBN 0 240 51597 8

For more information on all Focal Press publications
visit our website at www.focalpress.com

Composition by Genesis Typesetting, Rochester, Kent
Printed and bound in Great Britain

Contents

Preface to the third edition

This book has been specially designed to save you time and effort, to give you essential facts in an interesting, easily digested form. So let's start immediately by answering some basic questions.

What is this book all about?

It is a journey into the basics of budget program-making with the video camera; whether you are working alone, or with a small multi-camera crew.

It covers the techniques and organization involved in transforming the ideas in your head into a persuasive presentation on the screen. It is an introductory workbook, showing you how to use your video and audio equipment effectively.

Whether your aim is to instruct, inform or entertain, you will find here sure-fire methods enabling you to produce interesting results at minimum expense.

There is no substitute for hands-on experience, and the know-how you will develop as you work through this book will provide a firm foundation for your future studies. We shall be concentrating on the *practical* features of video program-making, so that you achieve encouraging, worthwhile results right from the start, even with quite modest facilities. This book will help you to get the best out of your equipment.

Who is the book written for?

It is designed for anyone, anywhere, using a video camera, wanting high-grade results on a modest budget.

It will be particularly helpful for a wide range of communications and audio-visual students using video in community colleges, high schools, university courses, training schools, etc.

You may be:

● taking an introductory course in TV production
● working on a class project

- using video in the classroom as a teaching aid
- making programs for work training, promotions, sales, staff instruction, etc.
- in a local access CATV group
- an enthusiastic hobbyist

The same underlying production principles apply whether you are on the beach, shooting the family vacation, or in a well-equipped studio making commercial instructional programs.

This text does not assume that you have a technical background, or any previous experience – or that you are really interested in the nuts and bolts of the equipment.

We are going to discuss the basics of good picture-making, and good audio, that underlie persuasive program-making. Why spend your time and effort making poor video programs that leave your audience bored, puzzled or sceptical, when you can create an interesting, even memorable production?

Do I have sufficient equipment?

Even if you have modest equipment, and little or no assistance, there is no reason why you should not make really successful programs. This book will help you to make the most of your system.

Its text is keyed to *low-budget production*. But 'low budget' does not mean 'second best'. High-grade results come from know-how and imagination.

Isn't all this equipment complicated to use?

Although you need to understand certain techniques to get the best out of your equipment, you will find that good handling quickly becomes a habit.

Television is a highly technical medium. But so is the technology behind your home TV, your calculator; your phone . . .! Concentrate on learning how to handle your equipment effectively, leave the expert to worry about the technicalities, and keep it up to top performance.

Why do we need to learn 'techniques'?

Great ideas do not automatically make great programs. It is not enough simply to show what is going on. The *way* you present your subject will influence how your audience responds. You need to choose your picture and sound carefully, to convey your ideas in an interesting persuasive way. Use them carelessly, and your production can become a *bore*!

How can this book be used?

As a conventional *class textbook* it can provide the material of course lectures, leaving students free to concentrate on what the instructor is saying, without the preoccupations of extensive note-taking. Any class-notes or supplementary information can be margin annotated to personalize the text.

Using this book as a *preparatory study text* students can learn relevant principles at their own pace before each tuition period. This not only relieves the teacher of repetitive formal lecturing on basics, but enables precious class-time to be devoted to group involvement. So there are increased opportunities for check-questions, discussions, demonstrations, practical work and critiques.

As a tutorial workbook, the text is ideal for *self-paced home study*, for its step-by-step coverage helps the reader, through theory and practice, to build up a self-assured appreciation of principles.

And then?

For those who want to explore aspects of television production in greater detail, there are the author's companion books, all published by Focal Press:

Television Production (13th edition)

Effective TV Production (3rd edition)

Video Camera Techniques (2nd edition)

TV Scenic Design (2nd edition)

Lighting for Video (3rd edition)

Lighting for Television and Film (3rd edition)

Remember!

The video camera and recorder give you an enormous advantage. You can check your results as you shoot! Unlike the film-maker, who has to wait for processing before seeing results, you can make sure that you have the best possible version, shoot alternatives perhaps, experiment, for the videotape is reusable. The result is that you can make comparisons in techniques, correct errors, and *learn faster!*

Terminology

It can be disconcerting to discover that the technical terms or expressions regularly used by one production group sound quite strange or idiosyncratic to another. Some refer to the person operating the camera as a '*cameraman*' (whatever their actual gender), while elsewhere this is a '*camera operator, camera person, videographer*,' or even a '*shooter*'. There are variations, too, in the terminology used to describe the camera's shots and various operations. Some people speak of '*filming*' with their camcorders, rather than '*shooting video*'. We've tried to include the commonest terms in this book; but obviously the best solution is to use those your team understands, and is most comfortable with.

A final word

Over recent years there have been exciting advances in equipment available for program-makers working on a modest budget. Digital technology and the extension of computer-based programs have transformed many facilities, allowing us to produce results comparable with costly professional equipment. Cameras and video recorders provide us with greatly enhanced picture and sound quality. Ingenious software allows us to create outstanding graphics and video effects with regular desktop computers. Precise editing techniques have become possible for video and sound, that previously required elaborate facilities.

Video Production Handbook has been updated and extended to reflect this world of opportunities. My sincere thanks to program-makers who have suggested various ways in which the text could be developed to suit current video courses.

As always, we are mainly concerned here with principles and practices; for these are the timeless essentials of persuasive video production. Even more know-how has been crammed into this new edition, to help your programs to have greater audience appeal and to aid you with the problems you will encounter in the real world.

The great thing about video production today is the way in which program-makers are increasingly stretching their facilities to develop polished, imaginative productions. In the end, what really matters is what you have to say and how you say it!

Chapter 1

The way ahead

The special features and opportunities of the video medium.

1.1 What is video production?

The differences between 'video production' and 'television production' have become increasingly blurred.

Most 'video production' is concerned with *non-broadcast* program-making. Productions are recorded *closed-circuit on videotape, distributed, and viewed by a small audience.*

Television productions, on the other hand, are usually broadcast, i.e. shown to a large public audience by over-air or cable transmission – either 'live' (during performance) or 'taped' (carefully edited video recordings).

In practice though, you'll find broadcast material packaged for home or closed-circuit viewing, and see video productions aired in broadcast programs (e.g. music videos and pop promos).

Television transmissions are obliged to conform to closely controlled technical standards. Equipment is in constant use for many hours daily, so needs to be stable, robust, reliable, and capable of continuous high-grade output. Video productions are made with equipment ranging from the most sophisticated professional broadcast standards, to low-cost consumer items.

There is no intrinsic reason though, why the screened end-products should differ in quality, style or effectiveness as far as the audience is concerned. Video programs today range from ambitious presentations intended for mass distribution, to economically budgeted programs designed for particular audience sectors. This book will help you, whatever the scale of your production.

Breaking the ice

1.2 The need for 'know-how'

Video production appears deceptively simple. After all, the video camera gives us an immediate picture of the scene before us, and the microphone picks up the sound of the action. Most of us start by pointing our camera and microphone at the subject hopefully, but find the results pretty unsatisfying. Why? Is it the equipment or us? It may be a little of both. But the odds are, that it is *us*!

As you may have discovered already, there is no magic recipe for creating attractive interesting programs. All successful production springs from a foundation of *know-how*.

1 Knowing how to handle your equipment properly. The effects of its various controls.
2 Knowing how to use your equipment effectively. The skills underlying good camerawork and sound pick-up.
3 Knowing how to convey your ideas convincingly. Using the medium persuasively.
4 Knowing how to organize systematically. Practical planning, preparing, and operations.

As you work through this book, the know-how you develop will soon become part of your regular approach to program-making. Knowing what your equipment can do, will enable you to select the right tool for the job, and use it in the right way. Remember, in the end, clumsy operation and inappropriate treatment get between you and your audience!

1.3 It's designed for you

Many people are scared of technology. There's even a name for it: *technophobia*! But however unfamiliar the various units may be at first, remember, most equipment has been designed for speedy uncomplicated handling.

After all, it is there for one fundamental purpose – *to enable you to communicate your ideas to an audience!* Video equipment is as much a communication tool as a typewriter or a telephone.

1.4 First impressions

We all feel a little stupid when we have to operate equipment for the first time! We are apprehensive about which controls to use, and exactly what will happen when we operate them. Some people adopt a 'try it and see' approach – but this can be pretty frustrating, even disastrous. It needs self-control to find out step by step, and patiently build up techniques.

And then there is that private embarrassment most of us have when all these new technical terms come pouring in. Our minds block off, our eyes grow glassy, and mental ear-muffs descend! Take heart, this phase soon passes. Don't let technology scare you off! It really is surprising how rapidly it all becomes a daily routine, as you acquire confidence and get the right results every time.

As for your equipment – if it has been well designed, adjusted and serviced, it will reward you with reliable performance (provided you treat it with care).

1.5 Learning basics

You don't need to know *how* equipment works, but you should know *what* it does if you are going to get reliable results.

Even with the most sophisticated video and audio equipment, you need to know the answer to only a handful of basic questions to use it successfully:

What is the equipment *for*?
What can it *do*?
What are its *limitations*?
Where are the *controls* and any *indicators* (lights, meters, etc.)?
How and when do I *adjust* them?
What is the *result* when I do so?
Can I cause any problems (or damage) by *misusing* them?

1.6 Remember the purpose

There is no short cut to experience. As you handle equipment, you grow increasingly familiar with its peculiarities.

But don't let slick handling preoccupy you. Many a raw camera operator, has tried to show panache by zipping around, fast zooming and cute composition – where an experienced one would have avoided these distractions, and held a steady shot, letting the subject work to the camera instead!

Smooth accurate operation is important, but *appropriateness* is even more desirable. In the end, it is *audience-impact* that really counts – the effect your camera treatment has on your viewer.

1.7 Resources

Nowadays, it is true to say that, for certain subjects, a single person with sufficient time, talent, experience, and suitable equipment, can make great video productions unaided at home. Topics ranging from coin collecting to electronics, from agriculture to archeology, can be treated effectively with minimal resources. However, decide to tackle drama or make a documentary, and it's a very different ball-game!

Clearly, the kind of equipment and technical knowledge you need for your production, will really depend on the sort of programs you are going to make. If for instance, you are using video as a living picture album, to capture memories of the family and recall enjoyable vacations, then you might even find that just a video camera and a videotape deck connected to your regular TV set will suffice.

But if you aim to make carefully staged packaged productions, with precise editing, music and effects, you will find that more flexible facilities are necessary. Successful productions usually depend on teamwork; each member of that team contributing their individual expertise and experience.

1.8 Simplicity

Don't get preoccupied with hardware! You do not need elaborate or extensive facilities to produce successful programs. Even the simplest equipment may provide you with the essentials you need. It really depends on the type of presentation you are involved in. For some purposes, one camera is ideal. For others, a dozen may be insufficient.

Of course, you may be hampered occasionally if you do not have a special gizmo that enables you, for example, to produce a multi-segment screen, or turn the picture upside-down. But surprisingly often there is another method of achieving similar or equally effective results. *What* you do is more important than *how* you do it. If you can get an effective moving shot along a hospital corridor by shooting from a wheelchair, rather than a special camera-dolly, your audience will not know – or care!

Sometimes extra 'goodies' on your equipment can tempt you to use them *because they are there*, rather than because you *need* them! You will see examples every day on broadcast TV where wipes, star filters or diffused shots are used in the wrong place, at the wrong time, just for the sake of variety; because they are readily to hand.

What appears at first sight to be sophisticated, stylish presentation, may have far less impact on your audience than a single still shot that lingers to show someone's expression.

The versatility of video

The video medium

- The TV camera provides you with an instant image in full color.
- Video cameras may be automated, and can be remotely controlled.
- Video pictures can span from the microscopic to the infinities of outer space.
- Video pictures from several sources can be combined (inset, split screen).
- The image can be modified and manipulated. (Color, tonal values, shape and form, sharpness, etc.)

Video presentation

- The video picture can be shown on screens ranging from pocket-size to giant display. From a single screen to a 'videowall' (multi-screen) display.
- The video signal can be distributed instantly by cable (wire, fiber-optic), wireless transmitter or infra-red link, satellite.
- Video pictures can be intercut, superimposed, or blended in various ways.
- All forms of photographic material can be televised (photo-stills, slides, film of any type).
- Video artwork can be created electronically (computer graphic).
- Titles, text, patterns can be generated electronically (computers, character generators).
- A video image can be printed onto paper in full color (photographic, printers).

Video recording

- The video signal can be stored in several forms (photographic, magnetic tape or disc – using analogue or digital recording).
- Video recordings can be played back immediately, and replayed many times. It can be stored indefinitely.
- Videotape can be wiped in selected parts, or completely. New recordings can be made on the erased tape.
- Videotape recordings can be reproduced at faster or slower speeds than normal. A single moment of action can be frozen ('still frame', 'freeze frame'). A day's events can be played back in a few seconds.
- Taped programs can be edited to omit faulty or irrelevant shots, enhance the presentation, adjust program duration, etc.
- Video programs can be transferred to standard motion picture film for projection.

Recorded sound

- The action sound normally recorded in synchronism with the picture on videotape recording, can be augmented or replaced (e.g. music, commentary).

Limitations

- There are many incompatible video-recording systems.
- Video tape is easily damaged or destroyed.
- Tape faults or damage result in picture defects of various kinds.
- To select individual shots from the tape, it is necessary to play or spool (fast wind) through it. Tape has to be rewound after play through.
- When tape is copied during editing or devising special effects, picture quality deteriorates.
- Tape wear develops during freeze-frame replay.

1.9 What facilities do I need?

Fundamentally, there are two extreme approaches to using equipment:

'I have this gear; now what can I do with it?' or

'I want to do a particular job. What equipment do I need for it?'

If truth be told, most of us tend to start by experimenting quite a lot. We seek opportunities to use all the various bells and whistles available, even where they are not really appropriate. After all, that's part of our natural learning process. With experience though, we generally develop a more discriminating approach.

Let's take a look at the sort of issues that affect the equipment you need.

When working with a larger production unit, one usually has access to a wide range of facilities. If extra items are needed, they are hired or rented from a production house (facility house). You've only to look through any manufacturer's or supplier's catalogue, or a video magazine, to see the endless variety of equipment available!

On the other hand, in a small unit production you usually need to work within the limitations of your *existing* equipment; unless it proves possible to augment it in some way. A lot is going to depend on the kind of program you are making, and on your particular approach to the subject:

- **Productional style**. Even an apparently straightforward situation can be tackled in a number of quite different ways. Each will have its merits and its drawbacks. Supposing, for example, you are shooting two people talking together (an interview, or general conversation). You can treat this formally, shooting them seated at a desk. Or informally, resting in easy chairs. But to create a more natural ambiance, you might have one of them working at a task (e.g. mending a fence) while the other looks on. Alternatively, they might be shot walking side by side along a pathway. Another familiar approach is to shoot them within a car as they drive to their destination.
- Think about these variants for a moment. In each case there are restrictions for the camera and sound treatment. In one situation, the camera can be held firmly on a fixed mounting; in another the camera

will probably need a wheeled dolly; while in another it will be necessary to carry the camera on a shoulder, or even attach it to the vehicle itself. Sound pickup problems, too, will vary. Clearly, how you shoot the action and where it takes place, will affect the optimum gear for the job.

● **Shooting circumstances**. You can find that equipment which is essential for some situations (e.g. an underwater camera) proves quite unsuitable for other projects. While you need a robust camera mounting for sustained shooting, it could be an encumbrance if you need to continually reposition your camera in crowded surroundings. At times, even a microphone may be superfluous if you are going to shoot 'mute', and add all the sound content to the silent shots during editing.

1.10 Is there a right way?

Creating a program is a very subjective process. Newcomers soon get the hang of the basic mechanics, but learning how to use equipment to persuade an audience and influence their reactions is another matter entirely. Some 'creative' or 'original' productional styles can be a pain to watch: e.g. a rapid succession of unrelated shots; or fast intercutting between different viewpoints, hoping to create an illusion of 'excitement' and 'pace' for a rather dull subject. After a while such techniques only succeed in annoying, confusing, or boring the audience.

Figure 1.1 The versaility of video

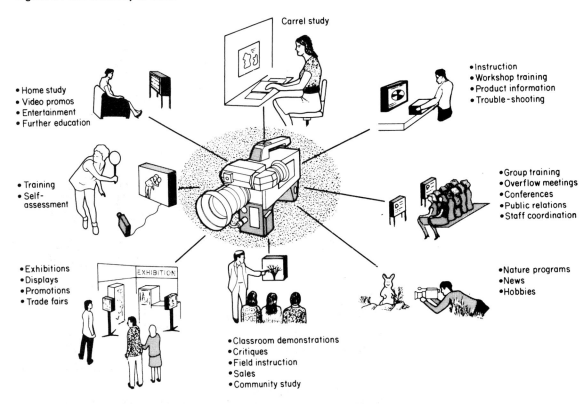

Carrel study

● Instruction
● Workshop training
● Product information
● Trouble-shooting

● Home study
● Video promos
● Entertainment
● Further education

● Group training
● Overflow meetings
● Conferences
● Public relations
● Staff coordination

● Training
● Self-assessment

● Exhibitions
● Displays
● Promotions
● Trade fairs

EXHIBITION

● Nature programs
● News
● Hobbies

● Classroom demonstrations
● Critiques
● Field instruction
● Sales
● Community study

You can learn a lot by studying videotaped TV shows; particularly those covering the topics you are interested in emulating. Review them over and over, and you will see that while some approaches are little more than stereotyped routines, others have an individuality and flow that is sympathetic to their subject matter. Adjust your own approach to suit the occasion, rather than imitate 'the way things are always done'. If what you are doing does not have the particular impact you are aiming at, it is *wrong*!

1.11 Your productional approach

Preoccupied with ideas about how you are going to tackle your subject, it's easy to overlook a lot of down-to-earth issues that have to be faced at some time or other, such as:

costing, availability of facilities, labor, materials, scheduling, safety issues, weather conditions, transportation, accommodation, legalities . . . and so on.

Again, a lot is going to depend on the program you have in mind. And at the same time, your opportunities must inevitably be affected by the expertise and experience of your production group, the program budget, the

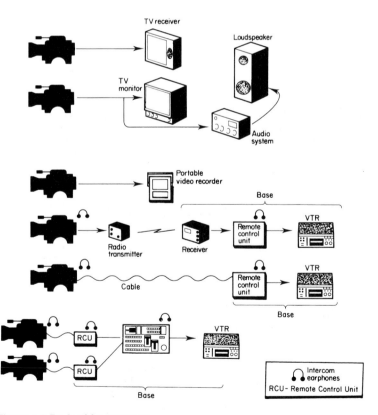

Figure 1.2 Basic video systems
The flexibility of video equipment allows you to arrange it in a number of ways

equipment you are using, the time available, and similar factors. But with a little imagination and ingenuity, you can often overcome limitations or at least leave your audience quite unaware that there were any. Later we shall be exploring typical stratagems that enable you to do just that.

At an early stage you should have given a deal of thought to your audience, settling such basic questions as

- **Who are you making this program for?** An individual to watch (at home or carrel study), or a group of people? Is it for the general public or for a specialized audience?
- **Is this to be a broadly-based program or for a specific audience?** Is it targeted at prospective customers (e.g. an advertising display) or for delivery to a student group, or an in-house symposium? Perhaps it is intended for home study?
- **What is its main purpose?** Is it to *entertain*? Are you seeking to amuse, excite, intrigue? Or is your show *imparting information*: e.g. to guide, to list statistics? You could be *demonstrating methods*: e.g. showing how to make or repair something. Are you aiming to *persuade* your audience: e.g. to visit a particular place; or encouraging them to make a purchase? Or even *warning* them against doing so?

The style you adopt for your production, the pace of delivery, how you give emphasis to points will all be determined by the program's purpose. You'll find a list of reminders in Chapter 10.

Technicalities

1.12 Equipment performance

Thanks to careful design, even the most complex equipment continues to perform faultlessly for long periods with little attention. But it is

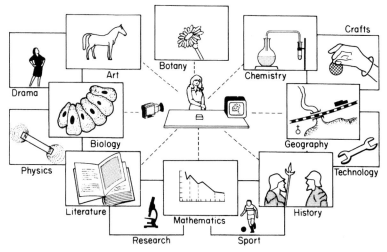

Figure 1.3 The classroom camera
Video in the classroom provides a valuable tool that can extend normal teaching opportunities.

good practice to make very regular checks, and carry out routine maintenance.

It is simple enough to check that parts are clean (lenses, tape heads), that controls are working correctly and ready for use. Even the simple action of running a head-cleaner tape through a recorder at intervals, will reduce the likelihood of problems during taping sessions.

Whether you carry out equipment checks yourself, make basic readjustments, or have the services of an experienced engineer to keep its performance up to specification, will depend of course, on your particular circumstances; on how much you understand about that particular piece of equipment, and the test gear you have. It is quite practicable for instance to adjust a series of preset controls on a vectorscope to place markers within their appropriate boxes, without having the slightest idea what is happening technically within the circuitry.

But remember, don't tweak controls unless you know what is going to happen, and you can correct any mistakes!

1.13 Technical basics

Although you don't need to know how your equipment actually works to use it effectively, it certainly does help if you have a general idea about the purpose of the various units in the video and audio system. So in Chapter 13 we shall look at a general outline of the way video works, and typical units you may meet in the video chain.

Chapter 2

Meet your camera

Get to know your camera's controls so well that you use them instinctively.

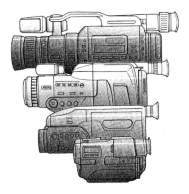

Figure 2.1 Consumer cameras
A wide range of excellent designs is available in the consumer market, from *palmcorders* to *lightweight systems*.

2.1 A range of designs

Video cameras today come in a variety of shapes and sizes, to suit all pockets and applications. They range from units as small as a peanut, to broadcast cameras that need a couple of people to lift them. Performance ranges from satisfactory to state of the art.

You can use a video camera as stand-alone unit, or combine it with others in a multi-camera production.

You can record the video camera's picture on a separate videorecorder – either a VCR (video cassette recorder) or a VTR (reel-to-reel system). This can be carried in a backpack, a shoulder bag, or on a small wheeled cart.

An increasing number of video cameras take the form of *camcorders*, with a VCR either built-in to the camera unit, or attached at its rear.

Another approach is to fix a radio transmitter to the camera, and to pick up both picture and sound at a mobile support vehicle/base station (a station wagon or truck), where the program is recorded and/or passed on to a studio center.

2.2 Cameracraft

It is very easy to operate any video camera. Designers have gone to a lot of trouble to make controls simple to use. Popular hobbyist cameras have been so automated, that you need do little more than point them at the subject, and press a button to get results. If you are shooting for fun, and just snapshooting around, that's fine. Why make camerawork any more complicated?

It really depends on whether you are aiming to use your camera as a *creative tool*. The weakness of automatic controls, is that your camera can only be designed to make *technical* judgments. And these are usually something of a compromise. It can't make *artistic* choices of any kind. Auto-circuitry can help you to avoid poor-quality pictures, but you can't rely on it to produce attractive, meaningful pictures. Picture appeal will always depend on how *you* use your camera, and the choices *you* make.

As you will see, good picture-making is much more than just 'getting the shot'. It begins with the way you handle your camera, and use its controls. It is not just a matter of getting the shot sharp, but of selecting which parts of the scene are to be sharp, and which are soft focus. It involves carefully selecting your viewpoint, and arranging the framing and composition for maximum impact; deciding what is to be included in the shot, and what is to be left out. It is the art of adjusting picture tones by careful exposure.

Automatic camera circuitry can help, particularly when shooting under difficult conditions, and save you from having to worry about technicalities at all. But it cannot create meaningful pictures for you.

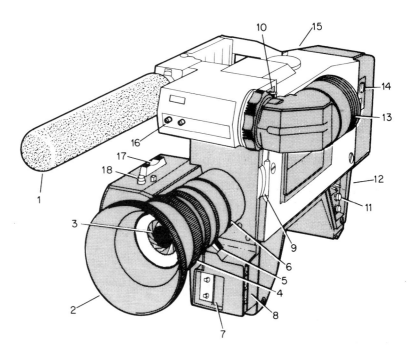

Figure 2.2 (A) Parts of the camera
Camera designs vary, but the following are typical facilities found in the video camera:
  1 Microphone – electret, unidirectional
  2 Lens hood
  3 Lens aperture (iris) – e.g. f/1.6 max.
  4 Focus control
  5 Manual zoom control
  6 Lens aperture control
  7 White balance adjust; black adjust
  8 Video gain (0 dB, 6 dB, 12 dB), color bars, camera standby/operate switch
  9 Color compensation filter – 3200 K, 5600 K, 5600 K + 12.5% ND, closed
 10 Viewfinder, adjustable – 1.5 in (37 mm) with LED indicators
 11 Power selection, intercom, audio monitoring jack
 12 Camera back: VTR connector, video output, camera cable, monitor video output, gen-lock connection for multi-camera set-ups
 13 Viewfinder eyepiece
 14 Snap-on battery pack
 15 Side of camera: mike input connector, external d.c. socket
 16 Viewfinder controls
 17 Power zoom switch
 18 Auto-iris on/off

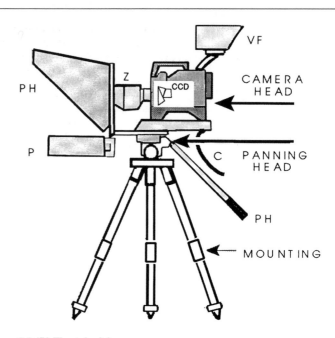

Figure 2.2 (B) The television camera
The *camera head* is fitted onto an adjustable *pan head* (*panning head*), which is attached to a supporting *mounting*.

A *zoom lens* (*Z*) focuses the scene onto *CCDs* (*image sensors*) which create the electronic picture signal.

A two-way *camera cable* (*C*) carries the camera's video to the distant control unit (CCU), which provides various technical supplies.

The *viewfinder* (*VF*) monitors the camera's picture.

The program script on the *prompter screen* (*P*) is reflected in an angled glass sheet within the *prompter hood* (*PH*).

A quick-release *wedge-mount* under the camera head slides into a corresponding recessed plate on the *pan head* (*panning head*). This device enables the camera to tilt and turn (*pan*) smoothly. Variable friction controls (*drag*) steady these movements. The head can also be *locked off* in a fixed position. *Tilt balance* adjustments position the camera horizontally to avoid its being nose- or tail-heavy.

One or two *pan* (*panning*) *handles* (*PH*) attached to the pan head allow the operator to accurately direct and control the camera.

The *camera mounting* support can take various forms: e.g. a *tripod*, *pedestal*, *jib*.

Camera features

2.3 Main features

Let's take a look at the main features of your camera:

1. The *lens system*, which projects a small image of the scene onto the camera's pick-up device.
2. This light-sensitive *CCD* (*charge-coupled device*) converts the image from the lens into a corresponding pattern of electrical charges which are read out to provide the video signal. (Earlier systems used various forms of *camera tubes*.)

3 The camera's *viewfinder* displays the video picture, enabling you to set up your shot, adjust focus, exposure, etc.

4 The way your camera is *supported.*

5 The camera's *power supplies.*

6 The *microphone* which is either fitted internally or clipped onto the camera. Intended for general sound pickup.

7 The *supplementary controls* which affect picture quality.

8 *Camera light/video light.* A small in-built or clip-on lamp used to illuminate the subject or supplement existing lighting.

9 The *power supply.* A DC supply powering the camera; usually from a built-in or attached battery, but may be derived from several other sources (Figure 2.8). The actual voltage may range from e.g. 3.6, 4.8, 6, 7.2, 9.6, 12, 14.4 volts.

The handbook issued with your equipment will give you details and specifications of your particular camera. There is a list of typical features in Table 2.1.

Table 2.1 Camera features

As well as the main lens control, the camera has various extra adjustments to ensure that shots taken under different conditions will match. Otherwise picture brightness, color, and tonal values could vary noticeably from shot to shot. Other features offer you extra facilities.

AGC (Automatic gain control)	Circuitry which automatically adjusts video amplification to keep it within preset limits. Reduced during bright shots, and increased under dimmer conditions, it *arbitrarily* alters overall picture brightness and contrast.
Animation	Control enabling a series of still shots to be recorded which, when played back consecutively, create an illusion of animation.
Auto-black	After capping up the lens to exclude all light, this switch automatically sets the camera's circuitry to produce a standard black reference level.
Auto-fade	Although you can manually adjust the lens aperture, to fade the picture out to a black screen, or up to full strength from black, it is not always easy to do this smoothly while holding the camera steady. So a facility is fitted to some cameras for doing this automatically at the touch of a button. This may fade the audio at the same time.
Auto-focus	A facility that automatically adjusts the lens focus for maximum sharpness on the nearest subject in a selected zone of the frame. Whether this is the one *you* want sharpest, is another matter. When you are shooting through foreground objects, or focusing selectively, or anything is likely to move between the camera and your subject, you should switch the camera to manual focusing.
Auto-iris	This device automatically adjusts the lens aperture (*f*-stop) to suit the prevailing light levels (light intensities). By doing so, it prevents the picture being very over- or under-exposed ('washed-out' or 'murky').
	However, there are times when the auto-iris 'misunderstands', and changes the lens aperture when it should remain constant, e.g. during zooming, or when a lighter area comes into the shot. Then it is necessary to switch the lens aperture control to *manual* or *aperture lock*, and operate it by hand.

Table 2.1 *continued*

Auto-white	This control automatically adjusts camera circuits' '*color-balance*' to suit the color quality of the prevailing light, and ensure that white surfaces are accurately reproduced as neutral. Otherwise all colors will be slightly warmer (red-orange) or colder (bluish) than normal.
	You simply press the *auto-white* button while shooting a white surface, or place a white plastic cap over the lens, or point the camera at the scene (averaging out its colors).
	If the color quality of the light is outside the circuit-adjustment limits, a warning indicator may show that a *color correction filter* (below) is needed on the lens to suit the illumination.
	Where white balance adjustment is entirely automatic, a *white balance lock* can prevent it from making wrong adjustments (e.g. when shooting large color areas).
	Some cameras use a *manual white balance adjustment*, which is turned while watching a meter or viewfinder indicator.
Backlight control	Control that opens the lens aperture an arbitrary stop or so above that selected by the *auto-iris* system to avoid under-exposure due to ambiguous readings.
Black stretch or gamma adjustment	Some cameras include an operator-controlled circuit adjustment to make shadow detail clearer and improve tonal gradation in darker picture tones. This is the opposite of 'contrast compression', which emphasizes the contrast in picture tones.
	With a higher gamma setting (e.g. 1.0) picture tones are more contrasty, coarser and dramatic. A lower gamma setting (e.g. 0.4) provides more subtle, flatter tonal quality.
Cable correction	When a camera is cabled to a central control unit, corrective circuits can be switched in to compensate for video losses (fall-off in definition) that increase with cable length.
Camera cable	This may be a short 'umbilical' multi-wire cable connecting the camera to a portable VCR (video cassette recorder), or a more substantial cable routed to a camera control unit (CCU or CPU). This cable provides power, syncs, intercom, etc., to the camera, and takes video and audio from the camera to the main video/audio equipment.
Color correction filters	Because the brain compensates, we tend to assume that most everyday light sources such as sunlight, tungsten light, quartz lamps, candlelight, etc., are all producing 'white' light. But in reality, these various luminants often have quite different color qualities. They may be bluish or reddish-yellow, depending on the light source and the conditions.
	Unless the camera's color system is matched to the prevailing light, its pictures will appear unnaturally warm (orange), or cool (bluish).
	How far auto-white adjustment is able to re-balance the camera's color response, to compensate for variations in the color quality of the prevailing light, depends on equipment design. For greater compensation you may need color correction filters. These are often fitted inside the video camera, just behind the lens (perhaps on a 'filter wheel'). Alternatively, you can fit a suitable filter over the front of the lens.
	Typical correction filters include *daylight*, *artificial/tungsten light* and *fluorescent light* (perhaps marked 6000 K, 4700 K and 3200 K). The filter wheel may also include or combine neutral-density (ND) filters to improve exposure.

Table 2.1 *continued*

Digital effects	A selection of prearranged settings allowing the picture's appearance to be changed in various ways.
Exposure modes	A series of pre-set exposure settings.
Exposure override	Switches from auto-iris system to manual to allow precise adjustments.
Focus ring/wheel	Manual focusing adjustment. (Quicker and more precise than automatic focusing.)
Haze filter	Ultraviolet (UV) filter clipped over the lens to reduce haze blur in daylight exteriors. Also serves to protect the lens surface.
Macro	Many zoom lenses have a *macro* position. This allows the lens to focus on very close objects; much closer than the lens' normal MFD (*minimum focused distance*). You cannot zoom with the lens in *macro mode*.
Photo mode	Facility enabling the camera to capture still pictures (freeze frames) of the scene.
Picture stabilizer	System which compensates for accidental irregular camera movements; camera shake.
Preset situations	Prearranged adjustments selected for typical occasions, e.g. portraits, sport action, snowy conditions.
Remote camera control	Small infrared hand control unit, providing remote control of camera/VCR unit.
Remote control	A system for operating the camera and/or its videotape recorder at a distance. 'Cordless' connections use an *IR* (*infrared*) link between the hand controller and the camera.
Remote VCR control	A trigger to remotely stop/start a videorecorder from the camera.
Reset to auto	Instantly switches from manual control to automatic (auto) system adjustments.
Reverse/normal switch	Reverses picture tones and colors for negative effects.
Self-timer	A device that automatically delays the start of videotaping, to allow you to get into the shot.
Shutter speed	To avoid movement blur and improve detail in fast action, a much briefer exposure rate than the normal 1/60 sec (PAL 1/50) is needed. A variable high-speed electronic shutter (settings from e.g. 1/125 to 1/400 sec) reduces blur considerably, but needs higher light levels, and is liable to produce unnatural break-up or flicker on some subjects.
Slow motion control	Where an interval timer ('intervalometer') is fitted, the camera records a brief shot at regular adjustable intervals (e.g. 10, 20, 60s). When replayed at normal speed, the time lapse effect will show a flower grow, or a day's weather, in just a few minutes.

Table 2.1 *continued*

Standby switch	A device used to save battery power, by switching off unused units when rehearsing or during standby. Some cameras have *auto switch-off* which cuts the system's power, when the camera has not been used for several minutes.
Sync – Int/Ext	When working alone, a video camera generates its own *internal* synchronizing pulses to stabilize the scanning circuits. These pulses are also combined with the picture video and sent to the camera's video output. In simpler camera designs, these sync pulses are imprecise, and rely on the TV receiver's circuits to compensate for any resulting jitter.
	In multi-camera production the camera is switched to *external sync*. It then uses the accurate synchronizing signals sent along the camera cable from a separate communal *sync generator*.
Time lapse facility	Still pictures taken at regular intervals create an illusion of animation when played successively (e.g. plants growing).
Title generator	A small keyboard used to provide titles and data (choice of colors) and inserts them onto the background scene. Several frames may be composed and stored ready for use. Although the print style limits its use, it is a convenient way of introducing titles/subtitles, and shot identification such as time, date, location, shot number (a built-in 'slate').
Video/RF output	As well as its normal *video output*, some video cameras have an *RF (radio frequency) output* that can be fed directly into a TV receiver or VCR's antenna (aerial) socket (e.g. Channel 3).
White balance override	Manual override controls for adjusting color temperature when shooting under variable light quality.
Zoom lens iris	Some lens systems can be switched to allow manual, auto-iris, or remote manual control at a CCU, by a video operator/shader.
	In addition, there will usually be various controls for selecting and setting – tape speed, clock, character generator (titles), etc.

2.4 The lens system

You will find two fundamental types of lenses on video/television cameras – the *prime lens (primary lens)* which has a fixed coverage or *field of view*, and the *zoom lens* in which this is adjustable.

If you look at the front of your camera's lens, you will see two important numbers engraved there:

The lens' focal length – or in the case of zoom lenses, its range of focal lengths. This gives you a clue to the variations in shot sizes the lens will provide.

The lens' largest aperture or *f/stop* (e.g. *f/*2) – the smaller this *f/*stop number, the larger the lens' maximum aperture, so the better its performance under dim lighting (*low-light*) conditions.

2.5 Focal length and lens angle

The term *focal length* is simply an optical measurement – the distance between the optical center of the lens and the image sensor, when you are

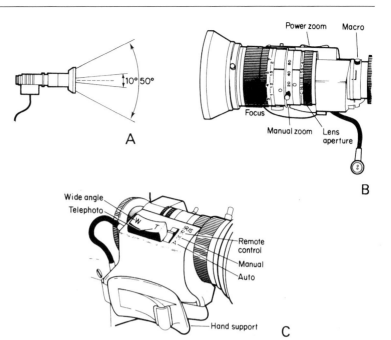

Figure 2.3 Camera lenses
Part 1 *Prime lens*. The prime lens (fixed focus lens, primary lens) has adjustable focus, and iris (aperture, stop), but its lens angle (focal length), is fixed.

Part 2 *Zoom lens*

(A)   The zoom lens has variable coverage. Changing the lens' *focal length* while on shot produces '*zooming* – '*zooming in*' as it is increased and '*zooming out*' as it is decreased. The range covered depends on lens design.

(B)   The main adjustments on a zoom lens include:
Focus
Lens aperture (f-stop, iris)
Focal length (lens angle)
A *macro* device may be fitted to provide very close shots.

(C)   The focal length setting can be adjusted *manually* by a ring on the lens barrel or a motor-driven *power zoom* device controlled by a two-way rocker-switch.

● Where *remote control* facilities are fitted, the lens can be adjusted by e.g. separate hand controls on the pan-bars.

focused at a great distance (*infinity*, ∞). It is measured in millimeters (mm) or inches.

Prime lens (primary lens) features – The various lens elements of a prime lens system are fixed. Only the *iris (diaphragm)* within the lens barrel is adjustable. Changing its *aperture (stop)* varies the lens' image brightness, so controlling the picture's '*exposure*'. *Focusing* is carried out by varying the entire lens system's distance from the CCD or film surface.

A prime lens designed to have a *long focal length* ('*long focus*') behaves as a '*narrow angle*' or *telephoto* system. The subject appears much closer than normal, but you can only see a smaller part of the scene. Depth and distance can look unnaturally *compressed* in the shot.

When the lens has a *short focal length* ('*short focus*') this *wide angle* system takes in correspondingly more of the scene. But now subjects will look much further away; depth and distance appear *exaggerated*.

The exact coverage of any lens will depend on its focal length relative to the size of a camera's CCD (or film) format. There are *field-of-view-tables* which show the lens' exact horizontal and vertical coverage for a range of camera distances.

If you are using a video or photographic camera with a single *prime* (*primary*) lens and want a closer or more distant shot of the subject, you have to move your camera nearer or further away. The only alternative solution is to have a selection of *prime lenses* of various focal lengths to choose from either fitting a suitable lens onto the camera as required or arranging several on a rotatable lens-turret.

2.6 The zoom lens

For everyday identification, one often refers to prime lenses by their *focal lengths*; i.e. a '*24 mil lens*'. But for many practical situations, particularly when working with scale plans of the action area (e.g. in a studio), it is much more useful to think in terms of *lens angles* rather than juggle with formulae. A transparent scale marked with lens angles immediately shows us how much of the scene will appear in shot from any camera position, and for any setting of your zoom lens. And no tables are needed. When talking non-specifically, we usually refer to a '*narrow-angle*' ('*telephoto*') lens setting or a 'wide angle lens'. Otherwise, we quote its horizontal coverage angle (e.g. a '*24 degree lens*').

Most video and TV cameras are fitted with *optical* zoom lens designs in which the focal length is adjusted by repositioning certain lens elements within the lens-barrel. Its adjustable *focal length* provides a *continuously variable lens angle*, enabling you to select any coverage within its range. You can leave the lens set at a chosen angle, or readjust it while on shot to produce the familiar *zooming* effects. (Increasing the focal length causes the picture to *zoom in*; while conversely, reducing it provides *zooming out*.) Designs currently vary from systems with a ratio of around 6:1 (sometimes written ×6) in which its longest focal length is six times that of its shortest, to those with a range of e.g. 20:1. A typical consumer camera will have a widest angle of around 28–38 degrees.

Lens design involves many technical compromises, particularly in small systems. The problems in providing high performance from a lightweight, robust unit at a reasonable cost has been a challenge for manufacturers. So the optical quality of budget systems is generally below that of an equivalent prime lens.

An increasing number of consumer video cameras are fitted with a lens system which combines *optical zoom* and *digital zoom* facilities. A camera might, for instance, have ×20 optical zoom and ×400 digital zoom. Depending on the quality of its design, an *optical zoom system* can give a picture of consistent quality throughout its range; the focus and picture clarity remaining optimum at all settings. In a *digital system*, the impression of 'zooming in' is achieved by progressively reading out a smaller and smaller area of the same digitally constructed picture. Consequently you are likely to see picture definition progressively deteriorating as you zoom in for fewer and fewer of the original picture's pixels are being spread across the TV screen.

When you want a 'closer' shot of your subject, or are trying to avoid something at the edge of the picture coming into shot, it is obviously a lot easier to zoom in a bit than to move your camera particularly if you're using a tripod or there are obstructions. In fact, many people simply stand wherever it's convenient, and just zoom in or out to vary the size of the shot. But as we shall discuss later in more detail, the *lens angle/focal length* setting does not just determine the image size. It also affects:

How much of the scene is sharp.
How prominent the background is in closer shots.
How hard it is to focus.
Camera shake.
The impressions of distance and depth in the picture.
The accuracy of shapes (geometry).

So as you'll see, any zoom lens really needs to be used with care; although people do ignore such distortions and varying perspective! The 'zooming' action, too, can be overused, producing very distracting effects.

2.7 Changing the lens system

The camera's zoom lens is usually attached to the camera head with a screw threaded *lens mount*. On some video cameras, it is possible to remove the zoom lens and fit a different lens system instead.

You may, for instance, want the highest picture quality for a particular purpose (e.g. high grade macro shots), and decide to use a 16 mm or 35 mm film camera *prime lens*. Or you might want to affix a special purpose periscope or microscope attachment.

To do this, you need a suitable lens mount. It might be a 1 in. or $\frac{2}{3}$ in. '*C-mount*' as used with 16 mm film cameras, or a $\frac{1}{2}$ in. '*D-mount*'. Adaptors also allow T-type, P-type or quick-release bayonet-types of lens fittings to be used with 35 mm camera lenses.

2.8 Zoom lens control (Figure 2.3, Part 2)

Your zoom lens has three sets of controls.

- *Focus adjustment.* You adjust focus by turning a broad ring at the front of the lens barrel. This moves the lens system in and out. A scale shows the distance at which sharpness is maximum – although as you will see, things nearer and father away may still look reasonably sharp. As well as *manual focusing*, many video cameras also include an automatic focusing device (*auto-focus*).
- *Iris or lens aperture adjustment (f-stop).* Along the lens barrel nearer the camera head, you will see another ring. This turns against a scale marked in *f-stops* or *transmission numbers*. If you look into the lens as you turn the aperture ring, you will see the opening of its small variable iris or diaphragm change. The size of this aperture controls the brightness of the image falling onto the image sensor (CCD). Again, you can adjust the iris manually, or with automatic circuits (*auto-iris*).
- *Zoom control.*

To adjust the focal length, you turn a third ring on the lens barrel (it has a small knob to make operation easier). A scale shows the selected setting. You can either choose a particular lens angle and shoot at that setting, or vary the angle while on shot to produce the familiar 'zooming' effect.

In a *pump zoom* lens (used for photographic cameras), a large ring on the lens barrel rotates to *focus*, and slides along the barrel to *zoom*; not usually the smoothest of movements!

You can switch most video zoom lenses from *manual* to *power zoom* operation.

A rocker switch actuates a small motor, which drives the zoom in and out between maximum coverage (wide angle) and minimum angle (telephoto). The speed of the zoom may be variable, depending on the switch pressure.

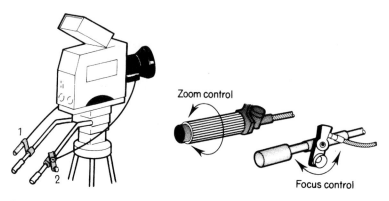

Figure 2.4 Pan-bar controls
When the camera is fitted to a mounting, the lens focus and zoom actions can be adjusted from extension controls on the pan bars, e.g. a twist-grip for zoom and a hand-crank for focus.

When a video camera is mounted on a movable dolly, it is not really convenient to reach round to the front of the camera to adjust the lens. Instead, flexible cables or an electrical servo system are fitted. These allow focus and zoom to be adjusted from behind the camera, by controls attached to the *pan-bars* (*panning handles*).

2.9 Altering the iris

For all practical purposes, it does not matter whether your lens system is calibrated in *f-stops* (based on the size of the aperture), or in *transmission numbers* (based on the amount of light it passes at various openings).

When the iris aperture is fully opened (probably around *f*/1.4) it lets in the most light. Its minimum opening when 'stopped right down' (under very bright lighting), may be *f*/22. Remember, the smaller the opening, the bigger the number. Some irises can be closed down until the picture fades out altogether.

When you alter the aperture of the lens, two things happen simultaneously:

● It changes the brightness of the lens image falling onto the CCD, so altering the picture's *exposure*. (See Chapter 3.)
● It will modify the available *depth of field*; so the sharpness of anything nearer and further than the actual *focused distance* will be affected.

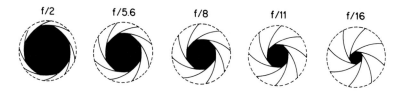

Figure 2.5 Lens aperture
The lens aperture is adjustable from a maximum (e.g. *f*/2) to a minimum (e.g. *f*/16).
Large aperture: small f-number, shallow depth of field, but less light is needed.
Small aperture: large f-number, increased depth of field, but more light is needed.

Figure 2.6
Part 1 *Depth of field*. Within the depth of field, things appear sharp, although focus is maximum at the *focused* distance (FD). Outside these distance limits (Df and Dn), things look defocused.

Part 2 *Aperture and depth of field*. As you stop the lens down (to a smaller aperture), the depth of field increases. (FD: focused distance). More of the scene is sharper; but the picture becomes dimmer.

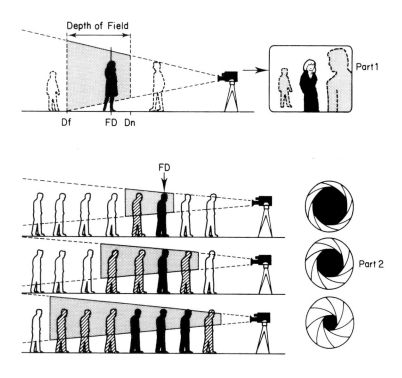

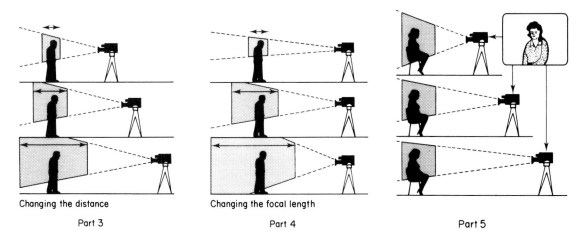

Changing the distance
Part 3

Changing the focal length
Part 4

Part 5

Part 3 *Distance and depth of field*. As you get farther from the focused subject, the depth of field increases.

Part 4 *Altering the focal length*. As you *decrease* the focal length (i.e. widen the lens angle or zoom out), the depth of field in the shot *increases*.

Part 5 *Depth remains the same*. If you alter the camera distance, then adjust the lens angle to get exactly the same size shot, the depth of field will be the same as before. Only the apparent perspective will have changed.

In practice you have three working options when selecting the lens aperture:

1 *You can choose the f-stop to suit the exposure.* Adjust the lens aperture to give a properly exposed picture, i.e. so that you can see tonal gradation and details clearly in the subject you are most interested in. If there is insufficient light, you will need to add more (Chapter 4). If there is too much light, so that the shot is overexposed, you will need to reduce the light falling on the subject, or cut down the lens-image intensity by reducing the lens aperture (*stop down*) or introduce a *neutral-density filter.*

2 *You can choose the f-stop to give the depth of field you want.* One usually concentrates on getting the exposure right, and accepts whatever depth of field results. But there will be times, especially in close shots, when you find that it is not possible to get all of the subject in sharp focus; in other words, there is insufficient depth of field. Then it is necessary to stop down (reduce the aperture), and increase the amount of light until the exposure is right. As we shall discuss in Section 3.10, you may want to select a *shallow depth of field*, so that only the subject itself is sharply defined. Or you can use *deep focus techniques*, in which everything in shot appears clear-cut.

3 If you have little or no control over the amount of light on the scene, or are moving around under varying light conditions, you may have little choice but to adjust the lens aperture manually for the *best average exposure*, or switching in the camera's automatic iris control and accepting whatever depth of field results. In the studio, where you have direct control of light levels, you can adjust the lighting to suit a convenient f-stop, or light to a comfortable lighting intensity and adjust the lens for correct exposure.

In a multi-camera production, cameras may be set to a local 'standard' f-stop and lighting balanced to correctly expose the pictures. Alternatively, the cameras' lens apertures may be adjustable remotely at a central control point (e.g. $\pm \frac{1}{2}$ a stop) to match pictures from different cameras shooting from various angles.

2.10 Lens accessories

There are two often-neglected accessories that fit onto the lens; the *lens cap* and the *lens hood*. The protective *lens cap* is an opaque metal or plastic disc which clips or screws over the front of the lens to protect it when not in use.

When you are not actually using your camera, get into the habit of clipping the *lens cap* over the end of your lens. The lens surface has a special bluish coating ('blooming'), which improves picture contrast and tonal gradation (by reducing the internal reflections that cause 'lens flares' or overall graying). This thin film is easily damaged by careless cleaning, or scratching (e.g. blown sand, grit). Your lens cap not only prevents anything from scratching or rubbing against the lens surface, but helps to keep out grit or moisture.

Although today's CCD image sensors are not as easily damaged by intense light sources as earlier camera tubes, it is still good working practice to avoid leaving your camera pointing at a powerful lamp or at the sun. It only takes a moment to cap up the lens during stand-down periods.

The lens hood (sun shade; ray shade) – This is a cylindrical or conical shield fitted round the end of the lens. When there is a strong light source just out of shot ahead of the camera it shields off stray light rays that could otherwise inter-reflect within internal lens elements. Although special lens-coatings considerably reduce these lens flares, the lens hood helps to avoid the spurious blobs of light, mottling, ray effects, or overall veiling that could otherwise develop.

2.11 The image sensor

The type of image sensor your camera has will affect the quality of the picture – its resolution (definition), picture defects, limitations.

Most video cameras today are fitted with CCD image sensors. The solid-state CCD has many advantages over camera tubes.

- It is small, compact, rugged, consumes low power, and has a long life.*
- CCDs have high sensitivity, and produce little 'lag' under low-light conditions.
- The CCD resolves moving detail well, and handles a wide brightness range (dynamic range) effectively.
- It produces pictures at switch-on (no warm-up time)
- There is no geometric distortion.
- Strong magnetic/radio fields (e.g. nearby radar) do not affect the system.

There are several types and sizes of CCD. A camera may have from one to four CCDs, their separate outputs combining to form the final color picture. The CCD's digital picture is made up of a total of some 225 000 to 2 million light-sensitive picture elements. Each element produces signal voltages corresponding to variations in the *intensity* of the light falling upon it. To generate *color* video signals, a color filter is introduced for each CCD; these red, green, and blue filters corresponding to the three primary colors, which combine to create natural color when their separate video outputs are blended together.

CCD performance has progressively improved, and various defects such as background blemishes, spurious streaks on highlights, smear on movement, flicker, strobing on fine line structures, etc. have been minimized; although they may be apparent under certain conditions. With small CCDs, there may be considerable depth of field; so everything in the picture appears sharp at all working lens apertures. Then it may not be possible to deliberately use *selective focusing* (i.e. shallow depth of field) to soften backgrounds.

2.12 Sensitivity

All camera systems must have a certain amount of light to produce good clear pictures. How much, will depend on camera design and adjustment, and on how light or dark the surroundings are.

Lighting intensities (light levels) are measured in footcandles or lux (1 fc is roughly 10 lux), and modern camera systems typically need around 75–150 fc (805–1600 lux) at *f*/4.

*Typical CCD sensors for a 4:3 picture format

2/3in. (17 mm)	8.8 mm horizontal × 6.6 mm vertical	. 11 mm diagonal
1/2in. (12.7 mm)	6.4 mm horizontal × 4.8 mm vertical	. 8 mm diagonal
1/3in. (8.5 mm)	4.8 mm horizontal × 3.6 mm vertical	. 6 mm diagonal
1/4in. (6.4 mm)	3.2 mm horizontal × 2.4 mm vertical	. 4 mm diagonal

The pixel area on a 2/3in. CCD is double that of a 1/2in. and four times that of a 1/3in. CCD.

A high-definition CCD image area is 14 mm horiz. and 7.9 mm vert. 16 mm diagonal.

But what if the surroundings are not sufficiently bright to get good pictures? You have two options. Either you can adjust the camera, or you can improve the lighting – e.g. move the subject nearer the light; adjust or add light.

The simplest solution is to open up the lens aperture to let more of the available light through to the CCD; up to the maximum lens-stop available (e.g. $f/1.4$.) But then the depth of field becomes shallower, and that may make focusing difficult for closer shots.

Another solution where there is insufficient light, is to switch in increased *video gain* (*video amplification*) in the camera system. Although the image sensor itself still lacks light, this electronic boost will strengthen the picture signal. Most cameras include two or three boost positions. A 6 dB increase will double the gain, while a 12 dB increase will quadruple it. With a 6 dB boost you may get very acceptable pictures with quite low light levels, e.g. around 15 fc (150 lux) at $f/1.6$; while with a high 12 dB boost, only about 8 fc (80 lux) would be needed. However, it is best to keep boost to a minimum wherever possible, for it increases picture noise (grain) and picture sharpness deteriorates.

So you see, a camera's sensitivity will depend on both the f/stop and the amount of boost switched in. A camera with a typical specification requiring 186 fc (2000 lux) at $f/8$ (3200 K, 89.9% reflectance), will only need 1.2 fc (13 lux) when opened up to $f/1.8$ and 18 dB gain. With the iris fully opened ($f/1.4$) even 0.7 fc (7.5 lux) will produce satisfactory pictures!

Even when there is very little light, it may still be possible to shoot action; although it is best to augment any illumination wherever possible. The simplest method is to work with full lens-aperture (smallest-stop number) and maximum video gain. Pictures will probably be grainy with video noise, rather smeary and losing detail; but there are times when that's unimportant if you are to get the right shot.

When shooting wildlife at night, the answer may be to illuminate the scene with infrared light (which animals and people cannot see), and clip an IR filter over the lens. The result is a monochrome picture with inaccurate tonal values, but you will capture the action without disturbing your prey.

2.13 The viewfinder

There are two forms of viewfinder: an *optical* or *eyepiece* type, and a fold-out rectangular *LCD screen*.

The optical or eyepiece viewfinder – This contains a small picture tube (typically 1.5 in. (38 mm) diameter), showing a magnified black and white image of the shot. With its flexible cup eyepiece held up against one eye all ambient light is shielded from its picture, so that you can not only frame up and compose the shot but get a good idea of exposure and relative *tonal* values. On some camera designs you can reposition the eyepiece onto whichever side of the camera is more convenient. It may also angle up and down (or swivel) so that you can still watch its screen even when using your camera above or below eye-level.

Like all picture monitors, optical/eyepiece viewfinders have brightness, contrast and focus (sharpness) adjustments. Some also have a *crispening* control that emphasizes detail in the viewfinder picture to make focusing easier. (Remember, *viewfinder adjustments* do not affect the camera's video picture in any way.)

A camera's optimum *configuration* can vary, depending on your particular shooting conditions. When moving around with a shoulder-mounted camera, you want it to be as light as possible, so a compact zoom lens, viewfinder and video/audio recorder are ideal. But when the camera is working from a fixed viewpoint, or fixed to a dolly, it is possible to fit a larger higher-quality zoom lens system, and a larger viewfinder.

The 5–7 in. (12.5–18 mm) diameter of an *open-screen* type of viewfinder (like a small TV monitor) is easier to watch for sustained periods, compared with an eyepiece continually held up to the eye. And focusing can be more precise than when watching a small image. A *hooded visor* is usually fitted around the monitor screen to shield stray light from falling on its picture. This type of viewfinder may be either black-and-white (monochromatic) or color. Because the structure of a monochrome monitor screen is virtually grain free, it is easier to maintain sharpest focus than on a color screen with its red, green and blue phosphor structure.

LCD viewfinders – An increasing number of small video cameras are fitted with a fold-out rectangular *LCD screen* (*liquid crystal display*) which is typically 2.5–3.5 in. wide, showing the shot in color. It is lightweight and conveniently folds flat against the camera body when out of use. But stray light falling onto the screen degrades its image, making it more difficult to focus and to judge picture quality.

In a studio, a small LCD screen can be tiring to watch for any length of time, particularly under bright lights, and a camera operator may prefer to use a nearby full-size picture monitor on a floor mounting instead, for more exacting focusing and composition.

Replay – The viewfinder on a camcorder not only shows you the video picture while you are shooting, but can be switched so that you can watch a replay of the shots you have just taped. You can check for any faults in camerawork, performance, continuity, etc., and re-shoot the sequence if necessary.

Some cameras have a switchable viewfinder feed that allows it to display test cards and data of various kinds, when checking camera performance; and to display *another camera's picture* superimposed upon your own. The last can be a very useful facility when two cameras are combining to create a special effect: for example, where one is shooting a map, and another is taking a shot of a city name. Thanks to the combined viewfinder image, the second camera can position the name accurately at the right spot on the first camera's map. If the second camera zooms in, the name grows dramatically, spreading right across the screen.

The only other ways of carrying out this trick, would be for the camera operators to watch the superimposition on a nearby picture monitor, or work from intercom instructions.

However, the electronic viewfinder does have its drawbacks.

- On a battery-powered camera, it consumes current all the time the camera is working. That is easy to overlook, especially if you have lengthy rehearsals, and review your recordings in the viewfinder.
- Because the picture is black and white, you may overlook the effect of *color* in the shot; inadvertently including a distracting brightly colored area perhaps.
- Because the viewfinder image is small, unwanted details can go unnoticed that will be very obvious when seen on a large TV screen.

2.14 Indicators

Even if you are operating your video camera in a completely automatic mode (*full auto*), you'll need information from time to time about such basics as how much tape you have left, and the state of the batteries.

Video cameras carry a range of indicators giving a variety of information and warnings – small meters, liquid crystal panels, indicator lights, switch markings. Most of the indicators are on the body of the camera, but because your attention is concentrated on the viewfinder much of the time while shooting, several are arranged within the viewfinder or on its screen.

Viewfinder indicators take the form of inserted titling displays, warning lights, superimposed patterns on the viewfinder picture. You will find a selection of typical indicators in Table 2.2. No camera has them all!

2.15 Audio circuits

Most portable video cameras are fitted with a microphone (usually an *electret* type) intended for general program sound pick-up. It may be built-in or removable, perhaps for use in a portable handgrip.

A foam sponge or cloth *windshield/wind gag/windjammer* cover over the mike reduces low-pitched wind rumble.

To position the microphone more effectively, it is sometimes attached to a short telescopic 'boom', which can be extended to reach out in front of the camera.

The sound pick-up is usually mono, although stereo microphones are increasingly used.

Sometimes, when shooting documentaries, the camera operator/director uses the mike to record information and sound notes as a guide track alongside the video. This can be a useful aid when writing the program commentary later.

An *audio monitor* earpiece jack, enables you to monitor your sound pick-up during recording. You should continuously assess sound quality, balance, background, etc. Quite often you will find that *background noises* which seem quite slight to the ear, prove very obtrusive on the soundtrack.

You can also use the earpiece to listen to a replay of the videotape soundtrack.

An *external mike* socket on the camera allows you to plug in a separate microphone; for better sound quality, and more accurate mike positioning. (It may also include a power supply for the extra mike.)

An *audio input* socket may be included, to allow a second sound source (e.g. music or effects) to be recorded on a separate track during video-taping.

When a camera is used in a multi-camera production, and cabled back to a central control point (CCU, CPU), *intercom* (*talkback*) *circuits* allow the camera operator to speak with the director and video operator, through a headset mike. Some cameras have a duplicate socket, for a second operator (e.g. a sound operator or an interviewer) to plug into the intercom circuit.

2.16 Power

Your video camera will normally require a low voltage d.c. power supply. This can come from a number of sources including: an on-camera battery pack, a battery-belt worn by the camera operator, the battery used to power the VCR, or a heavy-duty battery (car battery) on a small cart or trolley. When you are working near regular utility supplies (mains supplies), you can use a special adaptor to convert the 100–240 volts a.c. to e.g. 12 volts d.c.

Table 2.2 Typical camera indicators

	A variety of indicators of various kinds are fitted to video cameras, including the following.
Autofocusing zone selected	Shows whether autofocus is controlled by a small central area of the shot, or the nearest subject in the scene.
Back light exposure correction	System that opens the lens an arbitrary stop or so above the auto-iris setting, to improve exposure against bright backgrounds.
Battery alarm	Warning light showing that the battery is OK, or that it is getting exhausted.
Boost setting	Amount of video amplification (gain) being used.
Call light	Indicator light showing that the distant CCU operator wants to contact the camera operator on inter-com/private-wire system.
Date and time indicator	Displays details on screen, for insertion into picture.
End of tape warning	Shows that only e.g. 1 min of tape remains available.
Full auto-indicator	Shows that camera is in fully automatic mode (i.e. auto-iris, auto-focus, etc.).
Low light level warning	Insufficient light falling onto CCD, causing *under*exposure. (Open iris and/or increase boost.) An *over*exposure indicator light may also be fitted.
Manual aperture setting	Shows lens iris is in manually operated mode.
Manual focus correct	Lens focus is manually operated, and correctly adjusted.
Playback	Indicates that VCR is replaying the tape.
Shutter speed	Indicates which shutter speed has been chosen, to capture fast movement.
Standard or long play selected	Shows whether normal tape speed or half-speed (for tape economy) has been selected on VCR.
Tally light	A cue light showing that the camera is recording; or when used with a switcher unit, shows that this camera has been selected 'on-air'.
Time indicator	Shows running time (elapsed time/tape time used) and/or the amount of time remaining on cassette.
Titles	Small character generator provides titles, which can be superimposed on the picture.
Video/audio recording	Indicates that the VCR is recording (picture and sound).
Video level	Some cameras can superimpose a display on the viewfinder, which shows the video signal's strength and exposure.
White balance	Shows if color temperature adjustment is satisfactory.

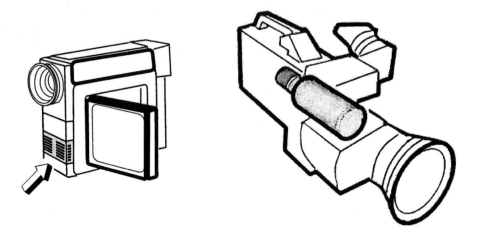

Figure 2.7 Camera microphone
Some smaller cameras have a built-in microphone (mono or stereo) within their bodies. But most have an external bar attachment into which a microphone shielded by a foam sponge cover (wind shield) is fitted.

When using batteries, there are a number of precautions that you should take if you are to avoid being left without power at a critical moment. The most obvious is to either switch your equipment off when it is not actually being used, or switch to a standby (warm-up) mode so that it is only using minimum power. (See Appendix A, Battery Care.)

Remember, the camera system (including its viewfinder), the videotape recorder, any picture monitor you may be using, an audio recorder, lights

Figure 2.8 Camera power
The camera can be powered in a number of different ways

1 Internal battery
2 Battery belt
3 Battery in shoulder pack
4 Battery on camera trolley
5 Car battery (Using cigar-lighter socket)
6 A.C. adaptor from public supply
7 'On-board' attached battery
8 Power from portable VCR

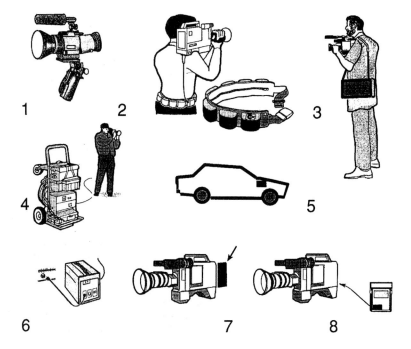

fitted to the camera, these are all drawing current. And when setting up shots, organizing action, shooting, doing retakes, reviewing the recording, writing up notes, it is very easy to find that you are squandering valuable battery power. Fully charged standby batteries are a must!

2.17 Camera arrangements

Video cameras are designed to suit a wide range of applications.

As you have seen, there are fundamentally two approaches to video production:

- Single camera shooting, in which a camera works quite independently.
- Multi-camera shooting, where a group of cameras work together.

This leads to a number of different configurations:

1 *Single camera*

- The camera may be completely self-contained; as in a typical *camcorder*. The camera carries its own battery power supplies and VCR system – either built into the camera, or attached to the camera body ('on-board').
- The camera may carry its own power supply, but its video (and sound) passes through a lightweight umbilical cable, to a *separate portable VCR*.
- In a variation, the camera is cabled to a portable VCR as before, but is *powered from the VCR unit*.

2 *Multi-camera*

- Each video camera may carry its own power supply and circuitry, sending its video signals to a pick-up point or base unit some distance away. (A system used on location for remotes.)
- Various forms of interconnection are used in these systems, including cable, radio mini-link, laser link, infrared link. Each has its particular advantages and limitations.
- The camera may be cabled to a central control point at a base station in the vicinity. This cable carries video and audio from the camera, together with the intercom, and provides the camera with power, synchronizing signals, scanning-voltages, etc., generated by units at the base station. (A system universally used in studios.)

Controlling the camera

2.18 Handling your camera

Pictures that are shaky, bounce around or lean over to one side, are a pain to watch. So it is worth that extra care to make sure that your shots are steady and carefully controlled. There may be times when your audience's attention is so riveted to exciting action on the screen that they are quite unconcerned if the picture does weave from side to side, or hop about. But don't rely on it! Particularly when there is little movement in the shot, an unsteady picture can be very distracting and irritating to watch.

As a general rule, you need to hold your camera perfectly still, unless you are deliberately *panning* it (i.e. turning it to one side), or *tilting* it (pointing it up or down) for a good reason.

Figure 2.9 The hand-held camera
Keeping the camera steady.

1 Legs braced apart, and elbows tucked in.
2 Seated, with elbows on knees.
3 Kneeling, with elbow resting on leg.
4 Elbows resting on the ground.
5 A *sandbag* or *beanbag* (containing tiny plastic balls) molds itself around the camera, supporting it firmly on rough ground.
6 Resting the back against a wall.
7 Resting the elbows on a low wall, fence, railings, car, etc.
8 Leaning your side against a wall.
9 Supporting one foot on a step or box.
10 Resting your body against a post.
11 Pulling up on a string (chain) fastened under the camera, with its lower end trapped under one foot.
12 Use a monopod (single-leg telescopic tube).

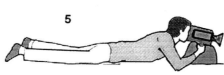

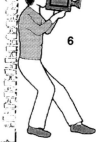

So what stops us from holding the camera steady? There are a number of difficulties. Even 'lightweight' cameras are still quite heavy (particularly if fitted with a lamp, battery, large zoom lens, etc.), and seem to grow heavier with time. Muscles tire. Body movements (breathing, heart beat) can cause camera movement. Wind can buffet the camera. You may be shooting from an unsteady position such as a moving car or a rocking boat. And on top of all that, if you are using a narrow lens-angle, any sort of camera-shake will be considerably exaggerated anyway!

To overcome or reduce this problem, and provide a stable base for the camera, several methods of camera support have been developed.

2.19 Supporting your camera

There are four basic ways of supporting your camera:

- Hold it in your hands.
- Rest it on your shoulder.
- Use some kind of body support.
- Affix it to some kind of mounting support.

Hand-held video cameras are extremely light. Depending on its design, you may steady the camera against your head while looking through the viewfinder eyepiece and/or support it with a molded pistol grip beneath the unit. This grip usually has a trigger-switch, which will start/stop/pause the video recorder during recording.

Many video cameras have a molded *saddle-type base* or *shoulder pad* that rests on one shoulder, while positioning the viewfinder in front of your opposite eye.

Lastly, you can attach the camera to a mounting of some kind (e.g. a *monopod*, *tripod*) with a screw-socket in its base. A quick-release *base-adaptor plate* may be fastened to the bottom of the camera, allowing it to be removed in a moment.

2.20 Hand-held cameras

The lightest, smallest video cameras are easily hand-held. So there's always the temptation to handle them casually and produce unsteady leaning shots. The secret to good camera control with a hand-held camera is to adopt a comfortable well-balanced position, with your legs apart and slightly bent and your elbows tucked into your sides. You grip your camera firmly but not too tightly or your muscles will tire and cause camera shake.

Some cameras have a vertical hand grip beneath the body of the camera. With others, your fingers go round the body of the camera while the other hand adjusts the focus control and steadies the camera. Larger camera units which are shoulder mounted are steadied by a hand slipped through a support loop on the lens system; within easy reach of lens controls including the zoom rocker-switch, and manual/auto-iris switching (Figure 2.3, Part 2C).

You can improve picture steadiness further by resting your elbows or your body against something really secure. This may be a wall, a fence or perhaps a nearby car.

The simplest aid, when you are hand-holding a camera, is a string or chain suspended from the camera-base. You hold its free end under your foot, pulling the camera gently upwards, to make it just that bit more stable.

Figure 2.10 The shoulder-mounted camera.

Part 1 A U-shaped saddle holds the camera firmly on the shoulders.

Part 2 *Hand positions*. With the right hand through the support loop (fingers operating power-zoom, and iris selection), and the left hand adjusting focus (perhaps iris), the camera can be supported firmly, even in difficult conditions.

Part 3 *Body brace* A body brace from the camera to the belt (or the chest) helps to support the camera firmly.

There are situations where you can use a special camera mount attached to a C-clamp, or an alligator spring-clip (gaffer-grip), to attach the camera to a firm nearby support such as scaffolding, fencing or furniture.

2.21 Shoulder-supported cameras

This familiar method of holding the camera is mainly used when the camera has to be very mobile, and able to change position quickly, or when shots are very brief. So we see it mostly when news-gathering, and at sports events, where the camera has to move around at the run, to follow action.

With the body of the camera on your right shoulder, and your right hand through a support loop at the side of the lens, your fingers are free to operate the power-zoom rocker switch, while your thumb can press the VCR pause switch. Your left hand adjusts the manual zoom lever, the focusing ring, f-stop (lens aperture), and the macro lever when necessary.

The comfort and success of this method depends largely on your stamina, and how long you are using the camera. Standing with upraised arms supporting a shoulder-mounted camera can be very tiring. So there are several body-braces and shoulder harnesses that help to keep the camera steady if you are shooting for long periods. A typical arrangement has a metal prop fixed beneath the camera, and resting on a chest pad or a belt support.

2.22 The monopod

This is a cheap, easily carried, lightweight mounting. It consists of a collapsible metal tube of adjustable length, that screws to the camera base.

Figure 2.11 Monopod
This lightweight extensible tube can be set to any convenient length and used in various ways.

Braced against your knee, foot or leg, the monopod can provide quite a firm support for the camera, yet allow it to be moved around rapidly to a new viewpoint. Its main disadvantage is that you can accidentally lean the camera sideways, and get sloping horizons. And of course, the monopod is not self-supporting.

2.23 The panning head (pan head, camera mounting head)

If you were to bolt your camera straight onto any form of mounting it would be held rigid, and unable to move around to follow the action.

So instead, you need to fit a *panning head (pan head)*. Not only does this enable you to swivel the camera from side to side (*pan*), and tilt it up and down, but you can adjust the freedom of movement (friction, drag), and lock the head in either or both directions.

Although you can control the camera on the panning head by holding its body, it is better to use a small panning handle (pan-bar) attached to the head to guide it.

Whenever you pan or tilt the camera, you need to feel a certain amount of resistance in order to be able to control it properly. If there is too little, you are likely to overshoot or twitch the camera at the end of a pan or tilt, and you will have difficulty in following action accurately. On the other hand, if too much effort is needed, panning will be bumpy and erratic. So the friction (drag) for both pan and tilt is generally adjustable.

Panning head for video cameras may use either friction or a fluid (silicon) to dampen movements. The cheaper, simpler friction head has disadvantages, for as you gradually exert pressure to start a pan, it may suddenly move with a jerk. And at the end of a slow pan, it can stick unexpectedly. With a fluid head though, all movements are very steady and controlled.

A panning head is usually fitted with *locking controls* that you can use to prevent it from panning and/or tilting. You should always apply these to lock-off the camera whenever you are leaving it unattended; otherwise there is the danger that the camera may tilt suddenly, and not only jolt its delicate mechanism but even overbalance the tripod altogether!

Locking controls are very useful too, when you want to avoid any trace of camera shake, e.g. when shooting a title card, or when heavy winds are likely to buffet the camera, or when you are holding a shot on a very narrow-angle lens.

Figure 2.12 Tripod
A simple three-legged stand, with independently extendable legs. Height cannot be adjusted during a shot. It can be set up on rough uneven ground. A spider (spreader) will prevent the feet from slipping, or sinking in soft ground.

2.24 Using a tripod

A tripod is a very compact, convenient method of holding your camera steady, provided you use it properly. It has three legs of independently adjustable length, that are spread apart to provide a stable base for the camera.

Unscrewing the tripod from the camera usually takes a little time. So most people leave the tripod attached and just close its legs together when they move to a new position. If you have a quick-release mounting plate fitted to your camera, the tripod can be removed rapidly.

Tripods are certainly not foolproof! In fact, you need to take certain precautions to avoid disaster, so here are some useful tips:

Don't leave your camera on its tripod unattended, particularly if people or animals are likely to knock against or trip over it! Take special care whenever the ground is slippery, sloping or soft.

To prevent the feet of a tripod from slipping, they normally have either rubber-pads for smooth ground, or spikes (screw-out or retractable) for rough surfaces. (Be sure though, not to use spikes when they are likely to damage the floor surface!)

If the ground is very uneven (e.g. on rocks or a staircase), you can fix the tripod legs at different lengths so that the camera itself remains level when you pan around. Otherwise horizontals will tilt as you pan! Many tripods are fitted with spirit-levels to help here.

A very lightweight tripod is a false economy. It is intended for small photographic cameras, and will be far too flexible and insecure for a video camera.

Because any tripod fitted with the camera tends to be top heavy, you should always make sure that its legs are *fully* spread, and resting on a firm surface. When a tripod is set to full height (e.g. 6 ft (2 m)), it is particularly unstable. A low tripod (e.g. 2 ft (55 cm)) is effective for low-angle shots, but it may not be easy to see into the viewfinder. Most times, you will want to work with the camera viewfinder at around your natural eye-height. You adjust the camera's height, by selecting how far the tripod legs are extended before locking them. But do not try to vary height by altering the distance apart of the legs. Some tripods have a central camera-support column that can be raised or lowered by a hand crank, although not while actually shooting.

There are several techniques for improving a tripod's stability. Simplest is a central weight (e.g. a sandbag or bag of stones) hung by rope beneath the tripod's center. The legs can be tied to spikes in the ground. Or you can use a folding three-blade device known as a 'spreader' or 'spider', which provides a portable base. On very soft ground, sand or mud, the tripod is best used on a flat triangular wooden base.

2.25 The rolling tripod/tripod dolly

One practical disadvantage of the tripod is that you cannot move it around while shooting. However, fix the tripod to a castered (wheeled) base or 'skid', and you have a rolling tripod. This useful economical general-purpose *dolly* can be pushed around easily on a flat level floor. Uneven surfaces, though, will shake the picture. If the floor slopes at all, it can be very difficult to control the rolling tripod while dollying.

Rolling tripods may be fitted with *brakes* (to prevent wheel movement), *direction locks* (to hold the wheels in a chosen direction), and *cable guards* (to prevent the wheels overrunning cables).

Figure 2.13 Rolling tripod/tripod dolly
A tripod on a castered base (skid/skate/rolling spider). The height is preset with a hand-crank (or pneumatic). Caster foot-brakes and cable-guards may be fitted. Easily wheeled on a flat smooth surface, steering may be erratic.

Although it sounds obvious, before you move a rolling tripod, remember to check that the brakes are off, that the wheels are free, and there is no cable or obstruction in your path. You will find that it helps if you give a slight push to align the casters in the appropriate direction, before you dolly. Otherwise the picture may bump a little as the tripod starts to move.

Although widely used in smaller studios, the rolling tripod does not lend itself to subtle camerawork. Camera moves tend to be rather approximate. Camera height adjustments are made either by resetting the tripod leg-heights, or with a central hand-cranked column adjustment. So height changes while on shot are not practicable.

2.26 The pedestal

For many years, the *pedestal* (or '*ped*' as it is widely known) has been the all-purpose camera mounting in TV studios throughout the world. It can support even the heaviest studio cameras, yet still allow a range of maneuvers on smooth, level floors.

Basically, the pedestal consists of a three-wheeled base, supporting a central column of adjustable height. A concentric steering wheel is used to push and steer the mounting around, and to alter the camera's height. Thanks to compensatory pneumatic, spring, or counter-balance mechanisms within the column its height can be adjusted quite easily and smoothly, even while on shot, from as low as 2 ft to a maximum height of around 6 ft (0.6–1.5 m approx.).

Moving around at maximum or minimum height can require some dexterity for it is not easy to follow the viewfinder throughout the move. There can be occasions when a second operator's assistance is needed to help push the pedestal and to look after the camera cable.

The three rubber-tired wheels can be switched into either

- a '*crab*' *mode* in which all three wheels are interlinked to move together,
- or a '*steer*' or '*dolly*' *mode* in which a front wheel steers the mounting while the other two remain fixed.

Simpler types of lightweight pedestal have hand-cranked central-column height adjustment, so any height changes on-shot can look quite jerky. The mounting is steered around by its *pan* (*panning*) *handles.*

Figure 2.14 The pedestal
Pedestals of various designs are widely used in the studio and on location. Lightweight versions like that shown combine stability with mobility.

2.27 Jib arms

In the golden days of filmed musicals large *camera cranes* came into their own: birds-eye shots of the action ... swooping down to a group ... sweeping along at floor level, taking shots of dancing feet ... climbing to follow the action as dancers ascended staircases ... In the right hands, such camerawork was certainly impressive!

Small camera cranes are still used in some larger TV studios, but they need skilled handling, and occupy a lot of floor space compared with the ubiquitous pedestal mounting. A much less costly, and more convenient mounting where you want wide variation in camera heights, is the increasingly used *jib arm.*

The long extensible *jib* (*boom, beam*) is counterbalanced on a central column. This column may be supported on a tripod, a camera pedestal, or a four-wheeled platform. The video camera is fixed into a cradle at the far

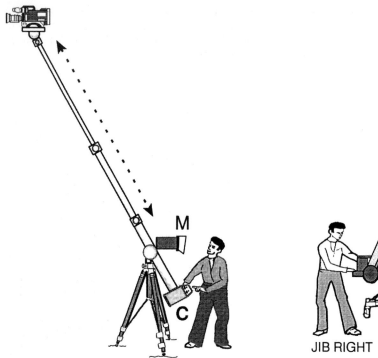

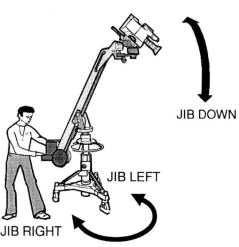

JIB UP

JIB DOWN

JIB LEFT

JIB RIGHT

Figure 2.15 Jib arms

Part 1 This lightweight jib arm can be extended to pre-set lengths. The camera is remotely controlled from a control box (C) at its lower end, while the operator follows an attached picture monitor (M).

Part 2 You can swing the main beam of the jib up/down (*jib up*, *jib down*) or turn it left/right (*jib left*, *jib right*). Where its camera is remotely controlled as in Part 1, separate *panning* and *tilting* are also possible.

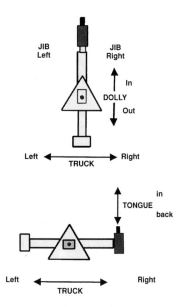

JIB Left   JIB Right

In
DOLLY
Out

Left ← → Right
TRUCK

in
TONGUE
back

Left ← → Right
TRUCK

Part 3 (Left) Where the complete jib arm on its mounting are moved around, its movements are described as *dollying* (*tracking*) in and out, or *trucking* (*crabbing*) sideways, or *tonguing in/back* when the mounting is set across the action area.

end of the jib, remotely controlled by the camera operator who stands beside the mounting, watching an attached picture monitor. You will find a wide range of jib designs; from the lightweight mountings used with smaller cameras (maximum camera height e.g. 10 ft (3 m)) to heavy-duty jibs that will reach up to e.g. 40 ft (12 m).

The *small jib arm* is particularly convenient, for it is easily assembled and, when necessary, disassembled and transported. Moreover, it can be used equally effectively in the studio or in the field. The length of the jib is pre-adjusted before cranking it up to working height on its tripod; which may take up a floor area of as little as 6 × 6 ft (2 × 2 m). Even when it is used on a smooth floor, it's generally inadvisable to move the jib's tripod mounting around in an attempt to follow action, for when fully extended it becomes less stable.

The jib has various operational advantages. It can reach out over obstructions, which would bring a rolling tripod or pedestal to a halt. It can take level shots of action that is up on a *platform/parallel/rostrum* while other mountings working from nearer floor level can only shoot the subject from a depressed angle. However, as you swing the jib arm, the camera *always moves in an arc*; whether it is being raised, lowered, or turned sideways. It cannot travel parallel with subjects moving across the action area. Whether you can turn and raise/lower the jib while on shot, and keep moving subjects in focus in a well-composed picture, will depend on your skills and luck.

2.28 Telescopic columns/motorized elevator pedestal

In this mounting, the remotely controlled video camera is positioned at the top of a vertical column, which is fixed to a wheeled tripod base. The camera's lowest height is determined by the length of the column, but it can be raised by an internal motorized system to an appreciable height, depending on its design. Typically this may be 40 ft (12 m) or more. Telescopic columns are great for those really high shots of a race track, a sports event, a golf course.

2.29 Special mountings

Several devices are available, that can help you to cope with those awkward occasions when you need to secure the camera in unusual places. Typical equipment that can prove handy for smaller production units include:

- *Camera clamps* Metal brackets or clamps of various designs, which allow the camera to be fastened to a wall, fence, rail, door, or other structure.
- *Camera spigot* This is a tubular fitting which slots into the top of a regular lighting stand or a suspended lamp clamp.
- *Car rig* A mounting fitted with strong suction cups which can be attached to any reasonably flat smooth surface, such as the exterior of a car.

2.30 Other mobile mountings

A number of other types of camera mounting are used in video production.

The *Steadicam-Jr* is a special stabilizer that takes the shake and shudder out of even wide camera movements. While carrying a camera weighing up to 4 lb (1.8 kg) it allows you to take smooth traveling shots while panning, tilting, walking, running, climbing, etc. A $3\frac{1}{2}$ in. LCD color screen (treated to reduce reflections) allows you to monitor the shots, and a small camera light (videolight) (3200 K) helps out in those awkward corners.

The main theme you will find running through this book is *it's the result that matters, not how you get it!* You need to be able to support your camera firmly. Your audience does not know or care whether you are using a tripod or are resting it against a handy post.

You could take a moving shot, from a car, the back of a motor cycle, a hospital trolley, wheelchair or even roller skates or skis. It is the result that counts – although some methods are a lot safer and more convenient than others!

2.31 Handling care

It's very easy to hazard your equipment, especially when shooting on location. Although some units are pretty rugged and almost foolproof, others are easily damaged or fouled up. A moment's oversight can leave you with unreliable performance, or even put your equipment out of action altogether: a camera momentarily rested on the ground, a spilt drink, the

Figure 2.16 The Steadicam-Jr
A compact balanced support, that holds the camera rock steady, even when you are moving around. It incorporates a video light and an LCD color monitor.

jolts and vibration of a traveling vehicle. It takes just a moment to protect your camera with a waterproof cover ('rain hood') against wind-blown dust and grit, sea-spray, or rain. Extreme cold, heat or moisture can create problems too. A car's trunk (boot) can become an oven in the hot sun. High humidity can wreak havoc with videorecorders.

Moving from a cold exterior to warm surroundings, is liable to result in condensation (dew) in VCRs, and can cause tape or machine damage. Wrapping up the equipment (even in a plastic bag) may help. Similarly, when moving from an air-conditioned interior into a hot sunny exterior.

There's always the temptation to wonder what is inside, or wonder what would happen if . . . Resist it! Always bear in mind the old adage: 'If it ain't broke, don't fix it!' It's a good general principle not to open up equipment unless you do really know what you are doing. It can easily cause additional faults. There is nothing more annoying or time wasting, than wrestling with equipment to make it work, and wondering: 'Am I doing something wrong, or has it "gone on the blink"?'

Chapter 3

Using your camera

Why put up with the second best, when your camera can create interesting, persuasive images?

3.1 Why bother?

Have you seen how casually some people use their video camera? They adopt a 'point and squirt' approach, assuming that automatic circuits will take care of the problem. After all, they might argue, the camera is not gobbling up costly film. It is easy to discard anything you don't want.

It is only when they come to check over the results later, that they too often seem disappointing. Many shots are plain boring. The audience's attention will wander. Picture quality varies. Subjects are not all that clear. Editing looks clumsy.

This is a pity, considering that by mastering a handful of working principles, you can produce effective pictures with a professional polish!

3.2 What gets on the screen?

You will often hear the camera described as 'an extension eye' or 'the eye of the audience'. But these are very misleading over-simplifications. You can use your camera to *deliberately* create those impressions, but the camera doesn't automatically convey a true picture of any situation to your audience. If someone is at the spot, their eyes flick around, refocusing, taking in what is happening. They know where they are, and can decide for themselves what they look at. Everyone makes their own selection from the scene.

Your audience can only see what you have chosen to show them. Just that part of the scene selected by the lens is visible on the rectangular screen in front of them.

They can only guess at what lies outside the lens' 'angle of view'. Other things quite near the camera would fill the screen if the lens turned just a little; but they remain unseen, 'out of shot', for the camera is highly selective.

A hallmark of good directors is their ability to select from moment to moment exactly the right features within the scene that suit their dramatic purpose . . . yet at the same time convince their audience that this is exactly what *they* want to see at that instant!

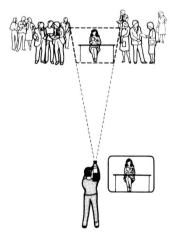

Figure 3.1 The camera isolates
The camera only shows what is going on in its 4 × 3 shaped segment of the scene. The audience does not know what is outside the field of view.

3.3 How close should we be?

A *close-up shot* is fine for revealing detail – sometimes too much!

- It encourages your audience to concentrate on a particular feature.
- But in restricting how much they can see you might frustrate them; particularly if they feel that they are missing something going on elsewhere.

But you have to take care not to thrust detail at your audience too blatantly as if to say: 'Now see this! Pay attention! Look at these details!' Good production techniques are based on *persuasion*. And there are many subtle ways of influencing exactly where your audience looks, without thrusting big close-ups at them all the time. You can do this by the way in which you arrange the composition of the picture, move people around or position the lighting.

A *long shot* shows your audience a wide view:

- It reveals a lot of the scene in front of the camera.
- It shows where the action is located.
- It helps the audience to follow movement.
- It lets them see how one thing relates to another.
- It can give them a good idea of space; unless you deliberately mislead them by exaggerating perspective by using a much wider or narrower lens angle than normal.

An overall view of this sort does have its disadvantages, too. Your audience cannot see subject details at all clearly. They can see the speed with which the player runs after the ball, but not the expression when he or she drops it!

Long shots have the advantage of allowing the viewers to select; to choose whatever attracts their attention in the broad view. But it also gives them the

Figure 3.2 Shots of people
Shots are classified by the amount of a person taken in:

ECU Extreme close-up (detail shot) – isolated detail.

VCU Very close-up (face shot) – from mid-forehead to above chin.

BCU Big close-up (tight CU, full head) – full head height nearly fills screen.

CU Close-up – just above head to upper chest (cuts below neck tie knot).

MCU Medium close-up (bust shot, chest shot) – cuts body at lower chest (breast-pocket, armpit).

MS Medium shot (mid-shot, close medium shot. CMS, waist shot) – cuts body just below waist.

KNEE Knee shot, three-quarter length shot – cuts just below knees.

MLS Medium long-shot (full-length shot, FLS) – entire body plus short distance above/below.

LS Long shot – person occupies $\frac{3}{4}$ to $\frac{1}{3}$ screen height.

ELS Extra long shot (XLS), extreme LS.

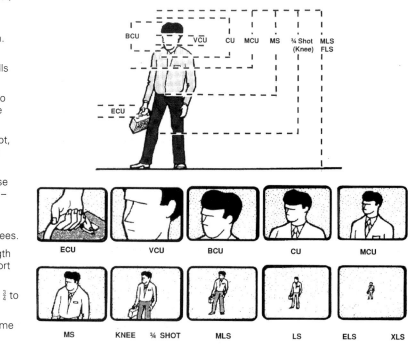

opportunity to gaze around and start thinking about whatever catches their interest, rather than concentrating on the particular point you may be making in your program at that moment.

Any well blended program treatment needs a series of closer and more distant shots, each carefully chosen for its purpose: to help your audience locate themselves, see what is going on, interpret action, see details, and so on.

3.4 How much can we see?

How much of the scene your camera shows will depend on:

- The camera's viewpoint.
- How far the camera is from the subject.
- The angle its lens covers.

As we saw earlier, the lens' coverage (*lens angle, angle of view*) varies with its focal length. The *zoom lens* can be adjusted to any focal length within its range. If it is a 6:1 (six to one) system, then its widest angle will be six times the narrowest. (Its shortest focal length is $\frac{1}{6}$ of its longest.) Currently, optical zoom lens systems fitted to popular cameras, have a zoom range of around 10:1 to 18:1. But as we saw earlier (Section 2.6) an additional '*digital zoom*' facility can bring the overall zoom coverage to some 400:1.

It is arguable whether such extreme zoom ranges are really practical, for apart from the likelihood of camera shake, picture quality deteriorates, atmospheric haze can mar close shots of distant objects, and perspective is grossly flattened. However, there will be times when it is quite impracticable to move closer with a 'normal' lens angle, and then you will be glad to be able to zoom in for that special shot, whatever the picture's shortcomings.

Some larger zoom lenses are fitted with an *extender lens (range extender)*. This can be flipped in when you want to push the zoom range beyond its normal upper limit, perhaps effectively doubling it – although with a noticeable light loss (e.g. $1\frac{1}{2}$ stops) and degraded definition.

Another way of altering the maximum or minimum angle of your lens system is to clip on a *supplementary lens (diopter lens)*. A $1\frac{1}{2}$ times *teleconvertor* lens will effectively make a 1:6 zoom lens' narrowest angle that of a 1:9 lens. A *wide-angle conversion lens* will increase its widest coverage.

An *adaptor ring* can effectively double the original lens' focal length. It screws between the original lens and the camera body. Results can be quite good, but definition falls off when you zoom in to detail, using the narrowest lens angles.

In fact, each of these methods of altering the lens performance has its limitations, but they do provide ways of extending your present system.

Finally, as you know, you may be able to replace your lens with a photographic prime lens that has a more appropriate fixed focal length.

3.5 Using a different lens angle

Let's look more closely at this matter of *lens angles*, the ways in which they affect your camerawork, and your audience's interpretation of the pictures.

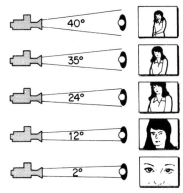

Figure 3.3 Lens angles
Changing the lens focal length alters its coverage in proportion. Using a focal length three times the present one, the lens angle will be one-third of the original, so the subject appears three times as large in the picture. It is the equivalent of having reduced the camera distance to one-third, and only one-third of the original scene is now visible.

'Normal' lens angle If the angle from your eyes to the sides of your TV screen is reasonably similar to that of the camera's horizontal lens angle you will get a realistic impression of space, distance, and proportions as you look at the picture. With today's variants in screen size and shape, this angle is by no means precise, but for all practical purposes we can assume that it is around 20–28°.

But what are the disadvantages if you shoot with a lens angle that is appreciably different from 'normal'? Well, some interesting things can happen. With some subjects, your audience may not even notice anything amiss. But where there are lots of visual clues from which to judge proportions and perspective (e.g. inside a building; a room; a group of people) differences between pictures shot with different lens angles will be obvious.

There are directors for whom the entire process of program-making is a mechanical routine. They would probably contend that:

'The public have now become so inured to the conventions of film and television production techniques that they accept what they see without a qualm. In any case, it is a lot more convenient to use the zoom lens to alter shots, rather than keep moving cameras around in a fast-paced show. In the field, particularly where cameras are obliged to work from static positions, there is no option but to rely on the zoom.'

With experience you will form your own judgments.

A *narrow angle* or *long focus* lens (long focal length) will give a telescopic view of the scene. This shows a relatively narrower segment, which is magnified, and appears closer.

A narrow lens angle has great advantages when you cannot move the camera closer (or do not want to). But there are snags too. It often has the effect of flattening subjects, squashing space, and compressing depth. It can make things look unnaturally close. Movements too are affected. Even fast-moving subjects seem strangely slowed by a narrow-angle lens, as they move up to, or away from the camera.

You will find that it is difficult to hold a camera steady when using narrower lens angles, for even the slightest vibration is magnified, and shakes the picture. (Rest the camera on something firm, or use a tripod or some other type of mounting.)

A *wide-angle* lens, on the other hand, shows us a much greater area of the scene. But now everything in the picture looks unusually distant. The lens seems to emphasize space and depth. Movements towards and away from the camera (or forward/backward camera moves) seem faster than they really are.

The wider the lens angle (i.e. the shorter the focal length), the easier it is to hold the camera steady, and to move around smoothly while shooting. But don't let that tempt you to use a wide-angle lens all the time. Otherwise, your subjects will look too distant. If you move in close to them to compensate, subjects will look very distorted shot on a wide-angle lens.

3.6 So why move around?

If you can make things appear closer and further away simply by varying the lens angle why bother to move your camera? Why not just alter the zoom setting? It's far less trouble!

Figure 3.4 Adjusting proportions
If you widen the lens angle, then move the camera closer to bring the main subject to its original size, other subjects in the scene will appear further away; relative proportions in the picture will alter.

Narrow the lens angle, and the reverse happens.

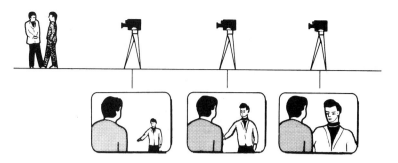

Although, at first glance, changing the lens angle *seems* to give more or less similar results to those you get when repositioning the camera, if you look at the picture critically you will see that there are distinct differences in the results. You'll find these summarized in Tables 3.1 and 3.2.

It's a good working principle to use a *normal lens angle* as far as possible and to move your camera viewpoint rather than just zooming in and out with a stationary camera. Actual camera movement gives life to a picture. Whenever a camera moves, we see *parallactic changes* in the picture. Various surfaces become progressively hidden as the camera moves past; others are gradually revealed. Although this effect becomes most obvious when traveling past a series of columns or through a group of trees, it is one of those natural everyday phenomena that helps us to interpret the three-dimensional world about us. It is even more pronounced when the camera *trucks/crabs* sideways.

Whenever you zoom, you are simply blowing up and reducing exactly the same shot. The natural displacement effects that make shots from a moving camera so persuasive, are simply not there. Zooming is an entirely *artificial* device; an optical trick, albeit a very useful one.

There will certainly be times when you deliberately widen or narrow the lens angle for practical or artistic reasons. Don't hesitate to vary the lens angle as you need, to overcome a problem or to get an effect. Don't just alter it *casually*. If you are shooting a parade from a balcony, and are getting useful group shots with a normal lens angle, you might increase to a wide-angle to take in the lengthy procession or change to a narrower angle to show details. With a constant lens setting your shot opportunities would be much more limited. And you certainly couldn't rely on running up and down to new viewpoints to provide the variety of shots you need.

Supposing you want to show details on a distant statue located way up at the top of a building. You will certainly need to use a really *narrow lens-angle* (*long focal length*). There will be foreshortening. It's quite unavoidable. Space will be squashed, and the form of the building itself appear distorted. That is just hard luck! But if you are taking oblique shots on a *narrow angle lens* when alternative camera positions are available, such distortions are quite unjustified. Yet it happens!

On the plus side, the way in which a *wide-angle lens* exaggerates space offers invaluable opportunities in a crowded studio or where the budget is slim. A wide-angle lens can make the smallest setting appear quite spacious. Even a couple of scenic flats linked together can create the illusion of an entire room if you shoot them strategically with a wide-angle lens!

In the real world, working with a zoom lens has great practical advantages, and you will find these summarized in Table 3.2.

Table 3.1 Care when choosing the lens angle

The lens angle (which varies with focal length) affects a number of things simultaneously. How noticeable these effects are in the picture depends on the subject and the scene.

How much of the scene is sharp?	● When using a *wide lens angle* (*short focal length*) most of the scene will *usually* appear sharply focused because there is considerable depth of field. ● With a *narrow lens angle* (*long focal length*) the depth of field is considerably less, and only subjects located within this restricted zone will really be sharply focused. **The depth of field varies with:** ● *The actual lens angle (i.e. the focal length of the lens)* The zone's depth **in**creases as you **in**crease the lens angle. ● *The lens' aperture (i.e. the f-stop it is working at).* The zone's depth **in**creases as you **de**crease the lens aperture; i.e. as you *stop down*. ● *The distance at which the lens is focused.* Depth **in**creases as you focus further away; i.e. **in**crease the camera's focused distance.
How prominent is the background in closer shots?	● With the lens aperture stopped down (i.e. a *large f*-stop number) the depth of field will be *greater*. ● With the lens aperture opened up (i.e. a *small f*-stop number), the depth of field will be *reduced*. ● Backgrounds are likely to be defocused if the lens is working wide open.
How hard is it to focus?	● The *longer* the focal length at which the zoom lens is set, the more difficult it is to focus accurately because the depth of field becomes considerably shallower and reveals focusing errors. In close shots of a nearby object it may be hard to get the whole of it sharply focused. ● Working with a *wide-angle lens*, the depth of field is much greater and focusing is correspondingly easier. But there are still drawbacks. It can be difficult to judge exactly where you are focused if there is considerable depth of field. And when set to a wide angle, you have to work closer to the subject in order to get an appropriate image size on the screen. Then there can be problems with geometric distortions and camera shadows on the subject to be faced.
Camera shake	The *longer* the focal length (narrower angle), the more sensitive the camera becomes to shake and shudder; particularly when you are standing still shooting a stationary distant subject.
The impression of distance and depth in the picture	Because distant planes appear closer when shot on a *narrow-angle lens* (*long focal length*) a distant back wall will look much nearer and the room appear smaller. Any planes that are at an oblique angle to the camera (e.g. a side wall) will become foreshortened. Three-dimensional subjects look squashed as their depth or thickness along the *z-axis* (i.e. near-to-far direction) is compressed. Conversely a *wide-angle lens* will cause these same dimensions to appear stretched or deeper than usual. All planes will look abnormally far away. Impressions of size and space are exaggerated.
The accuracy of shapes (geometry)	The *wider* the lens angle, the greater the distortion in closer shots of three-dimensional subjects.
Problems when zooming	When using the zoom lens, several kinds of problems can arise: ● Some zoom lenses do not maintain constant focus throughout the zoom travel (design or poor adjustment). Then you will need to refocus whenever you alter the lens angle, even if the subject-to-camera distance has not changed. ● The depth of field available when zoomed *out* is greater then when zoomed *in*. So when zooming in to a closer view (tighter shot) you will probably find that a subject which appeared to be sharply focused with a wide-angle setting (greater depth, focusing less precise) becomes soft focus (*defocused*) as the angle narrows and depth is restricted. (See Section 3.13.) ● The smoothness of all camera movements and adjustments (panning, tilting, focusing changes) deteriorates as the lens angle is reduced. When following a moving subject with a narrow-angle setting, accurate constant framing may become impossible (e.g. a distant bird held exactly in center-frame as it wheels and dives). Camera shake increases at narrower lens angles.

Table 3.2 Why change the lens angle?

To adjust framing	**A slight change in lens angle:** Where you want to exclude (or include) certain foreground objects, and repositioning camera or subject would spoil proportions; Where a normal lens would not provide the required size or framing without repositioning the camera or subject.
For otherwise unobtainable shots	**Using a narrow-angle (long-focus) lens:** To shoot remotely situated subjects – where they are separated from the camera by uneven ground or inaccessible: Where the camera is isolated – on a camera platform (tower), shooting through scenic openings: Where the camera cannot be moved – static tripod, obstructions. **Using a wider-angle (shorter-focus) lens:** Where the normal lens does not provide a wide enough shot – space restrictions: To maintain a reasonably close camera position (e.g. so talent can read *prompter*) yet still provide wider shots.
To adjust effective perspective	Altering lens angle and changing camera distance to maintain same subject size alters relative subject/background proportions and effective distances **Using a wider lens angle (short-focus lens)** – enhances spatial impression, increases depth of field. **Using a narrower lens angle (long-focus lens)** – reduces spatial impression, compresses depth, e.g. bunching together a straggling procession.
Insufficient time to change camera distance	**Altering apparent camera distance (shot size) by changing lens angle:** During fast intercutting sequence: When camera repositioning would involve complicated moves.
To provide simpler or more reliable operations	**Zooming in/out instead of dollying** may produce smoother, easier changes in shot size (but perspective and handling affects change). Zooming provides **rapid changes in image size** more safely than fast dollying (for dramatic effect or to suddenly reveal detail). **Zooming in/out on a flat subject** is indistinguishable from dollying, but avoids focus-following problems. Lens angle changes can avoid close-up cameras coming into picture.
To increase production flexibility	Where dollying would distract talent or obscure the camera action from audience. When using only one camera.
To produce distortion	For grotesque close-ups or to flatten modeling.

3.7 The zooming process (see Section 2.8)

There are several different methods of controlling the lens' zooming action. A camera operator working on a drama production may prefer a *manual zoom system* which allows the shot's coverage to be subtly readjusted as

Figure 3.5 Zooming
Zooming simply magnifies and reduces the picture. It does not produce the changes between planes that arise as you move through a scene (dollying; tracking).

Increasing the focal length narrows the lens angle, filling the screen with a smaller and smaller section of the shot (zooming in).

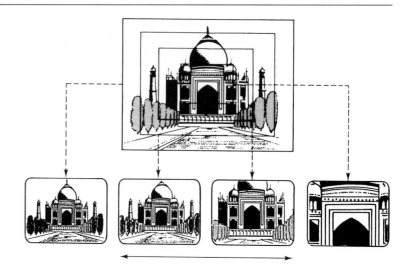

picture composition varies. But for the split-second decisions and fast zooms involved when shooting a sports event, *automated systems* can prove a lot more convenient.

Controlling zooming

Let's look at regular methods of controlling zooming:

- *Barrel ring* Turning a ring on the *lens barrel* varies the zoom lens' focal length. This is a precise method, giving you total control over the zoom action throughout. Watching the viewfinder picture, you judge for yourself the amount of angular change you need and the speed of the zoom.
- *Shot box* This is a *press-button control unit* which may be attached to a pan-bar (panning handle) or fitted at the back of the camera head. Each button switches the zoom lens to a particular chosen angle. (You can select and adjust these angles beforehand.) When you want to zoom, you press the appropriate button and the lens angle changes automatically at a speed selected by another variable control. The particular advantage of this arrangement is that you can set up a series of shots in advance, knowing that you will obtain exactly the same coverage during taping as you had during rehearsal. In newscast or interview situations where people remain in predetermined positions this method can simplify operations considerably.
- *Power zoom* Many zoom-lens systems can be controlled by a two-way *rocker switch* (Figure 2.3) which activates a small motor. This will drive the zoom towards either the *wide angle* or the *telephoto (narrow angle)* end of its range, stopping where needed. The zoom speed may be adjustable or vary with finger pressure on the switch. The power zoom is widely used and particularly adaptable to all types of production in the studio and in the field.

  Where this facility is fitted you will generally have the switchable option of selecting between *remote–manual–auto* methods of iris control using the same hand.

The smooth zooming action of a motorized system is very convenient. Some manual designs are difficult to operate smoothly over a wide range.

Some are limited to a single speed of travel, others have the choice of two speeds (*fast/slow*) or provide *variable speed*. One limitation is that instead of being able to vary zooming speed during a shot you are restricted to that of your particular system. A motorized zoom system may take from e.g. 5 seconds to 20 seconds to travel from maximum angle to minimum angle (or vice versa).

Two other drawbacks make motorized zoom systems unpopular with some users. They consume the camera's *battery power* every time you use it. And some designs are quite noisy (like some *auto-focus* systems) and are liable to be overheard by the camera microphone, whirring away as they operate.

● **Remote control** Here the *manual zoom controls* are fitted to the pan bar(s). They are of several types which allow you to control the zoom action precisely as you judge from the viewfinder picture the speed and extent of zoom needed.

The zoom in use

How successful any zoom-lens system is in practice often depends on the type of production. While a large zoom ratio may be useful when shooting a documentary, it may prove excessive in the studio, where you are generally working with only a limited part of that range. Operationally, the zoom operation may feel '*coarse*', so that even a slight movement of a manual control produces a considerable change in the lens angle. Conversely, some systems are so '*fine*' that it takes appreciable readjustment to cover the zoom range. Results generally depend on the maximum zoom range available and the design of the zoom controls.

Zooming is a great facility when used discretely. If you are shooting a ball game, and zoom in to a closer shot as the action grows more tense, even the most perceptive viewer is not going to be disturbed by any variations in perspective! Zoom in rapidly so that the camera seems to swoop into the scene, particularly if it is on a jib arm arcing over the action, and the result is dynamic!

But use a similar zooming action at the wrong time, and you may well antagonize your audience. Rapid *in–out* zooms can be nauseous! Zoom back as someone approaches the camera, and tension will fall.

Try for yourself the effect of dollying in towards a person while zooming out at a corresponding speed; i.e. keeping them the same size in the frame throughout. The result is quite bizarre, but it certainly demonstrates the extent to which the lens angle and camera distance can affect your shot!

3.8 Focusing

Focusing quickly becomes a reflex action. You adjust for the sharpest image, turning the control just a little to keep subjects sharp ('follow focus') if they begin to soften. But as we shall see, focusing is not always as straightforward as that.

To begin with, a lens cannot focus on subjects closer than its 'minimum focused distance' (MFD). And with a long-focus (narrow-angle) lens, that could be as little as a foot and a half (0.5 m) away. You cannot focus on subjects nearer than that. At very narrow angles, the MFD may be several yards/meters from the camera!

At the other end of the scale you have the *macro lens* systems, which are designed to provide a sharp image almost up to the actual lens surface. But it is difficult to avoid a camera shadow when lighting such close subjects.

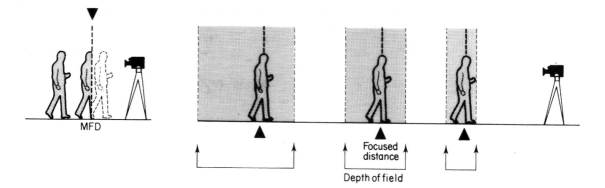

Figure 3.6 Following focus
The camera cannot focus on anything closer than the *minimum focused distance* (MFD).

For a 'long focus' lens (long focal length; narrow angle), the MFD may be some distance from the camera. With a 'short-focus' lens (short focal length; wide angle), focusing may be possible right up close to the camera lens.

As the subject gets closer to the camera, the depth of field becomes shallower, so focusing is more critical. How noticeable a fall-off in sharpness is depends on the amount of fine detail and tonal contrast in the subject.

When you are using the macro setting, the lens' zoom action is inoperative.

3.9 Auto-focus

Most video cameras are fitted with an *automatic focusing* facility. This is a really useful device for those occasions when you are extremely preoccupied with following action, are not sure where the subject is going to move to next, are shooting in a hazardous situation, and might get the focusing wrong in the heat of the moment. But why not switch auto-focus in all the time, so that it frees you of that chore altogether?

Well, if you rely entirely on automatic features in the camera to control your pictures, you must expect results to vary. The auto system simply sharpens focus to maximum in a selected zone of the shot, irrespective of what is appearing there. So you need to use it with care.

Camera systems have different degrees of sophistication. Some have a two- or three-step focus zone (small angle, to full frame width). Some include an *auto-focus check*, so that you can check the auto effect while still in the manual mode. There are even 'fuzzy logic' circuits which readjust focus as a subject moves around within the shot, or the shot is altered.

There are several different design approaches for auto-focus systems including: *infrared light* (IR), *ultrasonic (piezo) control, digital AI, auto-tracking, fuzzy logic*, and an '*eyeball focus*' system. Each has its advantages and limitations. Even if you are not particularly interested in the various technologies involved it is as well to know about the practical limitations of your camera's system if you are going to rely on auto-focus to keep your pictures sharply focused.*

*For more details on '*autofocus*' see page 594 of *Television Production* (3rd edn) by Gerald Millerson.

● In the infrared system the camera sends out a brief burst of IR light which is reflected from the nearest object and detected by an IR sensor. Circuits interpret the return beam's angle (triangulation) and adjust the lens focus.

- The ultrasonic (piezo) system emits a short bleep of inaudible sound, and measures the time taken to return. Circuits calculate distance and adjust the lens accordingly.
- One electronic system examines the video signal and adjusts the lens focus for maximum sharpness by checking the strength and contrast of the video signal, which fall off as the picture is defocused.

Each of these methods can work well most of the time, but there are situations where they can produce very surprising results!

Different auto-focus systems can be fooled by the subject or by conditions, and give inaccurate results:

Infra-red. Small subjects, surface color (especially black), shiny angled surfaces.
Ultrasonic. Subjects behind glass, water, etc. Broken-up foreground (trellis, foliage, branches). Metallic noises. Rain, snow, fog.
Electronic. Dim lighting, low contrast or flatly lit subjects.

Keep a lookout for problem occasions:

- When the subject is not in the center of the picture. If you place two people either side of the frame, auto-focus may sharpen on an unimportant distant object in the center of the screen, and leave the subjects soft-focused.
- You may want to focus on someone near the camera and a distant person at the same time, but auto-focus may sharpen on one or the other – or neither!
- If you shoot a subject through a foreground framework (e.g. trellis or branches) the system will focus on this foreground rather than the more distant subject.
- If you are following someone who is moving around within a crowd the auto-focus system is liable to continually readjust itself; focusing on nearby people instead as the shot changes.
- If you zoom to change the size of the shot, the auto-focus system may refocus as you recompose the picture.
- If you are shooting a distant view, and anyone (or anything) moves into the shot, closer to camera, the system may refocus on them instead, and defocus on the real subject. If, for example, you are panning around a scene and look past a foreground tree, the system may readjust to focus on the tree.
- There could be times when the background behind subjects becomes confusing or intrusive, due to ambiguous focusing.

If you meet such situations, the best solution is to switch to *manual* focusing, to avoid problems. Nevertheless, if you use it wisely, auto-focus is a very useful facility.

3.10 Depth of field

Strictly speaking, when you focus a lens, only objects at that distance on the focusing scale will appear really sharp in the picture. Anything nearer or farther away becomes increasingly defocused.

In a distant view, everything seems pretty clearly defined. But refocus the lens onto something a few feet away, and you will find that only a limited amount of the shot appears really sharp. Now focus on something very close to the camera, and sharpness becomes restricted to a very shallow zone indeed.

How obvious this effect is varies with the amount of detail there is in the scene.

The focused zone, which is called the *depth of field*, varies with:

- the *distance* at which the lens is focused,
- the *focal length* of the lens (or the setting of the zoom),
- and the lens *f*/stop (*aperture*).

Alter any of these, and the depth of field changes.

Depth is *greatest* when:

- the lens is focused at a distance,
- you are using a short-focus (wide angle) lens,
- the lens aperture is stopped down (e.g. *f*/16).

Depth is *shallow* when:

- you are focusing on close subjects,
- using a long-focus (narrow angle) lens,
- the lens aperture is opened up (e.g. *f*/2).

Don't be misled into thinking that you can use a wide-angle lens to improve depth of field in a shot. When you change to the wide-angle, the subject will look smaller, and by the time you have got closer to compensate, the focused depth will become the same as before! And now you will have distortions and exaggerated depth too!

3.11 Maximum sharpness?

Should one always try to get everything in the picture as sharp as possible? Not always. There will certainly be situations where you *do* want to see everything in the shot clearly. You may be showing widespread action, as in a ball game. Or the camera could be looking around an interesting building. Or you may want to compose your picture in depth, and have your shot include both a person near the camera and another some distance away, all sharply focused.

Then you could use a wide-angle lens, stopped down as far as the light levels will permit.

There will be other times, though, when you want your audience to concentrate on a particular subject, and disregard the surroundings. And you can achieve this, by deliberately *restricting* the depth of field, using a larger lens aperture and/or a narrower lens angle. Now, thanks to the limited depth, your subject will appear sharp against a defocused background, where anything likely to confuse or distract merges into an indistinct blur.

3.12 Difficult to focus?

Sometimes you will find that there is insufficient depth of field to focus clearly on the *whole* subject. That is a particular problem in close shots. Stopping the lens down would help of course, but there may not be enough light for you to do so, without under-exposing the picture. Yet you are unable to increase the light level. What do you do then?

Well, there are several regular compromise solutions here.

The best method, may be to sharpen focus on the *most important part* of the subject, and leave the rest defocused.

Figure 3.7 Limited depth of field

Part 1 If the depth of field is too limited for your purposes, you can:

Part 2 *Stop down* – increasing focused depth, but higher light intensity is needed.

Part 3 *Focus on one subject* – letting others soften.

Part 4 *Split focus* – spreading the available depth between both subjects (now none is really sharp).

Part 5 *Move subjects close* – so that they are roughly the same distance from the camera.

Part 6 *Use a wider lens angle* – so that depth increases, but subjects now appear smaller (Figure 2.6).

Part 7 *Pull the camera back* – so that depth increases, but the shot is now smaller.

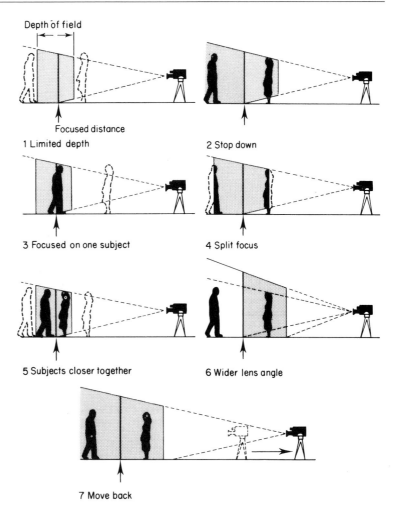

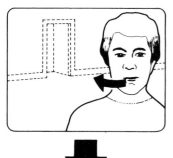

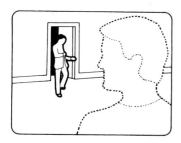

Figure 3.8 Pulling focus
As he turns, you refocus on the visitor.

Alternatively, you might *split focus*, and choose a compromise focusing distance so that all subjects are clearly enough focused in the circumstances.

Sometimes you can *pull focus* (*throw focus*) if this is appropriate. Supposing, for example, that you are shooting two people at different distances from the camera, and cannot get them both in sharp focus. You might start by focusing hard on one, then at a suitable moment, alter focus while still on shot, to sharpen on the other person. The method works, but the effect of changing focus in this way can be very dramatic. So it's a technique you need to reserve for the right occasion!

Finally, you could improve matters by moving the subjects, or altering the camera position, so that they are both about the same distance from the camera and within the available depth of field.

3.13 Pre-focusing the zoom lens

The zoom lens is a fine tool for the creative camera operator, but it holds some nasty pitfalls for the unwary. At the very moment you are

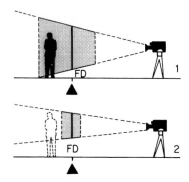

Figure 3.9 Pre-focusing the zoom
If you have not focused the lens accurately in a long shot, the picture will become defocused as you zoom in.

Part 1 Although focus appears satisfactory here, this is due to the available depth of field (wide lens angle).

Part 2 But on zooming in, the depth becomes restricted (narrow lens angle), and is insufficient to keep the subject sharp.

concentrating on following some tricky action you are most likely to meet up with its sneakiest traps!

It's one thing to read about such potential pitfalls on the printed page and quite another to encounter them 'for real' during action shots; so we've summarized them here! You have been warned.

You soon discover that it is a lot more difficult to *hold shots steady* when you are working at the narrow-angle (long focus, telephoto) end of its range, than when you are zoomed right out (widest angle, shortest-focal length). That is really what you would expect of course (Section 3.5), but to find that camera handling varies from moment to moment can be unnerving at first, especially when you zoom into a close detailed shot and then find that you cannot keep it steady!

The way the available *depth of field* changes throughout the zoom lens' range can pose practical focusing problems.

When you are zoomed out, there is normally considerable depth of field available, and focusing is easy. Usually, so much looks sharp in the picture that you can't judge exactly where the 'best' focus is. But zoom in to a close shot, and depth becomes relatively shallow.

In fact, there is always the danger that instead of being focused exactly on the subject as you thought, you were really focused some distance nearer or farther away! Consequently, when you zoom in from a good sharp long shot to a close-up, you may find it completely defocused, and then have to fumble to correct focus, while on shot!

The only solution to this dilemma is to remember to *pre-focus the zoom* (Figure 3.9), before you take the shot. All this involves is taking a trial close-shot of the subject immediately beforehand so that you can focus crisply, then zoom back to the wide shot (without changing your distance), ready to start shooting the action.

Some cameras are fitted with a rapid auto-check facility for the zoom lens. At the press of a button you can preview what your 'zoomed-in' shot will look like; allowing you to check focus and judge whether you need to correct the focus setting in anticipation. Let go of the button, and it returns to your current shot. This is speedier than turning the zoom control manually to zoom in, rocking the focus control to check, then zooming out again to find your original framing.

That sounds fine, but if you have been shooting a bank of flowers, then suddenly decide to take a big close-up of a butterfly that has just landed on a nearby blossom, you are unlikely to be pre-focused. In this situation, you can only hope, and correct the focus on the close-up surreptitiously. If the shot is badly defocused, then focus it correctly, and cut out the fuzzy picture during editing.

Exposure

3.14 What is 'exposure'?

The CCD in any video camera requires a certain amount of light to function effectively and produce attractive pictures. But it can only handle a fairly limited range of tones. When your shot contains a wide range of tones (*brightness values*) you cannot hope to reproduce them all absolutely accurately in the final picture.

● If the amount of light from a surface exceeds the CCD's upper limit, it will reproduce as white in the picture. It will *block off/burn out/clip* to a blank white.
● Conversely, where a surface reflects too little light, it will fall beyond the system's lower limit and crush to an overall black tone.

The average brightness of the lens image falling onto the CCD is primarily determined by the *lens aperture (f-stop)*. So the trick is to adjust the stop so that the tones you are most interested in, usually people's faces, are clearly visible. This process is called '*adjusting the exposure*'. '*Correct exposure*' is a very subjective choice.

Photographers and film-makers regularly use a light-meter to estimate their film's exposure. the meter is calibrated to measure the intensity of light falling on the subject (*incident light*), the average amount of light reaching the camera (*reflected light*), or the specific amount of light being reflected from a surface (*photometer*).

No-one can judge whether a **film** shot is going to turn out right until it has been processed (i.e. developed and printed). So it's extremely important for the film maker to calculate the *correct exposure* before shooting, otherwise entire sequences could be wildly wrong. (Notwithstanding such careful estimates, laboratories may still need to compensate for minor exposure inaccuracies during the printing process.)

On the other hand, when making a **video** production you have the enormous advantage that you can always see there on the screen exactly what you are taping. You can continually assess the picture, and if it is over- or underexposed, immediately compensate! In video/television production the camera itself is your light-meter! So you will only need to measure light values:

● When adjusting light intensities in the studio, to suit the lens aperture you have decided to work at. (As a general guide, you may assume that the video camera's sensitivity is roughly equivalent to a film speed of ASA 100.)
● To check the intensity of prevailing light (incident light levels) before pre-adjusting the lens aperture to suit.
● To check whether the intensity and contrast of lighting are reasonably consistent throughout the action area for various camera positions. If they are not, you will need to readjust the camera's exposure as it moves around.

Let's take a practical example. Perhaps you are shooting someone standing out in the open air. You adjust exposure by altering the lens aperture, until they look good in your viewfinder; or better still, on a high grade picture monitor. Their face tones in particular, should appear quite natural – neither too light nor too dark.

Now look carefully at the picture, and you are quite likely to find that their white shirt reproduces as washed-out and without detail, or the trousers look black, with no signs of modeling in the material at all. Perhaps you can simply accept the results. But if this is a fashion shot, showing off the quality and attractiveness of the clothing, it would scarcely be acceptable.

You can seldom expect to show good tonal gradation in *everything* in the scene. There will usually be something in the shot that crushes out to white or black.

How successfully you can expose a shot will depend not only on the range of tones appearing in it, but on the effect you are aiming at. You might deliberately 'underexpose' a picture to make it look more shadowy and mysterious. You might 'overexpose' a picture of the seashore, to create a high-key effect.

In the studio, one can control tones by careful selection, by lighting or by adjustments. But elsewhere, particularly on location, you have to make the most of what is available, and at times the lens aperture you select may have to be something of a compromise.

If parts of the location scene reproduce as large blank white or black areas in the picture, there may not be much you can do about it. The obvious remedy is to reframe the shot, or change the camera position, to keep them out of picture altogether. If you have lighting equipment available, you may be able to lighten darker tones or shadowy areas. Occasionally you can mask off a troublesome surface (e.g. have someone standing in the foreground obscuring a large blank white wall). If it is only a small object that catches the eye (e.g. sun reflected in a table mirror), you may be able to re-angle it, or remove it altogether. Choosing the optimum exposure may involve a certain amount of compromise.

3.15 Underexposure and overexposure

When a picture is *underexposed* all of its tones will appear that much darker. Results are usually dull and lifeless. Detail and modeling may be clear in light tones (even clearer than usual), but mid to dark areas look muddy and merge to black.

There is always a certain amount of 'noise' in any video picture, but when it is badly underexposed, a grainy sparkling 'snow' over the darker tones becomes very obvious and degrades its quality. The effect worsens in the videotape recording and any subsequent re-recordings of that tape.

It is worth remembering too, that when the camera receives insufficient light from the scene, other picture defects also develop such as *lag* (image smearing on movement), and picture noise.

To remedy underexposure, you open up the *lens aperture* to provide the camera's CCD with a brighter lens image. (But at the same time of course, this will reduce the depth of field to some extent, and could make focusing harder, particularly when using a narrow-angle lens.)

Increasing the *video amplification* on a camera cannot really compensate when the camera sensor is not getting enough light for maximum performance. It just boosts the video signal. But it will certainly strengthen the reproduced picture, perhaps even making it look bright and well contrasted.

When a picture is *overexposed*, all of its tones will appear unusually light. Even fairly light tones in the scene will block off, while darker areas of the scene will often be easier to discern than normal. Stopping down a little improves reproduction in light tones, but reduces the visibility of shadows. However, you cannot compensate electronically for *grossly over-* or *underexposed areas*. They will remain detailless. Again, lowering the video gain setting is not a solution. It will simply reduce the overall brightness of the picture.

3.16 Automatic exposure

If judging exposure is a matter of artistic choice, how is it that so many video cameras are fitted with an automatic iris? Well, leaving aside those people who would otherwise be careless about exposure, the auto-iris is a very useful facility when you are in a tight spot. It continually adjusts the lens aperture to maintain an average video signal.

Under typical location conditions, whether in the open or within buildings, light levels can change considerably as the camera alters its viewpoint. Try walking around with a light-meter, and you will see its needle bouncing up and down as you reposition. So your camera may well need to be stopped down to *f*/16 in a sunlit courtyard, yet have to open up to *f*/2 as you move inside a house.

Strictly speaking, therefore, if you are following along with action that moves from the exterior to the interior, you would need to keep an eye on your viewfinder, and adjust the exposure to match these different light levels.

But surely, you will say, you are already having to follow *focus* as you move, and keep the shot properly framed. How can you accurately adjust exposure at the same time? A very valid point! That is why even experienced cameramen under these conditions will leave exposure to the auto-iris, and concentrate on focusing and composing the picture.

Ideally, you set the lens aperture to suit your main subject. If the same subject appears in a succession of shots in the same scene, you want the exposure to be *constant*, not yo-yo about as incidental background tones vary. Yet changes of this kind are really unavoidable when using an auto-iris.

It is easy to fool an auto-iris. If you bring a lighter tone into the shot (e.g. open a newspaper or take off a jacket and reveal a white shirt), it will close down a little, and darken all the other tones in the picture, including the face you are really looking at. Take the light area out of shot, or pan away from it, and the auto-iris will open up. Picture tones will lighten. Take a long shot, and face tones may look dark, but zoom in to a close shot, and because other picture tones are now excluded the face reproduces much lighter.

Under certain conditions, the auto-iris can cause bad underexposure. Normally, if you are shooting inside a room, the system will open up and produce successful pictures. But suppose the person you are filming moves over to the window. The auto-iris will see the intense daylight, and stop the lens down. As a result, the person now appears as a silhouette, while the sky is well exposed.

Some cameras have a *backlight* control that you switch in under such conditions. This opens up the iris an arbitrary stop or so above the auto-iris setting, to improve the subject's exposure. This may overexpose lightest areas, but the person will now be more clearly visible.

Although the auto-iris system is by no means infallible, these variations are often preferable to badly overexposed or underexposed pictures. And in practice, they may be too slight to worry about, or even pass unnoticed. For all that, they are still there. It depends how critically you are watching the final result.

3.17 Practical solutions

As you have seen, when shooting a scene which contains a variety of tones it may not be possible to accommodate the entire range. You might have to accept that the lightest and/or the darkest areas will be lost in detailless highlights or shadows. So is that it? Well, there are possible remedies.

Sky filters

When shooting in the field you may discover that although your main subject is properly exposed, distant skies are far too bright and distracting. This can be a particular problem where you have dark-toned foreground subjects.

A *sky filter* can often overcome this dilemma. Its upper section has a neutral gray tint which reduces the brightness of the image in that part of the picture. So it will '*hold back*' the overbright skies while leaving anything in the clear lower section unaffected. Some sky filters have quite a *sharply defined* transition between their upper and lower parts. That's useful for pictures of a seascape or open terrain, for it will more clearly define the clouds and add to the picture's impact. However, when using this type of filter you need to take care that this artificial-looking division coincides with the horizon if it is to look 'natural'.

Sky filters which have a more *gradual* tonal transition, give a softer, less clearly defined blend between the treated and untreated areas; so their positioning in the frame can be less critical.

You can use a graduated color filter to create a deliberate effect. One half of the filter may be orange and the other half clear or blue-tinted. Some color filters have a central horizontal orange or yellow band which, with care, may simulate the effect of a sunset.

The main disadvantages of this otherwise useful device, are that

- You need to anticipate, and fit a sky filter for a specific shot.
- You cannot tilt or pan the shot; or the effect will be very obvious.
- You should, wherever possible, make the visible division coincide with a feature in the landscape; particularly for hard-edged types.

Tonal adjustments

How successfully can your video system reproduce the scene you are shooting? You might expect that the tones you see on the screen would correspond exactly to those in the scene. However, in practice video and film systems have a tendency to exaggerate or to reduce apparent tonal contrasts in the reproduced picture. At the lightest and darkest extremes, these systems cannot distinguish between subtle differences in brightness, so those tones appear merged into dense shadow or blank highlights.

As we saw earlier, if you have difficulty in seeing detail or tonal differences in shadows, and try to improve things by opening up the lens aperture, the lightest tones will probably become overexposed. Extra video amplification will not help either. So some cameras include a *black stretch* control, which will make shadow detail clearer and improve tonal gradation in darker tones. There may be corresponding circuitry to improve reproduction of lightest tones.

In Chapter 13 we shall be looking at various ways in which the camera system's response can be adjusted: to make the picture lighter or darker, increase or decrease the contrast, etc.

Handling your camera

3.18 Why all these rules?

There are a lot of 'do's' and 'dont's' in this section. You could simply follow them, but it would be better to try shooting situations in which you *deliberately* break each of these principles. Then re-shoot the same scenes the right way. If you sit down and critically compare the results, they should speak for themselves!

3.19 Panning and tilting

If you cannot get a sufficiently wide shot of your subject to show it completely, or you feel that the distant view does not have enough detail, there are two general solutions.

You can take a series of separate shots which are then intercut to build up an overall image in the minds of your audience. However, you must avoid this sequence simply developing into disjointed random 'potshots'.

Alternatively, you can pan your camera carefully and systematically over the scene, to relate various parts. Take care, though, to avoid a series of brief erratic pans or long 'empty' pans that wander over unimportant things. See that each pan has a clear purpose and finishes by settling on an interesting feature of the scene. Above all, do avoid panning from side to side over the scene, as if you were using a water-hose. Although this can be a great temptation, it is not something you are likely to do more than once when you have played back the results!

Like all camerawork, panning and tilting should be smooth and controlled. Above all, avoid overshooting, i.e. panning enthusiastically but going beyond your final point then having to correct the situation by reversing the pan a little. It draws attention to the error. Ideally, you want to bring each movement to a smooth finish. If your pan has a jerky start or finish, or is hesitant, or its speed is uneven, or it wavers up and down, the result can look pretty crude in the finished production.

Figure 3.10 Camera movements
Although some camera movements have alternative terms (dolly, truck, arc – track, crab), others are universal. People often speak of 'panning' up/down as well as panning sideways.

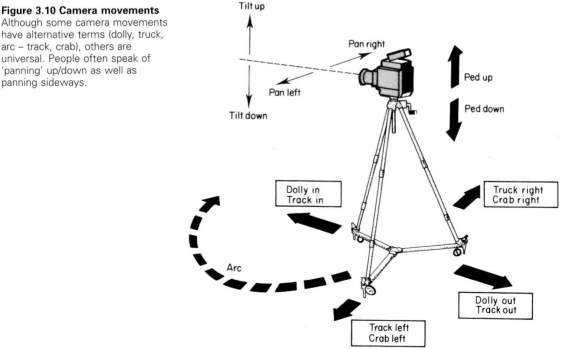

Don't be tempted to pan around too quickly, for your picture will only become an indecipherable blur. Most of us fall into that trap at first, when shooting a landscape. We pan around briskly, trying to show everything, only to find that the result on the screen is extremely disappointing, as details become broken up ('strobing') during the movement.

Try panning across a scene, so that an object takes around five seconds to travel from one edge of the screen to the other. That is about the fastest rate to avoid movement break-up.

Very occasionally, you can deliberately use a rapid *whip pan* (*zip pan*) for startling dramatic effect, but it is really one of those ideas that you try, then seldom use again!

If your camera is hand-held or shoulder-mounted and you want to follow action over a wide arc, do not try to rotate your body by turning on your heels. Instead, position yourself facing mid-way, ready to make a smooth balanced movement, and twist your body to follow the action. The result will be much more controlled. Keeping your knees slightly bent can help.

When you are using a tripod, remember to check that it is level before panning, or you will find the framing moving upwards or downwards as you pan.

3.20 Following moving subjects

There is a lot more to taking shots of a moving subject than simply keeping up with it! The way you cope with movement is a hallmark of good camerawork.

When you hold your camera quite still, anything moving around in the shot can very soon reach the edge of the frame and pass out of sight, particularly if it is moving quickly in a 'tight' shot filling most of the screen.

There are several ways of dealing with this situation:

- You can let the moving subject *pass out of the frame altogether* ('exit'). And you will certainly do this if you want the audience's attention to pass on to a new subject.
- You can *widen the shot*; zooming out or moving back to include the movement. That is often the best solution, if you have someone pacing to and fro, or waving their arms about.
- You can *pan and/or tilt* to keep the subject in shot, for example, to follow somebody as they move around a room. But don't use too close a shot here. Not only will the subject itself look very cramped in the frame, but you'll find it quite difficult to follow the action smoothly.
- You can move the camera position (e.g. arc round) so that the subject remains in shot.
- You can move along with the subject ('traveling shot') keeping it in frame as you go.
- Instead of following the movement, you can let it leave frame, and then pick up the action from a new viewpoint.

If you are shooting with a *single* camera the last option listed above means that you have to stop recording, get over to the next position, set up the new shot, and re-start recording again. In the meantime, you're missing some of the action. Unless, of course, you can have it repeated, and take up the action from just before you moved to your second viewpoint.

If you are using *two or more* cameras you need not miss any of the action; just cut to the second camera at the right moment.

Which of these methods you choose will depend on which you consider is most appropriate, both artistically and practically.

3.21 Framing movement

At first sight, it seems logical to keep a moving subject exactly in the middle of the picture. However, you will find that the picture looks unbalanced and rather boring. Instead, when you are panning with a moving subject, try to position it lagging just a little behind center-frame all the time ('offset'). The picture looks more dynamic. The faster the movement, the greater the offset.

Above all, don't let the subject 'hop around the frame' through uneven panning. (This can happen if there is *insufficient drag* on the panning head.)

Worst crime of all, don't have the subject 'popping in and out' of the shot, as you lose it and find it, while trying to keep up with it! (This will most likely happen if you try to follow a fast-moving subject in a close shot on a narrow-angle lens, or if you have *too much drag* on the panning head.)

3.22 Walking

If you are going to use a shoulder-mounted camera a lot it is a good idea to make practice recordings, as you move around on shot – towards the subject, away from it, in an arc, sideways. It is not easy as it seems, to keep level steady well-composed shots in sharp focus.

When your subject moves away, the obvious thing to do is to walk with them. But beware! Unless you have checked over the route beforehand, ensure that there are no carpets, steps, cables, people or posts. You may meet unseen hazards as you concentrate on the viewfinder picture. That is why experienced cameramen develop a habit of flicking a glance around, to check out their surroundings, and nearby action, and try to keep both eyes open when using an eyepiece viewfinder.

There is always a certain amount of bounce in the camera's shot as you walk, especially if you are moving at all quickly. This unevenness may be unimportant, even dramatic if you are following someone over uneven ground, through a crowd, or pushing through a forest. But it can be quite distracting if you are walking around within a building.

If you have a cable between the camera and a second operator (e.g. carrying batteries, sound equipment, video recorder, or a light) fast moves can be difficult. But at least you have a person nearby who can warn you of hazards in your path – particularly when you are moving backwards!

If you are going to take shots while moving around, or traveling over rough terrain, the most practical way to avoid camera bounce is to attach it to a special stabilizer unit such as the *Steadicam* fitting. This continually compensates for irregular random movements (Section 2.30). There are also several ingenious forms of optical or electronic *image stabilizer* which diminish vibrations and smooth-out variations.

3.23 Shooting from vehicles

Whenever you are shooting from any vehicle there are a number of points worth bearing in mind.

Where possible, it is best to hand-hold the camera, and shoot through an open window. Resist any temptation to rest the lens or the camera on the glass or the vehicle's body, for vibration can damage the equipment and blur the picture. Smeary, rain-speckled, dusty or tinted windows can degrade picture quality to a considerable extent, especially if sunlight is falling on them. Your pictures will show flattened contrast, defocused blurs and changing color values, that become particularly obvious when intercut with other shots.

Your position in a vehicle will influence the audience-impact of your pictures. Facing forwards, subjects appear to move towards the camera, getting closer and closer and increasingly clearer. So this is a powerful viewpoint that provides continual interest. A rear view, however, shows everything moving away from the camera, and audience interest tends to fall. No sooner does something come into shot than it quickly becomes too small to see properly. Side windows are a good way of shooting distant subjects, but anything close rapidly zips across the screen out of focus.

Shooting someone inside a moving car can need a certain amount of agility! A wide-angle (short-focus) lens is essential, to enable you to get sufficiently wide shots of the driver. Typical camera positions include: seated beside the driver, crouched in the passenger's foot space, or leaning over from a rear seat. Cameras can also be mounted outside the car, using bolt-on brackets or suction-held pads (limpet mounts).

Picture-making basics

3.24 Practical conditions

There are no absolute 'rules' for effective picture-making. In fact, if you arrange your pictures too systematically the results can look very mannered and artificial. But there *are* certainly a number of situations to avoid!

During a busy shooting schedule there simply isn't time to linger, experimenting over the composition of each shot. You have to make quick decisions. But if you understand compositional basics you will know what to look out for, and realize how to adjust the shot for the most appropriate effect. Once you recognize the sort of thing that makes pictures unsuccessful, and many are a matter of common sense, you will avoid them instinctively.

Unlike a painter, who can arrange objects on the canvas to suit his/her ideas, a video camera operator usually has to make the most of what is there already. But that does not mean that you cannot control what the viewer sees! You can do a great deal to change a picture's appeal: by selecting your viewpoint carefully, by the lens angle you choose, or by the way you frame the shot. Sometimes you will be able to reposition items to improve the picture further.

3.25 Selecting the shots

Whether you shoot the subject with one camera, or intercut between two or more, you must create a smooth-flowing sequence of pictures that makes sense to your audience. This will not happen automatically.

The worst thing you can do is to take a series of random 'good shots' of the subject without any thought about how they are going to be interrelated on the screen. You could finish up with a collection of unrelated bits and pieces. For reliable results, you should aim to work out beforehand what you want to show, and how you are going to show it. Try to plan ahead.

3.26 Persuasive shots

Picture-making is not about creating *beautiful* pictures, it is about providing *appropriate* pictures. There will even be moments when you quite deliberately introduce an *ugly* shot, to shock your audience with harsh reality. The color camera too easily glamorizes. A scene of squalid decay can become 'a vision of interesting textures and hues' in the evening sunlight.

A well-chosen sequence of shots does much more than just *illustrate* the subject for your audience. The pictures you choose and arrange are expressing your point of view; how you have interpreted a situation; what you want to say about it. That is what program-making is all about. It is almost as if you were there beside them guiding their choice and interpretation of events.

When you show them pictures of a bustling marketplace, you may be making the unspoken invitation; 'Look around at anything that happens to interest you'. More often though, you want to draw their attention to certain aspects of a scene, so you invite them through the shots you select, to concentrate on an interesting feature: 'See how this object differs from that one. Notice the intricate details there'. Or on another occasion you might be saying: 'See how she is reacting to what he said. See what she is doing . . . watch how she is doing it'.

3.27 What is it all about?

As each shot appears on the screen your audience is seeing and hearing it *for the first time*. In an instant, they have to interpret what you have selected to put there. It is not surprising that they can occasionally become confused!

Unless you are careful, they may 'look at the wrong thing', as their attention alights on something else in the picture that is more prominent, more colorful or more interesting!

The duration of a shot is important, too. If you hang on to any shot for too long, your audience will certainly begin to lose interest.

If your shots are too brief, they may 'flick past the eyes without entering the brain'!

Your aim is to help your audience to understand; to guide their thoughts, whether you are describing a technical process or telling a joke. You do not want to confuse or distract them by irrelevancies. You need to present a logical sequence of ideas that can be followed easily. Your audience cannot ask what you meant, or turn back to re-read what you said. They have to get the point first time round.

If you do not take the trouble to choose shots carefully, people have to look around each picture, trying to decide what it is all about, correctly or incorrectly. If they do not have any idea what they are supposed to be looking at (or don't find it interesting), they will look at whatever draws their attention. Random pictures produce random thoughts.

Very occasionally, you may actually *want* to puzzle or intrigue your audience, in order to create a dramatic or comic build-up of tension. The camera enters a quiet room. They are left wondering . . . they see a threatening shadow of someone standing there . . . but a moment later realise that it is only coming from garments on a coat-rack. They have been fooled.

But, in most situations, if your audience is left puzzled, wondering where it is, or what it is supposed to be, or why you have switched away from something they found interesting to this new unexplained scene, then something is very wrong!

Some directors do this all too often when they try to introduce some variety, or do 'something different'. The shot cuts to a building reflected in a puddle, or some wayside flowers, or watches a dog sleeping beside the road . . . that seems to have nothing to do with the story! Even shooting the subject through a decorative foreground screen can be puzzling at times.

Looking at production techniques critically, one soon spots current vogues. Intriguing or interesting at first perhaps, but they soon degenerate into repetitive doggerel:

- Loud music with a strong rhythm introduced for its own appeal, but quite unrelated to the program subject.
- A prominent repeated song lyric that has only a specious connection to the program subject.
- A rapid succession of apparently unrelated shots, cut to the beat of fast music.
- Continually swooping in and out on audience shots to capture reactions.
- Lengthy computer graphics at the start of a show that result in the production's opening shots becoming an anticlimax!
- The continual use of superficial shots (e.g. showing the personality's car driving to the next location) that interrupt the program flow.

Best of all, form a list of your own pet distractions. We can all learn from others!

If a shot is appropriate and helps the story onwards, it can be as unusual as you like. But if your audience is distracted by it, or begins to think how interesting the *shot* is, rather than the subject, then it has failed.

3.28 Clutter

If you do not guide your audience's attention to particular features of the scene they are just as likely to finish up looking at the wrong thing or becoming bored.

When a picture is absolutely full of things (a crowd of people, shelves of articles, or a wall of paintings), it is hard for the viewer to concentrate on any one of them properly, or even see them clearly. You may simply be trying to say: 'Aren't there a lot of different versions?', or 'See how big the collection is!'. But you could finish up with an audience who feel that they are missing out, for they can't see any of the items clearly.

It is often far better to *isolate* the item you want to show:

- Get closer (tighter framing).
- Change the camera's viewpoint.
- Use a shallow depth of field, so that only the main subject is in focus.
- Move it apart from the rest.
- Use contrasting tones.
- Use strong compositional lines.
- Position the subject higher in the frame.
- Use lighting to isolate it (light pool, shadows).

3.29 I can't see it properly!

There will be occasions when you will deliberately set out to intrigue, to mystify, to keep your audience guessing. You might use diffusion or dramatic lighting to make your subject look strange, mysterious or just different or choose an unusual camera angle. But these are the exceptions. Most times you want your audience to see the subject clearly; especially in a demonstration, or when someone is pointing out special features of an article.

Look out for those moments when the viewer *cannot see* what you are trying to show them, because the shot is too distant, or something is shadowing the subject, or even someone's thumb is over the label we are supposed to be reading.

Close-up shots are great when we want to show detail. But sometimes a close shot can prevent your audience from seeing *sufficient* of the subject. It may show a few cogs, when we really need to see much more of a piece of machinery, to see how it works.

Another hazard is overexposure. It can bleach out detail in light-toned subjects – particularly when back-light bounces off a paper being shown to camera, and we cannot see what is written on it.

All this is very obvious, but problems of this sort happen regularly, and very frustrating they can be too!

Composing pictures

3.30 Theory and practice

There is an old joke about a centipede who walked around happily until he was asked how he knew which leg to move first. Trying to work it out, he fell in a ditch, unable to budge. Many of us feel that way when we try to apply the *rules of composition*. They sound so complicated and so restrictive, they seem to turn the pleasures of picture-making into a mathematical process.

Let's forget about learning 'rules', and consider instead what we do and do not *like to see* in pictures. By following this path, we shall meet all the most important compositional principles we need to know.

3.31 The brief shot

As we look at a *still* picture, whether it is on the printed page, a projected slide, or hung in an art gallery, there is an opportunity to linger. We can scrutinize it for as long as we want.

On TV and film screen, shots do not encourage browsing. Each is there only for a brief time, from a fraction of a second to perhaps half a minute at most. Then it is replaced by another. Each shot has to make its point rapidly. Each creates its impact.

3.32 'Dull' is in the mind

What makes a shot dull? A lot depends on your *attitude* to what you are seeing. Any shot is dull when you personally find little worth looking at in it; when you could not care less who the people are, or where they are, or what they are doing. That's why other people's vacation slides may lack some of the appeal for you that they have for those who took them.

A shot may seem to show just a boring stretch of ocean. But if the commentary tells us: 'At this dangerous spot, after years of painstaking searching, divers found the Spanish treasure ship . . .' we look at the picture with new eyes, although in reality there isn't anything special to see! You

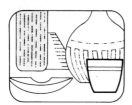

1. Avoid confusion

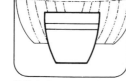

2. Get closer

3. Alter your viewpoint

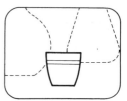

4. Reduce the depth of field

5. Isolate the subject

6. Use contrasting tones

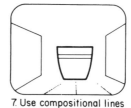

7. Use compositional lines

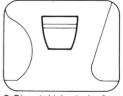

8. Place it higher in the frame

9. Isolate it with lighting

Figure 3.11 Concentrating attention

will meet this sort of thing regularly. Without the influence of the commentary, such shots could be an instant yawn. But because our interest is aroused, and they are only there for a short time, they attract and hold our attention.

So the appeal of any picture depends partly on what it *shows*, partly on what it is *about*, and partly on how *interested* you have persuaded your audience to be in it.

A shot of open desert may quickly pall, but when the audience sees a tiny moving shape in the distance, its curiosity is aroused. What happens if you continue to hold that shot? Usually, people lose interest. But in different circumstances, using exactly the same shot, they may be on the edge of their seats, waiting perhaps to discover which of the travelers has managed to survive.

If there is *too much* to see in the picture the eye flits around hopefully, but probably finishes up concentrating on nothing. If there is *too little* in the shot attention soon falls.

When there are no visual accents to grab the attention the eye wanders. But if you can arrange things so that your main subject stands out from its surroundings, then your audience will concentrate on it, and is less likely to heed other things in the picture.

3.33 Clever shots

It is tempting to devise shots that are *different*; shots that make the eye stop and wonder. Wildly distorted perspective from a close wide-angle lens, very

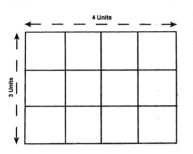

(a)

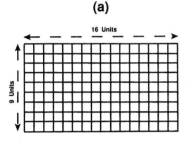

(b)

Figure 3.12 (A) Frame Shape
(a) The proportions of the regular TV picture are 4 units across and 3 units vertically. (So if a picture is 18 in. (45.7 cm) wide, it is 13.5 in. (34.29 cm) high.)

(b) In the later 16 by 9 format, a picture which is 18 in. (45.7 cm) across is 9 in. (22.9 cm) high.

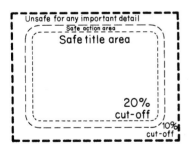

Picture borders. The picture edges are usually lost on the screen (due to over-scanning the picture tube). To ensure that no important action, or titling is lost, keep it within the borders shown.

low angle shots, or pictures using weird reflections are fine when you need them for a dramatic or comic effect. But unusual viewpoints don't just make a picture look different; they draw attention to themselves. They distract you from the real subject.

3.34 Fitting the frame

The TV screen has a horizontal rectangular shape, and many subjects fit comfortably into this format. So we can get quite a close shot of them, filling all of the screen, without losing parts outside the frame area.

Others are too tall for the screen. So you can only show them completely in a long shot, or shoot them in sections, either by panning over them, or by intercutting a series of close shots. Sometimes when the subject does not fit the screen, you have to select an oblique viewpoint to get it all into the picture.

Once you get fairly close to any subject, you are bound to lose parts of it outside the frame of the picture. Most TV receivers are adjusted to get the maximum picture size possible, so they cut off the edges of the shot. If you do not want your audience to miss anything important, such as titling, you need to compose the shot to keep these details within the 'safe area' of the screen.

If you shoot a person so that the frame chops off their heads, hands or feet the result looks odd. But alter the shot slightly so that the frame cuts partway along their limbs, and the effect seems natural enough.

There is nothing unusual about seeing a person leaning against a post, but adjust the shot so that they seem to be resting on the frame of the picture, and it appears comic.

It is interesting to see how the frame of the screen affects how comfortable we feel with the picture. If you take a shot in which the subject just fills the screen, it will look cramped and hemmed in by the frame. Go a little closer, so that parts of the subject are cut off, and all is well. Take a shot in which the subject only fills a small part of the screen, and we may get the impression that there is 'too much air around them'.

There are circumstances, of course, when you will deliberately aim at a crowded-screen effect, or isolate the subject, for dramatic reasons, but not for regular shots.

3.35 The rule of thirds

If you divide the screen into even proportions (halves, quarters), either vertically or horizontally, the result is generally pretty boring. You should avoid, for example, an horizon located exactly half-way up the frame.

You will often find the 'rule of thirds' quoted as a useful aid to composing the picture. Here you draw a grid on the monitor, dividing the screen vertically and horizontally into three equal parts. Then you compose shots so that main subjects come on these lines or where they cross. This routine is purely mechanical; for subjects' positions really depend on their size, shape, tone, the background, their relative importance, and so on. In time, you will instinctively compose shots with these features at the back of your mind. In the meantime, this 'rule' can be a helpful starting point.

3.36 Well-balanced shots

A good sense of balance is important to us in daily life, and we apply it instinctively to everything we do, even picture-making. It is easier to

Figure 3.12 (B) Fitting the frame

Framing people. Don't let the frame cut people at natural joints; intermediate points are much more attractive. Avoid having people seem to lean or sit on the edge of the picture.

Tight framing. If you frame shots too close to contain the subject's actions, it will keep moving in and out of the picture. The result is very cramped and distracting.

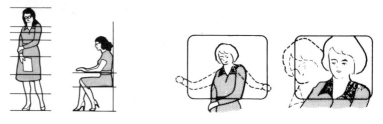

demonstrate than to talk about, and in a couple of minutes with a camera, you can see how it affects the way you arrange your pictures.

All you need is a reasonably small subject such as a vase or a pile of books on an empty table, with nothing else of interest nearby. Take a shot in which it takes up about one-third of the frame height, and comes in the center of the picture. Figure 3.15 (A) shows the idea, but results on your own screen will be a lot more convincing. What do you notice about this arrangement? Well, it probably looks a perfectly ordinary, stable, rather dull composition.

Tilt your camera down a little (B). The vase is now in the top of the shot, and you become aware of the space below it in the frame. The picture has become somewhat top-heavy.

Tilt up (C) until the vase is right at the bottom of the shot. Now the empty space above at the top of the picture has become prominent, and the frame is rather bottom-heavy.

You are seeing how the height at which you locate the subject in the frame, alters the feeling of the picture's vertical balance.

Figure 3.13 Headroom
Keep a check on the distance between the top of heads and the top of the frame. If this headroom is too little ('tight'), the frame will appear to crush down on people, and parts of heads may be cut off by the receiver overscan. Too much headroom ('loose') unbalances the shot, and may attract the audience's attention.

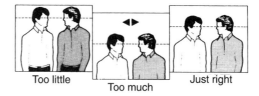

This idea is particularly important when shooting people. If you do not have enough space between the top of a person's head and the top of the picture (too little 'headroom'), the frame will seem to crush down on them. Have too much space, and one's attention goes up to the space, to see what is there.

So when taking shots of people, always look out for the headroom. It will be considerable in a long shot, and reduce correspondingly as your shot gets closer. As a very rough guide, you can think of keeping the eyes about a third of the screen height from the top of the picture, but as you will discover, headroom is influenced by whatever else is visible in the top of the picture.

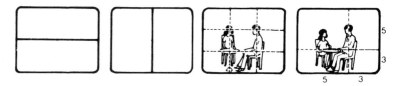

Figure 3.14 Proportions
An equally divided frame allows only formal balance – usually dull and monotonous. Thirds can lead to quickly recognized mechanical proportions. Dividing the screen in a 2:3 or a 3:5 ratio achieves a far more pleasing balance.

A   B   C   D

Figure 3.15 Picture balance

Part 1 The frame position of even a simple subject can affect whether the picture looks balanced, top-heavy, bottom-heavy or lop-sided.

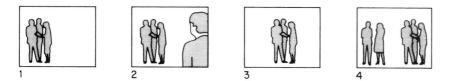

1   2   3   4

Part 2 A group that would look lop-sided and unbalance the picture (1) can be counterbalanced by another mass in another part of the screen (2). If centered (3), the picture is balanced, even without other subjects, but continual centering gets monotonous. Different sized masses can balance each other, but take care not to split the audience's attention (4).

3.37 Good balance

Looking at a well-balanced picture, we see that it has a settled, stable look. An unbalanced shot, on the other hand, has an insecure, uncertain feel to it.

That might be just what you want. An unstable, incomplete look increases tension and creates a dramatic impact. An easy way to achieve this is to make the picture top-heavy or lop-sided. But usually you will want to arrange shots so that they look balanced and complete.

Back to our experiment. Center up the subject as you did originally, then pan left a little so that it is over to the right of the frame (D). If there is nothing else in the frame the picture will look lop-sided, heavy on the right. Pan right until the subject is on frame left, and now the weight in the picture has moved across the screen. If you use a dark-toned subject the effect is more pronounced than with light tones.

You can do this experiment with light- and dark-toned pieces of card on a flat surface. The effect will be similar. If you zoom in (or get closer) so that a subject occupies more of the screen, it not only becomes more prominent, but its 'weight' in the picture increases. The farther you place it from the center of the frame, the greater is its effect.

When you have several subjects in the shot, the overall impact will alter, depending on their relative sizes and tones. Obviously, a large subject a long way away may appear smaller than a tiny object close to the camera. It is the effect that counts. You can actually balance a large subject on one side of the frame with several smaller ones on the other side. It is all a matter of their relative sizes, tones and distance from the center of the frame.

There you have the secret of interesting, well-balanced pictures; not shots which are continually, monotonously centered every time, but shots which are balanced across the frame, depending on the tones and proportions of the subjects we see there.

3.38 Juggling proportions

You can vary the relative proportions and positions of things in a picture very simply, by:

● *Adjusting the camera's distance* As you realize, the closer things are to the camera, the larger they appear in the frame. Even a slight change in the camera's distance can affect the apparent size of foreground items considerably, while anything in the background remains about the same size in the picture.
● *By changing the camera height* As you lower the camera's viewpoint things in camera foreground become more prominent, until they dominate the entire picture. But raise the camera a little, and you may shoot past them altogether. The viewer may not even realize that they are there!
● *Adjusting the lens angle* Use a *wide* lens angle, and everything looks much smaller and further away than usual. Size diminishes rapidly with distance from the camera. Even items relatively close to the lens appear further away than normal. The wide-angle shot generally emphasizes distance and depth; noticeably distorting subjects in the foreground. Conversely, when you use a *narrow* lens angle, the reverse happens. Everything looks much nearer than usual. Relative sizes do not seem to change much with distance. Even things that are far off, still look pretty close. Depth appears reduced.

So by selecting a suitable lens angle and adjusting the camera's distance, you can have quite a useful degree of control over proportions in the shot.

3.39 Grouping (unity)

When you are showing a number of items in the picture try to avoid having them scattered around the frame. It is better to centralize viewers' attention by grouping subjects in some way, otherwise your audience is likely to gaze around at random. Grouping creates a sense of unity in a picture, pulling its subjects together.

Sometimes you can create this grouping by deliberately positioning your subjects to suit the composition. At others, you will deliberately select your camera's viewpoint in order to frame the subjects in a way that will create unity.

3.40 Camera viewpoint

Where you place your camera relative to a subject, will have a strong influence on what it looks like to your audience, and how they feel about it.

The smaller a subject appears in the frame, the less important it seems to become and the less detail is visible. Its surroundings become more prominent, and can take attention from the subject itself.

Although closer shots emphasize the subject, you need to take care that they do not become so enlarged on the screen that the effect is overpowering! Really close shots often lose scale, and make the audience forget the true size and proportions of the blown-up area.

Looking down at any subject tends to make it look less impressive than looking up at it. Although steeply angled viewpoints are usually too dramatic for most purposes, even a slight variation from an eye-level position can affect the impact of a subject.

3.41 Distortions

Controlled distortion is a technique of cunning cameracraft. You might, for example, use a close wide-angle lens to distort a Halloween mask and create a frightening effect. Or you might use this technique to make quite a small group of trees look like a threatening forest.

But take care that you do not distort the shape of things badly, by accident. You might, for instance, be shooting an oil painting high up on the wall of an historic house. Either to avoid light reflections or to get an unobstructive view, you may decide to take close shots of it from a side position, on a narrow-angle lens. You get a shot, but look at the results! A squashed version that does little justice to the original!

Shooting in a small room, you may have to use a wide-angle lens to prevent everything looking too close. But beware! It is quite likely that now the room looks larger than life, and if people appear in the shot, you could too easily make them appear plump, fat-faced or large-nosed with receding hair, due to wide-angle distortions.

Anticipating editing

3.42 Continuity

Every time you set up your camera to take the next action shot, give a thought to *editing*. Otherwise you are liable to finish up with a series of shots that do not join together smoothly. This is particularly liable to happen when you re-angle the camera, and repeat the action.

The most frequent problems are:

- Part of the action is *missing*.
- The action shot from another angle does not *match* that from a previous shot of the subject.
- The *direction* of the action has changed between successive shots.
- The *shot sizes* are too similar, or too extreme.
- Action leaves the frame, and re-enters it on the same side.
- Successive shots show continuity differences; e.g. with and without eye-glasses different attitudes/expressions, dressed differently.

3.43 Improving flexibility

When you are shooting, you can help editing flexibility in various ways:

Avoid over-brief shots

- Always tape the *run-in* and *run-out* to an action, to allow editing leeway. Not just the instant the action starts.
- Where possible, start and finish a long panning shot with a 'held' (static) shot.
- When shooting 'continuous action', it can be helpful to begin each shot with the end speech and action of the previous shot.

Extra editing material

- Always shoot some *cutaways* showing the surroundings, general scene, bystanders' reactions, etc.
- Consider whether specific reaction shots/nod shots would be appropriate.

Table 3.3 Common faults while shooting

- Wrong color temperature. (Picture bluish or yellowish.)
- Soft focus.
- Focused on wrong subject.
- Camera shake, unsteady camera (tiredness, windblown).
- Sloping horizons.
- Headroom wrong. (Too little or excessive.)
- Cut off top of head or feet.
- Subject leaning on the frame.
- Subject size. (Too distant or close to see properly.)
- Successive shots too similar.
- Cutting to new camera angle, but similar shot size.
- Inappropriate camera height for the situation.
- Disproportionate number of long shots or close shots.
- All subjects composed center-frame.
- Too much sky in the shot.
- Shots do not interrelate. (Too many isolated subjects.)
- Subject obscured. (Foreground intrusion.)
- Distractions. (Other objects, background, people waving.)
- Background distractions (posters, traffic).
- Background objects sprouting from heads.
- Shots too brief (or too lengthy).
- Start of action missed.
- Zooming excessive or distracting.
- Panning not smooth, too fast, or overshoots.
- Speaker's eyeline slightly offset. (Gives a shifty look.)
- Person handling objects badly. (Obscuring, moving around.)
- Poor lighting. (e.g. Black eyes, hot top, half-lit face.)

- It is sometimes helpful to shoot the same scene at a leisurely pace, and at a faster pace (e.g. slow pan, faster pan) to allow editing choice.

Faulty takes

- Do not record over (wipe) an unsuccessful shot. Parts of it may be usable.
- If an action sequence goes wrong, it is sometimes better to retake it entirely. At others, change the camera angle (or shot size), and retake the action from just before the fault onwards (a 'pick-up' shot).

Overall shots

- Always begin shooting with a wide 'atmospheric' shot of the scene (*establishing shot*); even if it is not used eventually.
- Consider taking an overall *cover shot* of the action, then repeating action while taking closer shots.

Table 3.4 Filters

Several forms of *filter* are used with video/television cameras:

- Squares or discs of plastic sheet.
- Laminated types having a gel (gelatin) layer sandwiched between two sheets of glass.
- Squares or discs of glass.
- Other materials.

These are usually clipped over the camera lens as required, but in certain cases they may be housed within the camera (e.g. in a *filter wheel*) for instant selection, or slipped into a holder (*matte box*) supported in front of the lens.

What does a filter do? You can use filters in several ways:

1. To reduce the image brightness in very strong sunlight, to allow a wider lens aperture.
2. To give the picture an overall tint, in order to
   - Correct the color temperature of the prevailing light.
   - Simulate lighting conditions such as candlelight, sunset, firelight, etc.
3. To reduce the image contrast overall.
4. To 'cut through' haze on location (i.e. improve image contrast).
5. To create an atmospheric effect such as fog, mist, haze.
6. To create a decorative effect such as rays around highlights (star burst).
7. To distort the image in various ways; e.g. ripple.
8. To soften the image; e.g. localized or overall diffusion.
9. To reduce an overbright sky; permits rest of a shot to be exposed correctly; or to enhance clouds.
10. To create multi-image effects.
11. To suppress light reflections or glare.

Types of filter

Neutral density filter   Obtainable in a series of densities from 80.0% to 0.01% transmission

Color correction filter   Compensates for the color quality of the prevailing light. A 'daylight filter' (light blue) matches the orange-yellow color quality of tungsten lighting to a camera set up to suit the bluish quality of daylight.

Color conversion filter   Colored medium giving the entire picture a color cast; e.g. a light blue filter simulating moonlight.

Low contrast filter   A filter with many fine particles, which holds back highlights more than shadows, so reducing tonal contrasts.

Ultraviolet (UV) filter   A coated filter which blocks the ultraviolet light, that creates glare and reduces picture contrast when shooting in the open air (particularly in snowscapes).

Fog filter   A filter which diffuses the image and simulates a foggy or misty effect. There are several types, ranging from clear glass or plastic with an etched or finely ground surface, to open-weave net material stretched across the lens.

Diffusion disc   Provides overall softening of the image, from slight 'defocusing' to strong diffusion. Created by ribbing, embossing or scribing the filter's surface.

Star filter   A clear disc with a closely scribed or grooved grid, which produces multi-ray star burst pattern (e.g. 4, 6, 8 ray) around highlights, point light-sources and specular reflections. On turning the filter, the ray pattern rotates.

Ripple disc   Clear molded glass with a 'hammered' or ripple surface, or plain glass lightly smeared with oil or grease.

Sky filter   A graduated neutral density filter. (See Section 3.17)

Multi-image filter   A molded prismatic or multi-faceted disc, producing several small repeat images around the central subject, or a series of vertical repeating strips.

Polarizing screen   A filter material which is selective to light direction. Clipping on the filter and rotating it to an appropriate angle (found by trial and error) you can selectively suppress light reflections from various shiny surfaces (e.g. glass, water, metal, road surfaces), and darken blue skies while making clouds more prominent.

Dichroic filter   A glass filter with a special surface coating that allows selected regions of the light spectrum to be suppressed. Placed over tungsten lighting fittings to 'convert' the light to a color quality resembling daylight (i.e. from a lower to a higher color temperature).

With care, effects involving color and contrast can be simulated successfully enough by adjusting the camera channel. You can also devise your own versions of some filters by treating clear glass or acrylic sheets. *But never attempt to touch the lens surface itself* (e.g. with oil, grease, pen)! Fashion items such as nylon stockings, scarves, nets have all been used as diffusers. Burning a small hole in the middle of a net filter can provide a clear central subject with diffused edges to the frame.

Figure 3.16 The imaginary line

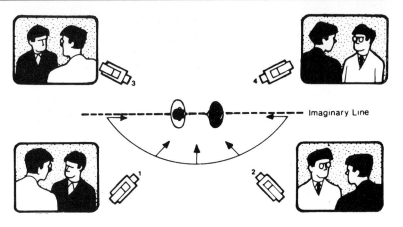

Part 1 *Intercut facing shots.* Shots can be intercut (cross-cut) between cameras located on same side of the imaginary line; i.e. between 1 and 2, or 3 and 4.

But inter-switching between cameras on opposite sides of this line, causes jump cuts (1 and 3, 1 and 4, 2 and 3, 2 and 4).

Part 2 *Crossing the line.* Reverse cuts arise very easily, when the camera crosses the line of a subject's route (the *imaginary line* or *action line*). Here the camera has moved to a new unobscured viewpoint on the other side of the path, so the direction of the walk appears to change during editing!

Part 3 *Maintaining direction.* A subject should appear to be moving in the same direction on the cut. To avoid confusion (e.g. intercutting 1 and 3), insert a neutral head-on shot, or a cutaway to another subject.

3.44 Crossing the line

Unless you take care when arranging camera viewpoints you can easily upset the audience's sense of direction, and their impressions of spatial relationships. Having seen someone on the left of the screen, it is distracting to discover them on the cut, at the right of the next shot.

To avoid this happening, draw an *imaginary line* between two people, or along the direction of action (*action line*). Then be careful that cameras shoot from only one side of this line – never crossing it. You can dolly across the line, or shoot along it, or change its direction by regrouping people, but intercutting between cameras either side of this imaginary line produces a *reverse cut* or *jump cut*.

Chapter 4

Practical lighting

Good lighting can transform even a routine, uninteresting shot into an attractive, appealing picture.

4.1 Lighting for everyone

Don't be scared of lighting! A lot of people are apprehensive about doing the wrong thing and looking foolish. Others think of lighting as an unnecessary luxury for a small production unit. They assume it requires a lot of equipment, and kilowatts of power. It can, if you have to light a large-studio drama, or the inside of a stadium. But everyday video productions are not usually so extensive, and even quite modest facilities will still give you opportunities for some really worthwhile lighting treatment.

As we shall see, there are many situations where just one lamp, or a well-placed reflector, is all that is needed to make a picture spring to life. Even where production is on a larger scale, foresight and imagination can often make a little light go a long way. It is chiefly a matter of knowing what you are aiming at, what to look out for, and what you can do about problems you meet.

Why not simply go around shooting in whatever light is available? You could. On your good days, you will finish up with clear attractive interesting pictures, where realistic color makes the picture sing. But there will certainly be those other days when pictures are lifeless, drab, or crudely over-contrasty; when you can't see the subject clearly, or its texture is lost, or attention goes to the wrong subject; when everything looks uninteresting and dull; when video noise spatters the picture, and color smears in the gloom.

So much depends on where and when you are shooting. Are you inside a building (interior) or out in the open (exterior). Is it day or night? Are the surroundings well illuminated, or in shadowy gloom? Are you shooting quite localized areas, or taking spacious long-shots? And finally, a lot will depend on the sort of atmosphere you are aiming to convey to your audience: a realistic everyday scene or a moody dramatic situation.

Obviously, you are not going to introduce any extra lighting into a scene unless it is really going to enhance your pictures. Often, you will not have the time or the opportunity to make changes anyway. So we shall assume that, at most, you will only be toting around a handful of lightweight lamps.

There will be many situations, particularly in the open air, where you do not even need these, provided you know how to arrange your subject in the existing lighting.

4.2 The camera does not compensate

One of the most important things to bear in mind, when you are lighting, is the essential difference between the way your eyes and brain register the scene and the limited, literal way your camera reproduces it.

Your eyes and brain compensate (sometimes *over*-compensate) in many subtle ways, as the lighting of your surroundings varies. You seem to be able to see details in shadows; variations in color values pass unnoticed. You are still able to see a remarkable amount even when the lighting conditions are very poor.

Your camera cannot interpret. As you saw earlier, it responds to what is there, within its limitations. If a surface reflects too much light for the video system, whether it is a specular reflection from a shiny surface, or a very light tone, it blocks off to a blank white in the picture. Darker-toned furniture, clothing, foliage or shadows often crush-out to black on camera. If you are on the spot, looking at the scene, you have none of these problems. So you have to be alert to how the camera is really reproducing what you are seeing.

Loss of detail and modeling in certain parts of the picture may not be important, unless you particularly want to see features of a white wedding dress or a black velvet costume (Section 3.14). Where the lost tones do matter, you may sometimes need to 'doctor' the scene to make it appear normal on the screen, e.g. by lighting a dark background to bring it within the range of the camera system, or deliberately keeping it out of shot.

4.3 The key factors

Did you realize that you already know a lot about the principles of lighting? Although these everyday effects are so similar that you probably don't give a second thought to them, you already have quite a store of knowledge about the way light reflects from different surfaces, how shadows fall, how the appearance of things can vary under different kinds of light, and so on. You will be applying these various observations, as you light your production.

'Lighting' involves a lot more than simply having enough illumination around to let the camera see what is going on. Light influences what your subject looks like, how people feel about what they see, what attracts their attention. So we need to think about not only where to put our lamps, but the sort of light we are getting from them, and how all this affects the quality of our pictures.

For most everyday purposes, we simply refer to illumination as 'light', and leave it at that. But to use it successfully, we should take a look at some of its interesting characteristics.

1 The light's *intensity* (brightness), for this affects exposure.
2 The light's *quality*; whether it is concentrated 'hard' shadow-forming light, or diffuse 'soft' shadowless illumination.
3 Lighting *contrast*; the relative brightness of the lightest and darkest areas in the shot.
4 The *direction* of the light relative to the camera's viewpoint, and the effect this has on the appearance of the subjects.
5 The light's *color temperature*; the luminant's overall color quality.

When using *colored light* for effect, you are concerned with:

its *hue* (the predominant color, e.g. blue, green, yellow),
its *saturation* (chroma, purity, intensity), i.e. its richness or paleness,
its *luminance* (brightness, value), i.e. how light or dark it appears.

If you understand how to control (or compensate for) these various features, you will be able to create consistent high-quality pictures, even when shooting with available light. If you ignore them, results may be fine; but then again, they may be unpredictable.

4.4 The light's intensity

As you know, the camera requires a certain amount of light reflected from the scene to produce high-grade pictures. If there is too little, the shot is underexposed (all tones reproduce too dark). If there is too much, it will be overexposed (all tones reproduce too light). You can measure the intensity of the lighting with a light-meter, or rely on the camera's exposure-indicator, or on the appearance of the picture in your viewfinder.

The camera will not receive sufficient light if:

● the illumination falling on the subject is too dim (low light levels),
● your lens aperture (stop) is too small,
● you are using a filter that is too dense, relative to the tones in the scene, or its overall brightness.

Clearly, you will need less light to achieve good pictures in a white-walled room than a dark-panelled one. Remember, extra video gain can only partly compensate for underexposure, for although it boosts the picture strength, the CCD sensor itself is still getting too little light from the scene (causing picture noise, smearing, trailing effects).

4.5 If there is not enough light

If you are shooting inside buildings, or outdoors at night, you are quite likely to find that there is not really enough light around to get high-grade pictures. There are several regular solutions:

● Move the subject to where there is more light.
● Open up the lens aperture – but this reduces the zone of sharpness ('depth of field').
● Increase the camera's sensitivity ('boost' 'video gain') – but this will increase picture noise.
● Increase the local lighting, i.e. switch on more room lights.
● Add some of your own lighting to the scene.

4.6 If there is too much light

If lighting is too intense (high light levels), you may compensate:

● by moving the subject to where there is less light,
● by stopping the lens down (smaller aperture),
● by using a neutral density filter,
● by switching off some of the existing lighting,
● perhaps pulling shades or blinds.

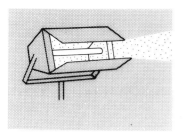

By partly closing the flaps you can limit the spread of the light.

Clipping a piece of diffuser to a barndoor flap.

Reduces the intensity of part of the light beam.

Similar to Pt 2 above but holding a sheet of cooking foil, cutting off the light completely.

Figure 4.1 Controlling the light

Otherwise, if you are using lamps to light the scene, you may:

- switch off some bulbs (in a multi-bulb light source),
- switch off some of your light sources,
- use lower-power sources,
- use a dimmer (although dimming a lamp lowers its color temperature),
- place diffuser material over a lamp,
- take the lamp farther away,
- flood (spread) the lamp's beam,
- use 'bounce light' instead of some of the direct lighting.

4.7 Hard light quality

Because the sun is so distant, it behaves as a localized *point source* of light. Its rays are therefore very directional and travel to us in straight lines. They cast distinct sharp shadows, which emphasize the texture and contours of any subject, especially when the light falls at an oblique angle. Because it is directional, you can easily block off this *hard light*, to prevent it falling on any surface.

Many man-made light sources, such as a match, a candle or a bare light bulb, also behave in this way. Because they are of very limited size, they act as point sources and produce hard light, irrespective of how powerful or weak they are.

Rather than allowing the light to spread around in all directions (as with a bare bulb hanging from the ceiling), many lighting fittings include a specially shaped 'parabolic' reflector, that directs light rays forwards in a narrow beam. They may also be fitted with a 'fresnel' ('stepped') lens to concentrate the beam further. This light-gathering improves the lamp's efficiency, and helps you to restrict the light to selected parts of the scene.

By adjusting the position of the reflector and/or the lens relative to the bulb, you can vary the spread of its beam, and to a certain extent, its intensity. Flaps or light-shields may be attached to the fitting, to cut off parts of the light beam. (These are known as barndoors, flags or snoots.)

The *good things* about hard light are:

- It is directional, so can easily be restricted to illuminate just those areas you want to light.
- It casts clear-cut shadows and shows up texture.
- Hard light can produce vigorous, bold, well-defined effects.
- The intensity of a hard light source, does not fall off appreciably with distance. So you can illuminate things effectively, with a lamp some distance away.

The *bad things* about hard light are:

- You often want to avoid distracting or ugly shadows (e.g. on the background behind someone).
- Results may look harsh, contrasty and unattractive.
- You may not want to emphasize texture (e.g. revealing the irregularities in someone's skin).
- Hard light sources have restricted coverage, so that you may need several lamps to cover a wide area.
- When you use more than one hard light source, the multi-shadows can be very distracting.

4.8 Soft light quality

Diffused light scatters in all directions. It occurs naturally, when the sun is obscured by cloud, and whenever sunlight is reflected from rough light-toned surfaces.

When subjects are illuminated by this *soft light*, there are no distinct shadows, only slight variations in surface brightness. So texture and surface contours are not very pronounced in the picture. You may not be able to see them at all.

There are several different types of fittings designed to provide soft light.

Some rely on diffusion material such as spun-glass sheet, frosted plastic or tracing paper (sometimes wire mesh) to scatter the light. (You can put a diffuser over a hard light source to reduce its intensity and soften its quality to some extent.) In others, the light from hidden lamps hits a reflector and scatters.

Another form of soft light uses a group or bank of open lamps. Their overlapping beams combine to give shadowless illumination.

At a pinch, you can create a compact 'soft light' source by placing two or three layers of diffuser (e.g. spun glass) over a hard-light source such as a lensless spot.

The good things about soft light are:

- It can produce subtle delicate shading.
- Soft light does not create unwanted shadows.
- Soft light avoids emphasizing modeling and texture.
- Soft light can illuminate the shadows cast by hard light sources, so that we can see details there, without itself casting further shadows.
- Soft light sources can cover a wide area of the scene.

The bad things about soft light are:

- It can flatten out all signs of surface shape and texture in the picture.
- Soft light spreads around, flooding all surfaces with light. It can be very difficult to restrict, and keep off selected areas.
- Soft light quickly falls off in intensity, as you increase the lamp's distance from the subject. So something fairly near the source may be over-lit, while another subject a little way away, is insufficiently lit.

4.9 Lighting contrast

The 'contrast' in a scene is simply the difference between the brightness of its lightest and darkest tones. If the range is too great for the camera to handle (around 20:1 to 30:1 max.), as it well might be when strong sunlight casts deep shadows, the extreme tones are lost in the picture. Many TV receivers can only reproduce a range of around 15:1 anyway.

The tonal contrasts that your camera sees will depend partly on the tones of the subjects themselves, partly on variations in the light's intensity, and partly on the shadows it casts.

Excessive lighting contrast produces a coarse 'soot and whitewash' effect, with burned-out highlights and detailess lower tones. Whether the result looks highly dramatic, or crude and difficult to interpret, depends on the situation.

When lighting is contrasty (e.g. lots of hard light from one direction, and no fill light), picture quality can alter considerably as you vary the camera's position. Shooting with the light behind the camera, subjects may look very

Figure 4.2 Light direction
As the position of the light changes, relative to the camera viewpoint, its effect alters on the subject. The direction you choose depends on which feature you want to emphasize or suppress.

Top: moving light upwards, and behind.

Bottom: moving light round and behind the subject.

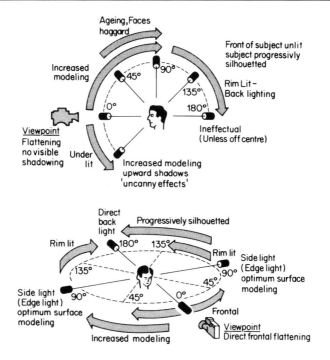

bright, flat and unmodeled. If you shoot towards the light, only the edges of subjects will be illuminated, while the rest of them remains unlit.

The other extreme is the effect you get when the scene is lit with soft shadowless lighting. Now everything is very subtly modeled – perhaps so subtly, that the picture looks uninterestingly flat, as if things had been cut out and stuck onto their background. Even if you move the camera around over a wide angle, the tonal quality of the picture remains reasonably constant under soft lighting.

In practice, you usually want to avoid the harshness that comes from a high lighting contrast, and the flatness that you get with a low lighting contrast. The best solution is to use a careful balance of hard lights (which creates a three-dimensional illusion), and some soft light, to illuminate any shadows (i.e. 'fill' them) without casting extra ones.

4.10 Light direction

The direction of light can have a considerable influence on what any subject looks like. The best way to demonstrate this for yourself is to sit in front of a mirror in a dark room, holding a flashlight. Then you will see not only how the effect changes as light from different directions, but you will begin to understand the ways in which light-direction affects portraiture.

First hold your flashlight beside your head, pointing it straight into the mirror. This is the equivalent of a light just beside the camera. Notice how this direct frontal light seems to flatten out the texture and shape of the front of your face. If there is a smooth or shiny surface behind you, the light bounces straight back into your eye (i.e. into the camera lens), and appears as a hotspot on the background. Even a rough surface, such as stone or concrete, may look smooth under direct frontal lighting. It reminds you too, how unpleasantly dazzling it can be for people if you light them this way.

Move your flashlight to above your head, shining straight downwards. See how the light emphasizes every wrinkle! The top of your head and your nose are now bright ('hot') and your eyes are hidden in dark sockets. You have instantly aged many years, and look dreadful! (So always try to avoid top, overhead, downward lighting, particularly when shooting people.)

Hold the flashlight down low, shining upwards, and the effect is spooky, because we are not used to seeing people lit in this way – except in horror movies. Now the eyes and the neck are strongly lit. Again, surface details are emphasized with upward shadows.

Take the light round to one side, and you will see how only half of your head is lit, and the surface texture and contours of your face are unattractively exaggerated.

If someone takes the flashlight and holds it behind you, shining onto the back of your head, you will see that only the edges of your head will be lit (i.e. hair, ears and shoulders if the lamp is high). This sort of *backlight* is very successful when lighting solid subjects, for it helps to make them stand out from their background, and creates a three-dimensional illusion. If the subject is of transparent or translucent material, the backlight will reveal this.

4.11 Three-point lighting

For most situations, you will find that the best results come from using three basic light directions.

The main light, or *key light*, is positioned slightly above and to one side of the camera. This is normally a hard-light source (a spotlight), and it reveals the shape and surface features of your subject.

A soft light (broad source) on the opposite side of the camera illuminates the shadows and reduces the lighting contrast. The more the key light is offset, the more important this soft *fill light* (filler; fill-in) becomes. If the key is nearly frontal, you may not need fill light at all.

Finally, a *backlight* angled down onto the subject from behind gives it solidity.

Wherever possible, you can add extra lamps to light the background behind the subject. But where space or facilities are limited, you may have to rely on spill illumination from your key and fill lights to cover background areas instead.

4.12 Measuring light levels

The most convenient method of measuring light is to stand in the *subject's position*, and point your light-meter towards a light source to measure the incident light. It is usually better to check and balance the final lighting set-up, than to switch on and measure individual lamps.

The best way to learn about appropriate light levels for your equipment, is by experiment. Set the lens aperture to e.g. *f*/4. Sit someone in front of the camera, and adjust the intensity of the key light (change power, distance, diffuser, dimmer) until their face and clothing appear attractively exposed, when viewed on a picture monitor (not the camera viewfinder). Light tones should not be crushed out, nor darker areas clogged.

Now read the key light's intensity, and you have a typical guide figure for future reference. Add sufficient fill light (offset at e.g. 5–30°) to relieve the shadows, without overlighting them – as *judged by your monitor picture*. Measure the fill light intensity (re-check the key-plus-fill brightness).

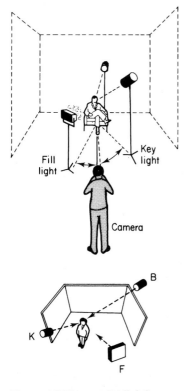

Figure 4.3 Three-point lighting
Basic set-up. Three lamps are used: The *key light* which models the subject, and is some 5–30° to one side of the camera (vertical angle of 10–40°). The *fill light* (*filler*) which illuminates shadows but ideally casts none of its own (diffused), positioned say 5–30° on the other side of the camera. The *back light* placed behind the subject, to outline it with light; up to 20° either side of the dead back position, facing the camera; vertical angle of 25–60°.

Area lighting. This principle can be used for lighting areas too.

Having noted these figures; repeat the operation for the back light. You now have useful working data for the future.

The amount of light produced by a particular lighting fixture, depends on its design, the quality of its light (how hard or soft), its power, how it is adjusted, the lamp's age and condition, its distance from the subject, etc. Forget formulae! Measure how much light *your equipment* gives at a typical distance under *your* working conditions, and use this as a basis for the number of units you need for a job.

4.13 Typical light levels

If you want to work with a lens aperture of *f*/4 (to get sufficient depth of field), you may need a typical light level from the key light of e.g. 100 fc (1076 lux). This is the main light source, that determines the exposure. Don't *underlight* if you can help it. Some people use minimum light, and boost the video to improve the signal, but this degrades picture quality. Worse still, you are unlikely to be able to judge tonal balance accurately at lower light levels. Your eye will overlook distracting shadows, that become all too prominent on camera!

The intensity of the *back light* should usually be similar to the key light (e.g. 100 fc/1076 lux); but it will vary with the subject. Strong back light when appropriate may look 'glamorous'; but hot edges around subjects can also be artificial and distracting too. Weak back light is ineffectual.

The amount of *fill light* (*filler*) you need from soft-light sources, will depend on how contrasty you want the final effect to be. A rough rule-of-thumb is *around one-half to one-third as bright as the key light (e.g. 50–33 fc/530–360 lux). It should seldom be similar (high key situations), and never stronger than the key.* Remember, the purpose of the fill light is to augment, to illuminate shadows, without casting fresh shadows.

4.14 Color temperature compensation

The color quality of light can vary considerably, from the orange–yellow of candlelight or small tungsten lamps to the bluish illumination of daylight; from the warm hues of sunset to the greenish quality of many fluorescent light sources.

For good color fidelity, your camera system's color response, and the color quality of the prevailing light, need to match reasonably well. If they do not, you will find that the pictures have a pronounced bluish or orange–yellow color cast.

You can *match the camera to the lighting* by switching in a compensatory color-correction filter on the camera, and/or readjusting the camera's white balance.

Sometimes you will meet a *mixture* of lighting, e.g. high color temperature daylight coming through the windows, and low color temperature tungsten light inside a room. Then you have the choice of:

- shutting out the daylight by pulling the shades and relying on your quartz/tungsten light alone (camera set to 'tungsten balance'),
- putting light-blue filters (or 'dichroic filters') over the quartz/tungsten light to raise its color temperature (camera set to 'daylight' balance),
- attaching large sheets of orange–yellow color filter material over the windows to match the quartz/tungsten light (camera set to 'tungsten balance'),
- simply shooting the scene with its mixture of daylight and unfiltered lighting, and accepting the results.

With the camera balanced to 'daylight', the daylight will look right and the tungsten over-warm.

With the camera balanced to 'tungsten', the daylight will look very blue, and the tungsten light will look natural. The color-quality of light (its *color temperature*) is measured in kelvins (degrees kelvin (K)). If you want accurate consistent color reproduction (e.g. when shooting for medical records), or need to match several video cameras, you can use a special color-balance meter to check the light, and then introduce appropriate compensation. But for most purposes, it is sufficient to switch the camera to its nearest color-correction position (e.g. 'daylight', 'artificial', 'fluorescent', or 5600 K, 3200 K) and white-balance to these conditions.

4.15 Using colored light

Because your video is in color, it seems reasonable to assume that you would use quite a lot of colored light. But, in practice, you will only find yourself needing colored light when creating decorative effects (e.g. for a display, a dance or musical routine, firelight or moonlight), or to change the appearance of backgrounds (to introduce some color on a plain neutral wall or drapes).

When you do need colored lighting, you clip a sheet of special color media over a light fitting. Make sure that the sheet is not going to restrict ventilation to the lamp (which will overheat and fail). And do not put it so close to the lamp that the color sheet is destroyed by the intense heat.

Various materials are available, but never use colored glass. Colored gelatine is quite cheap, but it burns up, quickly becomes very brittle and torn, and pales out in use. Special plastic sheeting (of acetate, polyester, mylar or acrylic) is expensive, but will last and can be re-used.

If you are shooting under tungsten lighting and want to create an overall warm look to your picture, all you have to do is to set your camera to 'daylight' color correction. Conversely, you can use a 'tungsten' setting when shooting in daylight, to give pictures a very cold blue wintry appearance.

4.16 Shooting in daylight

Although daylight provides us with a free, convenient light source, it isn't a particularly reliable one. Its intensity varies, and so does its overall quality. Clouds pass over the sun, and sharply defined shadows vanish. Instead we may be left with a much weaker, diffused light. Throughout the day, the color quality and the direction of the light alter, and the sun that was frontal in the morning can gradually change to side light by the afternoon. All this may make it difficult to cut together shots that have been taken at different times of the day, where the variations in lighting show in the edited version of the action.

What you always have to bear in mind, is that the effect of light depends on the *position of your camera*.

Strong sunlight, that is more than enough from one viewpoint, may only rim the subject from another angle, leaving it in deep shadow.

You really have four choices. You can:

● Move round your subject until the sun is roughly behind the camera (but then it may not be the background you want!).

- Turn the subject into the light.
- Wait for the sun to move round to a better angle.
- Add (or reflect) lighting to compensate.

Sometimes you will just have to accept things as you find them. Suppose, for example, you want to take shots of an impressive building. Sunlight falling at just the right angle would throw wall texture and its various features into sharp relief. Once in a while, the light will be just right, and produce exactly the results you are looking for. There are even tables to tell you where the sun will be at any time of the day. But don't rely on it!

Under dull overcast skies, everything can look uninterestingly flat. Perhaps you could try again later, when the sun is shining. It could be that the particular features you want to show never do get suitable sunlight anyway! If a wall is facing north, it never does get full sunlight. So you may have to shoot the subject as it is, and just hope that results will look all right on the screen.

4.17 Using reflectors

The cheapest way to improve a subject's lighting when shooting in sunlight is to use a *reflector*. This is simply a surface such as a board, screen, cloth or even a wall, that reflects existing light onto the subject from another angle. The quality of the reflected light depends on the surface you use.

A mirror surface (e.g. metal foil or metallized plastic) will reflect a distinct beam of light from a hard light source, creating sharp well-defined shadows. This light travels well, even when the subject is some distance away. (A mirror surface will even reflect soft light to some extent, if placed fairly near the subject.)

Unfortunately, the angle of a mirror-finish reflector can be critical. When the light shines directly at its surface, you will get the maximum effect. But as the surface is angled to the light, the reflected beam, which only covers a restricted angle anyway, narrows and becomes less effective. In a long shot, its limited coverage is seen as a localized patch of light.

If your reflector has a matte-white surface, it will produce a soft diffused light, which spreads over a wide angle. But this soft reflected light is much weaker, and will only travel a relatively short distance, depending on the intensity and distance of the original light source.

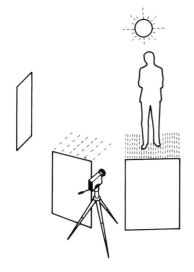

Figure 4.4 Reflectors
How effective a reflector is depends on its surface (polished, metallic surfaces are best) and on its angle to the sun or other light sources. If you use a reflector beside the camera, and reflect a source directly ahead of the camera, the intensity and coverage of the reflected light is maximum. As you angle the reflector to the source, its output and its coverage fall.

Reflectors are easily made from a board covered with aluminium cooking foil (smooth or crumpled and flattened) or matte-white painted, according to the type of light reflection you want. (A board faced with two different surfaces can be very useful.) The bigger the reflector, the more light will be reflected over a broad area, and big cloth or roller-blind reflectors (even portable cine-screens) can be used. But reflectors of this size are cumbersome to transport and support, and likely to vibrate in any wind.

Reflectors come into their own in strong sunlight. Over a limited area, you can use the reflected light to fill in deep shadows or to provide a frontal key light when the sun is behind the subject. Two or more reflectors can be used together. The main problems are in directing the light to exactly where you want it, and in supporting the reflectors perfectly still, at the right height.

However, as the only alternative is to use powerful lamps, or lights close in to the subject, it is an approach that is certainly worth trying when the sun's direction is appropriate, and tonal contrast is high.

Indoors, you can use reflectors to redirect light from windows into shadowy corners, or reflect sunlight as a filler. And when you are using backlight, a low reflector near the camera can provide useful filler, perhaps to lift the shadows under people's chins and eyebrows.

Finally, while on the subject, when you are shooting in bright sunlight, look out for *accidental colored reflections* from nearby surfaces. Even a smart green shirt may show its wearer with a green complexion!

4.18 Bounce light

It is a common trick in *photography* to point a flash-gun at the ceiling or a wall when photographing interiors to give the scene an overall wash of diffused 'bounce light'. (But don't use a colored surface, or the reflected light will have a similar hue!)

Although you can sometimes use the same idea when shooting video, and point your lamps at the nearby surfaces to get a soft 'base-light', remember that only a fraction of the lamp's output is reflected. So it is really a pretty wasteful, random method. If you use more powerful lamps in order to get stronger bounce light, ventilation can become a problem in a small room. On balance, it may be better to use a strongly diffused broad source instead.

4.19 Do we need to light it?

It is an interesting fact that, if you look around any everyday scene, your eye will often pass without a second glance, over incidental features that seem to stand out in a photograph. You overlook the reflections in a shop window, and concentrate on the items on sale within. You accept a bright blob of light on a tiled surface without a thought. You talk to people, and note their expressions and how they are dressed perhaps, and that is an end to it.

Now look at a video of the same scene, and you are likely to react quite differently. The reflections in the window seem to stop you seeing into the shop. The blob of light on the tiles has become an annoying distraction. You tend to look at the people in the picture in a much more detached, critical way, than in everyday life. You may well be struck by their shadowed eye sockets, how haggard they look under the steep lighting, the hot tops to their heads; you may become aware of ugly neck shadows, bright noses or ears, strongly lit shoulders, the long nose shadow that looks like a mustache . . . Various trivial aspects of the everyday scene now have quite a different impact on the screen.

This is why professionals go to so much trouble to re-adjust and light many scenes, where there is obviously insufficient illumination to produce acceptable pictures. It is not enough, for example, to be able to get shots of an audience at a concert; one wants the pictures to be *attractive* too. The available light is often in the wrong direction, or is too flat or too contrasty, or it only illuminates part of the scene clearly. The extra lighting seeks to correct these shortcomings.

4.20 Lighting options

Whatever sort of program you are making, you really have four choices as far as lighting is concerned:

1 You can shoot with the existing lighting, either from your chosen viewpoint, or after moving to another position where the subject looks better.

2 You can increase the intensity of the lighting already there, e.g. take shades off light fittings or replace the bulbs with others of higher power.
3 You can augment the present lighting with extra lamps of your own. These may be anything from a reflector or a single hand-held lamp to a number of lighting units.
4 You can rely entirely on the lighting equipment you have taken along, because either there is no other illumination there, or you have decided that it is unsuitable and switched it off.

Then you have the choice of either lighting the whole action area, or restricting your lighting to suit limited action in one small section at a time.

4.21 Economy lighting

Whenever you shoot in the light that just happens to be there at the time, whether it is daylight or artificial, there is always an element of uncertainty about the quality of the pictures you are going to get.

By lighting the scene, or supplementing the existing lighting, you have some control over the situation, and a far better chance of achieving consistently high quality pictures.

'Economy lighting' is a way of thinking, a matter of turning whatever lighting is available to your advantage.

You begin by asking yourself: 'Can I shoot the scene from the camera position I have chosen, with the present lighting?' Check on whether you can expose the picture properly. Is there good detail and tonal gradation in the subject you are particularly interested in? If part of the subject is in shadow, does that matter? Would some fill light from a reflector, or a hand-lamp beside the camera, help to show details in the shadows? Are there any distractions in the shot, such as a bright sky or a large defocused blob of color?

Perhaps the overall effect would look better if you were to turn the subject slightly towards the light. Then you might not need any fill light for the shadows at all.

Would it be better to wait for the sun to come out, or return another day when the light is right?

If you are shooting an interior and there is daylight around, can you make use of it in some way in your shot, e.g. to save you providing a key light, or lighting a background wall?

And here's a trick, when there is virtually no light, or it's impossible to get good pictures with your video camera. Use a *photographic camera* (either with flash or a time exposure), to take a slide of the scene. Then project this slide in a dark room, and shoot the screen with your video camera!

4.22 Makeshift equipment

If one is on a tight budget there is a natural temptation to improvise. There are occasions when you can for a short time put a higher-powered bulb into a hinged desk-lamp or a ceiling light-track, clip on a sheet of cooking foil to shade off the wall, and a piece of tracing paper to soften the light. But these makeshift arrangements take a while to set up, easily come adrift, and are very temporary. And they are not particularly safe. Time soon passes, and the fitting overheats.

Lightweight lighting fittings
Supports
4.23 Gaffer grip/gaffer clamp/alligator ('gator') clamp/clip-light

This large spring-loaded or screwed clamp has a support (5/8 in. (16 mm) spigot or socket) to hold a small lamp such as a PAR holder (the bulb incorporates a parabolic aluminized reflector) or a lensless spot.

You can use the gaffer grip to clip a light to any firmly based object, such as a door, table, chair, rail, post, window or treads/step ladder (light-stand, scenic flat).

This can be a very useful compact device, enabling you to secure lamps in out-of-the-way places, when space is restricted.

Take care when lighting

When lighting your productions, it is easy to become preoccupied with the effects you are creating and to overlook some of the very practical hazards that await the unwary. There are a number of things that you should look out for, just in case.

Equipment condition

Check out your lighting equipment to make sure that it is all in good condition. Lamps should be fitted firmly in sockets (never handle lamps with the bare hands). Check that nothing is coming loose, cables are not frayed or cut and that the plug and its connections are OK.

Grounding/earthing

All electrical equipment should be properly grounded (earthed), otherwise you are liable to get a severe electric shock under certain conditions.

Electrical overload

Take care that all your lamps are individually fused, and that you do not connect too many lamps to one outlet and/or overload the power supply. There may already be other equipment using the power circuit you want to plug into, and yours might exceed its capacity. So enquire before connecting to other people's supplies. Find out where fuses or cutouts are located, and who is responsible for them.

Hot lamps

Lamps can get extremely hot, especially quartz lights. So take care when working near lamps that are lit, or only recently switched off. Not only can you burn yourself, but the lamp's filament is fragile when hot and can be destroyed by even a slight knock.

If a hot lamp is within a couple of feet of a surface (0.5 m), there is every chance of scorching or setting fire to it. Wood, drapes, paper and plastic are particularly vulnerable. Cables should not rest against a hot lamp, for they can be burned up. Color media over lamps reduce the amount of air ventilating them, and themselves fume and smell when overheated, perhaps even catch fire.

Take particular care when using overrun photographic lamps (Photoflood, Nitraphot), or high-rated tungsten lamps (150 W) in domestic light fittings such as wall-brackets, ceiling lights, table lamps or desk fittings. They may overheat and damage the fitting and nearby surfaces.

Falling equipment

Light fittings can fall down or overbalance all too easily. Where possible, it is advisable to attach some form of safety bond (wire or chain) from the lamp to a secure point, to hold it (or anything attached, such as a barndoor) if it should fall.

Can anyone passing underneath a lamp hit their head on it, or move it, or burn themselves on it?

A lamp fitted to a lighting stand (floor stand) can be a hazard if it is anywhere near people. They may kick it out of position, fall over it, or knock it over!

Whenever you are using a lighting stand, it is best to place a weight on its base (perhaps a canvas sandbag, or bag of stones, even a rock) to prevent it from moving or toppling over. Very high lighting stands (over 6 ft (2 m)) are extremely unstable.

Floor cables

Remember that people can trip over cables strewn around the floor, so it is advisable to tuck all cables away neatly (e.g. near a wall), or cover them over (mat or board), or hang them (wall hooks, gaffer-taped/duct-taped) to firm non-decorated wall surfaces.

Water

Take great care when water is around. If rains falls on a lamp, it is liable to explode or short out the supply, unless the equipment is suitably designed to avoid this. Any water on the ground can cause short circuits, or electrocute the unwary, if it gets in the wrong places!

Gator grip

Figure 4.5 Gaffer grip (gaffer clamp, clip-light)
Clamps on any firm narrow beam, pipe, door, chair.

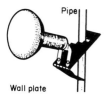

Pipe

Wall plate

Figure 4.6 Profiled wall plate
Tapes to any firm surface, hangs on pipes.

Figure 4.7 Lightweight stand
Collapsible extending stand used to support small lighting fixtures.

4.24 Wall-plate

The wall-plate can be a very adaptable method of positioning lightweight lamps on location. It consists of a flat metal plate, fitted with a porcelain lamp support on a directional swivel.

You can hang it onto any nearby pipes, wall-fittings, etc., by its hook-shaped edges. You can even tape the plate onto a door or wall, using gaffer tape/duct tape (a plastic-faced fabric tape with a contact-adhesive coating), provided the surface is reasonably smooth, clean and dust-free.

4.25 Lightweight lamp tripod/stand

This can be a collapsible/folding type, or it may dismantle into sections for transport. How sturdy your tripod needs to be, depends on the size of the lamp fitting you are going to use and the maximum height you intend to use it at. If the tripod is too flimsy, it will be top heavy and easily upset, even by the weight of the lamp's cable. With more robust types, you can attach two or more lamps to a tripod when necessary.

4.26 Spring-loaded support pole (Jack tube, Varipole, Acrow, Polecat, Barricuda)

This telescopic fitting consists of one long tube, spring-loaded within another. When wedged between wall and ceiling, or between two side walls, or in a window-opening, it can be used to support all forms of lightweight lamps. 'Cross-tubes' ('cross-beams') can be added to interlink two or more poles.

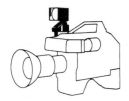

Figure 4.8 Camera light
A lamp clamped to the top of the camera.

Lamps

4.27 Camera light (video light)

A small portable quartz-light can be attached to the top of many video cameras (video light), it may be powered from a battery belt, a battery pack, the camera's supply, or an a.c. adaptor (for a utility/mains supply).

Power ratings are typically 100–350 W. A 250 W/30 volts lamp may run for 30 min from a battery supply, while a 350 W lamp would only last for around 20 min.

Its main advantage is that it always lights whatever the camera is shooting, and does not require another pair of hands. Portable lighting of this sort can provide a very convenient key light when shooting under difficult conditions, especially if you have to follow someone around as, for example, they arrive at an airport. (There may be no other solution!) And again, the lamp can provide modeling light for close exterior shots on a dull day, or fill light for hard shadows when shooting someone in sunlight.

The chief disadvantages here are that the lamp adds to the camera's overall weight, and its light is extremely frontal and so tends to flatten out the subject. Its light will reflect in spectacles and any shiny surfaces (windows, plastic) near the subject, as an intense white blob. People facing the camera may find the light dazzling.

Some camera lights have a fixed coverage, while others are adjustable (e.g. 6–35°). But the illumination is invariably localized, and when using a wide-angle camera lens, subjects may move out of the light beam. Furthermore, its illumination does not carry evenly. While anything near the camera is easily overlit, anything farther away remains virtually unlit. This can be very obvious in long shots. Some camera lights have an autosensor intensity control, which nominally adjusts their intensity to suit exposure and the prevailing lighting conditions. Like all automatic systems, its performance is variable.

4.28 Hand-held lamps (sun gun)

A hand-held lamp separate from the camera, requires the assistance of a second person, but this can have several advantages. Apart from not burdening the camera operator with its weight, the assistant can anticipate where to point the lamp, and avoid the 'searchlight effect' that can occur as a camera-light pans around. The assistant can probably hold the lamp high (not easy for any length of time) at a better angle to light the subject and avoid direct 'kickback' reflections.

The hand-held lamp may be more powerful, e.g. from 250 W to 1000 W. It may be battery or a.c. powered. Some designs have a cooling fan; those without tend to overheat.

In daylight, a *dichroic filter* or color-compensating filter medium is used over the lamp to raise its color temperature.

4.29 Open-bulb fittings

For small scale situations, unprotected open bulbs in simple supports (clip-light, wall plate) can be quite useful. But they are very vulnerable, easily broken, and offer no protection if the bulb explodes. It is difficult to control the spread of the light and prevent it from washing over the entire scene.

An *overrun tungsten* photographic lamp typically has a brief bright life of 2, 6 or 10 hours, and uses respectively 275, 500 or 1000 W. (Their boosted

Figure 4.9 Hand-held lamp
Positioned by a second operator.

light output is the equivalent of a regular tungsten lamp of 800, 1600 or 3000 W.)

An *internally silvered reflector spot lamp* can be used individually, or in multi-lamp floodlight banks. It is available in focused (hard, spotlight) and diffused forms. There are standard versions (100/300/500 W; 3200 K; 100 hours life), and overrun versions (275/375/500 W; 3400 K; 3/4/6 hours life). Their greatest shortcoming is that the light is not of even intensity overall (central hotspot).

Remember, each lamp casts its own set of shadows, so a two-lamp fitting, for instance, will produce disturbing double shadows for everything it lights.

The more robust *PAR* lamps are very widely used, individually or in banks, both inside buildings and out of doors. They have moulded heat-resistant ribbed (optical) or clear fronts, giving 'pre-focused spot' or 'flood' coverage.

There are also types with an elliptical beam shape, concentrating the light in a horizontal field, e.g. $6° \times 12°$ to $30° \times 40°$. With a power range of 75–1000 W, and 5200 K or 3200 K color temperature versions available. PAR lamps offer an effective economical lightweight light source. Clip-on light shields can help to localize the illumination.

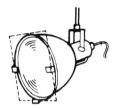

Figure 4.10 Scoop
A basic softlight source, once universally used in studios.

4.30 Scoop

Before more effective equipment became available, TV studios used *scoops* for many years to provide frontal soft light for action areas and to illuminate cycloramas and backdrops. The scoop is a cheap rudimentary light fitting, requiring little maintenance except an occasional clean. But it is inefficient and bulky; particularly when grouped. It consists of a large aluminum bowl with a central bare lamp. In some designs this lamp may be front-shielded so that only reflected light emerges. Unfortunately, the light from scoops spreads uncontrollably, spilling around over nearby scenery. Attempts to reduce this by clipping on strips of diffuser material or metal bring little success.

4.31 Skypan/open pan

The *skypan* or *open pan* consists of a large round shallow parabolic reflector with a central open lamp. Used since the early days of motion picture lighting, it has undergone various modifications to the reflector's surface, including white, silver, dimple patterns, ridges, and small glass bead reflectors to disperse the light. Its lamp may be fitted with a front shield to internally reflect the light, and a metal skirt around its edge to reduce side spill-light. There has been some renewed interest in this design as a general all-purpose illuminator, but by its nature it lacks finesse, for its light spreads uncontrollably, and falls off rapidly with distance.

4.32 Broad

The lightweight broad (broadside) has a short trough containing a reflector and a tubular quartz light of 500–1000 W. The bulb may have a frontal shield to internally reflect the light.

Although the broad is widely referred to as a 'soft' light source, due to its small area, it produces quite discernible shadows. Nevertheless, it is an extremely useful wide-angle broad light source, that can be hung conveniently in various ways, supported on stands, or laid on the floor, arranged singly or in groups.

Figure 4.11 Broad
Soft light source with a linear (tubular) quartz-light.

Two-leaf or four-leaf barndoor shutters, that can be closed to reduce the spread of the light, are often fitted to broads.

Figure 4.12 Umbrella reflector unit
Light from a central lamp shines *into* the interior of the umbrella, and is reflected in a more diffused form. Although this device is inefficient, and its illumination spreads uncontrollably, its portability makes it a handy accessory.

4.33 Umbrella

This fitting consists of a small central lamp facing into an open white or silver-coated umbrella (about 40 in. (100 cm) open). Its light weight and portability make it a particularly useful soft light source when shooting 'on-the-move' in the field. Its soft light spreads over a wide angle, and cannot be restricted, but is sufficient for close working and in when shooting in confined surroundings.

4.34 Multi-lamp sources

Several softlight sources use groups of lamps which combine, so that the shadows cast by each are 'lit out' by its neighbors.

A *strip-light* or *cyc-light* consists of a row of two to six units joined in a long trough. Each unit has a tubular bulb with a curved metal reflector. You can use the strip-light to illuminate 'backgrounds or translucent screens from the floor.

In a studio, strip or eye lights are often suspended to light backgrounds from above, but they are rather too cumbersome to support in this way in a lightweight lighting rig.

Multi-lamp *banks* are excellent soft-light sources. A typical design has one to three panels of grouped PAR internal reflector lamps. Each panel can be independently switched and turned to adjust the brightness and spread of the unit. Either 650 W or 1000 W PAR lamps may be fitted, in groups of 4, 6, 9, 16 or 24.

The *floodlight bank* ('Minibrute', 'Maxibrute', etc.), is mainly used as a booster light for exteriors, and for large-area illumination. Large side-flaps may be fitted to restrict the light spread.

Soft-light sources that rely on internal reflection to produce light scatter, produce quite diffused light, but are relatively inefficient.

Large units fitted with a bank of fluorescent tubes are favored by some people as a cheap soft-light source. But in practice the color quality of their light does not blend well with other sources. The exception is when small fluorescent banks are used as booster-light in a store already lit by a ceiling of fluorescent tubes. They are quite cumbersome and vulnerable in use.

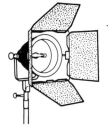

Figure 4.13 Lensless spotlight (external reflector spotlight; Redhead; Blonde)
Lightweight efficient focused unit. Light spread about 42–82°. Light output of 800 W per unit comparable with 2 kW fresnel spot (3200 K). As a keylight, typical distance 2.5–3 m. As a backlight, typical distance 1.5 m.

4.35 Lensless spotlight/open-bulb spot

This type of light fitting is very widely used in video/television production, particularly by mobile units, on location. It has a variety of names, including lensless spotlight, open-bulb spot, external reflector spot, reflector spotlight. Redhead (250 W, 600 W, 800 W), Blonde (2000 W).

The fitting is open-fronted with a plastic body, and contains a bare quartz-light (tungsten-halogen) bulb with an efficient adjustable reflector behind it. Its light beam is somewhat uneven (particularly when spotted), but this type of spotlight has many advantages.

It is extremely portable, compact, and efficient. The output of an 800 W version is comparable with a large 2 kW fresnel spotlight covering the same area. So there are many advantages where ventilation and power are limited. Moreover, it will spread over more then 80° (compared with a typical fresnel spot's 60° maximum) and that is a valuable feature where the lamp-to-subject distance (throw) is short.

Diffuser and/or corrective color filters are easily clipped to its barndoors.

Figure 4.14 Groundrow (striplight; cyc-light)

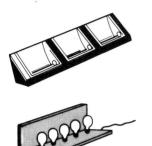

Part 1 A series of tubular lamps with curved reflectors, or constructed from a row of domestic tungsten lamps (150 W).

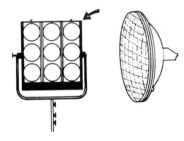

Figure 4.14 Part 2
Floodlight bank ('mini-brute')
Housing a series of switchable PAR lamps, groups may be hinged, and have side flaps.

4.36 Fresnel spotlights

In TV and film studios, where the lamps have to be positioned a fair distance from the subjects (e.g. over 15 ft (6 m)), the large heavy-duty fresnel spotlight is universal, suspended from ceiling bars or battens. (Typical power: 2–5 kW.)

Mobile small-unit video production teams need compact lightweight equipment that can spread light over a wide area, even when quite close to the subject. So for them, the fairly restricted beam-spread of the heavier fresnel spotlight has limited use, although it has a more even light coverage, and more precise adjustment than the lensless spotlight.

Practical lighting

4.37 The general approach to lighting

● As you will have discovered earlier (Section 4.10), if you move a lamp from near the camera's position over to the right, any prominent feature on the subject's surface (e.g. someone's nose) will cast a shadow over to the left. As you increase the lighting angle, such shadows spread across the surface, emphasizing its shape and texture. The greater the light's angle, the coarser its effect.

At the same time, the shadow of the subject itself also moves across the background, growing broader.

As you go on moving the lamp round it, less and less of the subject is illuminated, until eventually, by the time you have put the lamp right round to the side of it, only half is lit. The surface details that are caught by the light stand out prominently (a useful technique when lighting low-relief subjects such as coins).

As you raise the lamp, shadows grow downwards. Similarly, when you move a lamp upwards diagonally, shadows develop downwards diagonally in the opposite direction.

● From these basics, we can see some obvious principles to follow, whatever we want to light:

The lamp should not be *too close to the lens*. This flattens out surface modeling and causes light reflections.

● The angle should not be *too steep*. It creates crude, gaunt, unattractive top light.

It should not be *too far round to one side*, unless the subject is facing that way. This can result in harsh surface modeling, and a bisected half-lit effect.

Choose the lamp direction that suits the subject and its surroundings best. And don't forget to look out for any reflections or shadow that might be distracting.

The final lamp position is often a compromise. It depends on what you are lighting, and what you want it to look like. As a general guide, if you are lighting a *person*, do not have the lamp flat-on but position it at an angle; a little to one side of their nose direction, and a little above their eyeline. Clearly, the best position for the lamp depends on which direction they are facing. If they are going to turn their head around between full-face and profile, you will need to key them roughly half-way between these two positions.

When you are lighting an *object*, you have far greater freedom of choice as to where you place lamps, for its appearance is usually less critical than when lighting people. If, for instance, you are shooting a vase inside a glass case, you might be very concerned with avoiding reflections of the light and the camera, and deliberately steepen the lighting angle, not because it shows the vase best but because it avoids the problem. You might then use an upwards reflector to relieve the shadows.

- A prominent shadow on a light surface behind a subject can seem perfectly natural, or it may cause the picture to look crudely unbalanced. If you try to 'light shadows out' with another lamp, you are likely to overexpose the background and the subject in the process. Instead, you could either move the subject farther away from the background, or raise the lamp a little to push the shadow downwards.
- As you move a lamp *farther away* from a subject, its light spreads over a greater area, but its intensity falls.

If you take a lamp *close* to a subject, you will get a higher output from it, but its light beam will cover less of the scene. You are likely to find that the subject's brightness alters rapidly if it moves at all.

Very close lamps (e.g. for maximum depth of field on close-up work, and macro-photography) are not only uncomfortably bright, but quickly overheat nearby surfaces.

For many everyday purposes, a lamp distance of around 9–15 ft (3–5 m) from the subject, suits most situations.

- Having settled on a particular lighting angle, you will find that the farther a lamp is from the subject, the higher it will need to be.

The highest you can position any lamp is often decided by the local situation, such as how high someone can reach up with a hand-lamp (stand on a box?), or the maximum safe height of your lighting stands, or even the height of ceilings (do not get too close!).

- Avoid lighting arrangements where people move in and out of light, unless this is for a dramatic effect. Lighting should generally cover the action area, plus a safety region, in case people move beyond their expected positions.
- Find out as much as you can beforehand about what is going to happen. Then set up your lighting rig to suit this action. If you can watch the action being rehearsed before shooting, use this opportunity to check your lighting treatment on camera. Do not just watch the rehearsal and *then* light the scene. Otherwise, you will probably have insufficient time to do so properly, as well as missing the opportunity to check for lighting defects.
- During rehearsal, look out for hotspots and dark areas, both on people as they move around and on the background. To adjust the lighting *balance* (i.e. the relative intensities of the various lamps) you may have to put a scrim in a light to dim it a little, or spot up another to increase its intensity.

Provided a lamp is high enough, you may be able to cut away part of its diffuser, so that the part of its beam lighting nearby subjects is reduced, while its full light falls on more distant subjects.

Figure 4.15 Using daylight
Place the subject in a good position, facing towards the light, and adjust your camera position to suit.

4.38 Shooting without lamps – in lit surroundings

● Having selected the camera viewpoint you prefer, is the lighting *intensity* right for the lens aperture you want to use (i.e. is the exposure OK)? Does the light *direction* show the subject well? Is the *balance* between lighter tones and shadows satisfactory?

If these aspects are all right, but the overall light intensity is too low, open up the lens aperture and/or increase the camera's sensitivity (gain).

● If the light direction does not show the subject well, can you angle it or move it, to catch the light better?
● Is there any extra lighting available where you are shooting (e.g. some ceiling lights) that will lift the general illumination?
● Do you have a reflector that would serve as a key (hard, polished surface) or fill light (matte-white surface) to improve the shot? If you are taking a very close shot, even a sheet of paper, or plastic, or a metal tray may be pressed into service.
● Would it improve the lighting quality if you moved the camera viewpoint round towards the present main light source?
● If the background is underlit, is there sufficient light to take a closer shot of the subject excluding most or all of the background? Can you put in a dummy background (e.g. a sheet of cardboard) behind the subject to show it more clearly, or more attractively?
● You may even be able to move the subject to another place where the light is more suitable, e.g. take a statuette, standing in a dark corner of a room, outside into the daylight.
● Will the light be better or different later? Sometimes it is better to wait for clouds to pass over the sun, to reduce its intensity, than to shoot in bright sunlight with its harsh shadows and high contrast.

4.39 Using one lamp – the only light available

Whatever you are lighting, the priorities are: the subject's key light, then a fill-light to illuminate its shadows, then a backlight if needed, and finally lighting for the background.

If you have a single lamp, and this is *the only illumination there is*, you will have to use it relatively frontally.

A *single soft light*, such as a 'broad', will provide a more attractive effect than a hard light source, particularly if you use a diffuser (scrim) of tracing paper, frosted plastic, or even a fine wire mesh in front of the lamp. This will cut down its light level, but improve the pictorial effect. Although this soft light will scatter around, at least it prevents nearby areas falling into deep shadow.

If you use only a *single hard-light source*, results can be over-contrasty, leaving your subject unattractively isolated in a pool of light, within dark surroundings, or casting a strong obtrusive shadow.

4.40 Using one lamp – in lit surroundings

A lot depends on how satisfactory the existing lighting is. Your single lamp can be used in several ways:

1 As a *key light*. Your lamp can bring up the light level on the subject, to improve its exposure, or to provide clearer modeling in it, or to provide a low-intensity highlight that adds sparkle, glisten or glitter to it (e.g. eyelights).

You might let your key light flood over the background, to improve its general visibility.

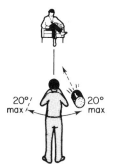

Figure 4.16 Using a single lamp
Place it up to 20° either side of the camera.

Take care not to illuminate a close-up subject so strongly that you have to stop the lens down, to adjust exposure for this increased local light level. If you do this, the overall brightness of the rest of the scene will appear to fall.

Under sunny conditions, you will often achieve more attractive pictures if you shoot towards the sun, which becomes a 'backlight'. Then for closer shots, you can use your lamp (or reflector) to key the shadowed side of the subject facing the camera.

Where subjects are positioned facing across the picture, you can use a key light from the side to produce maximum modeling. This side light does not suit forward-facing subjects, but when it can be used, you will not need backlight, to separate the subject from its background.

2 As a *fill light*. A single lamp or a reflector can help to illuminate the dense shadows cast by other lighting. It is best to use soft light, so that it does not produce additional shadows of its own. But soft light rapidly falls off in intensity, with increased distance. So if you are quite a way from the subject, you may have to use hard (or softened) light to reach it.

3 As a *back light*. Sometimes you will find a subject that is perfectly well illuminated under the existing lighting, but the picture lacks that extra quality backlight can add.

Even when shooting in the open on an overcast day, a single added backlight can improve picture appeal considerably.

You may be able to position the lamp directly behind and above the subject, by suspending it, or clamping it to a sprung-bar. Or you might use your lamp on a tall stand, which could be hidden behind a chair, for example, so that it is not obvious when it appears in shot.

4 As *background lighting*. Although your main subject may be well lit, you will often be able to improve the appearance of its background by careful additional lighting.

If for instance, you angle light onto items in the background, this will bring out their shapes and textures, and give the whole scene a more three-dimensional look.

Where the background has areas that are too dark to reproduce well, you can light them to make them clearer.

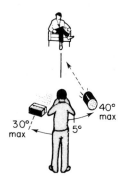

Figure 4.17 Using two lamps (facing the camera)
Use one as the key light (5–40° offset), the other as fill light (0–30° offset the other side). If the head is angled, 'light along the nose'.

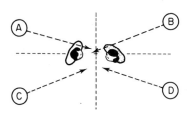

Figure 4.18 Lighting two people with two lamps
Several arrangements are effective, Keys at A and B, C and D, A and D, C and B.

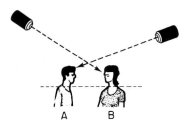

Lamps may be shared as key A/back B, and key B/back A. The lower part of light beams may need diffusers to avoid over-intense backlight.

4.41 Using two lamps

As you might expect, when you have two lamps, the choices increase considerably. You can use them separately (e.g. as two separate key lights for two people), or combine them (as a key and a filler for one subject) in the various permutations above.

Sometimes one lamp will serve more than one purpose, and light the background as well as keying the person. A spread backlight may be angled to one side, so that it lights not only the main subject but also other subjects in the shot, and perhaps shines directly onto a side wall that will be seen later in other shots.

4.42 Using three lamps

By now, you will have realized that just because you have three light sources, you do not necessarily have to provide three-point lighting. You use the lamps according to the priorities of the situation. You might use two lamps as combined key and back lights, and the third for the background. As always, it is the effect on camera that matters.

4.43 Limited lighting

There are regular situations where you will usually need *very few* lamps:

● When you are shooting in well-lit surroundings (daylight or interior lighting) and, at most, have only to supplement the existing illumination.
● When you have only a small localized area to shoot (e.g. a tabletop).
● When you are working in a small light-toned room.
● When the camera remains still throughout the shot (all the action taking place within the frame).
● When the action does not require the camera to pan around the scene (just zoom or dolly, in and out).
● When the background is not more than about 10 ft (3 m) behind the subject. (The more you see in depth, the more you may have to light.)
● When you are working at maximum lens aperture and increased sensitivity (video gain).
● When you are lighting each shot in turn; i.e. the lighting set-up does not have to satisfy a series of shots from different viewpoints.

4.44 Using multi-lamp lighting

You are more likely to need *several lamps* to light the scene:

● When you have to provide the entire lighting for a wide shot (no other light available).
● When your lamps are of low power or have a very restricted spread.
● Where you have to light a large subject area evenly (e.g. for shots throughout an audience).
● If action moves over a wide area (e.g. dance), and people and background need to be lit throughout.
● Where a series of subjects are spread around, and cannot be lit by one lamp. (Each may need its own individual lighting.)
● If there is extensive background area (e.g. a large cyclorama or wall) that has to be evenly lit. One lamp will not cover it, and you need to blend several lamps together.
● Where backgrounds are a considerable distance behind the subject (i.e. the shot takes in a wide area).
● When there are a series of planes (e.g. one set of arches or screens behind another) which may need individual lighting treatment.
● If you want to show detail or modeling in dark background tones.
● If the camera moves around, and shows a series of background areas.
● When the subject is to be shot from several different directions.
● Where subjects are to be lit with separate patches of light, e.g. on each piece of furniture in a display, instead of one light flooding over them all.
● For lighting effects, such as patches of dappled light, light patterns, colored lighting, lighting changes (e.g. morning to night) or a series of lamps each lighting a small selected area.
● In an awkwardly shaped location, where one lamp cannot reach a series of action areas.
● When you need a considerable depth of field in the shot (i.e. the lens stopped well down).

Natural light for interiors
With daylight coming in the window from exactly the right direction, the side-light creates a fine atmospheric effect.

Waiting for the right light With a bright overcast sky, the details are clear enough, but the shot lacks appeal.

Sunlight from the side casts attractive shadows, and gives The Alamo dimension and depth.

Reflections The camera operator is concentrating on the window display. But his audience is probably also watching what he is doing, as he stands reflected in the window!

Rim lighting
These shots remind us of how effective rim lighting can be in revealing outline and texture.

By keeping the light localized, the attention is concentrated.

The illusion of light
The shadows from this wicker globe
are falling on a flat wall behind it –
yet create the illusion of curved
planes. A reminder of the power of
light to deceive.

High contrast in exteriors
Where contrast is high, you may not
be able to expose the lighter areas
and the shadows successfully.

Above: the importance of viewpoint
A feature that is almost incidental in the long shot
appears impressive in a closer low shot.

Left: the audience only knows what they can see
From this close viewpoint, we see a row of charming
period houses, but the shot has excluded their
surroundings. Pull the camera back (below), and the effect
is destroyed.

Exotic locations
When your program requires a
scene at a distant location (e.g. a
Japanese Tea House) there may be
a suitable equivalent near at hand in
a local park!

(Fairmount Park, Philadelphia).

The commentary must explain
Pictures are not always self-evident.
Unfamiliar subjects, such as these
natural formations, need an
explanatory commentary

(Pamukkale, Turkey).

Avoid overcrowded pictures
If you try to show too many things
in the picture, none will be clear
enough to see properly.

Chapter 5

Audio techniques

Audio gives your pictures a convincing realism. It makes your audience feel involved in what they are seeing. Without it, they are watching moving shadows.

5.1 The essential component

Don't underestimate the valuable contribution that sound can make to your programs. In a good production, sound is never a casual afterthought but an essential part of its appeal.

People often think of television as 'pictures accompanied by sound'. Yet when you analyze most worthwhile television and film productions, you will find that for quite a lot of the time, it is the *sound* that is conveying the information and stimulating the audience's imagination, while the picture itself is really a visual accompaniment! In a radio broadcast, we conjure up mental images of time, place and people, from just a few audio clues without any picture at all.

Sounds are very evocative. Supposing, for example, you show a picture of a couple of people leaning against a wall, with the open sky as a background. If you accompany that picture with noises of waves breaking and the shrill cry of seabirds, we quickly assume that they are near the seashore. Add the sound of children at play, and now we are sure that there is a pleasure beach nearby.

Replace all those sounds with the noise of battle, explosions, passing tanks, and they are immediately transported to a war situation! They might even appear particularly brave and unflappable, as they remain so calm in this tumult!

In fact, all we really have here is a shot of two people leaning on a wall. The wall itself might have been anywhere – up a mountain, in a desert, or a replica in a studio. The location and the mood of the occasion have been conjured up by the sound and our imagination.

As we shall see, successful audio is a blend of two things:

● Appropriate *techniques* – the ways you use your equipment,
● Appropriate *artistic choices* – how you select and blend sounds.

Both are largely a matter of know-how, combined with experience.

5.2 The nature of sound

The world about us is filled with such an endless variety of sounds that it is difficult to believe each can be resolved into a single complex vibration pattern. When several sources sound together, their separate patterns combine into an even more complicated form. Yet our eardrums, the microphone diaphragm and the loudspeaker, all follow this combined vibration; and more miraculous still, our brain interprets the result.

The simplest possible sound vibrations make a regular *sinusoidal* movement, and you hear such pure tones from a tuning fork, a flute, or an audio oscillator. The faster this oscillation, the higher will we judge the *pitch* to be. Very slow vibrations (subsonic, below about 15 times a second) and extremely fast vibrations (ultrasonic, above about 20 000 times a second) fall outside our audible range. We measure the frequency or rate of these vibrations in *hertz*.

The stronger the sound's vibrations (the greater their *amplitude*), the *louder* it seems. Very slight vibrations will be inaudible, while extremely loud sounds can become painful to listen to, as they exceed our 'threshold of feeling'.

Few sources emit 'pure' sounds. Most are a complex combination of the main note (the *fundamental*) and multiples of that note (*harmonics* or *overtones*). The apparent 'quality' of a sound will depend on the proportions or relative strengths of these harmonics.

Broadly speaking, you can judge whether a particular note is being played by a double-bass, an oboe or a bassoon by its overall quality. If the response of the audio system is not even over the whole audible range (due to filtering, or limitations in the equipment), the proportions of the harmonics can become changed. Then the quality of the reproduced sound may no longer be recognizable as the original instrument.

5.3 Acoustics

You have only to compare sound in an empty room with the difference when that same room is furnished or filled with people, to realize how acoustics alter sound quality. If you understand the basics of acoustics, you will be able to avoid many of those problems that await the unprepared.

When a sound wave hits a *hard surface* (plastic, glass, tiles, stone walls, metal) little is absorbed, so the reflected sound is almost as loud as the original. In fact, when its higher frequencies have actually been reinforced by this reflection, the sound bouncing off the surface can appear brighter and sharper.

When a sound wave meets a *soft surface* (drapes, couches, rugs) some of its energy is absorbed within the material. Higher notes are absorbed most, so the sound reflected from this sort of surface is not only quieter than the original sound wave, but lacks higher frequencies ('top', 'highs'). Its quality is more mellow, less resonant, even dull and muted. Certain soft materials absorb the sound so well that virtually none is reflected.

Where there are a lot of hard surfaces around (as in a bathroom, a large hall or a church), a place can become extremely reverberant or *live*. Sound waves rebound from one surface to another so easily that you hear the original and the reflected versions completely intermixed. This can cause considerable changes in the overall sound quality and degrade its clarity.

When surroundings are very reverberant, you will often hear reflections, seconds after the sound itself has stopped; in extreme cases, as a repeated echo. Whether reverberations add richness to the original sound or simply

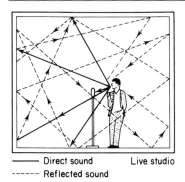

——— Direct sound   Live studio
----- Reflected sound

Figure 5.1 Acoustics
Live surroundings. When a room
contains predominantly hard
surfaces, the sound is strongly
reflected. Many of these reflections
are picked up by the microphone,
reinforcing and coloring the direct
sound pick-up.

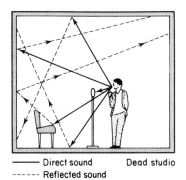

——— Direct sound   Dead studio
----- Reflected sound

Dead surroundings. When surfaces
in a room are very sound-absorbent,
the direct sound waves strike walls,
floor, ceiling, furnishings and are
largely lost. Only a few weak
reflections (if any) are picked up by
the microphone.

confuse it, will vary with the design of the building, the position of the sound source, the pitch and quality of the sound, and your own position as you listen to it. So there are opportunities for considerable variations here!

If on the other hand, the sound is made in a place with many absorbent surfaces, both the original sound and any reflections are quickly muffled. Under these *dead* conditions, you hear the direct sound, with few reflections from the surroundings. Even a loud noise such as a hand clap or a pistol shot, will not carry very far, but dies away rapidly.

We all know how dead the sound seems to be when we are out in the open. Because the air quickly absorbs it, and there are few reflecting surfaces, open-air sound is weak and does not travel very far. A microphone will often have to get much closer to a subject than normal, to pick up sufficient sound, especially if someone is speaking quietly.

Open-air sound has a characteristic quality that we immediately recognize; an absence of reflected sounds, combined with a lack of top and bass. This effect can be very difficult to imitate convincingly in the studio, even when we surround the subject with highly absorbent acoustic panels.

Acoustics can influence where you position your microphone. To avoid unwanted reflections in live surroundings, you need to place the mike relatively close. If you are working in dead surroundings, a close mike is necessary, because the sound does not carry well. When the surroundings are noisy, a close mike helps a voice to be heard clearly above the unwanted sounds.

However, there can be problems if you place a mike *too close* to the source. Sound quality is generally coarsened. Bass is over-emphasized. We become very aware of the noise of breathing, sibilants (*s*), blasting from explosive *ps*, *bs*, *ts*, and clicks from teeth striking together. Close to an instrument, the mike will reveal various mechanical noises such as key-clicks, bow scrape, etc.

5.4 Mono sound

In everyday life, you are used to listening with the aid of two ears. As your brain compares these two separate sound images of the external world, it builds up a three-dimensional impression from which you estimate the direction and distance of sound.

Non-stereo TV sound is not as sophisticated as this. It presents a 'single-eared' *monaural* ('mono') representation of sound in space. Your only clue to distance is loudness, while direction cannot be conveyed at all.

Many of our audio techniques are really methods of overcoming the limitations of mono sound systems. Listening to mono reproduction, we are not able to distinguish between direct and reflected sounds, as we can when listening in stereo. Instead, they become intermixed, so that the sound is often 'muddy' and less distinct. In mono sound, therefore, we become much more aware of the effects of reverberation.

Because your audience cannot easily distinguish direction and distance, you have to be careful when positioning the mono microphone that:

● You do not pick up too many sound reflections.
● You avoid a louder sound masking a quieter one (particularly in an orchestra).
● Extraneous sounds do not interfere with the ones we want to hear.

5.5 Stereo sound

Stereo sound creates an illusion of space and dimension. It enhances clarity. Because the loudspeakers in television receivers are quite close together, the effect is more limited than in most hi-fi systems. Sound quality and realism are enhanced, but our impressions of direction and depth are less obvious. Stereo can even make us more aware of the restrictions of screen size, and incompatibilities of perspective when shots change (e.g. from long shot to close-up at a concert).

To simplify sound pick-up, and problems of 'stereo space', many practitioners mix central *mono* speech, with *stereo* effects and music. Where you use a stereo/microphone, you must be careful to maintain its direction (i.e. mike left to camera left), and to hold it still; otherwise the stereo image will move around. In a stereo system, reverberation appears more pronounced, and extraneous noises (e.g. wind, ventilation, footsteps) are more prominent; for they have direction, rather than merging with the overall background.

5.6 Microphone care

Whilst most people regard the *video camera* with a certain apprehension, there are those who tend to dismiss the microphone (the '*mike*' or '*mic*' as it is familiarly called) all too casually. They clip it onto the guest's jacket with an air of 'that's the audio attended to' or wave a hand-held microphone around importantly as a status symbol or a pop-music prop rather than a delicate tool. Yet when you stop and think about it, the microphone and how it is used is really at the heart of your program's sound! If your microphone is inferior, if it is damaged, if it is poorly positioned the program sound will suffer. And no amount of 'compensatory tinkering' with audio equipment further on in the sound chain will compensate. *Your program sound all begins with the microphone*!

You do not need to know how various types of microphone work, to use them properly. They all convert sound waves in the air into a fluctuating electrical voltage (the audio signal). It does help though, if you are aware of their different characteristics.

Although most microphones are reasonably robust, they need careful handling if they are to remain reliable and perform up to specification. It is asking for trouble to drop them, knock them, get liquid on them, or overheat them near lamps.

5.7 Directional features

Microphones do not all behave in the same way. Some are designed to be *non-directional* (omnidirectional), and can hear equally well in all directions.

Others are *directional*, so can hear sounds directly in front of them clearly, but are comparatively deaf to sounds in all other directions.

A further design has a *bi-directional* or 'figure-of-eight' pattern, and can hear equally well both forwards and backwards; but it is deaf on either side of it.

The advantage of an *omnidirectional* mike is that it can pick up sound equally well over quite a wide area. So it is great when you want to cover a group of people, or someone who is moving around. The snag is that it cannot discriminate between the sound you want to hear (the speakers), and unwanted sounds such as reflections from walls, noises from nearby people or equipment, ventilation noise, footsteps, etc. The more reverberant the

Table 5.1 Coping with acoustics

When surroundings are too 'live'
To reduce acoustic reflections:
  Move the microphone closer.
  Pull drapes.
  Add thick rugs.
  Add cushions.
  Use upholstered furniture.
  Drape blankets on frames, or over chairs.
  Add acoustic-tile panels.

When surroundings are too 'dead'
To increase acoustic reflections:
  Move the microphone further away.
  Open drapes.
  Remove any rugs.
  Remove cushions.
  Remove upholstered furniture.
  Add board or plastic surfaced panels.
  Add floor panels (wood, fiberboard).
  Add artificial reverberation.

surroundings, the worse the problem. All you can do is to position your mike so that it is closer to the wanted sounds than to the extraneous noises.

When you point a *directional* mike at the sound you want to pick up, it will tend to ignore sounds from other directions, so provides a much cleaner, 'garbage free' result. On the other hand, you need to aim the directional mike carefully, and make sure that the person speaking does not move out of the main pick-up zone, otherwise he or she will be 'off-mike'. The sound will become weaker, there will probably be high-note losses, and you are likely to hear what you *are* pointing at, instead!

There are several different forms of uni-directional pick-up pattern. The *cardioid* or heart-shaped pattern is broad enough for general use, but not overselective, while the *super-* or *hyper-cardioid* response has also a limited pick-up area at its rear, to receive reflected sounds.

Line microphones such as the 'shotgun' or 'rifle' mike can be hand-held (or attached to larger cameras), and are valuable where you want to isolate a person within a crowd, or to exclude nearby noises. Around 22 in. (0.54 m) long, the shotgun mike covers a 50° angle, and is usually fitted with a foam-plastic or artificial fur wind-screen/windshield to reduce wind noise on the mike.

Finally, there is the *parabolic reflector*, a metal dish of up to 2–3 ft (0.6–0.9 m) diameter which provides a very sensitive, highly directional system (10–40°) for long-distance pick-up. Because of its size, it is liable to rock in the wind if it is not firmly secured.

Figure 5.2 Directional response
Non-directional (omnidirectional) response. Equally sensitive in all directions, generally rugged, and not too susceptible to impact shock, cannot be placed to distinguish between direct and reflected sounds, so must work close to the sound source.

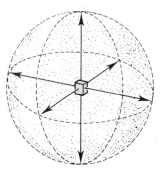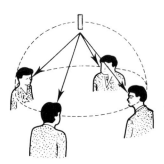

Cardioid response. A broad heart-shaped pick-up pattern (e.g. 160°), insensitive on its rear side. (Better coverage of close sources than a simple half-eight pattern.)

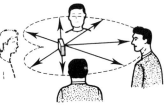

Highly directional response. Used wherever you want extremely selective pick-up, to avoid environmental noises, or for distance sources.

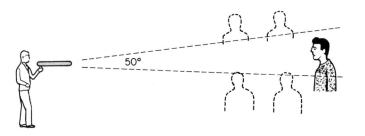

Bi-directional response. Sensitive ('live') on either face (e.g. 100° coverage for each), but deaf ('dead') at the sides. Useful for two-person pick-up, while suppressing reflected sound waves.

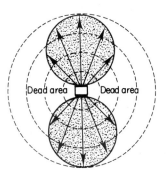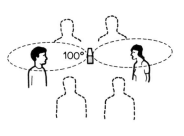

5.8 Popular types of microphone

Dynamic (moving-coil) microphones are pretty rugged, provide good quality sound, and are not easily overloaded by loud sounds (e.g. nearby drums). They can be hand-held without causing unwanted 'handling noise', and used in all types of microphone mountings.

Although this type of mike is sensitive in all directions (non-directional), it does tend to be quite directional at higher frequencies. In other words, anything to either side of where you are pointing the mike is liable to lack top to some extent.

Electret microphones are very popular in video production. Not only are they relatively inexpensive, but they are small and adaptable. The electret microphone can be used as a personal mike clipped or pinned to someone's clothing (e.g. tie, lapel or shirt), either singly or in pairs ('dual-redundancy', with one as an emergency standby). The electret capsule can also be used on a small boom or fishpole fitting, or within a parabolic reflector.

Its sound quality is good, although as you might expect, it can become somewhat muffled, when worn underneath clothing as an 'invisible' microphone. The unit uses a small battery to power its tiny enclosed amplifier.

Unfortunately, the electret microphone's performance (high note response; sensitivity) tends to deteriorate with time, and background hiss increases. High humidity, moisture, heat and dust can lead to failure.

The *pressure-zone* microphone (PZM) is a plate-mounted electret capsule that can be attached unobtrusively to any flat surface (table, floor or wall). Its high-quality output and sensitivity have made it increasingly popular for speech and music. However, because it is virtually non-directional, it is liable to pick up unwanted reflected sounds.

5.9 Other types of microphone

The *condenser* or *electrostatic* microphone produces the highest audio quality, and is ideal for musical pick-up. It can be fitted to a sound boom, a stand, a fishpole, or used slung over the action area. Its main disadvantages are that it is relatively large and liable to be overloaded by very loud nearby sounds. It also needs a special power supply.

The *ribbon* microphone (figure-of-eight pick-up) again provides very high quality sound. Its main drawbacks are its size and fragility (for wind causes rumbles, and can damage it), and the way it overloads with close loud sounds.

Supporting the mike

5.10 Camera microphones

If your camera is fitted with a microphone you will be able to pick up the program sound as you shoot without the aid of a second person, at least in theory. A lot depends on the situation and the type of sound involved. Nothing beats a separate, high quality microphone placed in exactly the right place. However, if you are shooting on your own, or moving around in a crowded market-place, or having a series of impromptu interviews in the street, the camera mike has a lot in its favor.

The simplest form of camera microphone is a small omnidirectional *insert mike*, built in at the front of the camera itself. This picks up the sound from all round the camera, including any noises from the camera zoom lens and auto-iris, and the camera operator's grunts and breathing. With care though, this basic microphone is useful for general atmospheric background sounds (traffic, crowds), and about adequate for close speech.

With most camera mikes, you will usually find that if you try to pick-up speech more than about 4–6 ft (1.2–1.8 m) away, background noise or acoustical reflections can sound unacceptably high.

Some types of video camera are fitted with a *zoom mike*. This ingenious unit combines electret capsules to give it an adjustable pick-up angle. Linked to the zoom lens system, it behaves as a *non*-directional ('omni') mike when the lens is zoomed out to its widest angle, and narrows to '*ultra-uni*directional' when the lens is fully zoomed in to its narrowest angle. Nominally therefore, it matches the sound pick-up to the shot, giving close-up sound when zoomed in for close-ups, and long-distance sound when zoomed out for long shots.

At first sight, this seems a great idea. But as you know, the lens angle you choose depends on your shooting conditions, and the 'perspective effect' you want. This has nothing whatever to do with the mike coverage-angle you would use to suit the acoustics, the action spread, and the mike distance.

Let us take an example. Supposing you are shooting a person singing in an echoing church. Using an automatic zoom-mike, the long shot sound (non-directional) would be accompanied by very strong reflections – so loud perhaps, that the singer's voice is masked by them. In close shots, the sound would appear localized and relatively dead, for the narrow-beam mike is not picking up the reverberation. But what you really want is clear sound of constant quality, with just a slight change in *volume* (if any) between the distant and close shots.

However, if you are shooting unassisted, and unable to put a microphone in the optimum place, the results can be satisfactory enough for many purposes.

A further type of camera microphone uses a regular *shotgun/rifle mike* attached to the top of the camera, and plugged into the camera's external mike socket. This is an excellent arrangement where you want high quality 'long-distance' sound pick-up from a subject in the picture. The main disadvantages here are the way the volume and quality of any background sounds will change as you pan around the scene, as they enter and leave the microphone's pick-up area. As always with directional mikes, you have to make sure that it is aimed accurately.

5.11 The hand mike/baton mike

Unless a microphone is designed to be held in the hand, your will hear quite a lot of handling noise (scraping, thumps, clonks) as you move it around, especially if the audio gain (amplification) has had to be increased for weaker sounds.

The hand-held mike (*stick mike*) is a familiar sight on TV, in the hands of interviewers, singers and commentators. It is a very simple, convenient method of sound pick-up provided it is used properly. Otherwise results can be erratic.

The hand mike is best held just below shoulder height, pointed slightly towards the person speaking. But don't exaggerate this pointing technique. Make it as unobtrusive as possible. If whenever you ask a question, you jab the mike at your victims, you are liable to unnerve them in no time at all!

Figure 5.3 Hand microphone
The hand microphone is widely
used for interviews, commentaries
and stage work. If the mike has a
cardioid directional response,
extraneous noise pick-up is lower. If
it is omnidirectional, it may need to
be held closer (e.g. 9 in. (23 cm)).

Techniques:
1 Normally held just below shoulder
  height. Pointing the mike at the
  speaker improves sound quality,
  but can be distracting, and may
  place the mike too close.
2 Avoid low mike positions, as they
  pick up more background noise.

To reduce the low rumbling noises of wind on the microphone, and
explosive breath-pops when it is held too close to the mouth, it is advisable
to attach a plastic-foam shield a *windshield* or *blast filter*. Whenever
possible, aim to talk across the microphone rather than directly into it, to
avoid quality changes (particularly if the mike is directional for higher
frequencies).

Some people hold the mike around waist height, to prevent it being visible
in the picture, but you will generally find this results in weak pick-up, poor
quality, and more intrusive background noise.

Where a hand microphone has a *cardioid* response, this helps to reduce the
amount of extraneous sound overheard, so it can be used about 1–1.5 ft
(30–45 cm) from the person speaking. But if you use an *omni-directional*
hand mike, it will normally have to be held rather nearer, say 9 in.
(25 cm).

Hand-mikes are not foolproof, and there are several points worth bearing in
mind whenever you use one. Although it is fairly rugged, treat your mike
gently. When you are not using it, or you need to put it down to handle
something, choose a safe place where it will not roll off or get trodden on!
You may able to tuck it under your arm temporarily, but this can cause loud
thumps as you do so. If you put the mike in a pocket, there is every chance
that the cable will pull it out. And don't be tempted in an idle moment to
swing or hang the mike by its cable – this leads to broken connections!

Cables need care. If you are going to walk around holding the mike, make
sure you have enough free cable to do so, and that passers-by are not liable
to stand on it, or trip over it. You can often lay the cable out of sight, and
use gaffer tape (duct tape) to fasten it against the floor or the wall.

As you move, hold the cable in your other hand (or under an arm, or clipped
to your clothes) rather than pull it along by the mike itself. When the cable
gets fouled up, don't heave on it to release it. If you cannot retake the
sequence, and someone out of shot does not rescue you, just accept that you
are trapped, and make the best of it!

If you are using several microphones, and want to confirm that a circuit is
working ('hot', 'live'), or are checking which mike is connected to an audio
mixer channel, scratch its end mesh or casing. Never blow into it, for this
is liable to cause damage.

5.12 The shotgun (rifle) microphone

As you can see in Figure 5.4 the *shotgun microphone*, which is also called
a *rifle* or *gun mike*, consists of a slotted tube (10 or 18 in. (25 or 46 cm)
long) containing an electret microphone at one end.

The shotgun microphone is designed to pick up sound within quite a narrow
angle (around 50°), while remaining much less sensitive to sounds from
other directions. So even if you stand some distance away from a group of
people, you can select a particular person while considerably reducing
sounds from others nearby.

Unfortunately, the shotgun microphone cannot maintain these directional
properties throughout the audio range. At lower frequencies it loses this
ability to discriminate. The narrow forward-pointing pick-up pattern
becomes increasingly broader, until from about 2 to 4 kilohertz downwards
the microphone has a more overall heart-shaped (*cardioid*) coverage (see
Figure 5.2).

It is easy to overlook that the shotgun microphone is always quite sensitive
to *lower-pitched sounds from all directions*. Where low-pitched extraneous

Figure 5.4 Shotgun/rifle microphone
The popular shotgun or rifle microphone (without and with its windscreen/windshield) is quite directional (50°). In a one-person unit, the shotgun mike is often attached to the top of the camera. Otherwise it is hand-held by a second operator. It can also be used in a sound boom (with or without a windshield).

noises such as traffic rumble become especially troublesome, you can often improve overall sound intelligibility by switching in a *bass-cut* filter to reduce lower frequencies but remember, this will affect the sound quality of the main central subject too. When you are shooting in very '*live*' (reverberant) surroundings, a shotgun microphone has advantages, for it will pick up the subject's sound successfully, while reducing unwanted reflections although how effectively will depend on the pitch or coloration of the reflected sounds.

The shotgun microphone is quite adaptable, and is regularly used as:

- a *hand-held microphone* supported by a pistol grip attachment,
- fastened to the end of a *fishpole*,
- in the swiveled cradle support of a regular *sound boom*,
- as a *camera microphone*, fitted to the top of the camera head.

Most people working in the field fit a shotgun microphone with a windshield (*wind-gag, windjammer, wind muffler*) of synthetic fur-type fabric. This furry overcoat with 'hairs' around 3 cm long can appear quite bulky, but it is a very effective method of suppressing obtrusive wind noises. An alternative design of *wind-filter* is a tubular plastic-sponge or fabric-tube fitting. Although much lighter, this may prove rather inadequate except in the lightest breeze.

5.13 Using the shotgun (rifle) microphone (Figure 5.4)

Of course, it's obvious! You just point the microphone at the subject. But that's not always easy to do, particularly if the subject moves or your viewpoint happens to become obscured. When your microphone's central axis is not in line with the speaker or instrumentalist, they will be '*off-mike*'. Then you are liable to find that *sound levels* (intensities) fluctuate, quality varies, or the sound loses definition (lacks '*top*'). Worse still, you might inadvertently pick up the wrong source instead!

There can be other unexpected traps for the unwary. Supposing you are using a shotgun microphone selectively, to pick out soloists in a choir. If you slowly pan a live microphone across to each soloist in turn, you are liable to get some very odd sound variations as other singers en route pass in and out of its main pick-up area.

The hand-held shotgun How do you choose the best position from which to pick up the sound? Well, you need a clear idea of the way the action is going to develop. You may get this from a briefing beforehand or have to find out empirically from a camera rehearsal. Will your shotgun be used for long takes or for brief shots? It is one thing to stand in a fixed position for someone talking straight to camera, and another to have to follow action around as people and cameras move through a complete sequence.

Will you have an uninterrupted view of the action? Is anyone or anything going to get in your way or are you going to get in theirs? It's a good idea to check with anyone working nearby (e.g. a neighboring camera dolly), to ensure that you are not both going to land on the same spot while following the action.

Try to position yourself so that action works towards you, rather than away from you. Even moves across the action area can be embarrassing if they are walking away from your microphone. Whenever you or your subject moves around, the speaker can easily pass in and out of the microphone's main pick-up angle. If someone turns away from the microphone there is no way you can compensate or move onto their sound axis!

When fixed to a fishpole (fishing rod) This is a regular method of mounting the shotgun microphone, particularly in the field. It allows the operator to stand several feet away from the subject, reaching over any foreground obstacles, to place the microphone at an optimum angle. In Section 5.15 we shall be looking in some detail at various ways in which you can use the fishpole.

When attached to a sound boom Some small sound booms are designed to hold the microphone at a *fixed* pre-adjusted angle. If you fit a shotgun microphone to such a boom, take particular care to locate the mike's axis as exactly as you can, for there will be no opportunity to readjust its angle during the take.

A sound boom with a fixed arm length and a preset microphone are really only suitable for picking up someone in static position (such as an instrumentalist). It cannot cope reliably with *moving* subjects. If someone is going to walk from one spot to another, and you do not have a separate microphone for each area, simply swinging the boom arm after them is an uncertain solution. Not only will the mike's angle be wrong, but because the boom's arm turns in an arc, it will probably over- or undershoot them as they move.

Where the sound boom has hand controls that allow you to turn and tilt the microphone you may have a little more success in following the action. (Large sound booms allow you to extend and retract the boom arm, swing it up and sideways, and to turn and tilt the microphone at the same time; maneuvers that are necessary to position the mike accurately during a move!) It is better to avoid the situation altogether. If necessary, ask the person not to speak during the move, and to fade to another mike when they arrive. It may even be necessary for the director to arrange two separate camera set-ups, with a break between to move the sound boom into position. But do not trundle the boom over after them during the action, as is so often attempted.

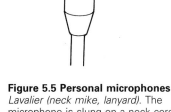

Figure 5.5 Personal microphones
Lavalier (neck mike, lanyard). The microphone is slung on a neck cord, about 6 in. (15 cm) below the chin.

5.14 Personal microphones

Rather than having a member of the sound crew following someone around with a microphone, it can be a lot more convenient to supply speakers with their own *personal mikes*. Then it seems, wherever they moved, we would be assured of successful sound pick-up. A *personal* microphone has many advantages; but it does have the disadvantage that there is no '*sound perspective*', i.e. the volume and quality of the sound do not vary with the apparent subject distance (length of the shot). However, for many types of production this lack of realism may not matter.

The most obvious type of microphone for someone to carry around with them, is the *baton microphone* (Section 5.11) which we see used so extensively in impromptu interviews. If handled correctly, results can be very satisfactory. But a baton microphone in the hands of the inexperienced, or someone working with their hands as they speak is quite another matter! To overcome such dilemmas, several special forms of microphone were developed.

Lanyard, lavaller, neck mike

An early approach to supplying a personal microphone was to hang a small dynamic microphone on a neckcord or lanyard around the speaker's neck, suspended at about the height of a necktie knot. A lanyard (lavalier) microphone may still be the answer where other approaches are impracticable; e.g. for a bather.

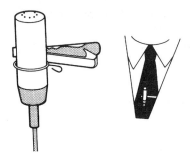

Figure 5.5 (Continued) *Tie clip mike (miniature capsule mike – electret or dynamic).* A single mike is clipped to the necktie, lapel or shirt. A 'dual redundancy' pair are used, where a standby mike is desirable. Presence filters (mid-range boost) may improve audio quality. Plastic foam windshields reduce wind-noise.

Clip mike/tie-tack mike

Smaller microphone designs developed, that have proved to be the solution to many sound difficulties. A small *electret* or a *dynamic* microphone with a clip attachment the '*clip mike*' or '*tie-tack*' mike has become a favorite device in productions where it is unimportant whether the viewer sees it attached to someone's tie or coat lapel. (Confusingly, the term '*lanyard/lavalier*' is also used for these clip-attachments.) Clip microphones are compact, unobtrusive and provide high sound quality. But you need to use them judiciously if you are to get optimum results. Clip the microphone to outside clothing (such as the tie, lapel, shirt or blouse) and noises from clothing-rub will be kept to a minimum. But tuck it away beneath a heavy sweater or coat, and understandably the sound becomes muffled and less distinct. Yet clip microphones are regularly misused this way!

A regular hazard when using a microphone clipped to a lapel is the way the volume and clarity of the sound can change as a wearer turns their head left and right; towards and away from the microphone. Wearing the microphone *upside down* reduces this problem to some extent, but may increase the chances of picking up extraneous noises from below (e.g. the sound of footsteps, whirring kitchen equipment).

If the wearer is inexperienced, it may be advisable to warn them not to touch or bang against their lapel mike, or to clasp items (especially animals!) against it.

As with all microphones attached to the person, you can only rely on a clip-on microphone picking up the sound of the individual wearing it. Where you have two or three people speaking, each will need to wear their own microphone which is connected to a separate audio circuit. Paradoxically, you can't assume that someone's microphone will *not* inadvertently overhear other sounds in the vicinity perhaps creating an echo effect. When working in noisy surroundings, unwanted pick-up can be a problem. A small foam windshield over the end of the microphone will reduce the rumble of wind noise.

When using more than one microphone in the same action area, make sure that they are all connected the same way round. If two or more have reversed connections, their *combined* outputs will be '*out of phase*'. The result can be a strangely hollow fluctuating sound quality.

Because electret microphones are so small, they are often treated very casually in everyday use. They get sat on, dropped, thrown down, inadvertently left attached or cast aside after use. But bear in mind that the microphone and its small connections are particularly vulnerable. *So it's advisable to check them regularly.*

A personal microphone's long trailing cable can be 'an-accident-waiting-to-happen' as it snakes across the floor to an audio input point on the camera's external microphone socket, the video recorder, an audio mixer unit, or a suitable audio wall-outlet in the studio. Secure it wherever possible, e.g. by sticking it to the floor with *duct tape (duck tape, gaffer tape)*, so that people do not trip over it.

When someone who is wearing a clip mike moves around, take the precaution of attaching the cable-end to their belt or clothing so that their mike cannot be pulled out of position. While some speakers accept this trailing cable quite willingly, there are those who feel tethered and manage to get it entangled or pulled off. Where possible, try to route the cable so that they 'walk into the loop' instead of dragging the cable behind them.

Having fitted someone with a personal microphone, try with their cooperation to arrange the cable so that it is not too distracting (avoid a 'wired-for-sound' look). Regular users will conceal the cable beneath a jacket or skirt, or run the cable down a trouser-leg.

Above all, remember at the end of the rehearsal and taping sessions to help people to detach themselves from the microphone and cable!

5.15 Wireless microphones (radio microphones)

Two forms of wireless microphone are widely used:

- **A wireless hand mike (baton)** This instrument is self contained and includes its own miniature transmitter and antenna (aerial). The transmitter's signal is picked up by a nearby radio receiver, and routed into the audio mixer. Although modern units are themselves very reliable, you need to take precautions for the best results. First of all fit new batteries before a session. (Typical battery life is about 4 to 6 hours.) Do not leave it to chance, assuming that there is enough capacity left from last time!

  Where two or more wireless microphones are being used in an area, it may be advisable to set them to different radio channels, to avoid mutual interference.

  When working near large metal structures, there can be difficulties with radio blackouts (dead-spots; drop-out), fading, distortion, or interference arising from radio shielding or multi-path reception. (*Diversity reception* using multi-antennae improves this dilemma.) Typically, the wireless microphone's range is around 440 yds (400 m).
- **A wireless clip mike** When someone is wearing a wireless clip mike on the clothing (usually on a lapel), its short cable is plugged into a small radio transmitter tucked away in a pocket or fastened to a belt. Free from the restrictions of an umbilical cable, the wearer can move around with ease. But as with all personal microphones, the sound technician controlling the program can do little or nothing if the microphone comes adrift or becomes badly positioned during the action, so it's necessary to take all possible precautions. The potential hazards above still apply.

5.16 Fishpole microphones

The *fishpole* or *fishing rod* fitting has now become a universal choice for sound pick-up on location, and in many smaller studios. Its adjustable lightweight aluminum pole is usually about 6–9 ft (2–2.5 m) long, carrying a microphone at its far end. The sound cable is taped securely along the pole.

Don't attach your microphone *directly* to the fishpole. For regular use, it needs to be housed in a proper shock-proof fitting (*cradle*) to prevent the rumbles of handling noise traveling along the pole and being picked up by the microphone.

Although you could use any suitable microphone at the end of the fishpole, most people fit a *shotgun* (*rifle*) microphone with a *windshield* attached. This makes the fishpole end-heavy, but as we saw in Section 5.13, it is essential if you hope to suppress wind noise. Plastic-sponge or fabric designs are much lighter but less effective. Again, background noises can often be reduced to some extent by switching in a *bass-cut* filter.

Whether you use your shotgun mike fitted across the end of the fishpole in a *'T' position*, or *set at an angle*, may be a matter of choice; but remember that the shotgun is a *directional* microphone, and for consistent sound quality it always needs to be held in an appropriate position, pointing to the sound source.

Figure 5.6 Using the fishpole

(B) Held high
Tiring if held up for long periods. Positioned to keep the mike out of shot; may be difficult to avoid visible mike shadows.

(C) Under-arm support
Favored for some situations; particularly for low pick-up positions.

(A) End on ground
Comfortable for sustained shooting
Best for stationary subjects.
It is not easy to follow wide movements.

Unlike the traditional *large sound boom*, which allows the microphone to be accurately positioned whatever the action, operating the fishpole effectively can be an acquired knack. Your aim is to position the microphone close enough to people without its coming into the picture or casting a shadow in shot. While a *small boom* microphone can occasionally dip into the top of the shot unobtrusively and be overlooked, the large furry *windshield* is immediately obvious. When poked up into the shot from below, it has been mistaken for a wayward animal!

Operating the fishpole

Until you get used to it, the pole can be a very unwieldy unbalanced implement when fully extended, for the weight is all at its far end. You can hold your fishpole in several ways (Figure 5.6):

1 *Above your head, with your arms fully extended along the pole to balance it*. This position can be tiring if you have to maintain it for long, but it may be the only solution where people are standing and/or walking about.

2 *With the end of the pole tucked under one shoulder*. This position is most suitable when picking up sound from people who are seated.

3 *Kneeling with the pole angled upwards*. This position would generally be used when picking up sound with the microphone held below the speakers' eyeline. The trick is to get the microphone close enough, without peeking in at the bottom of the camera's shot.

4 *With the end of the pole tucked into your belt*. Although sometimes recommended, this is really an unwise practice. Even when wearing a belt with an appropriate receptacle to support the pole's lower end, there is a real danger of the pole-end slipping out of the belt and causing severe personal injury. If held at a shallow angle the pole is insecure; while at a steeper angle, the microphone's position tends to be too approximate. Furthermore, you will usually find that holding a fishpole near one end does not allow sufficient control over the pole's movements.

Using a 'T'-mode fixing The fishpole is frequently used with a shotgun mike set at right angles across the end of the pole. You can operate it in several ways:

- Holding the pole vertically (preferably with its lower end on the ground), it is inclined forwards, angling the microphone downwards to point towards the subject. This method can be effective, particularly in a crowd, where obstacles get in the way of a more manageable hand-held shotgun microphone.
- Operators often hold the horizontal pole with spread hands, high *above* the action with the microphone pointing straight downwards; or low down out of frame, pointing upwards. Neither position is really optimum where people are speaking across the microphone, for the sound is likely to lack top and to be bass heavy as a result. If you are using this technique to pick up several people in a group, they will all be off-mike to some extent.
- Another approach is to stand to one side, with the fishpole across the action area; held so that the microphone points *across* directly towards the subject. If you are aiming to include a group of people speaking at random, you will need to work correspondingly further away to take them all in.

Using an 'angled mode' fixing You can also use a fishpole with the shotgun microphone set at an angle, pointing along the line of the pole, end-on to the subject. Using this method, you can direct the microphone more accurately; but there is a tendency to work with the pole at a lower angle than normal, and the possibility that it will dip into shot.

5.17 Small booms

Occasionally, a *small sound boom* is used for video production, to position the microphone over the action area. It consists of a pivoted telescopic rod (in principle, rather like a fishpole) balanced on the column of a castered tripod. It is usually possible to turn and tilt the microphone, with the boom preadjusted to stretch some 10–15 ft (3–4.5 m) towards the action. Although

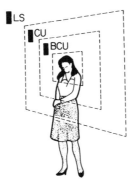

Figure 5.7 Microphone distance
You should aim to position the mike to suit the size of the shot, keeping it just above or below the frame limits,

BCU 0.3 m (1 ft)

CU 1 m (3 ft)

LS 3 m (10 ft)

Figure 5.8 Small studio boom
The pre-adjusted telescopic arm (counterweighted) is pivoted on a column of adjustable height in a swivel-castered tripod stand. The boom arm can be tilted and panned, the stand wheeled around, and the microphone can usually be turned and tilted. Boom stretch is typically 3–4.5 m (10–15 ft).

Figure 5.9 Desk microphone

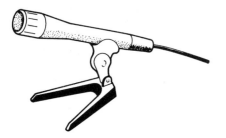 

Desk fitting. Fitted in a small stand, the mike can be used for people seated at a table.

Position. Typical mike positions are about 1.5–2 ft (0.3–0.6 m) from the speaker; 3–4 ft (0.9–1.2 m) between mikes.

Shock. A foam pad under the desk mike will insulate it from thumps and vibrations.

the base can be wheeled, the whole contraption tends to be rather top-heavy and to have a will of its own, even when the floor is smooth and level.

Smaller production groups seldom make use of the traditional *large sound booms* developed in film-making and used in larger TV studios. This equipment is costly, rather bulky, and requires experienced operation, but it does have the considerable advantage that you can position the microphone with precision under the most demanding conditions, and follow action very accurately.

5.18 Desk mikes

For someone seated behind a desk or table, you can clamp the microphone in a small support stand resting on a foam-plastic pad. This helps to isolate the microphone from any shocks if the person happens to kick the desk or thump on its top. To prevent the microphone being displaced accidentally, use double-sided adhesive tape to temporarily attach the microphone's fitting to the desk top. Similarly, it is good practice to tidy the microphone cable away (taping where necessary) to avoid its being pulled.

5.19 Stand mikes

There are several types of microphone stand, from robust bottom-weighted telescopic forms to unobtrusive versions with thin flexible or curved tubing intended for miniature mikes. Some have quick-release tops, allowing the mike to be removed and hand-held if necessary.

The stand mike is a useful general-purpose arrangement, when you do not mind the fitting appearing in shot, e.g. for center-stage announcements, a singing group or for miking musical instruments.

It has its disadvantages though. If people move around much, they easily get off mike. You have to rely on performer's getting to the right place and keeping the right distance from the mike. It is a good idea to give them taped foot marks on the floor to guide them. And of course, there is always the danger that they will kick the stand or trip over the cable.

Unobtrusively tape the sound cable to the floor if need be, with *duct tape/ gaffer tape.*

Figure 5.10 Stand microphone
The stand height is adjustable, and angled extensions can be fitted. A quick-release head allows the mike to be removed easily and used as a hand mike. Lightweight stands can be very unstable.

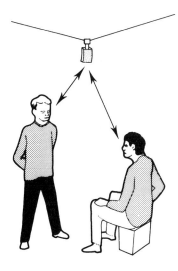

Figure 5.11 Hanging/slung microphone
Useful for area pick-up (audience applause, choir). But problems arise when people move around, or are at different distances from the mike (e.g. seated and standing).

5.20 Hanging or slung mikes

Sometimes the best solution to locating a microphone near enough to the sound source is to suspend it over them, e.g. above a choir, or part of an orchestra or an audience. Do not hang the mike by its own cable, but rig it securely with line (cord), using extra safety lines in case anything comes adrift and it falls down.

The hanging mike has several limitations. The mike will be visible in long shots (this may not matter). It usually has a fairly localized pick-up area (people may inadvertently move out of it). Its position cannot normally be adjusted during the production item. It may pick up quite a lot of extraneous noise. Its coverage of individual speakers in seated groups is poor. It can overheat and pick up hum from nearby lamps. It may cast a distracting shadow on the background.

5.21 Hidden mikes

When other methods of sound pick-up are difficult, a hidden microphone may be the solution to your problems. It can be concealed among a bunch of flowers on a table, behind props, in a piece of furniture, etc.

This idea too has its limitations. Although you can hide the mike, it may not be easy to prevent its cable being seen. Sound quality may be affected by nearby reflecting or absorbing surfaces. Because the mike covers a fixed localized area, you have to rely on a performer playing to the mike and not speaking off-mike.

Controlling dynamics

5.22 Dynamic range

Everyday sounds can cover a considerable volume range. Fortunately for us, our ears are able to readjust to an astonishing extent to cope with these variations. But audio systems can't do this. If audio signals are larger than the system can accept, they will overload it and become badly distorted. If on the other hand sounds are too weak, they get lost in general background noise. So if we want to reproduce audio clearly, with fidelity, it has to be kept within the system's limits.

A lot of sounds pose no problems at all. They don't get particularly soft or loud; that is, they do not have a wide dynamic range. When you are recording sound of this sort, there is little need to alter the gain (amplification) of the system, once it has been set to an appropriate 'average' position.

But one has to record sounds that vary in volume from a whisper to an ear-shattering blast. And the latter will certainly exceed the system's handling capacity, unless you compensate in some way. The obvious thing to do is to turn down the system's audio gain so that the loud parts never reach its upper limit. But now the quiet passages may be so faint that they are inaudible.

So somehow or other, you need to control levels, unless the sounds happen to have a limited dynamic range.

5.23 Automatic control

As you saw earlier when looking at video cameras, equipment today often allows you two options – either you can let it adjust itself *automatically*, or you can control it *manually*.

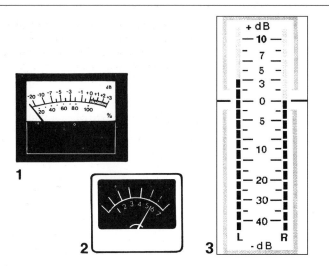

Figure 5.12 Volume indicators
1 Volume Meter (VU Meter)

Lower scale shows percentage modulation, where 100% is system's maximum limit. Keep your sound peaks in 80–100% (12–0 dB), only occasionally over (+1 to +3 dB) in the red area. Readings are unreliably low for loud transient sounds (e.g. percussion). The upper scale marked in decibels (dB), is used for calibration and line-up (with steady tone). Normal range is –20–0 dB.

2 Peak Program meter (European)
Designed specifically to indicate sound volume peaks. The PPM has fast-rise/slow-return characteristics, so its needle fluctuates less than a VU meter. Its easily read seven section logarithmic scale is akin to the ear's loudness response (unlike the VU meter).

3 Bargraph
Instead of a meter dial, this volume indicator shows a bargraph of *LEDs* (*light emitting diodes*), *gas-discharge devices*, or *plasma displays*.

In this example, both channels of a stereo system are monitored, showing the peaks of the audio signals. In more complex arrangements, twin bargraphs are used to indicate separate VU and PPM displays.

To avoid loud sounds overloading the audio system and causing distortion, most audio and video recording equipment includes *AGC (automatic gain control)* circuitry also called *AVC (automatic volume control)*. When the sound signal exceeds a certain level, the *audio gain (amplification)* is automatically reduced. You plug your microphone in, and the circuitry looks after sound peaks or so we hope.

There are two situations here. In the first, you have a completely *automatic* system, which amplifies all incoming sounds to a particular preset level. It 'irons out' sound dynamics by preventing over- or underamplification. Quiet sounds are increased in volume and loud sounds are held back. You have no adjustments to make and must accept the results.

This can be an effective enough way of coping with occasional overloud noises, but if the sounds happen to be so loud that they are continually '*hitting the limiter*', the results can be very distracting from an unpleasant strangled effect as sound peaks are '*pulled back*' to moments when quiet background sounds are overamplified, and surge in persistently whenever there is a pause.

In a second control system you adjust the audio gain *manually*. The trick is to ensure that your gain control is set high enough to amplify the quietest passages without running into overamplification of the loudest sounds. The AGC circuitry only limits sound peaks as an occasional safety measure, depending on your gain adjustment.

5.24 Manual control

The other method of controlling the audio level is to listen continuously to the program ('monitor' it) while watching a *volume indicator*, or *audio level meter*. As you watch, you re-adjust the system's gain (amplification) whenever necessary, to suit the incoming audio signal. That does not mean of course, that one should iron out the dynamics, by making all the quiet sections loud, and holding back all the loud passages. 'Riding the gain' in this way can ruin the program.

Instead, if you know sounds are going to be weak, you anticipate by gradually increasing the gain, and conversely, you slowly take back the gain before loud passages. Then the listeners are unaware that you are making changes to accommodate the audio system's limitations.

How quiet you allow the softest sound to be, can depend on the purpose of your program. If, for example, you are making a videotape that is to be used in noisy surroundings, or shown in the open air, it may be best to keep the gain up to prevent quietest sounds from falling below − 15 or − 20 dB. If you are shooting a piano performance, to be heard indoors, take care not to overcontrol the music's dynamics, and use the system's full volume range.

Because, unlike auto circuits, you are able to anticipate and make artistic judgments, the final effect can be far superior. The drawback to manual control though, is that you have to be vigilant all the time, ready to make any necessary re-adjustments. If you are caught out, results may be less satisfactory than the auto circuits would have produced!

There are several types of volume indicator, but the commonest on video equipment take the form of *visual displays* using bargraphs of LEDs (light emitting diodes) or *VU meters*.

A bargraph (Figure 5.12. Pt. 3) has a strip made up of tiny lit segments. This varies in length with the audio signal's strength. Calibrations vary, but it might for example have a decibel scale from −50 to +10 dB, with an upper working limit of about +2 dB. You simply adjust the audio gain control so that the sound peaks reach this upper mark.

The VU (Figure 5.12. Pt. 1) meter is a widely used volume indicator. It has two scales: a 'volume unit' scale marked in decibels, and another showing 'percentage modulation'. Although accurate for steady tones, the VU meter gives deceptively low readings for brief loud sounds or transients (e.g. percussion). So one could accidentally let the system overload.

Maximum signal coincides with 100% modulation /0 dB. Above that, in the red sector, sounds will distort, although occasional peaks are acceptable. The normal range used is −20 to 0 dB, typically peaking between −2 to 0 dB.

A further type of indicator, the *PPM* (*peak program meter*) is used only on certain professional audio equipment. It has a seven-section scale (4 dB per division), using 2–6 as its normal range. (Figure 5.12, Pt. 2)

We might summarize the situation by saying that if you need the audio system to look after itself, because you are preoccupied with shooting the scene, or are coping with very unpredictable sounds, then AGC has its merits, for it will prevent loud sounds overloading the system. If you have an assistant who can monitor the sound as it is being recorded, and adjust the gain for optimum results, then this has artistic advantages.

There are special electronic devices, called 'limiters' or 'compressors', that automatically adjust the dynamic range of the audio signal, but these are only found in more sophisticated systems.

5.25 Monitoring sound

Monitoring sound for a video program involves

- *watching*: checking the volume indicator, and seeing that the microphone does not pop into shot inadvertently,
- *listening*: on high-grade earphones or a loudspeaker, to check sound quality and balance, and detect any unwanted background noises.

If you are going to tape a performance straight off, without rehearsal, as with an interview, you should ask a performer to give you a few words before they begin, as a *voice-level* or *level-test* at the volume they are going to use during the taping. Alternatively, if they have a preliminary chat with an interviewer, you can normally 'take a level' then instead. Otherwise, you can judge the volume and dynamics from a rehearsal.

As you monitor the sound, get an impression of its possible dynamic range, while watching its peak on the indicator. (Even if the system is using AGC, there is often an indicator to prevent your 'undermoding' by having the audio gain setting too low.) If the results are not satisfactory, you may need to ask the speaker to talk louder or more quietly, or to reposition the mike. Finally, on a prearranged hand signal, when the recording has started, you cue him or her to begin.

5.26 The audio mixer

You need an *audio mixer panel* whenever you have a number of sound sources to select, blend together and control (e.g. a couple of microphones, audio tape, CD, VCR audio output, etc.). The output of this unit is fed to the VCR.

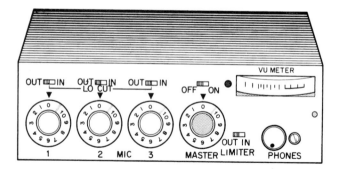

Figure 5.13 Portable audio mixer
Used in the field, to mix up to three mikes, the overall output is controlled by a master fader. An optional bass cut can be switched into any channel (to cut wind-rumble and improve intelligibility). A VU meter provides a volume indicator. This mixer includes a limiter, to prevent audio overload. A phones check-jack monitors the audio.

On the front panel of the audio mixer, are a series of rotatable knobs (or sliders). Each of these 'pots' (potentiometers) or 'faders' can adjust its channel's volume from full, down to fade-out (silence). In some designs, you can also switch a channel in or out ('key it') on cue.

When you plug the sources into the patch panel (connector strip) at the rear of the unit, you can choose which pot controls which source. Some mixers also include *channel selector switches* that allow you to reselect the channel controlled by a particular pot (e.g. either mike-1 or mike-2).

In a larger panel, as well as these individual channel pots, there may be *group faders* (group masters, submasters). Each of these group faders controls the *combined* outputs of several channels, and it may have its own group volume indicator. You could, for instance, use one group fader for all the mikes on an audience.

Finally, there is generally a *master fader* that controls the overall audio strength being sent to line (e.g. on the VCR). This can be used to fade the complete mix in or out. A master volume indicator shows the combined strength of the mixed audio.

Larger audio mixers include a *cue circuit* (audition, pre-hear), that enables you to listen 'privately' on earphones or a loudspeaker to the output of any individual channel, even when its pot is faded right out. So you can hear to set up a disc or tape at exactly the right spot, ready to be started on cue, without this being overheard on-air. You can also use the facility to identify circuits, making sure that the person at the other end is ready with their contribution.

The larger mixer panel will also include an *intercom* (production talkback) circuit that allows the sound operator to talk to assistants, and the director to communicate with the production team on headsets.

5.27 Using the audio mixer

Whether operating an audio mixer is a straightforward matter of 'just fading up a microphone or two and controlling the sound levels', or a complex process involving edge-of-seat decisions, will largely depend on the type of production, and how the director decides to treat it. For example:

- A *'live'* show, which is transmitted or taped 'as-it-happens', involves rapid decisions and simplified operations. There is inevitably a feeling of urgency, tempered with caution. When working on a production that is being taped 'scene-by-scene' there is time to set up complicated audio treatments. Anything that goes wrong can usually be corrected and improved.
- Where there are a number of contributory sound sources which need to be cued in at precisely the right moments, it will pose very different problems from a less complicated routine such as an interview.
- Is the program's soundtrack being compiled during performance, or later during a post-production session?
- Have the incoming sources already been controlled and prepared (e.g. as when using recorded material), or are you controlling live incoming sources which continually need to be individually monitored and adjusted (e.g. filtering and reverberation added)?

These are just a few of the issues that decide how complex your audio mixer needs to be, and how you will use it. Let's look at typical operations in some detail.

1 Cueing in and out. It is normal practice to cue a sound source, fade it in just before it begins (to the appropriate pot setting), and fade it out when it has finished.

If all the channels you want to cue are linked to a group fader (e.g. several mikes on a choir), this will control them simultaneously.

You can fade a source or a group in and out gradually (sneak in, fade-away) or rapidly (a straight fade-in, fade-out), whatever is most appropriate.

You should never leave a sound channel 'open' (live) when it is not in use. Apart from accidentally recording overheard remarks ('Was that all right?') and other unwanted sounds, it may pick up someone who is on another mike. Then you will have the sound from their mike, mixed with the 'off-mike' sound from the original microphone, which will produce an unpleasant echo effect.

2 Program continuity. Here we are concerned with selecting and introducing the right source at the right moment, and cutting each contribution as it is completed.

You can use either the channel pots for individual sources, or the group faders for a pre-balanced group.

As an example, imagine we are shooting a scene in a drama production. The audience sees a domestic interior, where music from the radio (*actually from a CD player beside the sound desk*) plays quietly. An actor is talking (*on live mike 'A'*) to another person (*on live mike 'B'*) who is out of shot. A nearby telephone rings (*fade up effects tape of phone ringing*). The actor turns down the radio (*we fade down the CD*) and picks up the phone (*we stop the effects tape*). Continuous background noises of a storm (*from another audio tape*) can be heard at a low level throughout the scene.

All these entries and exits would be carried out on individual channel pots. The different tape and CD machines may be operated by the person at the sound desk or by an assistant.

3 Creating a sound balance. If you are combining several sound sources, you will seldom want to add them all at their full original strengths. You will want to blend them for a particular overall effect.

Supposing you use a single microphone to pick up the sound from a musical group. With experience and good acoustics, this could work. But the chances are that it would pick up certain instruments much better than others. Loud ones would dominate; quiet ones would be lost. The overall balance would be poor.

Instead, you could use several microphones, devoted to different parts of the group. Then you would be able to increase the volume of weaker instruments (e.g. a flute) and hold back the louder ones (drums). With care, the result would sound perfectly natural and have a clearer overall balance.

Sometimes you will want to adjust the relative volumes of sounds to create an illusion of *distance*. If the sound of a telephone ringing is loud, we assume it is nearby; if it is faint, it must be some distance away.

You might deliberately *emphasize* sounds, e.g. by re-adjusting the pot controlling the crowd noise, to make it louder at an exciting moment, and give it dramatic impact.

The final balance you decide on is always a blend to suit your production.

5.28 Sound complexity

Preparing program sound can be simple and straightforward, or a highly complex business. It depends on the type of program you are making, how you decide to treat it, and how you go about the job. If you want to point your camera with its attached mike at the scene, and edit in camera, to get a finished product, you can do so, within certain limitations. But this is a very restrictive technique.

You do not have to have expensive, sophisticated audio equipment, to develop an effective, interesting soundtrack. With a certain amount of imagination, patience and careful organization, you can often achieve impressive effects cheaply and successfully with everyday facilities. But it is liable to be a longer and more laborious process. That is the price one has to pay.

5.29 Live sound

Practically speaking, there are really two live sound pick-up situations:

● The *repeatable performance*, in which you can re-record a sequence until it is just as you want it.
● The *once-only event*, in which you have just the one shot and must get it right first time.

The latter is the time when it may be wise to have a second microphone and a duplicate audio recording. If for example you are taping an important once-only speech, you could always at a pinch use track from the standby audio recorder together with audience shots ('cutaways'), rather than have an embarrassing gap in the program at the moment someone knocked the camera or pulled the main mike cable!

When you are recording an item 'live', as it happens, you need to monitor the program carefully, keeping a lookout for any errors or defects. It is too easy for something to go wrong, and remain unnoticed until afterwards. A fault that may be easily corrected at the time can be impossible to gloss over later, if you discover on replay that the sequence is unusable!

5.30 Recorded inserts

The great advantage of recorded material is that you know exactly what is in it – its contents, quality and durations. Even when there are unwanted sections, you can usually avoid them.

It can be more convenient, and a lot simpler, to audio tape an item beforehand ('pre-recording'), than to wait and include it live in the main taping session: piano music, for instance, played in the background of a scene.

Apart from various sound effects, recorded audio inserts have some less obvious uses too. In a drama for instance, you can play audio tape, to provide the voice of 'someone speaking in the next room', or at the other end of a phone 'conversation', and avoid using an extra microphone to take just those few words live in the studio. Audio tape can provide the 'voice-over' of a commentator or an announcer. Your audience will not notice the difference, whether the inserts are live or pre-recorded.

It is possible to manipulate recorded sound in many ways. You can cut bits out, play only selected portions, change the order of sections – even alter its speed or play it backwards if you really want to! And of course, you can add filtering, echo and distortion with a full knowledge that if anything goes wrong, you still have the original recording to go back to and try again.

There are several tricks you can play with recorded effects, to enable them to fit your particular needs. For instance, if you want to insert a recorded sound effect, but find that the version you have is too brief, you may be able to extend it by re-recording it several times in succession; so you could extend the drawn-out sounds of wind, seawash, a mob, machinery, traffic, etc. But watch out for any easily recognized feature though, such as a shout or the bleep of a car horn, that would become repetitious if repeated over and over.

You can create an illusion quite economically, by mixing suitable sound effects together. For instance, wind + rain + thunder + an automobile engine, can suggest that the car is traveling through a storm, although all the audience can see is the people inside it, and water on its windows.

By taking small parts of several effects, and joining them together, you can create the sound of something that does not exist! Thus you might combine the sounds of several different kinds of machinery (jet engine, sewing machine and slowed-down truck) to make the sound of a 'time machine'. A prehistoric monster might be contrived from the sound of several wild animals blended together, reversed, with speed changes.

5.31 Sync and non-sync sound

If the sound coincides exactly with the action in a picture, it is said to be *synchronized*, or 'in sync' with the action. This effect is most apparent when you can see anyone's lips as they speak, or their finger movements as they play an instrument, or watch actions that create noise (hammering or footsteps).

If after the picture and sound are recorded, they become 'out of sync' for any reason, the effect is usually distracting, annoying or comic.

If your audience cannot both see the action and hear its associated sounds simultaneously there can be no synchronizing problems. If someone's face is turned away from the camera as they speak, or we cannot see their finger movements as they play an instrument, or we do not see their leg movements as we hear them walking, sound and picture do not have to match at all accurately. We cannot judge whether the sound is accurately synchronized or not.

In fact, what we see and what we hear in the final program need not even be related! The back-of-head shot may be a mute 'cutaway', and a person at the piano may only be pretending to play, as the music comes from a recording. If you are using a piece of mute film or tape (no sound track, or with inappropriate audio) it is possible to simulate synchronization. A sound operator makes the appropriate noises in time with the original picture; a process known as *spot effects* or '*Foleying*'.

5.32 Why alter the soundtrack?

If you are shooting someone making a formal speech, the most appropriate technique may be simply to make a straightforward recording of what is taking place. But for many types of programs, this approach would be far too austere and ordinary.

You want to make your subject interesting, hold your audience's attention, give it a persuasive, convincing quality. And to do this, you may need not only attractive, well-chosen pictures, but carefully selected sound effects and music.

Let us take a dramatic example. Supposing that, at the time you were shooting a night scene, the location was disappointingly silent. Rather than leave the recording that way, you could make it more effective by introducing the sounds of night creatures such as owls, frogs, crickets, or even a quiet wind to build up a suitable atmosphere. Depending on what you choose, the same picture could be made to convey peaceful rest, anxiety, even impending doom – whatever is dramatically appropriate.

There are situations where, by altering the soundtrack, you can remedy what would otherwise be a disaster. Imagine shooting a documentary on the seashore, and finding that the speaker's words are regularly interrupted by persistent blasts from a nearby foghorn. The program seems ruined.

But all is not lost! You could take the videotape, and omit any shots that show the speaker close enough to reveal moving lips. You then get him/her to re-record the lecture (perhaps using the original videotape soundtrack to derive a script). Add the general, unsynchronized sound effects of sea-wash (without foghorns!), and use this new version to replace the original soundtrack. You now have a complete, unblemished program.

If you are showing a series of pictures that are really somewhat disjointed – various views around a city perhaps – you can link them together, and create a sense of continuity, by having the same background of sound effects or music behind the entire sequence.

5.33 Making the changes

When a video production is being shot in a studio you have the option of building up the program as you go (i.e. mixing in any recorded picture and sound inserts with the live pick-up from the studio microphones as you shoot), or shooting one sequence at a time, and combining them all during a later editing or post-production session.

The first approach has the advantage that you end up with a *complete soundtrack* on the video recording at the finish of the taping session. But there is a major disadvantage too. Any subsequent videotape editing will be interrupting a *combined* soundtrack. So, if for instance, you are videotaping a dance routine, and it is later decided to cut out 'the bit where a camera lost focus', or to put in an extra cutaway shot of the audience to hide a clumsy picture mix, the music soundtrack accompanying the dancers would change abruptly at that point. In the first case it would jump several bars while in the second there would be momentary silence!

To avoid such dilemmas, many directors prefer to keep their options open, and wait until they have *finished editing the pictures* before finalizing the soundtrack. And that involves detailed post-production work after the taping session.

However, where you *do* need to picture-edit a videotape program that already has a soundtrack with its pictures, there are two basic methods of doing this:

1 The simplest is to make a modified copy (a *dupe* or *dubbing*) of your program on another VCR.

To do this:

(a) Cable the *video* output of the replay machine to the video input of the record VCR. That will enable you to copy the original picture.
(b) You also feed the *audio* output of the replay VCR to an *audio mixer*. Other audio sources carrying effects or music are plugged into the audio mixer too.
(c) The output of the mixer is taken to the *audio* input of the record VCR. This will be carrying the original soundtrack, blended with the sound effects/music you are adding.
(d) Now you are ready to begin. Start the replay VCR, and the recording (dubbing) VCR, and introduce the extra audio sources as you go.

It is an easy, foolproof method, and if at first you do not succeed you can try again. The result is a *second-generation* copy of the original pictures, and a new composite soundtrack.

Because no copy can ever be as good as the original recording the picture quality on this version will inevitably have deteriorated somewhat during the copying, but it may not be apparent. However, you still have the original videotape with its 'first generation' picture and sound should you need it.

2 Another method of changing the soundtrack uses a facility called *audio-dub* on the VCR. This allows you to replace the original sound-track on a videotape, but leaves its pictures untouched.

You *lift off* the original soundtrack, make a new version, then *lay this back* in place of the old one, as follows:

(a) First you play your videotape program, making a copy of just its soundtrack, on an audio-tape recorder (from 'audio out' on the VCR).
(b) You then replay this audio-tape copy, through a mixer, blending it with the effects and music recordings you want to add. From the mixer's output, you record the new *master audio track*.
(c) Check this new track.
(d) When you are satisfied with the result, you load a VCR with your original videotape (set back at its start), and switch the VCR to *audio-dub*.
(e) Now you simultaneously play the new master audio track and record on the VCR. This will only affect the soundtrack of the original videotape. The result will be your new composite audio recorded alongside the original pictures, in place of the old sound.

The great advantage of this technique is that you have the original picture. So if you want to make copies of this program for distribution, you will get the best possible picture quality. (However, unless you keep an audio copy of its original soundtrack, you will have lost it during the 'audio-dub' process.)

There is a major snag though, if the program sound needs to synchronize exactly with the picture, e.g. close-up of people talking. Unless you are very careful(!) to ensure that the composite track starts at precisely the right moment, as you lay it back, you will get sound-sync errors.

Fortunately this situation is not as discouraging as it seems, for a surprisingly large number of programs do not contain (or can avoid) accurate sound sync.

At stage (b), instead of using a further audio recorder, you could have dubbed the mix straight back over the videotape's old audio track, but the method outlined is more flexible.

5.34 Discontinuous shooting

Most video programs are made up of a series of shots, taken in whatever order is most convenient, and edited together later to form the final program. This approach has both advantages and drawbacks. As far as the program sound is concerned, there are several complications.

First of all, although the various shots in a sequence have been taken at different times, you really want their quality and volume to match when they are edited together. Otherwise there will be sudden jumps whenever the shot changes. If, for instance, you take a shot of a person walking down a hallway, using a close mike, and then a side view of the same action using a more distant mike, the difference in the sound, on cutting from one viewpoint to the other, could be quite noticeable. The overall effect would draw attention to the editing.

When you are editing together a sequence of pictures shot at different times you may find that their background sounds do not match. Supposing we stop shooting for a few minutes to reposition the camera, adjust a light or to retake the action. Background noises often change quite considerably, but we do not notice for we are busy with the job in hand. When we start again, they are now different.

So sounds that we became accustomed to while shooting the scene, such as overflying aircraft, farm equipment, hammering or typing, can have a nasty habit of instantly disappearing and reappearing when the shots are joined together.

When you are on location, it is a good habit to record some general background noise on a separate audio tape during the shooting session. It is surprising how often this unsynchronized *wild track* comes in useful during audio editing, for use as background sounds.

Even when you are shooting under what seem to be quiet conditions, there is a certain amount of background noise from air-conditioners, equipment hum, etc. A wild track of this *atmosphere* ('atmos') can be used later, to cover any moments where there is a break in the soundtrack during editing.

There will be times when you decide that the sound you are getting on location is not really suitable for your particular program. It may be too noisy, too quiet, or you may find that you cannot get good sound pick-up. In these situations you may decide not to record it (to shoot 'mute'), or to replace the available sound with others you have recorded at some other time. A suitable wild track can be extremely useful here.

Perhaps, for example, you have shot scenes in a street market, and find later that instead of a general atmospheric hubbub you want to go behind (lay under) a commentary, your sound track is dominated by a few intrusive noises. You can replace the original sound with more appropriate wild track instead.

Wild track can help during those awkward moments when background sounds in successive shots do not match. It can serve as a bridge to disguise when silent and sound shots are intercut.

You might be cutting from someone speaking, to a silent shot ('mute') as they walk away. Wild track behind the entire sequence would give it continuity.

Even when the shot contains action that would seem to need synchronized sound (e.g. people walking around in the booking hall of a bus station), a wild track recording made at different time (or a different bus station!) will be quite convincing.

When we see and hear the finished results of all this trickery, the whole thing appears quite real and natural.

Getting organized

5.35 Preparations

So far we have been considering the nature of sound pick-up, and what you are aiming to do. Now we come to the very practical business of organizing exactly how you are going to tackle the job in hand. Even if your video program only involves one seated person speaking to camera, it is as well to anticipate, before you go ahead.

5.36 Working single-handed

If you are program-making single-handed, and have to operate the camera *and* arrange sound pick-up, you cannot control the sound manually. But the AGC circuits of the video recorder will prevent the soundtrack from being overloaded ('over-mod'). Where you have an audio gain control, take a sound level test beforehand, and check on the volume indicator.

Whether you are using a separate VCR or a camcorder, you can check the audio as you shoot with an earpiece plugged into a monitor-socket on the camera. (In some designs, there is a small in-built monitor loudspeaker in the side of the camera unit.)

As to the method of sound pick-up you use, a lot depends on whether you are shooting continuously or discontinuously (intermittently); whether you are editing the recording or not; and whether the talent remains still or is moving around.

If you are going to break the action down into a series of separate takes, and shoot *discontinuously*, you can obviously reposition the camera and the microphone to suit each shot, editing either in camera or afterwards. When you are shooting *continuously* though, sound pick-up may pose some problems – but there are several solutions.

5.37 Practical methods

At first sight, a camera microphone provides the simplest method of picking up program sound (Section 5.10):

- The microphone is there on the camera and doesn't require a second person to look after the audio.
- Wherever the camera points, the microphone will follow.
- There are no problems with microphone boom shadows.

But the camera microphone has a number of drawbacks too:

- Integral camera microphones seldom provide high-quality sound.
- The microphone is often too far away from the subject for the best sound. Its position is determined by the camera's shot; not by the optimum place for the microphone.
- The microphone's distance is the same for all shots. The camera may zoom in to a close viewpoint, or take a wide-angle shot, but the sound level remains the same.
- Where there are strong sound reflections from nearby walls, or loud background noises, the microphone really needs to be placed closer. However, if you move your camera nearer to achieve this, the subject will now appear much too close. Then the only remedy is to widen the lens angle to reduce its apparent size. But close shots with a close wide lens angle noticeably distort people and exaggerate space.
- The camera microphone cannot follow somebody if they turn away from a frontal position; e.g. to point to a nearby wall map. The sound's volume and quality will fall off as they move *off-mike*.

A properly positioned individual microphone will usually provide much better sound quality than a camera microphone. And where you have an experienced interviewer using a hand mike well, sound pick-up clearly presents few difficulties (Section 5.11). However, do not assume that you will get equally reliable results if you give a hand mike to an inexperienced person. Typically, they will feel ill at ease, and hold it incorrectly. You will usually see a similar response if you place them in front of a stand microphone. Remember, standing with a hand mike, or at a stand microphone is a very artificial, 'staged' situation, and in fact, this approach will not always be the appropriate solution.

A *desk microphone* is often the best form of sound pick-up where someone is seated at a table or desk (although rather less effective if they are standing). Whether you leave the microphone clearly visible, or hide it behind something on the desk-top, is up to you. Be warned though, against putting the microphone *inside* anything lying on the desk, for it will reduce the top (upper notes) and degrade the sound quality. If the speaker is going to turn to side, as well as face the camera, place the desk microphone mid-way between the head directions, so that the sound is similar for both directions.

As we saw earlier (Section 5.14), a *personal mike* is a very convenient method of picking up the sound for people who are not going to move around to any extent. It is best clipped on the clothing (tie, lapel or shirt front) whichever side the person is most likely to turn.

A cable can be a menace if the speaker is going to do anything energetic, or move in and out of a series of obstacles, e.g. within various pieces of sculpture in an art display. A wireless mike overcomes this dilemma, but of course it is a much more costly solution.

Whereas you can place a desk mike in position beforehand, you have to wait for the speaker to arrive to fit a lavalier/tie-clip mike. People who are unused to personal mikes may feel awkward and tied down by this unfamiliar appendage.

If someone is moving around over a wide area, you will not be able to cover them effectively with one static microphone. A very directional microphone, that is carefully aimed, could be successful, but this would involve a separate operator. So for the lone program-maker, the best solution may be to use two microphones, one for each action area. These are cabled to a small belt-worn audio mixer, and you fade from one to the other as the talent moves over to the respective mike.

5.38 Variations on a theme

As you will have realized by now, we need to be *adaptable* when deciding how to tackle a particular situation. If circumstances change, our method will often change too.

Supposing for example, there are to be a series of *live* events in a large hall. If you are shooting discontinuously, you could record the first, stop the recording, then reposition the microphone and camera for the second. When you are settled, you would recommence recording. This way, you could have a clean cut between the two shots.

Alternatively, to save time, you could keep the recording running, and relocate the shot and mike on the second event, and cut out the pause during post-production editing.

You can avoid editing altogether. At the finish of the first item (in sound and picture), you could widen the shot to reveal the new action area, where the performer appears busy preparing (mute). Move the camera in, and when the camera and microphone arrive, the person can speak on cue.

5.39 Anticipation or 'doing the obvious'

Anticipation comes with experience. When things go wrong, hopefully, one is prepared next time! You can be anticipatory in a number of ways.

Preparation

● Check through the script or any production planning sheet to ensure that you have all the equipment needed for that particular show.
● Check any audio recorded insert (music, effects, speech) you consider using, before the show. It may not be appropriate after all. Is the duration suitable too long or too short? Is the quality satisfactory? Will it require equalization (compensatory filtering to improve tonal balance, reduce wind noise, hum, rumble, etc.)? Is it damaged in any way (e.g. surface scratches on a disc)? Have you got the insert material arranged in the order in which it is to be used?
● Check all your equipment to make sure that it is working correctly. Don't rely on 'It was OK yesterday'! Is all equipment patching (plugging up) as you believe it to be? Confirm correct routing. Have someone at the audio mixer fade up each source in turn to confirm that all is well. Go to each microphone in turn, scratch its housing and announce its location (this is 'Boom A').
● Have a standby microphone ready in case the main microphone fails. If it is a special occasion, and you are relying on a lapel mike, it may be advisable to fit a second 'dual redundancy' clip mike too.
● Is the microphone cable long enough to allow the fishpole or boom to move around freely?
● Similarly, does anyone wearing a personal mike have it firmly attached with sufficient cable? (Don't forget to recover the clip mike and any transmitter afterwards!)

Of course these are all a matter of '*common sense*', but it is surprising how often the obvious and the familiar get overlooked. These are just reminders of regular routines, to which you will soon add your own.

In action

● Where are they going? What are they going to do there? Typical questions to which you want at least a general outline before rehearsals start. Without prior information, the most elementary mistakes are likely to happen. We learn from others.

An operator was standing to the left of the camera, poised with an extended fishpole . . . but the talent walked in the opposite direction, way out of reach of the microphone.

An actor seated in a chair . . . stood up suddenly, banging his head on the close microphone.

These are real situations that happened to an experienced team. More than an embarrassment, unplanned action can waste a lot of time, bringing everything to a halt. If the subject itself is totally unpredictable (e.g. animals and children) there still has to be a plan of campaign, to cope with the unexpected.

As well as position changes, you need to be prepared for any *loud noises* that are likely to arise during the action. One of the worst dilemmas is when someone who is quietly spoken stands by a noisy machine, explaining how it is used. If you hold back the audio gain to accommodate the machine-noise, they become inaudible. A friendly word beforehand, asking them not to speak while the machine is on, may solve the problem.

Another approach would be to shoot the action, then record the voice of the demonstrator separately afterwards while watching a picture replay. You could tape this speech on a separate audio recorder, and mix it with a lower-level version of the machine sounds to form the final soundtrack, and use 'audio-dub' to place it beside the videotape pictures.

It is very hard to avoid unexpected noises interrupting the wanted sound at some time or other, and either over-peaking and distorting, or shattering the viewer's concentration. Even apparently inoffensive actions can sound very exaggerated, when picked up on a close microphone. All you can do, is to warn people in advance if they are likely to be hammering (lower the audio gain at that point), or ask them not to clatter kitchen-ware, etc. If the result is unacceptable, you may be able to retake the shot, or even cut it out of the soundtrack, if the worst comes to the worst.

5.40 Improvizing

It might be argued that the more facilities you have, the greater your opportunities to do more sophisticated things. But many a hi-fi enthusiast has sufficient equipment to produce an interesting soundtrack for a wide variety of programs. And of course, with a little ingenuity, you can devise extra, useful facilities.

The same small electret microphone may be used in various ways:

- It can be clipped onto your subject, as a personal mike.
- As a table mike, its base can be inserted into a block of foam plastic if you do not have the right support.
- Attached to a thin vertical aluminium tube (isolated via a flexible joint) with a simple bottom weight, you have an improved stand mike.
- Held in a foam-plastic collar, clamped at the end of an aluminium pole, you have a 'fishpole'. (A monopole, or even a hand-held extended car radio antenna, has been used as an emergency fishpole, to hold the mike closer to the action.)
- Fix the electret mike facing into the center of a parabolic dish, and you have a narrow-angle reflector mike.

5.41 Audio dubbing

Dubbing, or recording an existing recording (i.e. making a 'second generation'), is a regular way of creating more elaborate background sounds. Now although sound quality will deteriorate to some extent whenever you make such a copy – and will worsen further if you go on and make a copy of that copy ('third generation') – things are not as bad as one might imagine in practice. With modern audio equipment and tape, these losses need not be great, especially if increased tape noise is lost in the background effects.

So we can take advantage of this fact, and by multi-dubbing, create quite complex soundtracks with modest equipment.

Some audio stereo recorders have the useful facility that they can be switched from 'stereo', to record two independent tracks of 'mono' sound side by side instead. Using this facility, you can prepare a different sound effect on each track of the audio tape. When you replay the tape (in 'stereo replay' mode), the two tracks will combine, in sync, and give you a composite mono soundtrack.

Some audio stereo recorders also allow you to dub from one track to another, as you play the tape and mix the sounds into a composite. You can then transfer this composite track, mixed with a further sound, back onto the first track, and so build up a detailed composite on one machine. All this takes time, but where you do not have several audio tape machines and an audio mixer, it does enable you to create very successful results nevertheless.

5.42 Anticipating sound editing

When you are shooting a scene, how can you anticipate and overcome the problems of sound editing?

- *Continuity.* Try to ensure that the quality and level of successive shots in the same scene match as far as possible.
- *Effects.* Keep a small audio recorder handy when you are shooting. It is good habit to record some general 'atmos' track, and typical background sounds (wild track) in case you need these later.
- *Sound effects.* If you have time, record any sound effects that crop up unexpectedly, that might be a useful addition to your effects library. Although you may be shooting a program on crops, any unwanted sounds of a passing fire engine, a police car, a dog barking, children playing, a shopping crowd or thunder, could all be used at the right moment in another program.
- *Question.* When you are shooting an interview, and the single camera and microphone are concentrating on the guest, the questions of the interviewer may not be audible on the videotape. So use your audio recorder to tape an interviewer's questions. These can be 'dropped into' the final soundtrack at the right moments, during the audio dubbing session.

This idea can be used too, to ensure sound continuity for *pick-up shots*, where a speaker moves from one location to another during unscripted speech.

Let's take an example of this last point. A lecturer has been telling us about the birthplace of a celebrity: '. . . he lived down there, at the bottom of this hill'. The scene changes, and the camera is now relocated inside the house. But in reality it took us half an hour to move the camera to the new location, and set up the lights. What were the lecturer's last words in the previous shot? Quicker than reviewing the videotape, we have the answer immediately on the audio recorder. When we are ready, the new shot begins: 'and in the kitchen of this house . . .'. Obvious enough perhaps, but a good way of ensuring that you do not later find yourself trying to edit together scenes that have no speech continuity.

5.43 Music and effects track

When your program is to be seen by audiences who speak different languages, it is worth taking the trouble to make a special 'music and effects' (M&E) audio track. This includes all atmospheric sounds, effects and music, but no speech. Commentary or dialogue in the appropriate language can then be added to this track as required.

If the video recorder has stereo facilities, you can tape a mono version of one language plus the M&E on one audio track of the videotape, and a different language combination on its other audio track.

5.44 Filtered sound

You can make considerable changes to the quality of sound by introducing an *audio filter* into the system. It can be adjusted to increase or decrease a chosen part of the audio spectrum, to exaggerate or suppress the higher notes, bass or middle register, depending on the type of filter system you use, and how you adjust it.

The simplest 'tone control' progressively reduces higher notes during reproduction. A more flexible type of audio filter has the various names of *audio baton, octave filter, shaping filter* or *graphic equalizer*. This can boost or reduce any segment(s) of the audio spectrum by changing the positions of a series of slider pots. The outline of these sliders shows the system's effective response.

Here are typical ways in which filtering can enhance the subjective effect of the sound:

● Cutting low bass can reduce rumble or hum; improve speech clarity; lessen the boomy or hollow sound of some small rooms; weaken background noise from ventilation, passing traffic, etc. Overdone, the result sounds thin, lacking body.
● Cutting higher notes can make hiss, whistles, tape noise, sibilant speech, and other high-pitched sound less prominent. However, if you cut them too much, the sound will lack clarity and intelligibility.
● If you cut bass and top, the sound will have a much more 'open-air' quality – a useful cheat, when shooting an 'exterior' scene in a studio.
● By slightly increasing bass, you can increase the impression of size and grandeur of a large interior.
● You can improve the clarity and 'presence' of many sounds, making them appear closer, by boosting the middle part of the audio spectrum (e.g. 2–6 kHz).
● Filtering can make the quality of sound recorded in different places more similar (e.g. shots of someone inside and outside a building). It can help to match the sound quality of different microphones.

5.45 Reverberation

As we saw earlier (Section 5.3) most everyday sounds we hear are a mixture of direct sound from the source itself together with '*colored*' versions reflected from nearby surfaces. The quality of that reflected sound is affected by the nature of those surfaces. If due to their construction or the material they are made of, they mainly absorb higher notes (e.g. drapes, cushions, carpeting) this reflected sound will lack 'top'. It may even be quite muffled. Conversely, where surroundings reflect higher notes more readily, these hard reflections will add harshness (edginess) to the final sound.

Where there are few sound-absorbing materials around there will be noticeable *reverberation* as sound rebounds from the walls, ceiling, and floor. If the time intervals between these reflections are considerable, we will hear a distinct repeat; i.e. an *echo*.

These are not just academic niceties. You are already familiar with how different a room in your own apartment sounds when emptied of furniture and when fully furnished. This is just a reminder of the way in which *room tone* will depend on its volume and shape, carpeting, drapes, easy chairs, etc.

Where there are *no* reflections as in open spaces away from buildings or other hard surfaces the resulting sound will seem *dead*. The only way we can simulate dead surroundings within a building is to use carefully positioned sound-absorbing materials.

In practice, you can enhance the appeal of many sounds by adding a certain amount of real or simulated *reverberation* to them. Music played in absolutely dead surroundings (e.g. an *anechoic chamber*) is not satisfying.

On the other hand, if there is too much reverberation, the result is a confused mixture of sound that reduces its clarity. A sound accompanied by rapid '*slap-back*' echoes can be very disturbing to listen to.

A number of techniques have been used over the years to simulate the effect of reverberation by mixing the original sound with a reverberant version. The simplest method is the '*echo room*' in which the sound to be treated is played over a loudspeaker in reverberant surroundings (e.g. a cellar, bathroom, corridor). A nearby microphone picks up the reverberating version. Cheap and effective, provided you do not also overhear unwanted sounds.

In *spring delay* systems the audio signal is routed to a transducer which vibrates a large spring. A pick-up head attached to the far end of the spring converts these vibrations into an audio signal. Large metal *reverberation plates* work on a similar principle.

In the most recent reverberation devices, *digitally stored sound* is re-read selectively over and over to give the impression of reflected sounds.

5.46 Program music

The role of music in film and TV programs is so established that we don't need to dwell on it here. Musical themes often remain in the memory long after the program itself has faded from the mind.

Music can have various purposes. For example:

- Identifying
  Music associated with a particular show, person, country.
- Atmospheric
  Melodies intended to induce a certain mood; e.g. excitement.
- Associative
  Music reminiscent of e.g. the American West, the Orient.
- Imitative
  Music that directly imitates; e.g. bird song.
  Music with a rhythm or melody copying the subject's features;
  e.g. the jog-trot accompaniment to a horse and wagon.
- Environmental
  Music heard at a particular place: e.g. a ballroom.

Musical jingles have been a highlight of many advertising campaigns. But music is regularly misused too! Here are a few reminders of how music can get between the program and your audience.

- Music that is played too loud (particularly opening music) causing listeners to grab for the volume control.
- Musical themes that are selected from standard classical works need to be chosen with care. Music lovers may resent hearing dissected globs of their favorite works.
- Some directors economize by repeating the same short musical passages over and over during a production.
  Even attractive melodies quickly pall.
- Try to avoid passing fashions in program music:
  - Loud repetitive percussion (hopefully intended to engender excitement).
  - Background music with lyrics containing a word or phrase that have just a tenuous connection with the program theme.
- Music that is continually fading up and down as the scene changes.

Probably the most elusive use of music is as a '*space filler*'. Where there is no sound to accompany the pictures (i.e. no dialogue or environmental sounds) there is a tendency to arbitrarily introduce music to '*fill the soundtrack*'.

A similar situation arises when there is '*voice-over*' dialogue but no apposite pictures; e.g. during explanatory narrative which is giving the audience background information on a topic. Because no pictures are available or appropriate, the director resorts to a montage of vaguely associative shots of views of countryside, townscapes, etc., or shots of shadow patterns, reflections, textures, trees against the sky, etc., that have nothing to do with what is being said, but overcome the alternative of a blank screen! These are often termed '*wallpaper shots*'! It is easy to dismiss the practice lightly, but where the picture or the soundtrack dominates this can be a real predicament for the director and the editor.

5.47 MIDI systems

You are probably familiar with the way in which *MIDI systems* enable us to 'play' a wide range range of musical instruments and sounds from a portable keyboard linked to a suitable computer program.

MIDI programs provide an impressive diversity of digitally sampled musical instruments; from various types of guitar, organ, drums, brass and woodwind to such fascinating instruments as the *bonang*, *oud*, *shamisen*, *gender* that are unfamiliar to most Western ears.

By altering the attack and delay times of an instrument you can considerably modify its sound quality. But when these musical instruments are played way outside their normal scale range they become totally unrecognizable. High-pitched timpani, a low-pitched piccolo, very low-pitched tubular bells, for example, take on a quite different character. They may even be combined to create sound effects!

Standard MIDI voices also include a wide selection of synthetic sounds with such intriguing voice names as '*shwimmer*', '*crystal*', '*popcorn*', '*planet*', '*stardust*', '*glisten*'. Carefully selected, they can add strangely evocative qualities to background or introductory music that are simply asking to be explored.

5.48 Sound effects

Appropriate sound effects give an unbelievable realism to an environment. It is an ironic fact that if you shoot a scene at an authentic location *but* everyday noises are missing the end product may appear artificial and contrived. Shoot the same scene in a well-designed studio setting, but accompanied by well-chosen sound effects, and the effect is totally convincing! The barely heard sounds of a clock ticking, wind whistling through trees, bird song, passing traffic, the barking of a distant dog, (or whatever other noises are appropriate) bring the scene to life. It is '*the real thing*'!

Sound effects can be so persuasive that even a diagram or model of a volcano, for instance, can make a stronger impact if accompanied by 'subterranean rumblings'!

Your sound effects can come from a number of sources:

- *The original sounds recorded during a scene*: e.g. a person's own footsteps accompanying the picture, which may be filtered, reverberation added, etc.
- *Re-used original sounds*: e.g. the sounds of wind, traffic, children at play, which were recorded during a scene, are copied (*dubbed*) and mixed with that same scene's soundtrack to reinforce the overall effect.

- *Substituted 'identical' sounds*: e.g. introducing sounds of your own footsteps for the original ones; keeping in time with those in the picture.
- *Audio effects library*: Effects from a commercial audio effects library on tape, disc, or CD.
- *Imitative effects*: Created manually, computer generated, or musical imitations.
- *Processing*: Taking any existing sound effect, and changing its character by filtering, speed changes, reversal, added reverberation, etc.
- *Sound sampling*: A system in which a sound is digitally recorded, and its character modified by shaping, stretching, reversing, repeating, etc.
- *MIDI*: MIDI systems offer a useful collection of digitally recorded everyday noises of varying pitch and duration. Even if your productions give you few opportunities for such novelties as 'Jingle Bells' rendered by the melodic voices of barking dogs, the MIDI vocabulary includes such practical opportunities as:

Rain; thunderclaps; wind noises; stream; dog barks; horse's hooves; bird twittering; telephone ringing; door squeaks; door slamming; a car engine . . . starting . . . stopping . . . passing . . . crashing; siren; train; jet plane; laughing; screaming; a punch; heartbeats; footsteps; machine gun; explosion; fireworks; applause; helicopter; breaking waves.

In this age of sophisticated electronics you should not overlook some of the traditional methods of creating sound effects. Basic but effective! Here is a wide field for experiment: the sounds of pouring sand, crumpling paper, plucking a stretched rubber band, flapping an umbrella. . . . Played slowly and/or backwards, filtered, they offer many surprising opportunities.

Why not try out the following?

Hollow muffled sounds. Either speak into, or use a small loudspeaker directed into, an enclosure such as a tumbler, basin, pan, tin box, plastic pipe, oven or cupboard.

Echo. Replay sounds into a tiled bathroom or empty room, re-recording them on another machine.

Fast repeat sounds; echoes. On many audio recorders a separate replay head lets you check the track as you record. (Others only have a single dual-purpose head.) There is a brief time lag as the tape moves past the record head to the replay head. So if you mix a little of this replayed sound with the incoming sound that is being recorded (i.e. 'Replay out' to 'Record in') you can get effects ranging from an 'echo' to a 'stutter'.

Low-pitched powerful voices. If you are using a multi-speed audio recorder (reel-to-reel) a further range of effects becomes possible through speed changes. Make an audio recording, speaking quickly, and replay the tape at a slower speed to create the voices of giants, monsters, etc.

High-pitched 'miniature' voices. Make an audio recording, speaking slowly and distinctly, and replay the tape at a faster speed to create the voices of tiny creatures, chipmunks, etc.

Threatening rumbling, thunder. Experiment with playing low-pitched taped music slowly backwards or disc slowly rotated by hand.

Low metallic gong-like sounds. Hold a suspended metal sheet, metal coat-hanger or fork against the microphone, and tap gently. (Perhaps replay the recording at a slower speed.)

Chapter 6

Backgrounds

The background is much more than 'whatever happens to appear behind the subject'. It directly affects the success of your presentation, and you need to select and control it with care.

6.1 The importance of the background

Video programs are shot in an extremely wide range of locations; people's homes, offices, factories, classrooms, halls, public buildings, campus studios, out in the streets, and the wide open spaces. Where we shoot the program may be vital to what we want to tell our audience, or it can be merely incidental.

To some extent, the importance of the background, depends on you; on the way you approach your subject and the style and form you adopt. A dramatic play can be presented successfully in front of black drapes, and shooting the same play on location, or in a built setting, might add little to its emotional appeal.

Shakespeare's plays were originally performed on an open stage with no scenery. It was in the imagination of his audience. Today, broadcast documentary programs whisk a speaker around the world, one exotic background following another in rapid succession. Yet this kaleidoscope of pictures often contributes nothing to our understanding of the subject. It just gets in the way of the words! Effective backgrounds are more a matter of making wise choices, than having a big budget.

6.2 The impact of the background

Most programs are about *people* – what they are saying and what they are doing. But the *background* for the action can play an essential part in a program's appeal.

Surroundings have a considerable influence on how we feel about what we are seeing and hearing. It is not just a matter of choosing a background that looks appropriate or attractive, but determining whether its audience-impact is right for the particular points you are making in your program.

We often overlook the considerable influence the surroundings have on how we feel about what we are seeing and hearing. The background we choose for our action, and the way we shoot it, can affect how persuasively points are put to our audience. It is one thing to see a person in a street market, recommending a type of medicine, and another when we see them wearing a white coat in a laboratory. The surroundings have swayed our reactions; yet they have nothing to do with the true quality of the product.

Having gone to a particular location, your camera cannot avoid being selective. You could, for example, take it to an off-shore oil rig, but depending on which parts of the structure you shot, you would give quite different impressions of the life there. The final emphasis could be on its huge geometric structure; the isolation of this group of workers in treacherous seas; it might appear as a scene of endless noise and tense activity. In the end, it is your shot selection and editing that will build up a concept in the minds of your audience. The result may be a fair cross-section of life there, or it could be overselective. Much depends on the point of view you adopt.

6.3 Real and unreal backgrounds

To your audience it is quite unimportant whether the background behind the action is real or the result of ingenious trickery. It is the effect that counts. But it is worth remembering that you can derive a background in a number of ways:

- *Use of actual place*. The action is really shot in the Sahara desert.
- *Use of substitute*. Shoot the action in a convenient home location that looks sufficiently like part of the Sahara desert.
- *Use of scenery*. Build scenery in a studio, that resembles the real thing.
- *Suggested location*. The camera shows location shots of the Eiffel Tower (part of a picture postcard), intercut with shots of someone standing against a brick wall. Thanks to sound effects of traffic, etc., the viewer assumes that this is shot in Paris.
- *Electronic insertion*. It is possible with various optical and electronic devices to insert the person standing in front of the camera into a separate background picture. With care, it can be done absolutely convincingly.

6.4 The neutral background

There are times when we want the background to provide totally *neutral* surroundings for the action.

In the extreme, this background could be just a blank white (*limbo*) or black (*cameo*) area, for we are concentrating on the performers.

However, we usually want something rather more interesting to look at than a plain area of tone, and TV solved this problem by creating the *neutral setting*; a background that is visually attractive, without actually reminding us of any specific style, period or place. You will see this sort of setting in broadcast talks programs, studio interviews, discussions; or in their more jazzed-up versions, for panel games and quiz shows.

Basically, neutral backgrounds are usually made up from scenic units, positioned in front of a *cycloramas* or *cyc* (pronounced 'sike').

The cyc provides an extremely useful general-purpose background surface for studios of all sizes. Whether you are improvising in a room, in a large hall, on a stage, or in a custom-built studio, the cyclorama can be the basis of a wide range of program backgrounds from the mundane to the spectacular. It can be scaled to suit your needs: anything from a few feet long to a complete wall around the staging area.

A cyc is usually made of a plain cloth, hanging from a batten, and stretched taut to form a smooth featureless surface by a further batten or pipe along

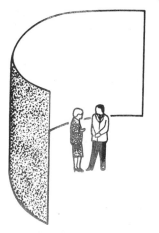

Figure 6.1 The cyclorama
Part 1 The cyclorama serves as a general purpose detailless background.

Figure 6.1 (continued)

Part 2 A ground row of cyc lights can be used to illuminate the cyclorama from below.

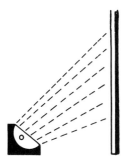

Figure 6.2 Paper cyc
Background paper can be hung or draped along the floor.

Figure 6.3 Open setting
A minimum amount of scenery or furniture, positioned in front of the cyc, creates a 'setting'.

its bottom edge. It may be straight or curved, vertical or slightly off-vertical. A simple horizontal board (*ground row*) will hide a row of strip-lamps to illuminate the cyc or back wall from below.

Typical materials for cycs include duck, canvas, filled gauze and sharkstooth scrim. Ideally, the surface should appear seamless, but if necessary you can hide the seams with a decorative strip, a column or a lightweight structure of some sort. Colors range from off-white, light gray, mid-gray, black, light blue, dark blue, to chroma key blue. Of these, light to mid-gray are probably the most adaptable.

The cyc is a very versatile facility. You can adjust its overall tone by lighting, project light-patterns onto it, hang lightweight cutouts in front of it or rear-light it to produce silhouettes. It can appear as infinite space.

Try to avoid tears, blemishes, creases or dirty marks on the background, for they can be surprisingly prominent, even in longer shots. If this problem does arise, you may be able to avoid shooting that area, rearrange the cyc, or hide the offending blemish with foreground scenery.

For smaller areas, seamless paper can form an effective background, with the roll fixed to the top of the wall and the paper curving onto the floor to form a continuous plane. At a pinch, any hung cloth sheeting can serve as a background.

6.5 Economical settings

If you are working on a tight budget and with limited storage facilities, you will have little opportunity to build much scenery. But that need not be a major limitation, for it is possible to develop very attractive scenic effects, simply and economically, by using just a few multi-purpose scenic units in front of a cyclorama or a background wall.

- *Lighting* alone, can change the appearance of a background to a remarkable extent, whether it is a plain wall or a cyc. You can light it evenly, shade it (bottom-lit from a ground-row), light it in blobs or dapples, project shadows or patterns on it, or use plain or blended color areas.
- You can form an *open set* by carefully grouping a few pieces of furniture in front of the cyc. Even as little as a sofa, low table, table lamp, potted plants, a screen, chair and stand lamp, can suggest a real complete room.

For training purposes, when one is concerned not with creating a realistic effect, but with the mechanics of production, quite a lot can be done using a few folding tables and chairs and a little imagination. A couple of tables side by side form a bench. A row of chairs become a sofa.

To suggest a doorway, a pair of upright poles on a wooden base is useful (bottom-weighted with sand or stoned-filled bags). Or you can use a hinged lightweight panel on a timber frame.

- Open *support frames* are quite simple to construct from lengths of tubular or angled aluminium or timber. They can be dismantled or folded, are easily transported, and require little storage space.
- Various materials can be stretched across these support frames to make *decorative screens*, and taped, wired, clipped or stapled on. Many materials can be used, including mesh, trelliswork, scrim, netting, cord, perforated board, wall-coverings, translucent plastic sheet, etc.
- You can attach *hang-on boards* to these frames, decorated in endless different ways, with surfaces selected to suit the program. Among a wide

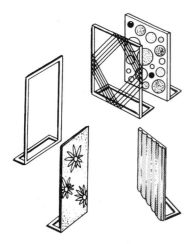

Figure 6.4 Support frames
A basic metal or timber frame can be used to support decorated surfaces, patterns, cutouts, perforated screens, etc. and drapes.

variety of possible materials are matte-black chalk boards, flock paper, thin painted board or plastic laminate and cardboard/strawboard.

These boards can be single- or double-faced, in light, medium or dark tones. Even a small selection can be rearranged in many different ways, to form single-tone, multi-tone or graded layouts. And of course, the units themselves can be positioned singly, in groups, or side by side, to form a complete background.

- The same support frames can be used as *drape frames* to display cloth or plastic drapes, arranged in pleats, folds, swags or stretched.
- To *decorate* these units quickly and cheaply, you can stencil or color-shade them with aerosol spray paints, form lines/patterns with color tapes, or add adhesive motifs (Christmas, Halloween, and similar decorations).
- *Modular units.* If you are constructing scenery that is only to be used on one occasion, then you can use cheap flimsy materials (e.g. cardboard shapes), and improvised units (e.g. paper-covered or painted cardboard boxes). The results need not look at all primitive on camera.

But for regular scenic units that can be transported, stored, and re-used, more substantial modular types are a must. These can be used singly or together, to form interesting variations, and are mostly demountable. The main units are 'box units', 'shell units', 'frameworks' and 'scenic flats'. You will see details of these modular units in Figure 6.5.

Figure 6.5 Modular units
Open frames with clip-on surfaces can be adapted to a very wide range of purposes. They can be re-structured to form display units, benches, desks, platforms, etc.

6.6 The location as a background

Location backgrounds make action look real and genuine in a way that it is hard to imitate in any studio.

But remember, all your audience knows of the location background, is what *you* show them. It is possible to go to an exotic place, and shoot someone against a tree that looks just like one back home! If you are on location, make good use of it. Ensure that there are sufficient visual clues for people to benefit from the particular atmosphere of the place.

6.7 Keep a lookout

When you are busy shooting action it is so easy to overlook things in the background that can become a nuisance in the final picture. On the spot, you just accept them as part of the scene. In the picture, they distract one's attention. Even major movies often have a microphone sneaking into shot at the top of the picture, or a shadow of the camera crew, or prominent lighting cables, in spite of all their vigilance.

Sometimes these odd things are puzzling or disturbing; at others they look funny – e.g. someone standing with a flagpole 'growing out of their head', or a circular ceiling light hovering like a halo. You may not be able to avoid them anyway, but they are worth looking out for. So here are some reminders of typical things that can spoil the picture.

Windows can be an embarrassment when shooting interiors. A large patch of sky in shot will push the exposure down if you are using auto-iris. Even if you expose the interior properly, this bright blank area still takes the eye.

Although you can use a corrective filter to compensate for the high color temperature of the daylight, its intensity can easily overwhelm your interior illumination and prevent you from getting a good tonal balance.

In addition to all that, if your audience has a good view of what is going on outside the window, there is always the chance that they will find this more intriguing than the real subject!

The simply remedy is to keep the window out of shot, or close the shades.

Reflecting surfaces in the background are difficult to avoid. But glass, plastic, even highly polished furniture, can be very troublesome. They can even reflect the camera and its crew. So instead of admiring the gleaming new automobile, your audience watches these interesting reflections in its door panel.

Worse still, shiny surfaces reflect lamps! If you are using a camera light, its beam will bounce straight back into the lens. When you move the camera, the blob of light will move with you.

Low-intensity reflections give sparkle and life to a surface. Strong light reflections are a pain, both technically and artistically. Apart from avoiding shooting straight-on to such surfaces, or keeping them out of shot, the quick solutions are to change your viewpoint, cover them up (e.g. position something or someone so that the highlight is not reflected), or angle the surface. You may be able to dull it down with a wax spray.

Any strong lights directly visible in the background, can be similarly troublesome. But unless you can control their intensities, or keep them out of shot, you will usually have to accept the results.

Flashing signs, prominent posters, direction signs and *billboards* are among the visual diversions that await the unwary camera operator. They are all part of the scene, but if you have a dramatic situation taking place anywhere near an animated advertising sign, do not be surprised if part of your audience's attention is elsewhere!

Even if you are shooting in a busy spot, it is often possible to find a quiet corner, where there are not too many interruptions. Try to avoid including a door or busy throughway in the background, or similar hurry-spots with a continually changing stream of people, for there will be constant distractions. Passers-by staring at the camera, and bystanders watching (particularly the hand-waving types!) are a regular problem, and there is little one can do, except try as far as possible to keep them out of shot.

 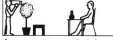 

Low camera viewpoint   Average camera height   High camera

Figure 6.6 Camera height

Low viewpoint. The camera's height affects the impression it gives. From a low viewpoint, the floor space is foreshortened; even small foreground objects appear large and may mask the shot. Space appears compressed. A lot of ceiling may be visible, or the camera may shoot over scenic backgrounds ('shoot off').

Normal viewpoint. From normal eye-height, we get a natural impression of size and distance. Small foreground items below chest height are unseen.

High viewpoint. From a higher camera position, the floor area becomes more prominent. The camera can see things on tables, etc., more clearly. It can shoot over quite large foreground items or obstructions, which are therefore not seen in the picture.

6.8 Camera height

The camera's height has a considerable effect on how much of the scene is visible in the shot. From a lower viewpoint you will see less of the middle ground, and this reduces the feeling of space and distance in the picture. Things nearer the camera become more prominent – perhaps overprominent.

When you see a very low viewpoint, even quite small foreground objects standing nearby can obscure the shot. But raise the camera just a little, and not only will it shoot over them but your audience will not even realize that they are there!

As you increase the camera's height, more of the middleground comes into view, and we get a greater impression of space and distance.

However, if you shoot a scene from a very steep angle, or use overhead shots, your audience will no longer feel that they are *within* a location, but will find themselves looking down, inspecting it instead.

6.9 Foreground pieces

You can *deliberately* arrange objects in the foreground of a picture to improve its composition, to increase the impression of distance, or simply to hide something in the scene.

You must have seen many an exterior shot with foliage hanging into the top of the frame. It is almost a visual cliché. But the camera operator has done this because the picture looks more complete, and gives a better sense of scale, than if there was just blank open sky. With this border, the picture tends to look more balanced, and no longer 'bottom-heavy'. When there does not happen to be a handy overhanging tree to shoot past, you can always hold an odd piece of tree branch above the lens so that it does the job instead! The effect is such an improvement, and your audience will never know!

Although the TV picture itself usually has a fixed horizontal 4 × 3 format (aspect ratio), you can use a foreground window, an arch, or a similar opening, to provide a border that alters the apparent *shape* of the picture.

By carefully framing foreground objects, you can hide all manner of things in the background that you do not want to see in the shot. They might be unattractive, or perhaps they would distract your audience. They might spoil the shot in some other way. If you are re-enacting an historical scene in a drama, it is very convenient to say the least, if a carefully positioned gatepost, bush, or even a standing person in the foreground, hides the modern signs, TV arrays, power lines, etc.

A shot through a castle gateway shows us the site of the ancient battle-field beyond. But because you have cunningly arranged for the gateway to form a border to the shot, your audience does not see the heavy trucks roaring along the major highway nearby. Instead of using the inappropriate sound from this location, you can lay down an effects wildtrack of birdsong or music, and the illusion is complete!

6.10 The location as the subject

We have talked about using location shots as the background to action. But supposing that, instead, you are making a documentary in which *the location itself* is the subject of your program?

There are interesting differences. Streets that were previously an incidental, unobtrusive backdrop, now become atmospheric opportunities to be explored with your camera. You will be drawing your audience's attention to various features: a window display, a quaint sign, the tourist sights, the people who live and work there. Your aim is to create a real living place in the minds of your audience.

You can approach this subject in a number of ways:

● You can have a guide who appears in most shots, and takes us around, explaining as we go.
● Alternatively, you can have a commentary spoken over the edited pictures, by someone who never appears.
● In place of a written commentary, you could insert the audio-taped voices of citizens and travelers you have talked to (before or after shooting).
● Lastly, you can rely on pictures and background sounds alone, to create an impression.

Each scheme has its appeal. You could combine them. The first somehow seems more personal, as someone guides us around, showing us the highlights. The audience feels involved in what is going on. We take any odd comments, observations, criticisms, as our guide's opinions; as part of their personality.

However, there are certain inherent difficulties in making the show this way. Moving about with your camera, and coping with people and traffic as you go, sound pick-up conditions may vary considerably, and it may be difficult to achieve reasonable sound continuity.

Occasionally, in particularly noisy surroundings, you may deliberately use long shots or over-shoulder shots of the guide, to avoid showing lip movements. You record dialogue at a more suitable moment, and insert it during editing.

The '*commentary over*' approach on the other hand, is much simpler. But there can be subtle differences. For example, a critical observation made to the camera with a grin or a shrug can appear like friendly banter, but the same remarks from an unseen commentator may seem sarcastic or fault-finding.

The method itself is very straightforward. You can shoot the pictures mute or with wild track, in any order you choose. Later you edit them together, and add commentary and effects at leisure onto the videotape soundtrack using 'audio-dub' facilities, either directly or via a prepared audio-tape.

Even for the broadcaster, it is not always practical or economic to shoot new material for every minute of every production. One regularly draws on *library shots* (*stock shots*), that have been excerpted from previous programs and retained for later re-use. You can follow this idea too, and explore still photographs or slides with your video camera when it is not practical to go out and shoot the real place, or when shooting conditions are difficult. But take care that you do not let a succession of animated still pictures degenerate into a 'moving slide show'.

6.11 Versions of 'reality'

As you appreciate by now, the camera does not 'tell the truth'. It *interprets*. Each aspect of the picture and the sound influences how your audience responds to what they see and hear. A slight change in the camera position can entirely alter the picture's impact. If the sun comes out, what was a drab threatening block of building can become transformed into an attractive, interesting piece of architecture. In winter, we see a dull-looking street planted with stark, lifeless skeletons of neglected trees. In spring, it becomes a charming avenue, where sidewalks are dappled with shade.

With this in mind, it is not difficult to see that you can present most places to convey the type of image *you want them to have!* Admittedly, there are places it would be difficult to make attractive. But it is possible to make a garbage heap look interesting, even beautiful, by using low shots, a diffusion disc over the lens, strong backlight, misty atmosphere, dreamy music, mysterious shadows, patches of color and interesting silhouettes against a sunset sky.

It is equally possible to make a beautiful situation look plain and tawdry, just by the way you shoot it, the way you edit the shots, and the sound accompanying them (hard top lighting, high-angle shots, sharp shadows cutting across attractive surfaces, no fill-light, crude mixtures of colored light, emphasize the ugly and the decaying, avoid the elegant).

You can shoot a location so that your audience envies its inhabitants, or pities them for having to live there. It can appear a fine place, or an eyesore. It's all a matter of what you choose to include, and what you omit; what you emphasize, and what you suppress.

Sound-effects and music can alter the feeling you convey. Use loud, harsh, discordant sounds, and you can build up an impression of noise, aggravation confusion and antagonism. Fast sounds suggest hurry and bustle. On the other hand you can use quiet sounds, soothing, happy, pastoral, associated with good things, and the overall effect is peaceful and contented. You can accompany a picture of children playing with joyous laughter, or angry screams and shouts, and suggest quite different things.

As the camera moves around, it can dwell on busy purposeful bustle, as people go to work, or it can linger on those who appear to be lounging around with nothing to do. (In reality, they might be waiting for a bus, but at the moment the camera captures them, they are 'aimlessly inactive'!)

You can suggest spaciousness by shooting with a wide-angle lens. Use a narrow-angle lens instead, and the same streets can look congested.

Under dull overcast skies and rain, a location can look a drab, miserable, unwelcoming place. Harsh, overhead sunlight with sharply cut shadows can produce a crude, hard appearance.

In most cities, one can find litter, decay, graffiti; but conversely, there will be signs of prosperity, attractive buildings, green spaces, fountains, wildlife, things that are amusing, others that are touching. How you select and relate the kaleidoscope of potential images will influence how your audience interprets the scene.

6.12 What can we do about the background?

If you are shooting in a studio, and the background is unsatisfactory for any reason, you can usually improve it in some way or other. But what can you do on location, if the background proves to be troublesome or unsuitable?

If you are a guest in someone's home, the answer may be disappointingly little. So much depends on the people involved, and on your own diplomacy. If they are not accustomed to appearing on camera, they will probably be disturbed if you suggest altering things around to any extent. They may even feel uncomfortable if they are not sitting in their customary chair. There is little point in doing things that will jeopardize the interview you are there for. But there are various little things you can do unobtrusively to improve matters:

- If you can use natural lighting, rather than introduce lamps, the person you are talking to will probably feel more at ease. But additional lighting cannot be avoided in most interiors if you are to get good pictures.
- Although you cannot change tones in the surroundings, you may be able to shade your lamps off a light-toned surface to prevent them appearing too bright (using a barndoor, flag, or partial diffuser). And you may also add a little illumination in dark corners.
- If there are reflections in a glass-fronted picture, and you cannot move your lamp or the camera to avoid them, slightly angling the picture may cure the dilemma. A wall picture or mirror can often be tilted up or down a bit by wedging a bunched-up tissue behind it. To avoid seeing the camera in a glass-fronted bookcase behind a speaker, you might slightly open its doors.
- Closing, or partly closing, the room drapes may help to adjust the lighting balance in a room.
- If you have to shoot a corridor or hallway, it can help if doors in a side wall are opened enough to let extra light in.
- Even if you are shooting in daylight, it may provide more interesting pictures if you have table-lamps or other room-light fittings on.
- You may be able to conceal low-powered lamps behind furniture or wall angles, to illuminate distant parts of the room; but take great care that they do not overlight, or even burn-up nearby surfaces.

6.13 Rearranging the background

If you are commissioned to make a program, it is much more likely that you will be able to alter the background to achieve the best effect. Again, this has to be done diplomatically, but if you gain the confidence of the people involved, and seem to know what you are doing, there should be no difficulties.

The simplest changes just involve moving around what is there already, to avoid any unnecessary distractions or unwanted effects in the picture.

Make it a regular routine to check that nothing is going to appear to be growing from the top of the speaker's head, or balancing on it, and that no vertical or horizontal lines cut through the center of the head or across the shoulders. These visual accidents can make the picture look contrived or comic.

Look out for reflection, ugly shadows, items that catch the eye (especially brightly colored objects that will be defocused in the shot) and anything that gets in the way of the shot such as a lamp or a vase of flowers on a desk. If there are books, posters, etc., in the back of the shot that might attract attention away from your subject, perhaps you can move or cover them to improve the picture. Otherwise you may be able to restrict the depth of field (larger lens aperture) to defocus them a little.

If you are shooting someone in an office, who is seated in front of a bright window, you may get better results if the window-blind is partially or completely lowered, or the drapes closed. Very occasionally, you could try moving the desk to the corner of the room or another wall, where the lighting is better, or there are no background problems.

6.14 Altering the background

You may want to improve the appearance of a room you are using to make it look more attractive on camera.

A certain amount of tidying-up and neatening is helpful to prevent a place from looking too muddled and disorganized. But do not get to the point where everything looks overtidy and unlived-in. Neat precisely positioned papers and magazines, decorative ornaments placed exactly in the middle of shelves, can ring a false note.

'Improvements' can easily get out of hand, as too many photographs of 'designed interiors' for houses, show! You find that all manner of bric-a-brac has been 'artistically positioned' in the kitchen, to produce an effect that no self-respecting cook would tolerate for a moment in their workplace! The result is pretentious and artificial.

But it is possible to enhance the feel of a room considerably, by making a few modest changes; adding a group of flowers here, an extra chair there, replacing a wall-picture perhaps. If you are not careful though, the place could become 'different' rather than 'better'.

If you really need to change the appearance of an interior considerably, to make it look like *somewhere else* (for a dramatic production perhaps), there are a number of quick, cheap and simple things you can do – successfully enough at least, to fool the camera:

- Rearrange furniture positions.
- Replace furniture with other pieces from nearby rooms, or lightweight portable units you have installed.
- Add or remove rugs.
- Hide a doorway with a folding screen, a vertical notice-board, or a drape on a frame.
- Tape lightweight drapes over the window or room features (niches, recesses, existing notice boards).
- Attach display posters to the walls.
- Insert a panel of heavy cardboard or laminate into a window opening, to provide a 'notice-board' or a dummy bookcase.

- Rows of dummy books come in forms ranging from printed card sheets, to actual book-backs attached to plywood. These can be used to provide an 'instant library'.
- Position indoor plants (e.g. ferns) to break up the background.
- Introduce notices and signs on walls, doors, etc.
- Add portable light-fittings (table lamps, stand lamps) – either 'non-practical' (not working), or 'fully practical' (working, and switched on).
- Add a dummy 'doorway' made from timber-finished laminate sheet, with a plastic-strip surround, attached to the wall with double-sided adhesive tape.
- A dummy window made of drapes on a frame, can be held against a wall behind an existing low bookcase.
- A wall-clock can be imitated by a clock dial (painted or attached hands) stuck to the wall with double-sided tape or plastic putty.

To be even more ambitious it is possible to get extremely realistic, three-dimensional moldings in the form of thin plastic PVC shells, that you can paint and attach to suit your needs. Low cost, featherweight and reusable, they range from decorative pieces (e.g. shields), display panels (guns, pistols, fish, wood carving), armor, wooden paneling, to stonework, brickwork, tiling, beams, rock-face, etc.

If you are shooting out in the open, there are relatively few things you can do cheaply and easily to change the background. It is possible of course, to carry around your own area of brickwork or stonework (plastic shell) to put in the foreground to hide unwanted bits of the background, or to introduce the odd foreground bush or branch. You might position a car, so that it hides an inappropriate building in the distance. But anything more than adding the odd sign to sticking a new shop name over an existing one, or scattering peat or sand over the road to cover markings, is usually out of the question for small-unit video on a tight budget.

6.15 Auxiliary backgrounds

Sometimes you will want to make changes to improve the *clarity* of the picture.

An arrangement within an exhibition or a museum, that looks excellent if you were walking around, seeing it from all angles, can look cluttered and confused in the camera's two-dimensional picture. Careful lighting can help, but it is seldom the complete answer.

If the subject you want to demonstrate or display is surrounded by a number of other (e.g. one bowl within a group), it will help your audience to concentrate on that particular piece if you are able to isolate it in some way.

Can you get a close-enough shot of the subject to exclude the rest? Would you be allowed to move the subject, and display it separately? Would it help if you restricted the depth of field, to defocus the other subjects into a blur?

The best remedy may be to introduce your own carefully positioned background. If for instance, you are shooting items that are inside a glass-sided showcase in a display area, you might attach a neutral-toned backing to the far side of the case to hide other items nearby. Similarly, by placing a board behind a group of flowers, you can isolate them from others in the vicinity.

You can often place portable lightweight screens round larger subjects, to block off their surroundings. Naturally, the number you need will depend on the area you are shooting and the camera position. Close shots only require a small backing.

If you are shooting at an angle to your background (e.g. at greater than about 50°), you are liable to shoot past its end, and see whatever lies beyond ('overshoot', 'shoot-off'). Rather than extend the background, it is better to curve it round or place 'wings' at its end.

It may not matter if you do overshoot, particularly if the rest of the surroundings are in darkness, or lit to a much lower intensity, but it is as well to check.

Sometimes, when you are shooting at night you can avoid the need for extra backings, by lighting just the localized action area and letting everything else merge into darkness. In a factory, warehouse or similar large enclosure, this avoids the audience seeing empty areas in the back of the shot. The overall result may not be as bright and interesting as you can get by using light-toned screens, but it can take less time and trouble.

6.16 Partial settings

This is a strategy for convincing your audience that a very modest setting is not only the real thing, but is much more extensive than it actually is. Yet the cost and effort involved are minimal.

If your camera does not move it can only see a limited amount of the scene in a mid-shot or a close-shot. So with partial settings, you concentrate on building up a section of the scene, just big enough to suit the camera's shot, and no more. Within the scene, you include enough features to allow your audience to interpret where the action is supposed to be taking place.

Do not underrate this idea. It has been used successfully in film and TV for many years. The result need not be at all crude or amateurish, for if you are only showing a scene width of around 9 ft (3 m), just a few items will quickly furnish the shot. Add a garnish of associated sound effects, and the combined image can be indistinguishable from the real thing.

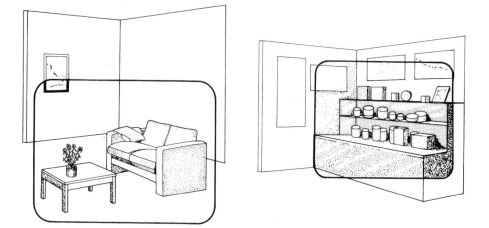

Figure 6.7 Partial settings
A few items can suggest a complete setting if the shot is fairly restricted.

6.17 Typical examples

You can create an 'instant store' by putting the appropriate sort of merchandise on a foreground table (the 'counter'), an advertisement or two on the back wall, and a shelf behind the salesperson, holding some more products.

Sometimes even a single feature in the picture can suggest an environment. A stained-glass window and organ music become a church interior. (The window could be a projected slide.)

You can form a convincing 'room' in a studio, with just a couple of flats or screens and a chair. Add an extra item or two, such as a side-table with a potted plant, a picture perhaps, and it begins to take on a particular character. If you hang a drape over part of the wall, one assumes a window there. Whether it is interpreted as being someone's home, or a waiting room for instance, largely depends on the way people in the scene behave. Lying back casually dressed, reading a paper, it is obviously their home. In outdoor attire, sitting upright and anxious, they are waiting.

Replace the plant with a typewriter, and the picture with a framed certificate, and magically, the setting has become an office.

You can ring the changes as simply as this in a real room of course, and make striking alterations at little cost, provided you keep your shot reasonably localized, using only a corner of the room or part of one wall.

Out on location, the same idea is still useful, i.e. restrict your shot, and 'doctor' the background. Suppose you are shooting a scene in a 19th century drama, where somebody visits their lawyer. You have found a house exterior of about the right period, but the rest of the street is so obviously a busy modern thoroughfare. Fortunately, all you need is a shot of the house doorway with a suitable name-plate alongside, and the picture explains itself to your audience. So you attach a name-plate to the wall for a few minutes, have the actor go up to the door, or pretend to leave the house, and your audience immediately accepts the location as the lawyer's office. It only needs the sounds of horse-drawn vehicles to replace modern traffic noise, and the period illusion is complete.

With a little care and imagination, you can create the impression of a particular location from a minimum amount of scenery. Paint a surface dull black, give it a pattern of rivets and a little rust-staining, set down a large coil of rope, and reflect light from a trayful of water, and you have a quayside scene that can be intercut with location shots. Add sounds of water lapping, sea birds, hooting tugs, and the effect can be really authentic.

If a scene is brief and the action limited (especially if it is a night shot), you can often get away with remarkably little scenery. Against a black background, even a few tree branches can convince your audience that they are seeing a wood. A person backed by black, lit by localized light, can appear on screen to be under a street lamp in a sleazy alley. Leaning on a horizontal pole against a light-toned background, someone is at the rail of a ship, if you build up the right expectancy in your audience and include appropriate sound effects.

It is incredible how seemingly trivial tricks can give a totally convincing effect on camera:

- The camera rhthmically tilting up and down that sells the illusion of *a ship at sea*
- The *wafting breeze*, that is really the result of an assistant waving a piece of board.

- The shuddering camera accompanied by things falling to the ground (pulled by unseen fishline), that implies an *explosion* or an *earthquake*. A hanging lamp swings alarmingly – tugged by an out-of-shot cord.
- The flickering flames of a nearby *fire* – that comes from a stick of rag-strips waved in front of a ground lamp.

These are just a few examples of how little ingenuity can apparently achieve the impossible, and create a strong impression in your audience's minds.

6.18 Creating depth

To get even more from your limited background you can include foreground masking pieces (see Section 6.9). If you shoot through a foreground bookshelf (a few books on a propped up board) to see just beyond, a table with piles of books and distant shelves of books (strips of printed book-backs attached to the wall), the result is a plausible bookshop. Keep the lighting shadowy and confined, to suggest an interior.

You can create an impressive sense of distance by using a series of planes between the camera and the background. If you can position larger items in the foreground, and small pieces in the distance (small pictures on the walls, small vases of flowers), the illusion is enhanced, particularly if you shoot the scene on a wide-angle lens.

6.19 Permanent sets

Many small studios use a combination of *temporary settings* that are designed and erected for a specific production, and *permanent settings* that remain in the studio for a long period.

A 'permanent' set has the advantage that it can be:

- erected (assembled; fixed together and firmly supported),
- dressed (various properties and furnishings added),
- lit (lamps arranged and adjusted),

and then left in position, while labor and resources are concentrated on other jobs.

When a studio is regularly staging a certain type of program, it may have a permanent setting installed, such as a kitchen, a laboratory, an office, a lounge or a news-desk layout, designed to suit these productions.

Another approach is the adjustable permanent set, which can be revamped to suit a wide range of productions: demonstrations, interviews, lecture, talks, documentary and travel programs, etc.

6.20 Adjustable permanent setting

The features of this type of setting can be altered in an unlimited number of ways:

1. Panels can be added and removed as necessary (hooked on, or slid along grooves). Double-sided, to give greater variety, they can have a range of tones, shades, textures, shapes, with different surface patterns, added contours, etc.

Sections can be prepared for use as chalk-boards, magnetic graphics (magnetic plastic sheet motifs, adhering to a steel surface) or as chroma key screens (see Section 13.10).

2. Wherever these panels are removed, the camera can see a set of permanently fixed screens, made of translucent frosted plastic sheet. You can use these screens decoratively in endless permutations.

Lit from below at the rear, by trough/strip-light/cyc lights, you have a shaded background. Use a sequence of red, green, blue filters on these lights (and separate dimmers for each color), and you can blend them to provide a very wide mixture of hues.

Add a corresponding series of overhead light-battens, and you can illuminate the screens evenly overall. Switch in only the blue circuits, and you instantly have a useful chroma key surface.

Suspend perforated, openwork or cutout panels in front of, or behind, the lit screens, and you have silhouetted shapes.

You can also use the screens to display rear-projected patterns. These are produced quite simply, by placing a piece of stenciled foil sheet a short distance in front of a ground spotlight, or by bouncing light off crumpled kitchen foil. Projector lanterns can be used, but require a greater distance ('throw') behind the screens, to project large-area patterns.

Also, of course, you can rear-project slides onto the screens, to provide pictures illustrating a program or to produce patterns. If the images from several projectors are combined to form a multivision/multiscreen presentation, with a series of adjacent displays, very large effects become possible.

3. Drapes (reversible) can be suspended at the front of the structure, and used fully stretched or pleated, in sections or overall.

4. Pull-down blinds can also be fitted to the structure to display program logos, station identification and similar material. A blue pull-down blind provides you with a local chroma key display screen when it is needed.

6.21 Facing reality

As you will have found by now, it is one thing to have armchair dreams about a program, and quite another to turn them into reality. Among the problems facing all program-makers are the inevitable limitations of budget and facilities. Some of the things you need, may not even be available.

When faced with such problems it is tempting to think small; to cut back on ambition, and do a simpler version. *Don't*! Do not immediately abandon your ideas. Instead, ask yourself if there is another way of tackling the situation to get virtually the same effect. How can you get round the difficulty?

What you are looking for are *imaginative substitutes*. You are producing *illusions*. However basic the materials really are, there need be nothing crude or trashy about the results in the finished program. There they can appear to be the real thing.

As an introductory example of this way of thinking, let's look at an actual setting that was used convincingly on air. The scene was the banqueting hall of an ancient castle. The king sat on a throne at one end of a long table, eating from golden dishes. That was the illusion.

What of reality? Two small foreground flags on wooden floor stands masked the edges of the shot, so we could not see the rest of the small studio. The 'wooden table' was of painted boards on trestles. The far 'stone wall' was of photographic wallpaper on a flat (black-sprayed slightly to 'age' it). The 'throne' was an old wooden armchair, with a red damask drape thrown over it. The 'gold dishes' were sprayed plastic plates. A 'lancet window' was painted, black on white, and stuck to the 'stone wall'. But nobody could recognize all this in the long shot they saw! Of course the scene would not have stood close shots, but under patchy lighting, we saw it as it was intended to be – the banqueting hall of an ancient castle!

One last word before we explore. Some of these ideas may seem basic, even crude – but they work. Try them for yourself! Often, the only alternative would involve more complicated methods, or expensive equipment. You may never need these particular effects, but they should encourage you to find ways round the 'impossible'. Remember, *it is the result that counts!*

6.22 Chroma key backgrounds

For many years, technical trickery called *chroma key* (*chromakey*; *Overlay*) has been used in television production. It's a method of inserting your chosen subject positioned in front of a plain blue surface into a quite separate background picture taken from any video source. With care, the subterfuge can be totally convincing, and your subject appears to be completely integrated into the background scene! *Chroma key* is increasingly available in video equipment, and we shall be looking at its potentials in some detail later, in Section 13.10.

Economic scenic materials:

A spray coating of color can transform the appearance of rope, plastic netting or plastic sheeting for decorative effect.

Paint sprayed through stencils cut in kitchen foil or perforated board, can decorate surfaces quickly and regularly. Similarly, you can hold suitable objects against a background, and spray silhouette outlines (leaves or tools).

Full-size photographic prints stuck to card can produce scenic miracles! In a front-on view, the camera cannot see that they are actually flat, so you can provide a wide range of articles to dress a room, either stuck-on to backgrounds or as free-standing cut-outs. In some cases, even a photocopied version will suffice. Typical items include: calender, certificates, wall-plate, clock, ornaments on walls and shelves, tools, machinery, equipment, plants, mirrors, book backs on a library shelf, paintings (use standard color reproductions in a photographed 'gold-frame'), view from window (a mosaic of several prints as 'panes of glass' build up the overall view), etc.

6.23 Titling

Your audience's first impressions of your show come from its opening titles! These don't have to be elaborate – even a chalked sign may be just the thing to arrest their interest. But they do need to be brief, clear, and appropriate in style. You can use rub-on letters, titling kits, scrabble, even a finger trace in the sand. Each can be effective when applied imaginatively.

Titling has various purposes:

Opening titles announce the show.
Sub-titles identify people and places.
Credits recognize those appearing in, and contributing to the program.
End titles draw the program to its conclusion.

Titling helps throughout the show: to announce the place or time, *to identify* a plant, *to display* data, *to clarify* how a term is spelt, etc.

Character generators (*CG*) are a regular graphics tool in video/TV production. Instead of having the camera shoot *title cards*, letters are typed on the character generator's computer-type keyboard can be electronically inserted, direct into the video picture. You can change the shape, size, color and design of the lettering, perhaps making it flash, flip, crawl (sideways), roll (vertically), animate etc. Lettering can be presented as outlines or as solid characters, given a black border (black edge), or a drop shadow around it. Having typed out your titling, you can arrange and store it, ready to be presented on cue at the press of a button.

For many video program makers the *personal computer* (*PC*) undoubtedly offers the greatest opportunities for titling. It can be used as a character generator as well as for many video effects. Suitable software can provide a wide range of fonts and backgrounds; even allowing quite elaborate treatments to be animated or processed in various ways.

Titling hints

- Video and television productions today may use either of two screen formats. The regular standard 4×3 proportions (4 units across, and 3 units high); and the later 16×9 picture format (16 units across, and 9 units high). Where your titling may appear in either screen shape keep details within the 4×3 area to avoid cut-off.
- Keep titling well away from the edge of the frame, to avoid edge cut-off.
- Simple, bold typefaces are best. Avoid thin-lined, elaborate lettering.
- Lettering smaller than about 1/10 screen height can be hard to read.
- Don't fill the screen with too much information at a time. It is often better to use a series of brief frames, or to use a *crawl*. (Continuous information moving vertically into the frame, and passing out at the top.)
- Leave a space between title lines of around 1/2 to 2/3 the height of capital letters.
- When smaller lettering is given a black-edged outline, it may become hard to read. The holes in 'Bs', 'Os', 'As', 'Rs', fill in.
- Lettering should generally contrast strongly with its background. (Usually much lighter.)
- Strongly saturated colors can be distracting, dazzling or cause unattractive effects, particularly against contrasting color backgrounds. (e.g. strong red lettering appears fuzzy.)
- Check the lettering does not merge with any pictorial background. Outlining often makes lettering easier to read.
- Check whether the titling is clearly readable in a monochrome picture. Different colors can reproduce the same shade of gray!
- If you set up titling or graphics in front of a camera (e.g. title cards), make sure that lettering appears level and centered!

Chapter 7

The basics of videotape recording

An outline of the principles

7.1 Various designs

There are continual developments in the design and format of video/audio recording systems. Some are mainly used for *acquisition* (i.e. shooting original material); others for *post-production editing*, *general editing*, and *archiving* (storage) work. Currently there are around twenty different incompatable videotape formats; and various obsolescent designs are still in use. All methods of recording store the picture (video) and its associated sound (audio) simultaneously. This can be done on magnetic tape (the usual medium), on a magnetic disc or in solid-state memory.

You will find videotape used in three formats:

- In the familiar *VCR* (*video cassette recorder*), all the videotape is wound onto two spools (supply and take-up), totally enclosed within a plastic *cassette*. The equipment automatically self-laces the tape through the system, so you do not need to handle it in any way.
- For short duration sequences – e.g. commercials or news inserts – tape is often housed in a *cart* (*cartridge*). This is a plastic container with an endless loop of tape wound onto a single reel. Broadcast organizations use carts stacked in *carousels*, which allow items to be played automatically in a prearranged sequence.
- In an *open reel/reel-to-reel VTR* (*videotape recorder*), the tape is stored on a single reel. It is laced through the recorder by hand, and wound onto an empty spool. You have to be careful not to damage or contaminate the tape, or it will spoil the recording.

7.2 Incompatibility

Although you do need to worry about design specifics it is as well to realize that there are important differences between formats. Tapes can only be recorded and reproduced on identical equipment standards.

Design features can vary considerably between video recorders. For instance, most record a composite video signal which incorporates both color and luminance (brightness) information. In professional camcorders,

Table 7.1 Summarizing videotape recording processes*

Several types of magnetic tape are now used: *iron oxide, cobalt doped oxide, metal particle, evaporated metal tape*; in standard widths of: 1/4 in. (6.35 mm), 8 mm (0.32 in.), 1/2 in. (12.65 mm), 3/4 in. (19 mm), 1 in. (25 mm).

Currently there are two approaches to videotape recording (*VTR*) – *analogue* and *digital*.

● The *analogue* system directly records the variations of the video and audio signals.

● The *digital* system regularly samples these waveforms, and converts them into numerical (binary) data.

Where a system includes both *analogue* and *digital* equipment, conversion (*analogue/digital* or *digital/analogue*) becomes necessary; e.g. *A/D conversion* of analogue video when using *non-linear editing systems*.

The video signals themselves may be recorded in *composite* or *component* form:

● In *composite* form they are encoded into a complex *NTSC, PAL,* or *SECAM* signal.

● In *component* form they are recorded as separate *luminance* (*brightness*) and *color* (*hue*) information, for improved picture quality.

CONSUMER FORMATS

The 8 mm series
● *Video* 8   The smallest, most compact systems, using 8 mm wide videotape. Results are comparable with VHS. Tapes are replayed either direct from the camera to the TV set/monitor, or with a separate 8 mm playback unit.

● *Hi-8*   An enhanced 8 mm development using metal tape, resolving about 430 vertical lines.

The VHS series
● *VHS*   The commonest consumer (domestic) format, using 1/2 in. wide tape.

Also available in compact form (VHS-C). Resolution is about 250 vertical lines.

● *S-VHS (Super VHS)* A development of the VHS system, providing superior sound and picture using high grade tape. Also available in compact form (Super VHS-C). Resolution is over 400 vertical lines.

PROFESSIONAL FORMATS

A wide range of professional video recorder formats now exists, including:

U-Matic (Type-E)
● *High band U-matic*   An upgraded improved high band [BVU] development of the incompatible earlier 'Standard' or 'Low band' U-matic system. Used for mobile/news-gathering video work.

● *A high band SP (Superior Performance) version*, using a different type of cassette with improved tape; has a resolution of around 330 lines. A system widely used for news gathering, location work, in-house corporate production units.

Beta series
● *Betacam*   Professional video recorder developed from the original Betamax domestic VCR design.

● *Betacam-SP (Beta SP)*   Later model, also widely used professionally.

● *Digital Betacam (PVW)*   Digital form. Other versions, including Betacam SX.

Type-B
Widely used in countries with 625-line TV systems

Type-C
Widely used in countries with 525-line TV systems

M-II [Type-M]
Very successful in analogue format. 344 lines resolution.

Digital systems include:
Type D-1: Type D-2: Type D-3: Type D-5: Type D-6: Type D-9 (DIGITAL-S): DVCPro: HDVS/HDD 1000: CamCutter

* You will find more details in Chapter 14 of *Television Production* (13th edn) by Gerald Millerson

the component colors are recorded separately from the black-and-white signal.

There can be further complication. For example:

● While a *S-VHS* machine will record/reproduce either a *S-VHS* or a *VHS* tape, a *S-VHS* tape will only replay on a *S-VHS* machine.
● A VHS-C cassette (which is a compact version of the normal VHS Tape housing) needs an adaptor to allow it to play on a standard VHS machine.
● There are variations in recording tape speeds. If you have for example, recorded a VHS tape at half speed, the replay VCR will need an identical speed selection.
● Some designs of video recorder provide only a medium quality mono sound, while others include very high-quality stereo audio.

Although there are so many video recorder formats, in practice, most of us use only one system, and few problems arise.

7.3 Recording principles

Virtually all videotape recorders use a similar basic method of recording – a 'helical scanning' system. Fundamentally, it works this way:

● The *recording tape* itself, is a thin plastic ribbon $\frac{1}{4}$ to 1 in. (6.35 to 25 mm) wide coated with a layer of tiny magnetic particles. Because these are dispersed at random, the tape is magnetically neutral at that stage.
● The *video recording head* behaves as an electromagnet. Fluctuating currents corresponding to the video, pass through the coil in the head, and produce a varying magnetic field.
● As the tape passes a fine slit in the recording head, it becomes magnetized according to the strength of the video signal at each instant.
● The result is a tape with a continuous magnetic pattern corresponding to the original signal fluctuations.
● When you reproduce the magnetized tape, it passes a *replay head*. The varying magnetic strengths of the recorded track induce tiny currents in the replay head, which are recovered as a video signal.
● Because we are recording such rapid fluctuations (high frequencies), the tape needs to move at a fast rate, to accommodate the fine magnetic pattern. (Otherwise the magnetic changes would be too cramped together and lost.)
● We could run the tape through the system at a very high speed, in order to spread out the pattern (e.g. 200 in. per second). But then a tape spool of a reasonable size would only last a few minutes.
● Instead, the VCR designer uses a trick, and spins the video head(s) themselves against the slow moving tape. Their combined speeds creates a fast *effective* recording rate, allowing high quality video to be recorded.
● This technique is known as helical scanning.

7.4 Helical scanning

This is a simple yet ingenious idea. The magnetic tape is pulled through the video recorder at a constant speed. In its path is a spinning drum, and the tape presses against this at an oblique angle. Just protruding from the surface of this drum, are tiny video recording heads. These scan across the tape, recording a regular series of long parallel slanting tracks.

Figure 7.1 Typical helical scanning system
The tape is wrapped in a slanting path round a drum. Within the drum, a disk head-wheel supporting recording (and erase) heads rotates, pressing heads against the tape at an acute angle as it slides past. (Designs include rotating upper drum or slot scanner with a narrow rotating center section.) Each head drum revolution can record one video track.

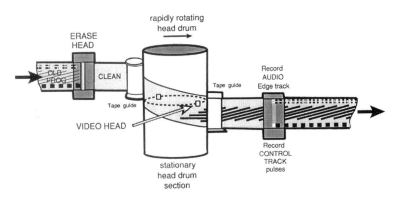

When you 'pause' the VCR, to hold a *freeze frame*, the tape stops moving, but the tape drum continues spinning, continually re-scanning the same track.

7.5 Cue pulses

Running along one edge of the tape, is the all-important *control track*. This is recorded during taping, and provides regular reference *cue pulses* (rather like a clock ticking), which accurately synchronize the tape movement and the scanning rate. On replay, these pulses ensure that the video heads re-scan the recorded tracks accurately, and so ensure color fidelity.

If you record a sequence on videotape, then stop, the control pulses cease at that point on the tape. When you next start to record, the pulses begin again. So at the moment on the tape where you stopped and re-started recording, the control-track pulses have been interrupted. When you replay the tape, this means that the synchronizing system is upset at that point, producing an unacceptable 'dirty cut' between shots.

Some videorecorders overcome this embarrassing situation by *back-spacing* a few seconds, every time you start to play or record. But as you will see, this can prove a hazard to beware of when *assemble editing*. You can accidentally lose the end of the previous scene! So check out how your particular equipment behaves.

Figure 7.2 Typical helical scan tracks
Various videotape recording systems have different track layouts. This typical analogue system shows the video slant tracks, longitudinal audio tracks, control, cue, and time code tracks.

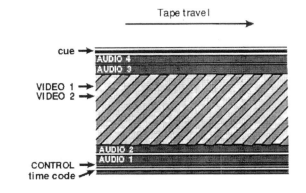

7.6 Audio on videotape

Audio is recorded on videotape in two ways:

- On a narrow track along the edge of the tape (*linear track*) as in the VHS and U-Matic systems. Sound quality is satisfactory for most purposes.
- By a special 'two-layer' method ('depth multiplex'), in which the picture (video) is recorded *over* the FM stereo sound signals, on the *same tape track* (using different head azimuths). This hi-fi technique is used in certain high-quality VCR audio systems, including Video 8, S-VHS, and Hi-Fi VHS.

Some VCRs have considerable audio flexibility. On S-VHS and Hi-Fi VHS systems you can make stereo audio recordings on both the linear and the multiplex soundtracks at the same time. It is even possible to record *different* audio on these two sets of soundtracks simultaneously. In Hi-8 systems, audio is recorded on a multiplex audio track only.

Although multiplexed audio has great advantages, for it provides near-CD quality sounds, it does have drawbacks when editing. Because it is inextricably tied in with the video track, you cannot 'lift off' and 're-play' ('lay back') the sound, as you can with the standard edge-track.

Table 7.2 Videotaping hints

Before loading a cassette:	• Check that its safety/protection tag has not been removed. If it has, cover the hole with adhesive tape. Otherwise you will not be able to record on the tape.
	• Check its label.
	• Check that the tape is *clean* (i.e. free to be used). If there is a previous program on the tape (now unwanted, and to be erased) note the fact. (It may save confusion during editing.)
	• Check that the tape is not slack; especially if it has been stopped/started and re-run several times. Perhaps the takeup spool needs turning clockwise slightly to improve tape tension; but do not over-tighten.
	• Check *humidity* (*dew*) warning indicator.
While recording	• Record at standard speed rather than half speed whenever possible. (Easier editing, and better sound quality.)
	• Keep a lookout for elapsed time, the amount of tape left, the state of the battery.
After recording	• Reset the tape counter whenever you change the tape.
	• Review the end of the take, to check that the recording is satisfactory – i.e. no head-clog.
	• If necessary, remind yourself of the end of the shot just recorded, in order to ensure good continuity and shot matching with the next take.
	• Consider whether you want to record further material on the tape now loaded. During editing, a great deal of time can be lost, shuttling to and fro, picking out required takes from a long tape.
	• When you take out the cassette, remove the protection tag (or pop out protect button).
	• Keep a log of all shots, with details of action, and indicator readings (or time code). If the take is faulty, note what is wrong.
	• After extensive recording, use a wet tape-head cleaner cassette. Some VCRs have a built-in head cleaner, but it pays to clean the entire tape path.

Table 7.3 Typical videotape recorder controls

SP/LP	Recording speed selection; *standard play* and *long play*. The latter allows twice the normal recording duration for a given tape length but at lower definition.
Standby mode	'Standby' automatically withdraws the tape from the cassette and laces it along the tape path, holding it stationary in readiness, without its making contact with the rotating video heads. This facilitates 'instant start' when you press *record* or *replay*. (Without this facility there is a delay on starting while the machine pulls the tape from the cassette and threads it through the tape path.)
Pause	If you press *pause* during **replay** the action will 'freeze', holding a *still frame*. (The tape stops moving, and the heads continually re-scan the same video track(s).) However, although some tape surfaces are more resilient than others, this inevitably wears the tape at that point; eventually causing surface damage and permanent drop-out. The loosened surface material can clog the heads.
	Most VTRs have an automatic cut-out system, that switches off the repeat-scanning after the tape has been stationary for about 2 minutes.
	If you pause while **recording**, the tape stops, but remains laced up, re-scanning the same small path. Press the pause button again, and recording continues. If you stop and restart the VTR during recording this can cause momentary disruption of the syncs at that point, and/or delay as the tape relaces. To avoid this, some people use *tape pause* during recording.
Fast forward, fast rewind	Running the tape at high speed, to reach a point further along the tape, or to fully rewind to the start of the tape.
Fast scan	Running the tape fast forward or in reverse while reviewing the pictures. With some VTRs you can still see pictures sufficiently well at quite high speeds (e.g. × 9) to follow action in color.
Jog	Playing the tape frame by frame; usually after selecting a still frame.
Shuttle	A variable rotating dial or ring, allowing the tape to be played/searched at selected speeds; forward or reverse. Alternatively, a series of preselected constant speeds may be selectable for continual jogging, slow motion, or fast motion effects.
Index search	This runs the tape on to an *auto-mark* introduced automatically at the start of each new recording. Alternatively, you can manually key in an electronic tag to identify a chosen section in the program.
Introscan	This winds the tape on to the next index marker tone and plays a few seconds of the program in order to let you identify that section. Unless stopped, it proceeds to fast-run on to the next marker.
Blank tape search	A facility for locating the next blank unrecorded section on a tape.
'Go-to' search	A fast-wind facility, taking the tape rapidly to a point which is a certain playing-time, or tape length, from the beginning of the reel.
Tracking control	Adjusts the accuracy with which the replay heads trace the recorded slant tracks by very slightly altering the tape tension and head drum speed. Mainly used when reproducing tapes made on another machine. Tracking errors only occur on replay, and include *skewing hooking/flagging* (in which the top of the frame curves left and right), picture tearing, picture break-up. Some VTRs include self-corrective auto-tracking systems.

Table 7.4 Tape care

Here are some tips for prolonging the life of your tape, ensuring good recordings, and avoiding embarrassing tape snarl-ups inside the machine. Many are very obvious, but we all get caught out at times!

- Store your tape at around 18–20°C (64.5–68°F); not above 40°C (104°F) or below about –10C° (14°F). The humidity of storage should be around 45–55% RH; not exceeding 85% RH. (Check the humidity indicator on a camera or VTR before loading the cassette.) Very low humidity can result in strong static charges which attract dust and produce permanent drop-out. Very high humidity causes stiction (i.e. tape tends to stick to revolving head-drum and become displaced). Tape surface deteriorates (heads clog). Avoid rapid temperature/humidity changes (e.g. moving from a cold exterior to a warm interior) and allow both tape and equipment to become acclimatized before use.

- Before loading a cassette check that you have an appropriate cassette and tape type, and that it has not been *protected against recording*. (Reposition the safety knob or tape over its tag opening.) Does the tape contain wanted program material?

- Before using a cassette check in its window that it has been rewound and that its tape has not been left slack from previous use. Insert a finger to gently turn the takeup spool a little clockwise to take up the slack. But do not *over*-tension.

- Clean the VTR's tape path, heads, and tape transport periodically, using a commercial head cleaner tape. This removes particles of coating and avoids head-clogging. (Fabric tape with *isopropyl alcohol* is preferable. Abrasive cleaning tapes wear heads unduly.) For maximum performance, it is advisable to clean the heads after each run; particularly for equipment such as digital VTRs, which uses faster tape speeds and multi-headed scanning drums.

- Store cassettes in their protective boxes to avoid damage and dust.

- It is best to rewind tapes to their start if they are not going to be used for some time. However, remember that if every new recording begins at the start of cassette, the early tape will become worn while the 'tail' remains unused.

- If a tape is frequently stopped, started and run back and forth it is liable to stretch, wind unevenly (cinching), and even develop edge-wear. (Preferably keep a 'straight-wound' original recording, and use a copy for shuttling during review/editing.)

- Even when treated carefully, all tapes wear in time; coating particles clog heads, drop-out causes visual defects. Check tapes before important recordings. Keep well-used tapes for off-line editing copies.

- Make sure that each recorded tape is clearly identified on the label (e.g. shot/scene numbers), use its safety device, and seal box (adhesive tape) to avoid accidental re-use.

- Remember that if a camera's battery voltage is allowed to fall too far there may not be sufficient power to withdraw the loaded cassette.

Where there are two sets of audio edge-tracks, one is often used as a *cue track*, to record a *timecode* signal.

7.7 Standards conversion

If you have a tape recorded in another country there are problems you should know about. A VCR designed for e.g. the NTSC system, will only record and replay with that standard. It cannot replay a tape recorded on a

Figure 7.3 Magnetic disk
The surface of the disk is magnetically sectioned into a series of concentric rings or *tracks*, which are subdivided into *sectors*. A pick-up head on its pivoted arm swings across the disk to write and read digitized data stored magnetically in the sectors, guided by additional data which locates its track and sector numbers.

different transmission system (e.g. PAL); even where both video recorders have the same format e.g. VHS. There is equipment that *can* reproduce different standards (perhaps in monochrome only), but it may require a multi-standard TV receiver/monitor to display the picture.

7.8 Magnetic disk recording

The familiar magnetic 'hard disks' used to record digital data in our computers have their equivalents in digital video and audio recording systems. All *magnetic tape systems* have the great advantage of being able to record for long periods at low cost. But, on the other hand, they have the major limitation that all the data is recorded successively along the length of the tape. So if you want to select a particular passage you must spool through the tape at speed to reach each selected point.

Magnetic disk systems are based on an aluminum or glass disk with a magnetic coating on each side. A tiny head on a pivoted arm arcs to and fro across the magnetic surface, recording or reading from the rapidly spinning disk's coating.

Initially, the surface coating on each side of the disk is unmagnetized. But it is *formatted* before use by recording a series of 'blank' concentric-ring magnetic tracks across the disk. Each ring (*track*) is subdivided into a number of separate segments (*sectors*). During recording, the specific track and sector location of all digital picture and sound data stored on the disk is noted!

Instead of having to spool through to find the right spot as on a tape the head on a *disk recording system* arcs across in a fraction of a second to the selected *track* and *sector*. After instantaneous selection, data can be replayed forwards or backwards at any chosen speed; even frame by frame (*jogging*). It can be replayed selectively in a prearranged order.

The benefits of such selectivity, coupled with the high quality of digital systems, makes magnetic disk storage a favorite for the future. At present it is only used to a limited extent within the video camera as a storage system, but it has become a preferred method for editing processes, as you will see.

Chapter 8

Editing

Through editing, the material that you have shot is blended together to form a convincing, persuasive presentation.

8.1 The need to edit

The simplest method of shooting a scene is to use one video camera and to record the action continuously from start to finish. These are occasions when you can do exactly this, and produce a satisfactory result. You do not *have* to edit the tape. It can be replayed straight away.

But even if you do zoom in and out at times to vary the shot, a long 'take' of this kind can become tedious to watch, particularly if it is from one viewpoint. Of course, if you are shooting a particularly fascinating subject, or the action is very exciting, you may get away with it; but don't rely on that! There will invariably be dull periods, and the lack of visual variety soon palls.

To hold the attention on the small screen, and build enthusiastic interest, we usually need to change the shot size, the viewpoint, and even the locale, quite frequently.

If you were shooting an event such as a marathon race, you would not expect to record every minute of the occasion. It would be impossible for the camera to be everywhere, seeing everything. Instead you select the highlights, such as preparations for the race, the start, difficult moments, the winning tape, talking to the contestants, etc. In other words, you excerpt from the action, and join the sections together to form a continuous presentation (continuity editing).

You shoot events in the order that is most convenient or practicable, then join these takes together so that they appear consecutive. The eventual 'running order' may be very different from the order in which you shot them (the 'shooting order').

- Sometimes you will shoot action through from start to finish – e.g. watching someone blowing a glass vase.
- You may deliberately shoot only sections of the total action, omitting unwanted action.
- You may have the action repeated so that you can shoot it from various positions.

- You may shoot all the action at one location before going on to the next, although the story line may intercut between them.
- You may shoot a series of *similar* subjects which have reached different stages – e.g. shots of various new-born foals, yearlings, colts, ageing horses edited together to imply the life-cycle of a *particular* horse.

As we shall see, *editing* has a much more subtle role to play than a simple 'jointing process'. It is the technique of selecting and arranging shots; choosing their order, their duration, and the ways in which they are to be joined together. Editing has a considerable influence on your audience's reactions to what they see and hear. Skilled editing makes a major contribution to the effectiveness of any production. Poor editing can result in your audience becoming confused and bored. The mechanics of editing are simple enough; but the subtle effects of the editor's choices, are a study apart.

8.2 The editing process

The simplest technique is to '*edit in camera*'. We shall look at this idea in Section 8.11. There are occasions when this approach can be quite successful, but it can be a very restrictive. You need to take care to record each shot in what is to be its final order, until you have built up your complete program. The result could be a finished 'ready-for-use' tape. But as you will see, there are many advantages in using *regular* editing techniques, where you take as many shots as you wish, in any order, and sort them out later in an editing session.

Film editing   The film editor physically handles lengths of film, viewing them on an editing bench, cutting out selected sections, and splicing these together in the chosen order, to build up the edited version. Where there are to be *mixes*, *fades*, *wipes*, etc., the editor makes appropriate wax markings at the joins to show the film laboratories the transitions required when they print the final version.

Videotape editing   This is a very different process. First of all, you do not *cut* your videotape if you are wise! Although it is physically possible to cut and splice videotape just as one edits *audio tape*, the result can be disastrous. Not only is the tape surface disrupted at the join liable to damage the VCR's tiny delicate heads, but it will replay as a major picture interruption (a wipe, with picture break-up). Instead, videotape editing is a *copying* or *dubbing* process, in which you run tapes to and fro to select the required scenes, and re-record the selected parts onto a fresh master tape.

8.3 Editing equipment

Preview monitoring

The director of a *live* multi-camera video production may need a stack of monitors in order to continuously check and select shots from all the available picture sources, but fortunately, this elaboration is not necessary for a *post-production* videotape editing session, where even a single preview monitor may be sufficient.

The minimum equipment you need for videotape editing is:

- A *videotape player* (*or recorder*) on which to play the tape from the camera.
- A *preview monitor* (perhaps a TV receiver) on which to watch this display.

● A *videotape recorder* with a clean (blank) tape, on which to copy (re-record) the sections you have chosen on the first machine's tape.

Though it can be more convenient if you use a second screen ('*master monitor*') on which to watch the output of the recorder and to check the results.

Where you have a *number* of picture sources (e.g. several VTRs, graphics, slides, titling, film) you have the option of switching a single preview monitor to each in turn or having one preview monitor for each source.

During an editing session we are more concerned with being able to *identify* shots rather than assess their technical quality, so it is practicable to dispense with a number of individual preview monitors, and instead to have a *single* monitor screen showing a *multi-frame display*. Of course, the individual picture from each source is quite small, but this kind of display has an important advantage. Instead of showing a *single* isolated frame from an action sequence it can present half a dozen or more *successive frames*, allowing you to make a comparative selection with great precision. Where these frames are identified by a *time code* the precise instant at which each frame was recorded is displayed.

● **Output monitor** Known variously as the *line*; *master*; *main channel*; *transmission monitor*, this shows the output of the switcher. There you can see the picture you have selected from the available sources and the result of any combined shots.

The basic switcher (vision mixer) controls

The *switcher* (*production switcher*; *vision mixer*) is the equipment that enables you to intercut or combine various picture sources and to introduce certain video effects.

The basic switcher includes two sets of switches:

● **The preview bus** Selecting a picture source on this row of push-buttons displays that channel on your *preview monitor(s)*; allowing you to check and adjust pictures, before switching them 'on air'.
● **The program bus** This row of push-buttons puts the selected picture '*on air*'; i.e. It routes that source to the system's *main output* (called *line; main channel; or transmission*) which is connected to the video recorder.

The simplest switchers do just that. They switch selected channels onto the main output. To make a **cut**, you press different switch buttons on the program bus and the on-air picture cuts from one source to another.

● **The fade** The *switcher unit* usually includes one or more *fader* levers. Equipment designs vary, but typically you select which sources (channels) are fed to the communal fader unit(s).

Fading up and down – When a fader on the switcher unit is set at minimum the picture from that video source (e.g. camera) is 'faded out'; i.e. you have a blank screen. Increase the fader's setting, and the picture strength grows progressively as you fade the channel up to maximum (i.e. 'fully faded up'). Move the channel fader from maximum to minimum will 'fade it out'.
● **The mix** If you fade one channel up while fading another down the result is a mix or dissolve (the filmic term) or a 'cross-fade' (a term more generally used in audio when mixing between sound sources).

- **Superimposition** If you are already looking at a picture (maximum fader setting) and then gradually fade up another video source as well this second picture will be seen superimposed on the first with growing strength. The actual results will depend on the relative tones and colors at each point in the two pictures. If, for instance, there is a dark area in the first picture and the corresponding area of the second shot contains a light-toned object (or light lettering) this new image will appear solid in the combined shot. Otherwise, superimposition produces a transparent 'double-exposure' effect. Light-toned areas break through the darker tones of other shots with which they are superimposed. Color pictures will show chromatic mixtures. If similar tones are superimposed, they will simply merge. You can fade one or more channels in/out of a superimposition, leaving the remaining picture at full intensity. Apart from those odd occasions when you want to create 'ghostly' effects, you are most likely to use 'supers' when introducing subtitles, or other titling.

In some video systems you need to take care when fading up more than one picture channel at a time. Their signals add, causing the combined picture to overload the system, crushing the lightest tones out to white. In that situation, you would need to balance the fader settings to keep below upper limits.

8.4 Editing opportunities

The kind of editing you do will depend very much on your facilities. So the first thing you need to know at this stage is:

- How do you make edits, with the particular equipment available to you? Some systems are simple to operate, but limited in what they can do. Other facilities are elaborate, but extremely flexible.
- Can you only make cuts between the shots you join together, or can you introduce mixes/dissolves, wipes, and other transitions?

If you know what opportunities you have, you can shoot the program accordingly.

On the other hand, it would be very unwise to record a series of shots in a random order, errors and all, assuming that you can sort this out during editing, only to find that this is the version you are stuck with! Yet this could be the situation if you are 'editing in camera'.

When you are editing a program, you have two major considerations.

On the one hand, you are concerned with organizing the material you have shot, into a coherent, flowing development. These are the *mechanics* of editing.

On the other hand, every choice you make, must directly affect how your audience responds to what they are seeing. You are influencing their interpretations, as you select and interrelate pictures. These are the *aesthetics* of editing.

8.5 Organization

Editing provides you with ways of correcting and improving the finished product:

- You can remove or shorten sequences that are uninteresting, irrelevant or repetitious.
- You can correct errors, by omitting faulty sections, and inserting 'retakes'.

- You can extract just the sections you need for your program.
- You can adjust the overall duration.

There is nothing inherently dishonest or deceitful about such editing, provided you do not distort or falsify the spirit of the occasion.

8.6 Editing begins

Editing begins with sorting through the available material, and:

1 Selecting the required shots.
2 Deciding on the order and duration of each shot.
3 Deciding on the cutting point (when one shot is to end, and the next to begin).
4 Deciding on the type of transition between shots.
5 Creating good continuity.

Let's look at these points in more detail.

8.7 Selecting required sections

It is normal practice to shoot much more than you finally expect to use. In *film-making*, professionals often have quite a high 'shooting ratio'; only one tenth or one twentieth of the total material shot is used in the final edited version! That is partly because they cannot check results while shooting, and partly to give more choice during editing.

When you replay what you have recorded, you will find that you have:

- good shots that you will use,
- shots that cannot be used due to defects or errors of various sorts ('no-good takes'),
- repeated shots (retakes to achieve the best version),
- redundant shots (too similar to others to use),
- JIC shots (that you took 'just-in-case' they would be useful as cutaways or insert shots/pick-ups during editing),
- shots that didn't work for some reason.

So the first stage of editing is to sort out what is available to use and what is to be junked, and form a list. If you kept a log while you were shooting, giving details of the shots, this will help considerably. Otherwise, you will have to play back the tape, and make notes to guide the editing.

You can identify the individual shot:

- visually ('the one where he gets into the car'),
- by shooting a 'slate' (clapper-board) before each shot, containing the shot number and details (or an inverted board, at the end of shots),
- by electronically inserted data printed in the picture at the start of a shot (a facility in some video cameras),
- By *timecode*; a special continuous time-signal throughout the tape, showing the precise moment of recording.

Once you know which shots you are going to use, the next step is to decide on the order in which you want to present them.

8.8 The order of shots

To edit successfully, you need to imagine yourself in the position of your audience. They are seeing a succession of shots, one after another, for the first time. As each shot appears, they have to interpret it and relate it to previous shots, progressively building up ideas about what they are seeing.

In most cases, you will show the shots in chronological order. If the shots jump to and fro in time or place, the result can be extremely confusing. (Even the familiar idea of 'flashbacks' only works as long as the audience understands what is going on.)

When you cut a series of brief shots together, the fast pace of the program will be exciting, urgent and confusing. A slow cutting rhythm using shots of longer duration, is more gentle, restful, thoughtful, sad, etc.

8.9 Cutting points

The *moment* you choose for a cut can affect how smoothly one shot leads to another. If the first shows a man walking up to a door to open it, and the second shot as a close-up of him grasping the handle, you usually have to make sure that there is:

- no missing time (his arm hasn't moved yet . . . but his hand is on the handle in the close-up),
- no duplicated time (his hand takes hold of the handle in the first shot . . . then reaches out and grasps it again in the close-up),
- no overextended time (his hand takes the handle in the first shot, and holds it . . . and is still seen holding it waiting to turn it, in the second shot).

There are various opinions as to whether the cut should occur before a movement, after a movement or during it. The smoothness can vary with the situation. But here we are talking about the finer points of the editing art.

There are occasions when we deliberately 'lose time' by omitting part of the action. For instance, a woman gets out of a car, and a moment later we see her coming into a room. We have not watched her through all the irrelevant action of going into the house and climbing the stairs. This technique of *filmic time* (*cinematic time*) tightens up the pace of the production, and leaves out potentially boring bits when audience interest could wane. Provided the audience knows what to expect, and understands, what is going on, this ploy is an effective way of getting on with the story without wasting time.

Similarly you can 'extend time' to create a dramatic impact. We see someone light the fuse of a stick of dynamite . . . cut to people in the next room . . . cut to the villain's expression . . . cut to the street outside . . . cut to him/her looking around . . . cut to the fuse . . . and so on, building up tension in a much longer time than it would really have taken for the fuse to burn down and explode the dynamite.

Again, you can introduce *filmic space*. We see a person getting into an aircraft . . . and cut to others at that moment at his/her destination, preparing to welcome him/her.

8.10 Transitions

In Figure 8.1. you can see the regular methods of changing from one shot to another.

The *cut* is the commonest, general-purpose transition, and can be made simply and directly, either during shooting ('editing in camera') or afterwards during editing.

Figure 8.1 Transitions
The cut (*straight cut, flat cut*). An instantaneous switch from one shot to another. A powerful dynamic transition that is easiest to make.

Picture 1

Picture 2

The mix (*dissolve*). An effect produced by fading out one picture while fading in another. A quiet, restful transition. A quick mix tends to imply that the action in the two scenes is happening at the same time. A slow mix suggests passing of time, or moving to a different place. Mixes are generally comparative. If a mix is stopped halfway, the result is a *superimposition*.

Picture 1

Picture 2

Superimposition
Picture 1 + Picture 2

Fade out. A gradual reduction in the strength of the picture, by stopping down (manually or motorized iris), or by fading out a video source. A slow fade suggests the peaceful end of action. A fast fade is rather like a 'gentle cut', used to conclude a scene.

A *fade-in* is the opposite process. A slow fade-in suggests the forming of an idea, while a fast fade-in introduces action without the shock of simply cutting from a blank screen to a full picture.

All picture tones progressively darken

Many video cameras have a lens iris (aperture), that can be fully closed. If you start to shoot with the lens closed right down, then open it up until you reach the aperture needed for correct exposure, the picture will *fade up* from a black screen to full intensity ('fade in'). Similarly, by closing the iris while shooting you can fade the picture from full down to a black screen ('fade out'; 'fade down'). Some cameras have an *auto-fade* button.

If you are using a *switcher* to control cameras you produce a fade by operating a fader control (rather as you would adjust the gain control/volume control on audio equipment).

A *mix* or a *superimposition* will normally need two video sources, and a switcher (vision mixer) to fade between them.

A *wipe* pattern is produced by a *special effects generator* (SEG). This can be either a separate unit or incorporated in a switcher.

8.11 Good continuity

If we see a series of shots that are supposed to show the same action from different viewpoints, we do not expect to see any radical changes in the appearance of things in the respective pictures. In other words, we expect *continuity*.

If a glass is full in one shot and empty in the next we can accept that, if something has happened between the two shots. But if someone in a storm scene appears wet in all the long shots, but dry in the close-ups, something is wrong! If they are standing smiling, with an arm on a chair in one shot but with a hand in a pocket and unsmiling when seen from another angle in the next shot, the sudden change during the cut can be very obvious. The sun may be shining in one shot and not in the next. There may be aircraft noises in one but silence in the next. Somebody may be wearing a blue suit in one shot and a gray one in the next.

These are all very obvious – but they happen. In fact they are liable to happen whenever action, that is to appear continuous in the edited program, stops and restarts.

There is an opportunity for the continuity to be upset when you:

- stop shooting, move the camera to another position, and then continue,
- repeat part of an action (a retake); it may be slightly different the second time, so cannot edit unobtrusively with the original sequence,
- shoot action over a period of time, e.g. part of it one day, and the rest on the next,
- alter how you are going to shoot a scene, after part of it is already taped.

The only way to achieve good continuity is to pay attention to detail. Sometimes a continuity error will be much more obvious on the screen than it was during shooting. It is so easy to overlook differences when you are concentrating on the action, and the hundred and one other things that arise during production. If there are any doubts, there is a lot be said for replaying the videotape to check back on previous shots of the scene, before continuing shooting.

8.12 Editing during shooting

Most lightweight video cameras have a switch that enables you to remotely start and stop the VCR, so that you can 'edit in camera'. This simply means that you tape the first shot, stop the VCR, set up the second shot; and then continue taping; and so progressively *assemble* your program.

Some VCRs provide a method in which you watch a replay of your previous shot, and switch at the appropriate moment, using an 'edit' or 'mode-change' button, from *replay* to the *record* mode.

In another method you play up to the cue point, and press the *pause* button on the VCR. This stops the tape moving, but continues to replay a still picture as the heads go on scanning the tape width. While the tape is temporarily paused, you switch the VCR to *record*, then release the pause button. The VCR begins recording the new shot without a disruption on the tape.

Most modern VCR systems produce a clean noiseless cut between two shots, on replaying the tape. (Unfortunately, some show momentary picture defects during 'in camera' cuts, due to sync problems.)

So where are the snags?

1. Well, you have to record the program in its final 'running order'; and that may not be convenient, or even practicable. Although you can *insert* a new item within the existing recording (wiping out that section of the original), you cannot do this with great accuracy.

2. 'Tight' accurately placed cutting is not really practicable, when 'editing in camera'. You need to make sure that you have sufficient material at the finish of each shot, and the beginning of the next, to avoid clipping the start or end of action during editing.

You need to make allowances too, for the fact that, unlike an audio recorder, the VCR does not start to replay or record immediately you press the appropriate switch. There is a momentary pause before the picture and sound appear. This delay is deliberate, to allow the machine to stabilize. It happens this way.

When we start a VCR, it takes a moment for its tape to get up to full speed, and its synchronizing system to settle down to produce stable pictures ('lock up').

So, many VCRs include a special *back-space editing* arrangement. Every time you press the play or record button, the machine starts by *rewinding* itself just a little (e.g. 5 s) before then running forward. Thanks to this brief back-track, the machine gives itself sufficient time for the system to stabilize, before it actually begins to replay or record. Picture and sound appear 'clean' and without slurs or disturbances of any kind.

That is fine, but if your last shot ended at a crucial moment (as the villain fires the gun), there is a chance that it will be chopped off, when the tape rewinds itself a little on starting the second recording. You will not know if you have lost the end of the previous action during the restart until you replay the sequence to check the edit. So make sure there is sufficient room at the end of each shot to accommodate this situation.

3. Probably the main disadvantage of 'editing during shooting' is that there is little leeway for mistakes. If you misjudge, previous shots can be spoiled. You need to re-record any unsuccessful shots straight away, and that involves running the tape back to the edit point ready for the retake, and checking each shot after recording it, to make sure that it is satisfactory.

A different method of editing is possible, when you have two or more cameras. The cameras are cabled to a switcher, where editing is carried out 'on the hoof' during the production, intercutting, mixing and wiping between shots at the required moments. The output of the switcher can be taped continuously, from opening to closing, as a 'live on tape' recording.

Alternatively, you can use a stop-start recording approach. If there are any faults during the production, recording stops, the tape is rewound to the end of the last good shot, and the recording and action are re-cued. This way, it is not necessary to carry out post-production editing, to correct and rearrange the recorded videotape.

The great benefit of all 'editing during shooting' approaches to production, is that you finish up with a *first-generation* recording. The picture quality represents the best the system can provide. And as a bonus, the videotape can be ready at the end of the shooting session.

8.13 Generations

Whenever we dub, with analogue VCR systems the quality of the copy can never be as good as the original recording. If you are using state-of-the-art professional VTRs the differences may be slight. But when a picture recorded on a domestic VCR is dubbed onto a similar machine, the quality losses are noticeable. At worst, video noise is more pronounced, detail is less clear, color tends to bleed or smear, there may be horizontal streaks across parts of the picture, edges of subjects appear ragged and color errors arise.

Copy this copy, and sound quality worsens, color disappears, and eventually both picture and sound break up completely.

The higher the quality of the system you are using, the less the deterioration during dubbing. There are more generations before losses become unacceptable. Thus tapes made with Super VHS for example, will survive editing and copying better than tapes made on the standard VHS system.

When you edit by dubbing, the composite copy that results is a *second-generation* version. If you make a straight copy of this final videotape, perhaps for distribution, this is a *third-generation* version. So it will unavoidably have lost some of the quality of the original *first-generation* recording.

Because the progressive deterioration at each dubbing is cumulative, we cannot disregard it if we want a high-grade end-product. Any multiple dubbing you do, to produce special video effects, can result in copies that are third-generation or so. If you include any 'library shots' in your program (i.e. material recorded for another production), which may themselves be third-generation, the final version seen in a distribution copy could be fifth-generation or more!

How far all this matters depends on the quality of the original. If it is really excellent, or ironically, if it is so poor that a little more noise will not make much difference, then the third-generation version can be quite acceptable. Much depends on the system used, and on the purpose of the program. If it is important to show detail in print, fine texture or subtle tonal difference, then results may not be acceptable in a multi-generation copy. If it is a news scoop of a once-only event, standards become flexible.

8.14 Electronic splicing

Some types of VCRs give you the option of recording in two different modes.

The first is the *assemble* (*assembly*) mode. When you use this system, it not only records picture and sound, but also records *new reference pulses* on the control track of the tape at the same time.

The second is the *insert* mode. Here, you record new video and audio, but the VCR leaves the *old control track* that is already on the tape, untouched.

The original idea was that one should use the 'assemble' mode when adding new shots *on to the end* of an existing recording. The 'insert' mode on the other hand, enabled you to slot some new material *into* an existing recording (e.g. replace a faulty shot) without interrupting the existing control track pulses, for that would cause picture disturbance on the cuts.

However, the disadvantage of the 'assemble' mode is that whenever you stop and re-start recording, the system begins to record a new set of pulses on the tape. So with certain recorders there could be a momentary hiccup in the recorded pulses at the editing point on replay, enough to cause a brief picture disturbance perhaps (frame roll or tearing).

When you are using such VCRs to assemble a tape shot-by-shot, you can use a simple technical trick to ensure maximum stability at each re-start. Take the videotape before the actual editing session, and record it throughout (without picture or audio) using the *assemble* mode. This will prepare the tape by laying down a continuous uninterrupted *control track* throughout. Rewind the tape.

Then for the editing session, switch the recording VCR to the *insert* mode and use this prepared tape to record the master program. (The video will be recorded without affecting the control track pulses already on the prepared tape.) As you record each shot in turn, to build up the program, the VCR will use these pre-recorded uninterrupted control pulses throughout as a reference, and all transitions will be 'clean' on replay.

In a more complex editing set-up, where you are using various pieces of video equipment interlinked (e.g. several VCRs, an SEG, etc.) there is always the danger that the video system's sync pulses might be disturbed at some time or other and upset picture stability on the master recording. To prevent this, a *time base corrector unit* (TBC), may be needed, which corrects any sync errors in the video signal before recording, and ensures absolutely accurate synchronization.

8.15 The editing process

Although it is simple enough to play one tape and make a copy on another, the mechanics can be tricky, and somewhat laborious, when you are aiming at any sort of precision. If your pictures show unrelated general shots of countryside, factory and city streets, and you are going to edit them together and put a commentary over the result, cutting points are not at all critical, so there are no difficulties. But if you have a series of brief shots containing tight action, that have to be intercut precisely, the dubbing operation can be very demanding.

Let us go through the basic mechanics of editing, so that we can see the potential problems.

1. First you have to select and locate the shot you want. Whereabouts is it, on which tape? (Section 8.6). You then run that tape up to the 'in-cue' point, and check how much you are going to copy. You now have in and out cues, and a duration. You know exactly when to stop the replay.
2. You load 'blank' videotape on the recording VCR, ready to make the copy.
3. To make the dubbing, you need to switch both machines on, so that they come up to speed, to *replay* and *record* simultaneously. (But remember,

Figure 8.2 Methods of videotape editing
Assemble mode. This method can be used to add a further scene to an existing recording (A), or to replace a faulty scene at its end (B). But because the VTR lays down a fresh set of synchronizing cue pulses on the control track, whenever it records in this mode, its pulse pattern is disturbed at each join.

Insert mode. In this mode, the original control track pulses are not erased and re-recorded, so there is no pulse disturbance at joins when recording new material. New scenes can be inserted within an existing recording, or added to its end, if an uninterrupted control track has been prepared beforehand.

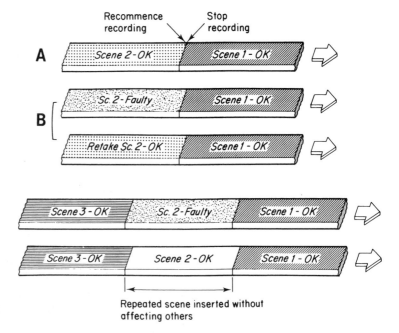

there is run-up period before a machine stabilizes, and this varies between machines.)

4. At the appropriate moment (the 'out-cue'), stop *record* and *replay* simultaneously.
5. If the next shot you want to copy is on the same source-tape, you must run it backwards or forwards to find the *exact cue-in point*. (Again, you will need to know the duration, and out-cue.) If the shot is on a different tape, you have to replace the cassette on the replay machine, and run it through to the new in-cue point.

There are several different ways of locating the 'in' and 'out' cue points on the master tape (the source-tape), as you run through it:

- A digital counter on the machine, showing how much tape has run through the system since it was reset to zero.
- A digital display that shows the lapsed time (in frames, seconds, minutes and hours) derived from counting the tape's control track pulses.
- Timecode, which accompanies the original recording, as a direct reference time showing exactly when each shot was taken (frames, seconds, minutes and hours).

A 'picture-search' facility helps one to reach the required cue-point, by fast winding to near the point, then using slow motion to get to the nearest frame. This sounds like a lot of work. And if you do it entirely manually, it certainly can be, especially if you make a mistake, misjudge or have to copy sections from several different tapes.

As VCRs have become even more sophisticated, tracking down the wanted material on a tape has become increasingly easier. Many of the tape access methods you will meet, are remotely controlled:

Manual

- *Search/shuttle*: allows the tape to be played forwards or backwards at variable speeds (briefly or continuously), from very slow to very high.
- *Jog-frame*: provides precision frame-by-frame searching forwards or backwards.

Automatic

- *Cue marks*. You can insert a 'bookmark' cue-marker during recording or playback, which will then automatically stop/start the tape at that point.
- *Time search*. This will run the tape to stop at (or play from) a particular time setting; either from the beginning of the tape, or from the current tape position.
- *Blank search*. This will search for a cued blank in the sound track.
- *Index search*: Automatically places index codes at the beginning of each new recording (take). These can be located by remote control.

8.16 Off-line and on-line editing

You can organize your editing selection in two ways:

Off-line editing. The best method is to play through tapes long before the actual editing session, selecting the takes you want to use, and making a list of your various editing decisions (in/out points, order of shots, transitions), perhaps preparing tapes in readiness.

On-line editing. Alternatively, you can leave your selection until the actual editing period. But that can be very time-consuming – and if you are paying for facilities, can be a very costly process!

8.17 Edit controllers

Thanks to ingenious devices called *edit controllers* a lot of this work can be automated.

The edit controller is a computerized switching panel. This 'magic box' remotely controls the VTR equipment, selecting and controlling the replay, rewind, and record mechanics. Designs range from simple editing aids to very sophisticated computerized equipment.

Edit controllers serve as 'intelligent interfaces', for they activate the right functions in the right order at the right moment. In doing this, they calculate and time all the machine processes, such as the run-up times, and synchronize the switching. You have to indicate what you want selected, and they do the rest – well much of it!

With this system you play through the source-tape and the recorded copy, to select the *in* and *out* edit points; and decide on the types of transitions needed (cut, mix, wipe). You then make a *rehearse edit*. This just plays the tapes, making a switch at the edit point, to show you on the screen, what that edit will look like. If the trial results are OK, the system will make the edit for real. You then check the final result.

Some systems will also provide *split-edits*, in which you can treat the recorded audio separately from the video. A *synchronizer unit* allows you to 'lift off' the original sound from the VT recording, add effects, commentary, music, and then 'lay it back' exactly in sync with the pictures. You may also be able to mix between two audio tracks on the same tape.

Where you are using a VCR with a multiplexed 'hi-fi' track (*Hi-Fi 8, S-VHS*) which is layered with the video track, the sound cannot be substituted in this way. Then you can only *audio dub* while copying.

More comprehensive editing systems give you an *edit decision list* display (perhaps with a printout), identifying the shots you have selected, their positions, timings, etc. This list is not only a valuable reference, but when confirmed, will rewind tapes to selected points, and automatically compile the dubbing to match (*auto-assemble*).

The 'edit decision list' may even remotely control a switcher (for transitions), an audio recorder (audio inserts), a character generator, a computer, etc. (for titling, graphics inserts, special effects).

The accuracy of the editing points will depend on the system. Where a *timecode reader* generates, reads and edits the tape using SMPTE time code, accuracy can be ±1 frame, with no tape slippage errors. Other methods may be more approximate; e.g. ±2–3 frames.

In a typical basic professional two-machine edit system two 'edit recorders' are used, with an 'edit controller' and two picture monitors. For economy, you can use a standard 'replay-only' or 'record-replay' type VCR to reproduce the tape, instead of using an edit recorder for that purpose.

Running tapes to and fro to their edit point can be very time consuming; particularly if one shot is near the end of the videotape, and the next near its beginning. That's why it is often better to use a series of short tapes. Then of course, you have to keep changing the cassettes!

8.18 Linear and non-linear editing

Linear editing As you saw earlier in Section 8.2, magnetic tape recordings have a major disadvantage. To select a particular part of the tape, you have to spool through the reel rapidly until you reach the selected point. Bearing in mind that one does not necessarily shoot scenes in the order that they will appear in the final tape, you can see that there could be a great deal of hunting, running the tapes to and fro to pick out the required shots (*shuttling*). When there are several retakes of the same action, there is always the problem of tracking down and extracting the right one from a group of 'N.G.' ('no good') shots.

Even where editing techniques are automated (Section 8.17), the process of picking out the required sections from the tapes, and copying them in the correct order onto a 'master tape', can still be extremely time-consuming. You can imagine that where you have several tapes shot on different occasions, with shots distributed in a random order, the mechanics can become tedious.

This linear editing process in which a master tape is compiled directly from the camera tapes can be speeded up to some extent if the original scenes are shot on 'short reels', each of which has, for example, only about 15 minutes of material. Then, provided you do not confuse reels, and do not mind continually swopping reels during the editing session, you are saved the 'dead time' wasted in running through long tapes.

Non-linear editing With the arrival of digital video recording, a different approach to editing became possible. Now, Instead of endlessly shuttling to copy individual shots, you copy all your videotaped material onto a magnetic disk. Admittedly that usually takes real-time (i.e. an hour to copy an hour's worth of material), but it is a straightforward routine that can be carried out while you are getting on with other jobs.

Now you have all the material you have shot on a single disk. Like the music on a CD recording, you can select any section(s) from the entire recording, in any order, at the press of a button. The system holds your choices as a temporary 'dummy' version, which you can change or accept. Run this choice to check if the results are satisfactory. Unlike linear editing, where any changes involve re-editing the material, it is quite easy to change your mind, and try another version. When you are ready, the system will dub off your choices onto the master tape.

The main control on the desktop editing console may take several forms: a shuttle wheel, a touch screen, a digital tablet, or a computer's mouse, keyboard, track-ball (tracker ball), or a light-pen. You can replay the picture and its associated sound forwards and backwards, in sync at adjustable speeds. You can jog frame-by-frame, jump to any point, or go straight to preset cue marks.

Some non-linear systems use a single color monitor, with switchable displays, to suit each stage of the editing. There may, for example, be a preparatory mode showing the shots available, and an editing mode displaying your decisions. Small display panels on the screen show details of the sound track, so that you can made precision changes (*cuts*, *inserts*) in the program audio. In another arrangement, the editing console has two monitor screens, and displays a visual log showing details of all the shots from which you can compile an edit decision list. Although these non-linear editing processes are not yet universally available, they promise to revolutionize future editing techniques.

8.19 Post-production editing

As you saw in Chapter 5, the program audio is usually a composite, made up of:

- the direct pick-up sound recorded during shooting (e.g. dialogue).
- any sound effects (background or synchronized spot effects),
- music,
- 'voice-over' commentary, announcements, etc.

Now is the time to combine and correct the program sound, and relate it to the picture.

It is worth remembering at this stage that either the pictures or the audio may be given *priority* during the dubbing process.

If you are, for example, making a complete record of a speech, the dialogue has priority. Although the camera will concentrate on the speaker, a single unchanging shot would become visually boring, even with judicious changes in shot-size. So you will probably include 'cutaway shots' of his/her audience, special guests, reactions, and so on. But the dialogue is continuous and unbroken – whatever picture editing you decide to do.

Where a speech is to be edited because it is too long for the allocated program time, or you are selecting the most important passages, the dialogue will be edited, and commentary or intercut shots of the audience interposed to disguise parts of the speech that are missing.

You may have a scene in which two people are supposed to be speaking to each other, although they were actually shot separately. For instance, all the shots of a boy stranded on a cliff would be taken at the same time (with dialogue). All the shots and comments of his rescuer at the top of the cliff would be shot at another time. During editing, the shots with their respective speech, would be intercut to give a continuous interchange.

There are times when the pictures have priority, and the sound has to be closely related to what we are seeing. You may have to adjust its start, its synchronism, its duration and its emphasis to match the pictures.

8.20 Good editing techniques

Editing, like so many of the crafts we have been examining in earlier pages, is an unobtrusive skill. If it is done well, your audience does not notice it, but is absorbed in its *effect*.

During an exciting scene, for example, when the duration of shots is made shorter and shorter as the tension grows, the audience is only conscious of growing agitation, and fast-moving action.

There are certain established principles in the way one edits, and although like all 'rules' you may occasionally disregard them, they have been born of experience. Here are a few of the most common:

- Do not cut between shots that are very similar or even matching (e.g. frontal close-up of person A to frontal close-up of person B.)
- Avoid cutting between shots of extremely different size of the same subject (e.g. big close-up to long shot). (*Continued on page 179*)

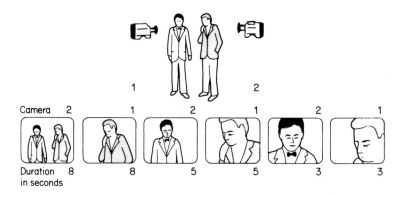

Figure 8.3 Intercutting
Tension can be increased by quicker cutting. Here an increasing cutting rate is combined with closer and closer shots.

Figure 8.4 Matching cuts
When pictures are intercut, take care to avoid the following distracting effects.

Part 1 *People*
A Mismatched camera height.
B Changes in headroom.
C Size jumps. Avoid cutting between shots of only slightly different size (e.g. a-b, b-c, c-d). The subject suddenly appears to shrink or grow! Aim at size changes of at least 4:3 or 3:4 (a-c, b-d).
D Transformations occur if identical size shots of two different subjects are intercut.
E Cutting over a wide angle, to a similar size shot, is distracting.

A

B

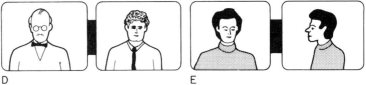

C   a   b   c   d

D   E

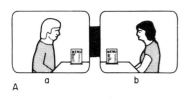

a   b

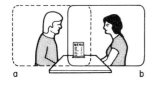

A   a   b

C

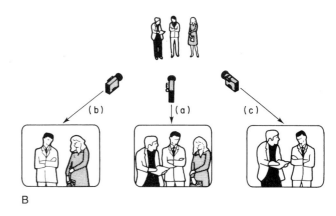

(b)   (a)   (c)

B

D

Part 2 *Jump cuts*
A If you have the same subject in two adjacent shots, it may jump across the screen on the cut.
B This can happen in group shots too (in shots (b) and (c)).
C Cutting between similar shots of the subject from slightly different viewpoints, can create a 'twist' on the cut.

D If continuity is not matched when shooting discontinuously, parts of the action may be missed or repeated.

Table 8.1 Anticipating editing
However good the pictures are, if they have been shot inappropriately they will not allow effective editing. Here are typical points to watch when shooting.

- Include *cover* shots of action wherever possible, to show the general view of the action.
- Always leave several seconds of *run-in* and *run-out* at the start and finish of each shot. Do not start taping just as the action is beginning or the reporter is about to speak; nor stop immediately action/speech finishes. Spare footage at the beginning and end of each shot will allow more flexible editing.
- Include potential *cutaway shots* that can be introduced when any sequence is to be shortened or lengthened; e.g. crowd shots, general views, passers-by.
- Avoid *reverse shots* (direction reversal). If it is unavoidable (e.g. when crossing the road to shoot a procession from either side). Include head-on shots of the same action.
- Keep 'cute shots' to a minimum, unless they can really be integrated into the program. These include such items as reflections, sunbathers, silhouettes against the sunset, animals or children at play, footsteps in the sand...
- Try to anticipate continuity. If there are only a few shots taken in daylight and others at night, it may not be practical to edit them together to provide a continuous sequence.
- Where there is going to be narration behind the pictures allow for this in the length and pace of takes; e.g. avoid inappropriately choppy editing due to shots being too brief. (Editors sometimes have to slow-motion or still-frame a very brief shot to make it usable!)
- Aim to include longer shots and closer shots of action, to provide editing opportunities. For example, where the action shows people crossing a river bridge a variety of viewpoints can make a mundane subject visually interesting; e.g. *LS* – walking away from camera towards bridge; *MS* – walking on the bridge, looking over, *VLS* – shooting up at the bridge from the river below; *LS* – walking from the bridge to the camera on the far side; etc.
- Try to avoid sequences that are straight into the sun in one shot and against it the next. They do not intercut well.
- Remember that environmental noises can provide valuable bridging sound between shots when editing. They can be audio-taped separately as wild track (non-sync sound).
- Where possible, include features in shots that will help the audience to identify the particular location or terrain (landmarks, street names). Too often, the walls and bushes behind closer shots could be *anywhere*.
- Keep an accurate camera log giving relevant shot details that could help the editor (time, place, identify action, indicate if a take is faulty, etc.).
- Wherever possible, use an identifying *board* or *slate* at the start of each shot. Failing that, announce the shot number so that the soundtrack carries identification. If an 'intro-ident' is missed, put one at the end of a take (showing the board upside down).
- If there are pronounced background sounds during a take, in some circumstances they can be cut out (overlaid) during editing and replaced by neutral sounds (e.g. 'atmos' wild track).
  But this is not always possible. Suppose you have just shot a single-camera interview in quiet surroundings. Finally, you shoot the reporter's questions to camera, but now there is high background noise. When the shots of the guest and the reporter are edited together the noise will mysteriously cut and reappear during the sequence.
- Most one-camera interviews shot while speakers walk around, are taken in three sections as (a) long-shots, (b) closer shots of the people speaking, (c) 'reaction shots/nod shots'. Make sure that mouths cannot be seen moving in (a) and (c). Check that the continuity of the action and positions in each version are reasonably similar.
- For the standuppers, check what is happening in the background behind the reporter. If the piece to camera is shot in several takes the background subjects could change noticeably between takes!

Figure 8.5 Point of view
The camera can change from a bystander's objective viewpoint to the performer's own subjective viewpoint. 1. We are simply following the man. 2. Here we become aware of what is happening around him. 3. We look at the scene with him. 4. A reaction shot as he greets the child 'through his eyes'.

- Cutting through an angle, to similarly sized shots of a subject (e.g. frontal to side view) produces unattractive jumps.
- If two subjects are going in the same direction (chasing, following), have them both going across the screen in the same direction. If their screen directions are opposite, this will suggest meeting or parting. (This arises if you intercut between camera positions on either side of the action's direction.)
- Generally avoid cutting between static and fast-moving pictures, except for a specific purpose.
- Take care if cutting *in* from a blank screen to full picture strength, or cutting *out* to a blank screen except for a deliberate shock effect.
- If you have to break the continuity of action (deliberately or unavoidably), introduce a cutaway shot. But try to ensure that this relates meaningfully to the main action. During a boxing bout, a cutaway to an excited spectator helps the tension. A cutaway to some garbage, or a bored attendant (just because you happen to have the unused shot!) would be meaningless, although it can be used as a comment on the main action.
- If someone walks out of shot (apparently exiting), don't re-discover them nearby in the next shot, taken from another angle.
- Avoid intercutting shots that make a person or object jump from one side of the screen to the other, on the cut.
- Intercut shots where a person is facing (or moving) left, then seen on the cut facing (or moving) right, are seldom acceptable, except to suggest confusion perhaps. 'Reverse cuts' arise if you alter your camera viewpoint during the action, and cross from one side of their route to the other ('crossing the line').

When you have the opportunity, do *all* these things deliberately! You will see how strange, how ambiguous, or how disturbing the effects can be, and you are less likely to do them again, except by accident!

Chapter 9

People

Your entire program could rest on how well people perform in front of the camera. How do you help them to give their best?

9.1 Talent

Although the broad term 'talent' is widely used to refer to those appearing in front of the camera, we must always remember how very varied this talent really is. It covers a remarkable spread of experience and temperaments; from the professional actor working to a script and playing a part, to the impromptu, unrehearsed interview with a passer-by in the street.

When you invite someone to appear in front of the camera, that is only the *beginning* of the story. Their performance can have a considerable influence on your program's success. So you will need to help them, to make their contribution as effective as they are able. Their particular role may be a major one, or it may be slight, but the impression they make on your audience can decide whether that part of your program wins or fails. The television camera is a great debunker. Under its scrutiny, brashness, pomposity and false bonhomie are weighed and found wanting; while sympathy goes out to those who are shy and ill at ease.

For all practical purposes, we can divide talent into the *professional performers*, who are used to appearing in front of the camera, and the *inexperienced*, for whom your program is likely to be a new, strange, exciting yet worrying event.

Professional performers usually work to a prepared format. Some, like an actor in a play, will learn their lines, their moves and the mechanics of the production. Others work from an abbreviated cue sheet near the camera, or a running text projected onto the screen of a prompter. Some will extemporize from guide notes, others will read from a printed script.

The best professionals can be relied on to repeat, during the actual taping, the dialogue, the moves, the pace and the timing that they gave in rehearsal. One knows what they are going to say, and that they can modify the delivery of their piece to suit the occasion, showing enthusiasm, vigor, calm detachment, patience or reverence. They can take guidance and instructions, and follow this through without being confused. They can improvise when things go wrong, and remain calm and collected if the unexpected happens.

Any program-maker using talent not used to working to a camera, has to make certain allowances, and take precautions that are not necessary where professional performers are involved.

How well inexperienced people fit into their roles in your program will depend to quite an extent on you. Do not expect them to have the self-discipline and efficiency of the professional. There is, after all, a scary novelty about finding yourself faced with an impersonal camera, a microphone pointing to pick up your slightest remark, unfamiliar people grouped around, the powerful lighting and sundry disruptions. The occasion can become very unreal to inexperienced talent.

9.2 Inexperienced talent

Many a person who appears to be a 'natural performer' in the finished program is really the product of a very understanding, yet wily director. Typical ways of handling inexperienced talent include:

- Careful planning, so that not much is required of the talent. You put them at ease by the way you make them welcome; by letting them know what you want them to do; making them feel that their contribution is an important and interesting part of your program; and assuring them that if anything goes wrong, there is nothing to worry about, for it can be taped again.
- Letting them do it their way, and editing the result.
- Letting them reminisce, for example, then selecting the most interesting or the most relevant parts.
- Keeping the tension down, by shooting when they do not know you are doing so.
- Interviewing them in a situation that is natural to them (e.g. their workshop) rather than in a formal studio setting.
- Wherever possible, avoid showing the talent just standing, waiting. They will feel more at ease (particularly in their own surroundings), if they have something to do; e.g. a cook might be cutting up some vegetables before speaking.
- Giving them a few instructions; e.g. telling them when, where or how to hold the items to the camera.
- Using plenty of cutaway shots, so that the picture is not concentrating on them all the time. As far as possible, we look at what they are talking about instead, together perhaps with intercut shots of the host smiling and nodding ('nod shots').

Figure 9.1 Guiding the talent
The experienced performer can help the inexperienced guest in many ways:

1 Putting them at ease.
2 Keeping an eye on the monitor shot.
3 Keeping the table clear of unwanted items.
4 Placing items on a pre-arranged mark.
5 Having the next item ready.
6 Positioning items to suit the camera.
7 Avoiding shadowing the item, or lens flares or reflections.
8 Aware of the running time.

It may be a wise plan to tape the rehearsal, and if possible, to run through the material several times, recording everything, so that you can select and combine the best parts of each version.

If sections do not join neatly for editing, the interviewer can record a question or a statement later, that will bridge what would otherwise be disjointed material. With care, this can be done quite ethically, even although it was not part of the original interview.

9.3 The presenter

Many of the problems of handling inexperienced talent can be reduced, if they are supported in the program by someone who is used to production routine.

This person, who serves as the host or presenter, will probably meet them beforehand, help them to feel at ease, introduce them to the camera, and gently guide them through the production. By interjecting such phrases as: 'Earlier, you were telling me about . . .' or 'I wonder if we could look at . . .' or 'Isn't the construction of this piece interesting . . .', they can move the program smoothly from one section to the next. Especially when you are shooting intermittently, or out of order – both very confusing to the novice – the guiding hand can be very welcome.

The host can help the guest with the mechanics of the situation. Instead of the nervous guest grasping something unreliably, partly hiding it and catching the light, or wobbling about in a very close shot, the host might tactfully do it for them by taking it to admire, then holding it quite still to camera at exactly the right angle, while looking in a nearby monitor to check the shot.

9.4 When there are problems

There are those sad occasions when the talent you have invited simply does not come up to expectations. They are so wooden, or so hesitant and nervous, that they do little justice to themselves. Or they over compensate, and become loud and verbose. There is often little opportunity to actually replace them, if you do not discover the problem until camera rehearsal.

It is a cruel solution, to see how bad someone is during rehearsal, then to say: 'I'm sorry, but there isn't time for your item after all. The program is too long'. It is far better to tape them, hoping either that they will be better next time or that part at least of this contribution can be used. It has been known for a director to record the item, then quietly junk it during editing.

But leaving aside these drastic methods (which can leave you with no material), it may be better to simplify or to shorten their contribution. Include lots of cutaways (e.g. close-ups of details on items being shown) that you can use to cover edits later. If necessary, you can take these after the main taping with the guest is over.

Another approach is to have the host present the items in the program, continually referring to the guest. For example, pick up an item, hold it to camera, and remind the guest of the information they discussed before or during rehearsal. At worst, the guest has to do little more than say: 'Yes' and 'No'!

As a last resort, if the combination is mainly a demonstration, you might keep most of the pictures of the items being demonstrated (e.g. showing steps in a cookery demonstration), and lay a commentary track over them, explaining what is going on, based on the original recording. In fact, if you see from rehearsals that there is little profit in taking shots of the guest speaking to the host, you might deliberately restrict shots to showing what he or she is doing, omitting shots of the speaker in anticipation of final voice-over treatment.

9.5 The camera's viewpoint

Because talent is expert at a particular subject, this does not mean that they can present it convincingly to the camera. Ironically, a presenter working from a prompter script may appear more authentic; even though the words were written by someone else.

How you can shoot action is influenced not only by the nature of the subject, but by the talent involved.

You may need to *sneak* shots as unobtrusively as possible, so that you do not intrude on the situation, and to avoid people playing up to the camera. If for instance, you are shooting children at play, or at work in a classroom, you are likely to get a far more accurate account of what really happens if they do not know you are there (unlikely!), or do not know that you are shooting them at that moment. Some program-makers contend, hopefully, that people simply ignore the lights and the microphone, and behave perfectly naturally after a while. But this is very challengeable.

The camera can behave rather like a bystander who moves around to get to a good viewpoint of whatever is going on. This happens in street interviews. At best, one hopes that someone who is being interviewed, will be preoccupied with the questioner, and barely notice the camera and microphone, although the curiosity of bystanders, particularly children, seldom lets them forget the artificiality of the occasion.

Inexperienced talent is seldom able to *speak to camera* completely naturally, without a certain amount of hesitation or over-playing, especially if they have to remember to cover particular points in order, and take various precautions as they go through their piece.

Even when someone is at ease speaking directly to camera, they may not *work to the camera* successfully. An inexperienced person holds something up so that *they* can see it, whereas what you really want is for them to handle it so that the *camera* can see the details clearly – and that can feel quite unnatural at times. They may need to hold the item awkwardly, to avoid fingers obscuring parts of it or casting shadows. They have to ensure that reflections do not prevent surface features being seen. And over-shoulder shots, looking at things from their viewpoint, are seldom the solution.

And here we come to the real decisions you will often have to make when working with people who are unused to the camera. Are you going to let them do things in their own way, and take what happens, hoping that they will do it more or less right? Are you hoping that something interesting will turn up while you are shooting? Or are you going to give them advice and instructions about what you want to see, and guide them until you get just that?

In practice, of course, the situation largely depends on the people involved, and on the amount of time (and patience) you have. Some people improve with practice, while others feel that they are failing and get worse. Some people gain confidence with rehearsal, others wilt. Some leave things out during repeats, others put more in. Some lose their naturalness, and begin to 'perform'. Some find it easier, others become more confused.

Figure 9.2 Bringing the scene to life
Empty shots. Without people, the scene looks empty, and desolate. With people, the scene becomes lively and interesting.

Foreground interest. The shot looks bleak, open, and uninviting. (You may want this effect.) But use a foreground tree to provide an upper border, and the picture looks more complete and attractive.

9.6 People passing by

From people as performers, let's turn to the importance of people as incidental passers-by in many kinds of scenes.

Supposing you are making a program about a town, describing its character and its special features and showing details of its buildings. If you shoot early in the morning before people are about, you have a better opportunity to get clear uncluttered views. But do they really convey its typical atmosphere?

On the other hand, if you wait until the town has come to life, and you have to shoot in the hustle and bustle of passing traffic, it may be difficult to get the shots you want, although the place now has exactly the right feel to it. A reminder then, that there may be advantages, in shooting various aspects to your subject at different times, according to the light, the weather, the passing crowd, and so on.

And finally, do not overlook how important people are in giving life to a scene. Rather than pan along an empty sidewalk, it is more interesting to follow someone who is passing. (Although there is the possibility that your audience may now wonder who this is, speculating on them instead of the real subject.)

A shot looking along an empty bridge, is all too likely to bore your audience within a few seconds. But have someone walk across that same bridge, and the scene immediately becomes more interesting. So you can hold the shot much longer, while a commentary tells us about its history. Whether you will have to provide your own 'passer-by', or wait for someone suitable to come along, is another matter.

Chapter 10

Organizing your
production

A lot of this is obvious; so obvious, that many program-makers overlook these essentials in their initial enthusiasm – and their product is less effective!

10.1 Art conceals craft

Watching a show on TV, our thoughts are normally centered on the program material: the story-line, the message, the argument. We become interested in what people are saying, what they are doing, what they look like, where they are, and so on. Unless we start to get bored, or the mechanics become obtrusive, we are unlikely to concern ourselves with how the production is actually *made*.

We 'believe' what we see. We respond to techniques, but remain unaware of them unless they happen to distract us. We even accept the drama of the hero dying of thirst in the desert, without wondering why the director, camera and sound crew do not help him!

All this is fine, but when you set out to make programs for yourself, you will soon realize the gulf between 'watching and enjoying' from the audience, and 'creating the illusion' by the way you use the equipment.

10.2 How techniques develop

You cannot just point a camera at a scene and expect it to convey all the information and atmosphere that the on-the-spot observer is experiencing. A camera is inherently selective. It can only show certain limited aspects of a situation at any time. If, for instance, you provide a really wide shot of the entire field at a ball-game, your audience will have an excellent view of the movement patterns of teamwork – but they will be unable to see for themselves who individuals are, or to watch exactly how they are playing the ball. A close shot can give details, even show how a player is reacting to a foul – but prevents the audience from seeing the overall action at that time.

10.3 The problem of familiarity

There is an essential difference between the way any director looks at the program and how the audience reacts. And that is not surprising when you stop and think about it. The director is completely familiar with the production and the circumstances in which it has been prepared.

Supposing, for example, the program is showing us a collection of priceless objects in a museum. There can be marked differences between the critical reactions of an enthusiastic viewer seeing a sequence for the first time and the director's own reactions.

From the audience's point of view: e.g. 'There were some unusual items in the display case, but the camera continued past them. Why didn't we have a closer look at the decorated plate, so that we could read the inscriptions? There seems to be elaborate ornamentation on the other side of this jug. But we don't see it! Why isn't it shown? Why aren't we looking at all the interesting things there in the background?'

The director could no doubt have explained: e.g. 'The camera picked out the most important details for the topic we were discussing. There isn't time to cover everything. When shooting the jug, this was the best viewpoint we could manage. The voice-over read the inscription to us. Nearby display cases prevented a better camera position. The museum was about to close, and we were scheduled to be elsewhere the next day...'

This imaginary discourse reminds us of several important points. First, there are many ways of interpreting any situation. A good director will have given the subject a great deal of thought before shooting, and rationalized how best to tackle the shoot. But most program-making is a matter of compromise between 'aesthetics' and 'mechanics'. Between 'what we would like to do' and 'what we are able to do'. Quite often, the 'obvious thing to do' is quite impracticable for some reason (e.g. too costly, insufficient time, beyond the available equipment, too elaborate, failing light etc.). In the real world, we shall discover great on-the-spot opportunities we had not anticipated. But we shall also encounter frustrating disappointments that oblige us to rethink our original plans.

The director, having spent a considerable amount of time on the project, is very familiar with each facet and knows the location. The audience, on the other hand, are continually finding out what the program is about; interpreting each shot as they see it often with only a moment or two to respond to whatever catches their attention.

The director was not only there at the shoot but has seen each shot on the screen many times: when reviewing the takes, when making editing decisions off-line, during post-production sessions, when assessing the show print or master tape. He or she knows what material was available and what they decided to junk.

The audience is seeing and hearing everything for the first, and probably the only time. They do not know 'what might have been'. They cannot assess opportunities missed. For them, everything is a *fresh impression*.

Our audience only sees as much of a situation as the camera reveals; quite unaware of things that are just a short distance outside the lens' field of view – unless something happens to move into the shot, or the camera's viewpoint changes, or there is a revealing if unexplained noise, from somewhere out of shot. When the camera presents us with impressive shots of a world-famous scene it may carefully avoid including crowding tourists, stalls selling bric-à-brac, waiting coaches . . . A carefully angled shot of a statue can produce a powerful effect on screen but a disappointing reaction when one stands on the spot, and sees its true scale, and its surroundings.

The director has a particular *dis*advantage. Being completely familiar with every moment of the production, it is not possible for the director or the production team to judge with a fresh eye. It might seem to the director that a particular point is so obvious, that only a very brief 'reminder' shot is needed at this moment. It may be decided to leave it out altogether! But for the viewers who are seeing all this for the first time this omission could prove puzzling. They may even misunderstand what is going on as a result!

To simplify the mechanics of production, scenes are often shot in the most convenient or rational order, irrespective of where they come in the final script (*script order*). This will all be sorted out during editing. While it is a very practical solution when shooting, it does have its drawbacks. Not only does 'shooting out of sequence' create continuity problems, but it can make it quite difficult at times to judge subtleties of timing, tempo, pace, inter-scene impact, that the viewer will be experiencing when looking at the final master tape (transmission copy).

Show a big close-up of odd detail without revealing the complete subject from which it comes, and it can leave the audience very puzzled. But the director knows, it obviously comes from that article over there!

You meet the opposite situation too, when a director holds a shot for some time, so that the audience can assimilate all the information in it, when in fact, they have lost interest in it, and their minds have wandered onto other things!

10.4 The problem of quality

When shooting pictures for pleasure you can be philosophical if the odd shot happens to be slightly defocused, or lop-sided, or cuts off part of the subject. It is a pity, but it doesn't really matter too much. You can still enjoy the results.

But when you are making a program for other people, any defects of this kind are quite unacceptable. They will give a production the stamp of carelessness, amateurishness and incompetence, so that it loses its appeal and its authority. Faulty camerawork and poor techniques will not only distract your audience, but can turn even a serious well-thought-out production into a complete farce!

10.5 Elaboration

How you can tackle any program will be directly influenced by your resources (equipment, finance, team-help, their experience, etc.), time, conditions, standards, intended market, and so on. There is no *correct* way to handle any subject, but there are usually a number of *bad* methods.

Suppose you want to discuss the problems of growing a particular crop. You could make an impressive program using special computer graphics, electronic titles, an expert walking through the crops speaking of problems, aerial views of the fields, time-lapse demonstrations, and so on. This would be an extremely expensive, time-consuming treatment requiring many resources.

Alternatively, you could use a very simple yet equally informative approach. The camera could explore a typical field, and show the program title finger-traced in the earth. It could look at typical crop features, with close-ups of specimens. A commentary could provide an explanatory 'voice-over' to pictures. If any additional sounds are required, they could be the natural ones of wind, birdsong, tractors, or whatever, recorded as wild-track at the site.

Elaboration does not necessarily result in greater audience appeal. Sometimes it distracts them from the real subject itself, and draws their attention to the clever techniques instead. It is a great temptation to do it *differently* not because it is better, but because the idea looks fresh and will attract attention. Is a weather forecaster any more informative because he/

she stands out in the rain beneath an umbrella, rather than beside a map in the studio? Some stations have thought so. Or is it an amusing gimmick to hold the audience's attention? Does it do that, or does it *divert* their attention instead?

10.6 Communication can be elusive!

There are no absolute 'rules' when creating a program, but there are quite a lot of well-established guiding principles. These have been discovered through experience. Occasionally you can deliberately ignore such guides, and create an interesting or unusual effect. But take care how you do so, for the audience response may not turn out as you hoped.

The human mind is great at seeing *relationships*, even when there aren't any! We all spend our time *interpreting* the world about us, frequently seeing meanings or significance where there is none.

In an experimental film made up of a random series of close-up stills from magazines' covers, the disjointed fragments of buildings, foliage and objects appeared on the screen as patches of color, progressive patterns and geometric forms. When this film was run at 24 frames a second and accompanied by any music, from Bach to Brubeck, the result was interpreted by the audience as an exciting animation sequence, with the visual theme changing to the beat of the music. Yet in reality there was no theme, no editing (for the film was as shot in the camera, frame by frame). It was all in the minds of the audience!

This example reminds us how frail the process of communication really is. The audience will at times accept and interpret visual/audio garbage, for they assume that it has a valid purpose, even if they cannot themselves understand what this is. We shall discuss this more fully later, with *visual padding* (in Section 11.9).

At other times although we select images and sound carefully, we find that the audience's attention has been taken by some odd irrelevant distraction in the background. They were reading the book titles on a shelf, and not listening to what was being said.

10.7 Begin at the end

Whether your program is a video 'family album', or a lecture on nuclear physics, the essential first step in program making is to think out *who* the program is for, and its chief *purpose*.

Your intended audience should determine your program's coverage and style. It is self-evident that the sort of program you would make for a group of specialist experts would be very different from one made for young children.

The conditions under which your audience is going to watch your program are important too. Most video programs are not made to be broadcast. They are to be viewed in classrooms, offices, factories, community halls, for home study, and so on. So the wise director tries to anticipate these conditions, for they can considerably affect the way he or she presents the program:

- How and where is your audience going to see your program? Will it be a seated group in a darkened classroom, watching a series of mid-sized monitors?
- Perhaps it is to be seen at an open-air meeting in a rural village, on a single monochrome receiver.
- Or it could be for close study by a student at a carrel.

If your program is intended to be seen in daylight it is as well to avoid dark or low-key scenes. The pictures displayed on many receivers/ monitors in daylight leave a lot to be desired. Tonal gradation is coarse, lighter tones block-off, smaller lettering bleeds and may be indecipherable, color is often either paled out or overemphasized. All this is frequently due to incorrect adjustment, as the users try to get the brightest possible picture.

Sound quality too is often poor, due to overload distortion. So keep the sound track simple. Loud background music is liable to distort, while quiet music may not be audible. Reducing the bass can improve the sound's intelligibility. (Listen to the sound quality of drums, thunder and an organ played over a small loudspeaker in the open air, and you will soon get the idea!)

You may need to anticipate the problems for an audience watching a distant picture monitor. Long shots have correspondingly little impact. Closer shots are essential. Small lettering means nothing on a small distant screen. To improve the visibility of titles, charts, maps, etc., keep details basic, and limit the information. White lettering on a black background is clearest, and you should be very cautious about using colored lettering on a colored background. (Try red on blue, or green on yellow, to see how bad the wrong choice can be!)

If your audience is watching on a monochrome monitor, you cannot use color to identify items, or directly demonstrate an effect that relies on color, such as a chemical change. They can only see tonal differences. When faced with this situation, make sure that you have an explanatory commentary, such as: 'You see how this light green solution is beginning to turn dark red ...'. Do not assume that your audience can interpret things for themselves in these circumstances.

Here are a number of reminder questions that can guide you to anticipate your audience's problems:

- Does your program rely on their previously established knowledge? How much do they know about the subject already?
- Does your program relate to others (e.g. in a series)?
- Is your audience going to see the program singly, or in a group?
- Are they watching it once only, from the beginning, or as a continuous repeat replay?
- Can they see the program as often as they want, and stop and replay sections (carrel viewing)?
- Is your program to be watched straight through, or will it be stopped after sections, for discussion?
- Is your program a step-by-step demonstration, in which you show a process which they carry out, or compare your version with theirs?
- Will there be any accompanying paperwork (e.g. map, graphs or statistics) to which your audience can refer? (You cannot expect them to hold detailed data in their heads, as they follow the program's argument.)
- Where possible, try to relate your program to the world of your particular audience, Is it likely to appear strangely foreign, abstract, too academic, too parochial, etc?
- Will there be other competing, noisy attractions as they watch, e.g. at an exhibition?
- Will your program soon be out of date? (Does this matter?)
- Is the program for a very formal occasion, or will a certain amount of careful humor sweeten the pill?

10.8 Develop a system

Great ideas are not enough. Ideas have to be worked out in realistic, practical terms. They have to be expressed as pictures and sound. In the end, you have to decide what the camera is going to shoot, and what your audience is going to hear. Where do you start?

Broadly speaking, you can approach program-making in two quite different ways:

- the *empirical* method, in which instinct and opportunity are your guides.
- the *planned* method, which organizes and builds up a program, in carefully arranged steps.

10.9 The empirical approach

Directors following the empirical approach get an idea, then look around for subjects and situations that relate to it. After shooting likely material, they later create a program from whatever they have found. Their inspiration springs from the opportunities that have arisen.

Let's suppose you are going to make a program about 'Safety at Sea'. Using the empirical approach, you might go along to a marina, and develop a production based on the stories you hear there. Or you could discuss the idea with coast-guards or life-guards, and find yourself following another train of thought. Again, visiting some commercial docks, you might discover material there of an entirely different kind.

After accumulating a collection of interesting sequences (atmospheric shots, wild track, interviews, etc.), you check through these, and get them into a meaningful order. Having done so, you then prepare a program that fits this material, probably writing a commentary as a 'voice-over' to match the edited pictures.

At *best*, this approach is fresh, uninhibited, improvises, makes use of the unexpected, avoids rigid discipline, and is very adaptable. Shots are interestingly varied. The audience is kept alert, watching and interpreting the changing scene.

At *worst*, the result of such shot-hunting is a haphazard ragbag, with little cohesion or sense of purpose. Because the approach is unsystematic, gaps and overlaps abound. Good coherent editing may be difficult. Opportunities may have been missed. The director often relies heavily on a commentary-over (perhaps with music) to try to provide any sort of relationship and continuity between the pictures.

10.10 The planned approach

This method of production, tackles the problem quite differently, although the results on the screen may be similar.

Here the director works out in advance, the exact form he or she wants the program to take, and organizes accordingly.

Fundamentally, you can either

- Begin with the environment or setting, and decide on how you can position cameras to get effective shots,

or you can

- Envision certain shots or effects you want to see, and create a setting that will provide those results.

A lot will depend too, on whether you are:

- *Interpreting an existing script* (as in drama). This will involve analyzing the script; examining the story-line and the main action in each scene, and visualizing individual shots.

or

- *Building up a treatment framework*. Considering how you are going to present a particular program subject (as in Section 10.18), and working out the kinds of shots you want.

At *best*, the planned approach is a method in which a team can be coordinated to give their best. There is a sense of systematic purpose throughout the project. Problems are largely ironed out before they develop. Production is sensibly related to what is feasible. The program can have a smooth-flowing, carefully thought-out, persuasive style.

At *worst*, the production becomes bogged down in organization. The program is stodgy and routine, and lacks any spark of originality. Opportunities are ignored because they were not part of the original scheme, and would modify it. The result may even be hack work.

In practice, of course, the experienced program-maker uses a combination of the 'planned' and the 'empirical' approaches; starts off with a plan of campaign, and takes extra opportunities as they offer themselves.

10.11 Storyboards

As you run through each scene in your mind, you can capture these imaginings, and turn them into practical program making, by preparing a *storyboard* as you go.

The storyboard is simply a series of rough sketches, that help you to visualize and to organize your camera treatment. It shows how you hope to arrange the *key shots* for each scene or action sequence.

You will find it a valuable aid, whether you are going to shoot action:

- Continuously, from start to finish.
- In sections or scenes, i.e. one complete action sequence at a time.
- Or as a series of separate shots or 'action segments', each showing a part of the sequence.

To begin, draw a grid of 40 mm by 30 mm frames. Now start to imagine your way through the first scene, roughly sketching the composition for each shot in turn. You don't have to be able to draw well to produce a successful storyboard. Even the crudest scribbles can help you to marshal your thoughts, and show other people what you are aiming at. If the action is complicated, you might need a couple of frames to show how a shot develops. In our example, the whole scene is summarized in just five frames.

Let's look at a very simple story line, to see how the storyboard provides you with imaginative opportunities.

The child has been sent to buy her first postage stamp.

There are dozens of ways to shoot this brief sequence.

You could simply follow her all the way from her home, watching as she crosses the road, enters the post office, goes up to the counter . . .

The result would be totally boring!

1

2

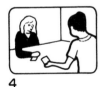

3

4

5

Figure 10.1 Analyzing action
When edited together, a sequence looks obvious and natural. But even a simple scene showing a child buying a stamp needs to be thought through. Note how shots 1 and 3 are taken on one side of the counter, and shots 2, 4, 5 on the other.

Let's think again. We know from the previous scene where she is going and why. All we really want to register, are her reactions as she buys the stamp. So let's cut out all the superfluous footage, and concentrate on that moment.

1 *The child arrives at the counter, and looks up at the clerk.*
2 *Hesitatingly, she asks for the stamp.*
3 *She opens her fingers, to release the money she has been clutching so carefully all the way from home.*
4 *The clerk smiles and takes the money.*
5 *A close shot of the clerk tearing the stamp from a sheet.*

You now have a sequence of shots, far more interesting than a continuous 'follow-shot'. It stimulates the imagination. It guides the audience's thought processes. It has a greater overall impact.

However, if this type of treatment is carried out badly, the effect can look very disjointed, contrived, posed, 'bitty', or mannered. It is essential that your treatment matches the style and theme of the subject.

You could have built up the whole sequence with dramatic camera angles, strong music and effects. But would it have been *appropriate*? If the audience knows that a bomb is ticking away in a parcel beneath the counter . . . it might have been. It is all too easy to over-dramatize, or 'pretty-up' a situation (e.g. star filters producing multi-ray patterns around highlights, diffusion filters for misty effects). Resist the temptation, and keep them for the right occasion!

This breakdown has not only helped you to visualize the picture treatment. You begin to think about how one shot is going to lead into the next. You start to face practicalities. You see for example that shots 1 and 3 are taken from the front of the counter, and shots 2, 4 and 5 need to be taken from behind it. Obviously, the most logical approach is to shoot the sequence *out of order*. Your storyboard becomes a shooting plan.

To practice 'storyboarding', videotape a broadcast motion picture off-air, and check through it carefully, making a sketch of each key shot. This way, you will soon get into the habit of thinking in picture sequences, rather than in isolated shots.

10.12 Why plan?

Some people find the idea of planning very inhibiting. They want to get on with the job. For them, planning, somehow turns the thrill of the unexpected into an organized commitment.

But many situations *must* be planned and worked out in advance. You will need for instance, to get permission to shoot on private premises, to make appointments to interview people, to arrange admissions, etc. You might occasionally have success if you arrive unannounced, but do not assume this. Other material turns up quite unexpectedly, or is quite impromptu, and you need to make the most of any opportunity. After all, you can always reject the result during editing, if it proves unsuitable.

10.13 Thinking it out

Most programs go through three main stages:

1 *Pre-production.* The preliminaries, preparation and organization beforehand.
2 *Production.* Rehearsals and shooting.
3 *Post-production.* Editing, additional treatment and duplication.

The amount of work entailed at each stage will be influenced by the nature of your subject. One that involves a series of straightforward 'personality' interviews must be a lot easier to organize than one on Arctic exploration, or an historical drama. But in the end, a great deal depends on how you decide to approach the subject.

Working to the highest standards, you can provide extremely stimulating programs using simple methods. Treatment does not have to be elaborate to make its point. If someone in the desert picks up his/her water bottle, finds it empty, and the camera shows a patch of damp sand where it rested, the shot has told us a great deal without any need for elaboration. A single look or a gesture can often have a far stronger impact than lengthy dialogue purporting to show how two people feel about each other.

It is important to realize right from the beginning, that it is largely in your own hands how difficult and complex a production becomes. Some ideas seem simple enough, but can be difficult or impossible to carry out.

Others look very difficult or impracticable, but are easily achieved on the screen.

For example:

'Let's zoom in to an extreme close-up'. (Impossible because the minimum lens angle only provides a chest-shot at this distance.)

'Make her vanish!' (Simple. Keep the camera still, have her exit and edit out the walk.)

10.14 Start with an idea

It is very unlikely that you will suddenly decide, out of the blue, to make a video program on a particular subject, such as 'building a wall'. Something has triggered the idea. Perhaps you realized that it could help a class you are teaching. Or a local store has asked you to make it to aid sales to the home handyman. Here is the starting point.

You know the *subject* to be covered (in principle at least), what the program is to be *used* for, and *who* the program is for.

The next question might reasonably be: '*How long* is it to run?' There is no point in settling down to a two-hour epic, if the client wants a two-minute repeat-cycle demonstration.

Consider how your audience is going to relate to your program. If it is one of a series, you obviously do not want to go over the same ground again unless it requires revision, or they may not see the other video.

10.15 Coverage

What do you want to cover in the available time? Or perhaps we should say, how much is it *reasonable* to cover in that time. If you have too many topics, it will not be possible to do justice to any of them. If you have too few, the program can seem slow, labored and padded out.

There is nothing to be gained by packing the program full of high-speed facts, for although they may sound impressive, your audience is unlikely to remember more than a fraction of them. Unlike the printed page, the viewer cannot refer back to check an item, unless the tape can be stopped and rewound when necessary, or is frequently repeated.

In most cases, it is a good general principle to structure a program, so that it has:

- An *introduction*, indicating what the program is to be about, also perhaps, its aim or who it is for.
- The *development*, i.e. the body of the program.
- A *conclusion*, summing up, perhaps reminding the audience of the main points, possibly referring them on to a further program in a series.

10.16 Building an outline

Now you can start to prepare the program outline. This begins with a series of *headings* showing the main themes you are going to discuss.

In the case of our 'building a wall' program, these might cover topics such as tools needed, materials, foundation, making mortar, method of laying bricks and pointing.

You now have to get a rough idea of how much program time you can devote to each section. Some will be brief, others relatively lengthy. You will no doubt emphasize some, and skip over others, to suit the purpose of the program.

The next stage is to take each of these topic headings, and note down the various aspects you want to cover there, as a series of *sub-headings*. Under 'tools', for instance, you would list those you need to demonstrate.

Now you have a structure for the program, and can begin to see the form it is likely to take.

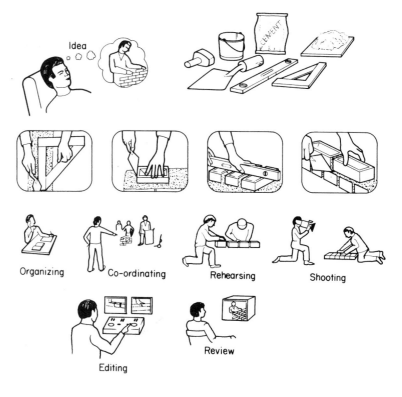

Figure 10.2 From ideas to finished shots
A reminder of the stages that a program has to go through, from the original idea, to the end product.

10.17 Broad treatment

Next in your planning process, you will be deciding how you are going to approach each of the sub-headings in your outline. Remember, you are still thinking things through. At this stage, you might decide to alter an idea, develop it, shorten it, or even drop it altogether.

It is a question and answer process. Let's imagine the situation:

What is the topic, and what is its purpose?

It is discussing 'animal hibernation in winter'.

How will you approach it?

It would be nice to show a bear preparing its den for hibernation, and settling down . . . show the hard winter weather with the animal asleep. . . . and later, waking up in the spring and foraging. All with a commentary over.

A good idea, but where are the pictures coming from?

Do you have any?

Are you using a film library's services?

Do they have that sort of material?

We could not afford that. It has to be a cheaper method. Perhaps we should forget it.

You could have an illustrated discussion, or a commentary, over still photographs and drawings (graphics, artwork).

That could be boring; like a slide show.

Not necessarily, for you can explore the still pictures with your camera, giving them a certain amount of movement. The secret is to keep the shots very brief, and to add sound effects and perhaps music. Supposing for instance, you had a still of a bear standing on its hind legs. Shooting its upper half, you turn the picture quickly, and create the impression that it has lurched forward. Pan towards a head, and it pushes into the frame. A series of intercut shots can look highly dramatic . . . if that's the effect you want. Anyway you could include some video of bears.

Where would we get these various pictures of the bear?

Stills could come from books (with permission). And you could shoot video in a zoo, or a museum.

. . . and so it goes on.

Note how each decision leads to another development. If you decide on the zoo, you then have to follow up how, when and where you are going to get these shots. If you prefer to use the museum specimen, does it have to be lit? Are there glass reflection problems? Can you get the viewpoint needed?

You may not be able to decide at this point, but will have to do some *research*, to see how feasible that particular idea is.

10.18 Finding out

There are, in fact, several stages during the creation of a program when you will probably need more information before you can go on to the next step.

Checklist 10.1 Typical research information

Lists can be very daunting, but here are reminders of typical areas you may need to look into, in the course of planning your production.

The idea

The exploratory process:
- Finding sources of information on the subject (people, books, publications).
- Arranging to consult these.
- Accumulating data.
- Selecting matter that is relevant to your idea.
- Who is your program for?
- What is the purpose of the program?
- Does it have to relate to existing program? (level; standards?)
- How long is it to run?
- Coordinating ideas into an outline, with headings, subheadings.
- Considering the program development, forming a rough script, or shooting script.

Practicality

Let's think about your ideas in practical terms:
- What will you actually want to see and hear at each point in the program?
- Where will you shoot the action?
- What sort of things do you expect to need for each sequence (e.g. items, furnishings)?
- How do you think of arranging the scene? (Action in broad outline.)
- Do you want any particular effects?
- Are other people involved (e.g. demonstrator, actor)? Do you know suitable people?

The mechanics

What you need to shoot the program:
- Are you using a single camera? Consider the ways you will shoot the action (shot breakdown; sound or mute, editing).
- If you are using more than one camera, consider the equipment needed for the treatment you anticipate (including post-production work).
- Do you need to make, hire or buy any production items (e.g. graphics, furniture)?

Feasibility

Check what is really involved:
- Are the ideas and treatment you are developing, reasonable ones for your resources?
- Is there another way of achieving similar results more easily, more cheaply, more quickly, with less labor?
- Can you really get the items you need?
- Will you be able to get to the location?
- Is there sufficient time (to do research; carry out schedule, etc.)?

Costs:
- What is your budget?
- You may need to research possible costs for a sequence, before including it in your production.
- Can you get advance payments for expenses?
- Do you have to pay in advance for services, purchases?

Assistance:
- Will you need assistance, manpower, expert aid or advice, extra transport, etc., to do the job?
- What talent is involved? (amateur, professional, casual?)
- Do you need professional services? (to make items, service, prepare graphics, etc.)

Facilities
- Are your available facilities sufficient for the shooting anticipated, and post-production work?
- Will you need to augment them?
- Will you need to borrow, hire, buy, adapt?

Problems:
- Try to anticipate any major problems such as whether a sequence can still be shot if the weather deteriorates.

- Is there any obvious danger factor (e.g. shooting a cliff-climb)?
- Will the situation you need for the program be available at the time you are shooting (e.g. snow in summer)?

Time:
- Will there be sufficient time to shoot the sequence?
- Prepare for eventualities. Instead of taking a couple of hours to shoot, it might take two days with an overnight stay, if things go wrong (high wind, rain, noise, etc.).

Administration

Various business arrangements and agreements:
- Permission to shoot, passes, permits, fees, etc.
- Copyright clearances, if you are using music, copying photographs, etc.
- Insurance may be necessary, to cover losses, breakages, injury, etc.
- There may be union agreements, and so *ad infinitum*.

Hiring

You might need to consider:
- Contractual arrangements for hiring performers,
- Operators, equipment, transport, scenery,
- Properties, costumes, services (e.g. editing suite, tape duplication), etc., etc.

Organizing

Another broad area, including such things as:
- Arranging transport, accommodation, food, storage.
- Return of borrowed/hired items.
- As you build up the program, you draw up a shooting diary, that helps you to avoid overlapped appointments, or wasted periods.

Remote survey (the 'recce')

The preliminary survey of the site of a location:
- Checking out the local conditions, anticipating any problems.
- Local organization.
- See Checklist 10.2 for details.

Your 'research' might amount to nothing more than hearing that Uncle David has a friend who has a stuffed bear that he would lend you for your program. You discover extra opportunities and problems as you search. They could even alter the way you eventually decide to treat the subject. You might encounter an enthusiast who can supply you with enough material to fill a dozen programs on the subject, or you might have to scout around for crumbs here and there.

As you work through the production process, you will find various areas in which you want information, or have to make special arrangements. In Checklist 10.1, you will find a very general indication of the sorts of things you might need to enquire into, although these can vary considerably with the nature of the production.

10.19 Remote surveys (the 'recce')

Fundamentally, there are two sorts of conditions under which you will be shooting: at *base* and away *on location*.

Your *base* is wherever you are normally centered, and shoot indoor work. It may be a studio, classroom, hall or a room. The sort of material you are likely to shoot at base includes 'formal' interviews, announcements to camera, table-top work, graphics, titles, etc., and perhaps demonstrations, musical items and talks.

You use your base all the time, so you know exactly what facilities are available (e.g. equipment, supplies and scenery), where things are, the amount of room free, and so on. If you need to supplement what is there, you can easily do so. (*Continued on page 200*)

Checklist 10.2 The remote survey ('recce')

How much detail you need about a location site, varies with the nature of your production. Information that may seem trivial at the time, can prove valuable later in guiding others.

Location sites can be interiors, under-cover exteriors or open-air sites. Each has its own problems.

Useful 'tools' for the visit

Note-pads, pens, maps (route, local), compass, measure, photo-camera (Polaroid), video camera/VCR for site check, light meter, stopwatch, flashlight, small audio recorder with mike, string, gaffer tape, protective clothing, radio intercom.

Sketches

- Prepare rough maps of route to site (include distance, travel time).
- Show position of location.
- Rough layout of site (e.g. room plan).
- Anticipated camera viewpoints.

Local conditions

- Contact local people for information and advice on the site, local conditions, etc. Their guidance can be invaluable.
- Are there any known local problems relative to the tide, wind, animals, low-flying aircraft?
- Is there easy access to site? At any time, or at certain times only?
- Any traffic problems? Do the public have access to site? Are crowds likely during shooting?
- On the shooting date, will it be market day, early closing, carnival, parade, etc.?
- Any obvious problems in shooting there? Dangerous? Protective clothing needed? OK if raining?

Selected viewpoints

- Check around location for best/most appropriate viewpoints.
- Are these what you want? Are they optimum positions? Is the required range of shots possible from them?
- Are the positions easy to reach, and safe to use? (Any precautions needed, e.g. rope, scaffolding?)
- Will the camera mounting be safe there? (stable, unlikely to move or fall?)
- Any obstructions? Any obvious distractions (e.g. large signs, reflections)?
- Are the viewpoints spread around? Easy access between them (e.g. top and bottom of a cliff)?

Other people on site

- Is anyone else using or working on site during scheduled shooting (e.g. people walking through, working, sightseeing)?
- Are people using equipment on or near site during shooting (e.g. machinery, lorries, excavators, fairground, tree felling, airfield)?

Aid needed

- Do you need assistance from site custodian, electrician, engineer, security?
- Local transport needed (e.g. truck, horses, boatman)?
- Are local police required (crowds), or fire services needed on call?
- Local addresses and phone numbers for police, fire, hospital, doctor, hotel, restaurant?
- Ensure anyone assisting you knows necessary details of when/where you are shooting.
- Are you shooting an event arranged by others (e.g. parade, ceremony, display)? If so, get their guidance about shot selection, times, durations, routes, etc. Will there be any rehearsals you could attend?

Permission needed

- Is site access restricted? Do you need to get permission (or keys) to enter site? From whom?
- Any parking problems? (Where to park?)
- Any payments, fees, gratuities involved? Any insurance needed (against damage or injury)?

Intrusions	• Do you need to take care in which direction you are shooting (distractions, anachronisms)? • Is the public likely to get into shot or prove an embarrassment (as passers-by or spectators, chatter, litter)? • Any animals wandering nearby (e.g. cattle, sheep, horses)? • Will you be creating hazards for other people (e.g. cables, equipment)? • Are there any possibilities of interference from high-power radar, strong magnetic fields, heat, medical equipment, etc.?
Lighting	• Will you be shooting in daylight? How will the light change throughout the day? (How will sun direction change? Is tonal contrast OK? Are light levels likely to be OK? Any deep shadows? Are you augmenting daylight with reflectors, or punch lights?) • Will you be shooting in artificial light? (theirs, yours or mixed?) Will they be on at the time you are shooting? • If you are lighting the scene, are appropriate supplies available nearby? • Estimate number of lamps, positions, power needed, supplies, cabling required (and its routing), and safety considerations. • Who is transporting, rigging, cabling, supplying lighting equipment? (local hire?) Does equipment need manning (e.g. following with reflector or spotlight)?
Sound	• Consider method of sound pick-up. • Any potential problems with acoustics, sound carrying, strong wind rumble? • Any extraneous sounds (elevators, phones, typewriters, machinery, children, aircraft, seagulls, plowing, etc.)? • Any playback needed (e.g. music for miming in sync with a recorded song)?
Wind and weather	• Alternative positions/locations if weather is bad? (shelter available?)
Continuity	• Do the light or weather conditions for the scenes shot on this site relate to material shot elsewhere (e.g. a studio interior setting)?
Set dressing	• Do any items need to be brought to the site to augment what is there, or alter its appearance (signs, graphics, posters, props, drapes)?
Time	• Consider the time taken for travel, setting up the unit, arranging camera/lights/sound/scenery. • Consider time and effort involved in moving from one camera viewpoint to another. • Consider the difficulty of shots or action, and possible time involved in retakes if they do not work.
Cueing	• Consider methods and problems of cueing action to start (e.g. when someone should enter a room). • Any arrangements needed, for lighting operator to switch lights on cue? • Any radio intercom needed?
Staffing/labor	• Consider labor requirements; especially if action is spread around a site.
Welfare	• Transport for performers and staff. • Feeding arrangements? • Accommodation needed (where, when, how many)? • Washing and personal comfort? • First aid arrangements?
Security	• Consider arrangements for security (e.g. personal items, equipment, props, etc.).
Travel arrangements	• Personnel, baggage, equipment.

A location, on the other hand, is anywhere away from your center. It may just be outside the building, or way out in the country. It could be in any sort of vehicle, down a mine, or in someone's home. 'Location' is a good broad catch-all term.

The main thing about shooting away from base is to find out what you are in for beforehand. You could simply arrive hopefully, and not have a single problem. But it is a lot better to be prepared!

The preliminary visit to any location (remote survey; site survey; location survey; 'recce'/reconnaissance) is an essential bit of program preparation. In practice, it can become anything from a quick look around, to a detailed survey of the site. What you find there may (probably will) influence the production treatment you have in mind.

In Checklist 10.2, you will find typical items you may need to check out, in preparation for your shooting schedule.

10.20 Developing the contents

To recap, we now have:

- The *main* subject of the program.
- An outline with *headings* of topics to be covered.
- Under each heading, we have *sub-headings* guiding us to the features we are going to discuss.
- Finally, we checked out whether these ideas are viable.

Do not regard this 'weeding out' process as one that stifles the imagination. It is a way of avoiding wasting time and money on profitless effort; a way of keeping one's feet firmly on the ground.

Now you are reaching the stage at which you should be thinking about how you are going to present these ideas.

At one point perhaps, you want someone to show a series of objects and pictures to the camera. How do you do this?

He could have them on his desk, and hold them up to the camera, one at a time. But wouldn't that be boring?

It might be. To some extent, it depends on his manner. If he is condescending, or lectures us, or goes through them mechanically, it certainly would be. But if he shows enthusiasm, and reveals them to us one by one, rather like bran-tub 'goodies', the result could be really interesting, in spite of the simplicity of the presentation.

However, to create visual variety, let's assume that he gets up from the desk and goes over to show us a picture on the wall. It is of a group of polar bears on an ice floe, and below the picture on a side-table is a carved group, and so on.

That's fine for the moment. It is beginning to sound like part of a script. The treatment seems quite *practicable*. A desk and side-table will be easy to get, and there was a picture in the book we looked up the other day...

Of course, you might well find that the first idea you have for a sequence is obviously *impracticable*.

Supposing your program includes a scene from a moment in history. It's easy to be ambitious, but the scene only lasts for about a minute. It tells how a raging mob besieges a house, battering at the door, throwing rocks ... Hardly the sort of thing one can tackle on a low budget! Isn't it out of the question?

Why not approach the scene *indirectly*? What if we watched the terrified expression of the person in the house, the camera getting closer and closer until the screen is filled by a single eye with a falling tear, as the noises of the mob, and the pounding (effects discs) echo louder and louder in his/her head? A commentary over sets the scene. Whether the result is poignant or corny, is up to you.

10.21 Freedom to plan

In practice, how far can you plan a production, depends on how much control you have of the situation. If you are shooting a public event, your planning may consist of finding out what is going on, deciding on the best visual opportunities, selecting viewpoints, etc. You'll have little or no opportunity to adjust events to suit your productional ideas.

If on the other hand, the situation is entirely under your control, you can arrange matters to suit your particular needs. Having rationalized your ideas, you then have to organize the contributory elements of the production, and explain your ideas to other people who are involved.

Single camera shooting. When you are shooting with a *single camera*, you will usually find yourself in one of two situations:

- *Planning in principle, and shooting as opportunity allows.* For example, you intend taking shots of local wildlife; but what you actually shoot, must depend on what you find when you get there.
- *Detailed analysis and shot planning.* This approach is widely used in film making. Here you examine the action in a scene, and break it down into separate shots. Each shot is rehearsed and recorded independently. Where action is continuous throughout several shots, it is *repeated* for each camera viewpoint.

  Shot 1. Long shot: an actor walks away from camera, towards a wall mirror.
  Shot 2. Mid shot: he repeats the action, approaching the camera located beside the mirror.
  Shot 3. Close shot: he repeats the walk as the camera shoots into the mirror watching his expression as he approaches.

When edited together, the action is to appear continuous. So it's essential to keep the continuity of shots in mind throughout.

It is regular practice to record the complete action in long shot, then take close shots separately. These can then be relit for maximum effect. Even when a person is supposedly speaking to someone else, it is quite usual to have them alone, repeating a speech to camera, to allow the camera to be placed in the best position.

Multi-camera shooting. When shooting with two or more cameras, a director tends to think in terms of *effective viewpoints* rather than specific shots. The results may be similar, but the strategy is different, for cameras have to be positioned to catch various aspects of continuous action.

When planning a multi-camera show, the director has to consider various mechanics, including:

- Whether one camera will come into another's shot.
- Whether there is time for cameras to move to various positions.
- The variety of shots possible in different cameras.
- Whether a camera needs to be released to move over to another setting.
- How the sound boom, lighting, etc., relate to the camera's movements.

It all becomes a lot simpler of course, if you record the program as a series of brief sequences (which are edited together afterwards), but that takes much longer.

Writing the script

10.22 The script's purpose

Most of us prefer to avoid unnecessary paperwork. If you are working entirely by yourself, you might possibly get away with a few notes on the back of an envelope. But planning is an essential part of serious production, and the script forms the basis for that plan.

- it helps the director to clarify ideas, and to develop a project that will work.
- It helps to coordinate the production team.
- It helps them to assess the resources needed.

Although you will meet professional crews on location (at a news event for instance) who appear to be shooting entirely spontaneously, they are invariably working to a pattern that has proved successful in the past.

For certain types of production, such as a drama, the script actually *begins* the production process. The director reads the draft script, which contains general information on characters, locations, stage directions, and all the dialogue. He/she envisions the scenes, assesses possible treatment, while anticipating the script's opportunities and potential problems. At this stage, changes may be made to improve the script, or make it more practicable. Next the director goes on to prepare a camera-treatment.

Another method of scripting begins with an *outline*. Here you decide on the various topics you want to cover, and the amount of time you can allot to each. You then develop a script based on this outline, and decide on the camera treatment for each part in turn.

When preparing a documentary, an extended outline becomes a *shooting script*, showing the location unit details of typical shots required. It may include any on-the-spot dialogue to be delivered to camera. All other dialogue (commentary) is developed later, together with effects and music, to suit the edited program.

10.23 Is a script needed?

The form of script you use will largely depend on the kind of program you are making. There will be situations, particularly where talent are extemporizing as they speak or perform, when the 'script' simply lists details of the productional group, facilities needed, scheduling, and shows basic camera positions, etc.

An *outline script* will include any prepared dialogue (e.g. opening and closing announcements). Where people are going to improvize, the script may just list the order of topics to be covered. (These may be written on a *cue board/cue sheet* and presented to them as reminders while they are speaking.)

If it is a multi-item program, then a *breakdown sheet/show format/running order** will prove useful. This lists the program segments (scenes), showing:

*Often wrongly called a *rundown sheet* – the term for a 'fact sheet' which summarizes information about a product or item for a demonstration program; details of a guest for an interviewer.

Table 10.1 Breakdown sheet/running order/show format

This lists the items or program segments in a show, in the order they are to be shot. It may show durations, who is participating, shot numbers, etc.

Example:

	CARING FOR THE ELDERLY	Total duration 15 min
1.	OPENING TITLES & MUSIC	00:10
2.	PROGRAM INTRO.	00:30
3.	PROBLEMS OF MOBILITY	02:20
4.	INJURIES	02:15
5.	DIET	02:45
6.	DAILY ACTIVITIES	03:40
7.	EXERCISES	01:20
8.	AIDS & GADGETS	01:15
9.	CLOSING LINK	00:25
10.	END TITLES	00:10
		15:00

- The *topic* (e.g. guitar solo).
- The amount of *time* allowed for each time – essential in a live multi-contribution show.
- The *names* of talent involved.
- *Facilities* – cameras and audio pick-up allocated.
- *Contributory sources* – details of any videotape or film inserts, etc. Where various items are already recorded on tape or film to be inserted into the program, the script will usually show the opening and closing words of each contribution (*in-words, out-words*) and its duration. This assists accurate cueing.

10.24 Basic script formats

Basically, script layout takes two forms:

- a single-column format,
- a two-column format.

Single-column or *filmic format*. In this arrangement, all video and audio information is contained in a single main column. Before each scene, an explanatory introduction describes the location and the action.

You can make any reminder notes in a wide left-hand margin, including transition symbols (e.g. X=Cut; FU=fade-up; SUPER 2=superimpose Cam.2.), indicate cues, camera instructions, make thumbnail sketches of shots or action, etc.

This type of script is widely used for film production, and single-camera video, where the director works alongside the camera operator. It is perhaps less useful in a multi-camera set-up, where the production team is more dispersed, everyone needing to know the director's intentions throughout.

Two-column format. This traditional TV format is extremely flexible and informative. It gives all members of the production team shot-by-shot

SINGLE COLUMN FORMAT

SINGLE CAMERA SHOOTING SCRIPT

FADE IN:

1. EXT: FRONT OF FARMHOUSE – DAY

    Front door opens. FARMER comes out, walks up to gate.
    Looks left and right along road.

2. EXT: LONG SHOT OF ROAD OUTSIDE FARM (Looking east) – DAY

    POV shot of FARMER looking along road, waiting for car.

3. EXT: FARM GATE – DAY

    Waist shot of farmer leaning over gate, looking anxiously.
    He turns to house,
    calling.

        FARMER:
        I can't see him. If he doesn't come soon, I'll be late.

4. INT: FARMHOUSE KITCHEN – DAY

    Wife is collecting breakfast things. Sound of radio.

        WIFE:
        You're too impatient. There's plenty of time.

5. EXT: FARM GATE – DAY

    Mid-shot of FARMER, same position. He looks in other direction.
    Sound of distant car approaching. Sudden bang, then silence.

    Etc.

TWO-COLUMN FORMAT

MULTI-CAMERA SHOOTING SCRIPT

SHOT	CAM (Position)	SCENE / ACTION / AUDIO
CAMS:	1B, 2D, 3A	SOUND: SMALL BOOM B

SCENE 4.   INT. BARN – NIGHT

15.	F/U 2 D L/S DOORWAY Zoom in to WS as FARMER enters	(FARMER ENTERS, HANGS LAMP ON WALL-HOOK BESIDE DOOR) FARMER: It's getting late. How is the poor beast doing?/	TAPE 7:WIND DISC 5:RAIN
16.	1 B O/S SHOT SON'S POV	SON: I don't think she'll last the night. She has a high fever./	
17.	3 A LS FARMER He comes into WS	(FARMER WALKS FORWARD TO THE STALL) FARMER: I called Willie. He's on his way. (FARMER KNEELS BESIDE COW)/ DISC 9:THUNDER	
18.	2 D CU SON	SON: D'you think he'll be able to get here?/	
19.	1 C CU FARMER	FARMER: If the bridge holds. But the river's still rising/	

Etc.
....

Abbreviations used:

F/U	Fade up	CU	Close-up
O/S	Over shoulder	WS	Waist shot
POV	Point of view	LS	Long shot
___/	Indicates point to 'cut to next shot'		

details of what is going on. They can also add their own particular information (e.g. details of lighting changes) as they need.

Two versions of the script are usually prepared. In the first (*rehearsal script*) the right-hand column only is printed. Subsequently, after detailed planning and pre-studio rehearsals, all production details are added to the left-hand column, to form the *camera script*.

10.25 The full script

When a program is fully scripted, it includes detailed information on all aspects of the production.

- *Scenes*. Most productions are divided into a series of *scenes*. Each covers a *complete continuous action sequence* and is identified with a number and location (e.g. Scene 3 – Office set). A scene can involve anything from an interview, to a dance routine, a song, or a demonstration sequence.
- *Shots*. When the director has decided how he or she is going to interpret the script, each scene will be sub-divided into a series of *shots*; each showing the action from a particular viewpoint. These shots are numbered consecutively for easy reference, in the order in which they will be screened.

In a live show, you shoot in the scripted order (*running order*). When taping a production, you can shoot in whatever order is most convenient (*shooting order*). You may decide to omit shots ('drop Shot 25'), or to add extra shots (Shots 24A, 24B, etc.). You may record Shot 50 before Shot 1, and edit them into running order later.

- *Dialogue*. The entire prepared dialogue; spoken to camera, or between people. (They may learn it, or read it off prompters of some kind.)
- *Equipment*. The script indicates which camera/microphone is being used for each shot (e.g. *Cam. 2. Fishpole*).
- *Basic camera instructions*. Details of each shot and camera moves (e.g. *Cam. 1 close shot on Joe's hand; dolly out to long shot.*)
- Switcher (*vision mixer*) *instructions* – i.e. cut, mix, superimpose Cam. 2.
- *Contributory sources*. Details of where videotape and film inserts, graphics, remotes, etc., appear in the program.

10.26 The drama script

Although a drama script too follows this arrangement, many organizations prepare the full script in two stages; the *rehearsal script* and the *camera script*.

The rehearsal script. This begins with general information sheets, including a cast/character list, production team details, rehearsal arrangements, etc.

There may be a synopsis of the plot or story line; particularly when scenes are to be shot/recorded out of order.

The rehearsal script includes full details of:

- Location – The setting (e.g. Lounge).
- *Time of day, and weather conditions* – Night, storm.
- *Stage instructions* – The room is candlelit, and the log fire burns brightly.
- *Action* – Basic information on what is going to happen in the scene (i.e. actors' moves, business (Joe lights a cigar.))

- *Dialogue* – speaker's name (character) followed by their dialogue. All delivered speech, voice over, voice inserts (e.g. phone conversation), commentary, announcements, etc. (Perhaps with comments; e.g. 'sadly', 'sarcastically'.)
- *Cues/effects* – Indicating the moment for a change to take place (e.g. lightning flash, explosion, Joe switches light out).
- *Audio instructions* – Music and effects.
- Information on titling, video effects, other contributory sources, etc.

The camera script. This is built up by adding full details of the production treatment to the left side of the 'rehearsal script', and includes:

- The shot number.
- The camera used for that shot.
- The position of that camera on the set (optional).
- Basic shot details and camera moves (e.g. CU on Joe. Dolly back to LS as he rises).
- Switcher instructions (e.g. cut, slow mix, superimpose Cam 2. etc.).

10.27 Hints on script-writing

There are no short cuts to good script-writing, any more than there are to writing short stories, music or painting a picture. You will learn techniques through observation, experience and reading. But there are general guides that are worth bearing in mind as you prepare your script. You will find a useful list on pages 207–209 (Hints on developing the script).

10.28 Be visual

Aim to present your material in visual terms as far as possible. Where you want your audience to concentrate on what they are hearing, try to make the picture less demanding at that point. If for instance, they are listening to a detailed argument, and trying to read a screenful of statistics at the same time, they may well do neither successfully. Your picture can strengthen or emphasize what they are hearing.

Programs vary in the way they distribute audience interest between the sound and the picture. A show may be mainly visual, with comparatively few words to script. Or conversely, it may rely almost entirely on what is being said, while the pictures are little more than an interesting accompaniment. There are even programs in which either the pictures or the sound are virtually unnecessary!

There will be times when you may find it hard to decide on any relevant picture to accompany the all-important sound, and then you may need to resort to a certain amount of improvised 'visual padding'! (See Section 11.9.)

10.29 Assimilation rate

Whatever type of program you are preparing, aim to develop it as a smooth-flowing sequence, making one point at a time. Avoid those tempting diversions that keep leading your audience well away from the main theme. As far as possible, try not to hop back and forth between one subject and another. Especially, you should avoid the three-ring circus effect, in which you are trying to cover several different activities simultaneously. Ideally, one sequence should seem to lead naturally on to the next. *(Continued on page 210)*

Hints on developing the script

How you set about developing a script will vary with the type of program and the way individual directors work. The techniques and processes of good script writing are a study in themselves, but we can take a look at some of the guiding principles and typical points you will need to consider.

The nature of the script

- *The script may form the basis of the entire production treatment.*
  Here the production is staged, performed, and shot as indicated in the script.
  As far as possible, dialogue and action follow the scripted version.
- *The scriptwriter may prepare a draft script (i.e. a suggested treatment).*
  This is studied and developed by the director, to form a shooting script.
- *The script may be written after material has been shot.*
  Certain programs such as documentaries may be shot to a preconceived outline plan, but the final material will largely depend on the opportunities of the moment. The script is written to blend this material together in a coherent story line, adding explanatory commentary/dialogue. Subsequent editing and post-production work is based on this scripted version.
- *The script may be written after material has been edited.*
  Here the videotape editor assembles the shot material, creating continuity, and a basis for a story line. The script is developed to suit the edited version.

Occasionally, the new script is replacing a program's original script with new or different text. When the original program was made in a different language from that of the intended audience, it may be marketed as an M&E version, in which the soundtrack includes only 'music and effects'. All dialogue or voice-over commentary is added (dubbed in) later by the recipient in another language.

Script writing basics

A successful script has to satisfy two important requirements:

- *The program's main purpose, i.e. to amuse, inform, intrigue, persuade, etc.*
  (i.e. the artistic, aesthetic, dramatic element of the script)
- *It must be practical.*
  The script must be a workable vehicle for the production team.

Fundamentally, we need to ensure that:

- *The script meets its deadline.*
  When is the script required? Is it for a particular occasion?
- *The treatment is feasible for the budget, facilities, and time available.*
  An overambitious script will necessarily have to be rearranged, edited, scenes rewritten . . . to provide a workable basis for the production.
- *The treatment will fit the anticipated program length.*
  Otherwise it will become necessary to cut sequences or pad out with added scenes afterwards to fit the show to the allotted time span.
- *The style and the form of presentation are appropriate for the subject.*
  An unsuitable style (e.g. lighthearted, jokey approach) will trivialize a serious subject treatment.
- *The subject treatment is suitable for the intended audience.*
  The style, complexity, concentration of information, etc. relative to their probable interest and attention span.

Ask yourself

Who is the program for?
- Age group? (e.g. Children, college classes, mature students.)
- A specialist audience? (e.g. Sales, teachers, hobbyists.)

- Where is it to be shown? (e.g. Classroom, home, public place.)
- Is it for private study (carrel) or mass audience?
- Display screen use? (e.g. Museum display, marketing, exhibition.)

What is the purpose of this program?
- Entertainment, information, instruction?
- To persuade? (As in advertising, program trailers, propaganda.)
- Is there a follow-up to the program? (Publicity offers? Tests?)

Is the program one of a series?
- Does it relate to or follow on other programs?
- Do you need to remind viewers of past information?
- Does the script style need to be similar?
- Were there any omissions, weaknesses, or errors in previous programs that can be corrected?

Does your audience already know?
- Are they familiar with the subject?
  Do they understand the terms used?
  Is the information complicated?
  Do you need to recap previous information?
- Would a brief outline or introduction help (or remind) them?
- Is your audience likely to be prejudiced for or against the subject, or the product? (e.g. necessitating diplomacy, careful unambiguous treatment?)

How long is the program?
- Is it brief? (Having to make an immediate impact.)
- Is it long enough to develop arguments or explanations, for a range of topics?

What is the program's emphasis?
- On *display and visual effect* (e.g. visual flim-flam),
- On *techniques* (e.g. training program),
- On *data* (e.g. economics),
- On *personalities* (e.g. interview),
- On *persuasion* (e.g. advertising spot).
- Should key points of topics be listed at the start and end of the main program? Or summaries included?

How much detail is required in the script?
- Is the script to be complete, with dialogue and action? (Actual visual treatment depends on the director.)
- Is the script a basis for improvization (e.g. by a guide or lecturer)?
- Is it an ideas-sheet, giving an outline for treatment?

Are you writing dialogue?
- Is it for actors to read, or inexperienced performers? (For the latter, keep it brief, in short 'bites' to be read from a prompter, or spoken in their own words.)
- Is it to be naturalistic or 'character dialogue'?

Is the subject a visual one?
- If the subjects are abstract, or no longer exist, how will you illustrate them?

Have you considered the script's requirements?
- It only takes a few words on the page to suggest a situation, but to reproduce it in pictures and sound may require considerable time, expense, and effort (e.g. a battle scene). It may have to rely on available stock library film.
- Does the script pose obvious problems for the director? e.g. Involving special effects, stunts, etc.?
- Does the script involve costly concepts, that can be simplified?
  e.g. An intercontinental conversation could be covered by an expensive two-way video satellite transmission or simply involve a regular telephone call, accompanied by photo-slides.

Does the subject involve research?
- The script may depend on what researchers discover while investigating the subject.
- Do you already have information that can aid the director?
  e.g. Have contacts, know of suitable locations, availability of insert material, etc.

Where will your picture come from?
- Will the subjects be brought to the studio? (This allows maximum control over the program treatment and presentation.) *Or* will cameras be going on location to the subjects – e.g. shooting in museums, etc.? Script opportunities may depend on what is available when you are shooting.

Remember

Start scripting with a simple outline
- Before embarking on the main script treatment it can be particularly helpful to rough out a skeleton version. This would include a general outline treatment, covering the various points you want to include, in the order in which you propose dealing with them.

Be visual
- Sometimes pictures alone can convey the information, and no commentary or accompanying sound.
- The way a commentary is written (and spoken) can influence how the audience interprets a picture (and vice versa).
- Pictures can distract. People may concentrate on looking instead of listening!
- Avoid 'talking heads' wherever possible. Show the subject being talked about, rather than the person who is speaking.
- The script can only *indicate* visual treatment. It will seldom be specific about shot details, unless that is essential to the plot or situation. Directors have their own ideas!

Avoid overloading
- Keep it simple. Don't be long-winded, or use complicated sentences. Keep to the point. When a subject is difficult, an accompanying diagram, chart, or graph may help to make the information easier to understand.
- Do not give too much information at a time.
- Do not attempt to pack too much information into the program. It is better to do justice to a few topics, than to cover many inadequately.

Develop a flow of ideas
- Deal with one subject at a time. Generally avoid intercutting between different topics, flashbacks, flashforwards.
- If the screen has text to be read, either have an unseen voice read the same information, or leave the viewer time to read it.
- Do not have quite different information on the screen and in the commentary (distracting, confusing).
- Aim to have one subject or sequence lead naturally into the next.
- Where there are a number of separate different topics, consider how they are to be related; e.g. speaker walks from one display to another; a decorative transition.

Pace
- Vary the pace of the program. Avoid a fast pace, when imparting facts. It conveys an overall impression, but facts do not sink in. A slow pace can be boring or restful, depending on the occasion.
- Remember, that your audience cannot refer back. If they miss a point, they may fail to understand the next – or even lose interest.

Style
- Use an appropriate writing style. Generally aim at an informal, relaxed style – avoiding slangy colloquialisms.
- There is a world of difference between the style of the printed page, and the way people normally speak. Read from a prompter, it produces unnatural, stilted effect.
- Be very careful about introducing humor in the script!

Figure 10.3 Overfamiliarity
The director knows how interesting the location is ... but does he reveal it to his audience? Or is it a 'pillar-through-the-head' to them?

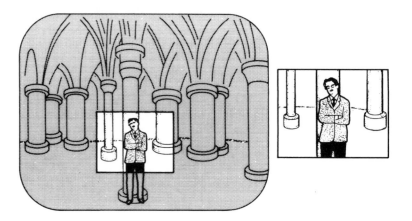

There were a number of important points in the previous paragraph, and if you presented ideas at that rate in a video program, there is every chance that your audience would forget most of the information. Unlike them, you can read this at your own pace, stop and re-read whatever you like. They usually cannot. An essential to remember when scripting, is the difference between the rates at which we can take in information in different media.

A lot depends, of course, on how familiar your audience already is with the subject and the terms used. Where details are new to them, and the information is complicated, it is better to linger rather than leap ahead. Ironically, something that can seem difficult and involved at the first viewing, can appear slow and obvious a few viewings later. That is why it is so hard for program-makers to estimate the effect of material on those who are going to be seeing it for the first time. They have themselves become so familiar with it, that they know it by heart.

Simplify! The more complex the subject you are dealing with, the easier each stage should be. If the density of information, or the rate at which you deliver it is too high, it will confuse, bewilder or just encourage your audience to switch off – mentally, if not actually.

10.30 Relative pace

You will soon find as you build up a sequence of pictures, and an accompanying soundtrack, that both the picture and the soundtrack have their own natural pace. it may be slow and leisurely, medium-paced, fast or brief. If you are fortunate, the pace of the picture and the sound will be roughly the same. However, there will be occasions when you find that you do not have enough picture to fit the sound sequence, or you do not have enough soundtrack to put behind the amount of action in the picture.

Often when a commentary has explained a point (perhaps taking 5 seconds), the picture is still showing the action (perhaps 20 seconds). We need to let the picture complete, before taking the commentary on to the next point. In the script therefore, a little dialogue may go a long way, as a series of interjections, rather than a continual flow of verbiage.

The reverse can happen too, where the action in the picture is brief, e.g. a locomotive passes through the shot in a few seconds, quicker than it takes us to talk about it. So we need more pictures of the subject, from another viewpoint perhaps, to support the dialogue.

Even when picture and sound are more or less keeping the same pace, do not habitually cut to a new shot immediately the action in a picture is finished. Sometimes it is better to continue the picture briefly, in order to allow time for the audience to absorb the facts, rather than press on with fast cutting and a quickfire commentary.

It is all too easy to overload the soundtrack. Without pauses in a commentary, it can become an endless outpouring. Moreover, if you have a detailed script that fits in with every moment of the picture, and the commentator happens to slow down at all, the words can get out of step with the key shots they are related to. Then you have the choice of cutting parts of the commentary, or building out the picture (e.g. with cutaway shots) to enable picture and sound to be brought into line.

10.31 Style

The worst type of script for video, film or radio, is the sort that has been written in a formal literary style, as if for a newspaper article or an essay, where the words, phrases and sentence construction are those of the printed page.

When you read this sort of script aloud, it tends to sound like an official statement or a pronouncement, rather than the fluent everyday speech we are really aiming at. Not, of course, that we want a script that is so colloquial that it includes all those hesitations and slangy half-thoughts one tends to use, but certainly one that avoids complex sentence construction.

It takes some experience to be able to read any script fluently, with the natural expression that brings it alive. But if the script itself is written in a stilted, fussy style, it is unlikely to improve with hearing. Try to present your material as if you are talking to the individual in your audience, rather than proclaiming on a stage, or addressing a public meeting. Probably the best way to achieve this, until you are more used to the style needed, is to prepare it by chatting to an audio recorder, as if you were explaining the subject to a friend opposite. And talk in the present tense rather than the past, for it is more vital.

The way you deliver information can influence how interesting it seems to be. The mind boggles at: 'The retainer lever actuates the integrated contour follower'. But we immediately understand: 'Here you can see, as we pull this lever, the lock opens'.

If your audience has to pause to work out what you mean, they will not be listening closely to what you are saying. You can often help them by anticipating the problems; with a passing explanation, or a subtitle (especially useful for names), or a suitable diagram.

10.32 Copyright and contracts

Whenever you want to make use of material prepared and created by other people – a piece of music, a sound recording, video tape, film, a picture in a book, a print, a photograph, etc. – you are liable to pay a fee to the *copyright holders*, or an appropriate organization operating on their behalf, for copyright clearance.

The copyright law is complex and varies between different countries, but it protects the originators from having their work copied without permission. So you cannot for example, prepare a video program with music dubbed from a commerical recording, with inserts from TV programs, magazine photographs, advertisements, and so on, without the permission of the respective copyright owners, and appropriate fees. These fees will depend on the purpose and use of your program. (There are exceptions when the program is only to be seen within the home, or is restricted to permitted study use.) In most cases, you can trace the copyright obligations through the source of the material you want to use (e.g. the publisher of a book or photograph); e.g. through the *ALCS* (*Authors' Licensing & Collecting Society*).

Agreements take various forms. They may be restricted or limited. You may have a license, and/or pay a fee for use. For music and sound effects, you may pay a royalty per use ('needle time'), buy the rights to use an item or a package ('buy-out method').

Organizations concerned with performance rights for music (copyright clearance for use of recorded music, or to perform music) include The Harry Fox Agency (New York), ASCAP (American Society of Composers, Authors and Publishers), SESAC (Society of European Stage Authors and Composers), BMI (Broadcast Music, Inc.) the MCPS (Mechanical Copyright Protection Society Ltd, London), the Performing Rights Society (PRS).

When clearing copyright for music, both the record company and the music publishers may be involved.

Music in *public domain* (e.g. old traditional songs) will not itself be subject to copyright, but any arrangement or performance will.

Whenever you hire talent (e.g. actors, professional talent) or use services (e.g. scaffold construction) contractual agreements arise. Union agreements may also be involved. So, before committing yourself in any way, find out exactly what is entailed both financially and legally.

Apart from general shots, whenever you want to shoot in the street, it is wise to let the local police know in advance. You may cause an obstruction, or contravene local by-laws. Strictly speaking too, if you are shooting people, you must get their permission in writing (with their name and address) on a *release form*. Terminology varies, depending on the purpose for which you are shooting the scene, and the nature of their contribution; but the release form is couched in legal terms generally authorizing you to use their performance – free or for a fee.

Chapter 11

Production techniques

Watch broadcast programs carefully, and you will see the whole gamut of techniques: dull routines, imaginative interpretations and pretentious flim-flam.

The production team

Production groups vary in size, according to the organization and the complexity of the production. Titles and responsibilities differ. In some groups there are strict demarcations, in smaller units work is shared. Here are typical key positions.

Producer
Usually responsible for overall business organization, budget. May originate and write the production. (In smaller units the producer will often direct the production too.)

Director
Responsible for interpreting and staging the production. Advises, instructs and coordinates the production team. Chooses, hires and directs talent. Guides and cues performance; either directly or through the *Floor Manager*. Instructs cameras, switcher, sound specialists, etc. Supervises post-production editing.

Director's assistant
Production Assistant (PA), Assistant or *Associate Director*. Exact function varies. Takes director's notes (*re.* changes, retakes, performance, etc.), checks timings, gives routine cues (e.g. countdown for film insert), warns of camera moves and upcoming action, etc., while the director guides performance and cameras. Also general liaison between the director and crew.

Floor Manager
The director's representative and contact in the studio. Cues talent. Checks and directs floor crew. Responsible for general studio organization, safety, discipline, etc.

Switcher
Production switcher (vision mixer) operator. Job done by the director, a specialist operator, or the *Technical Director*.

Crew Chief
Technical Director. Supervises technical facilities and operations crew. May operate switcher. May instruct operational crew during production.

Cameras
Camera crew responsible for all camera operations on a production.

Lighting
Lighting director designs, arranges, and controls all lighting treatment. Supervises *electrician(s)* who rig and set lighting equipment.

Audio
Audio engineer or specialist operator responsible for the sound balance, and technical/artistic quality of program sound. Supervises personnel operating microphones and all audio equipment.

Video control
Picture-quality control (adjusting video equipment) carried out by a specialist operator, or a *video engineer* (*shader*).

Make-up
Artist who designs and applies all make-up treatment.

Set design
Specialist designer who conceives, designs, and organizes the entire scenic treatment for a production (perhaps including graphics). Supervises scenic crew in erecting and dressing settings.

Videotape
Engineers/operators recording and replaying videotape machines. Videotape editing may be done by a specialist editor.

Video engineer
Technicians responsible for the maintenance and adjustment of all electronic equipment (cameras, sound).

Floor crew
(*Stagehands, grips*) Operatives who set up and dress settings; operate cue cards, prompting devices, etc.; may assist in moving equipment, etc.

11.1 Single- and multi-camera production

There are two radically different ways of shooting a video production:

- Single-camera production, in which one camera is used to shoot the entire show.
- Multi-camera production, in which two, three, or more cameras are interlinked to a *production switcher* (*vision mixer*), and their outputs selected or blended as required.

Each of these techniques has its particular advantages and limitations. Some types of program cannot be shot so effectively on a single camera (e.g. sports and games); while for others, a multi-camera approach can seem 'over the top', overpoweringly inappropriate (e.g. an interview in someone's home). From the director's point of view, the production techniques are markedly different. For a live production, a single camera would be unnecessarily inhibiting. But for a taped production, the director can adopt techniques that are similar to those of the film maker as far as time and facilities allow.

Single-camera production A single lightweight camera is independent, compact, and free to go anywhere. The director can be right there on the spot beside the camera, seeing opportunities, and explaining exactly what he or she wants to the camera operator. (In the case of documentary

Table 11.1 Prepare to record

- Check details of the next shot.
- Mark clapper board with scene and shot numbers.
- 'Is everyone ready?'
- 'Quiet please!'
- Start VCR and audio recorders.
- Show clapper board (5 s).
- 'Action!' (Cue; action begins).
- End of action. 'Cut!' (Action stops, talent wait.)
- Stop recording.
- Check recording (end only, or 'spot check').
- Note final frames for continuity, log shot details (identification, duration), label tape.

  either

- 'TAKE IS OK. LET'S GO ON TO SHOT 5'.

  or

- 'WE NEED TO RETAKE THAT SHOT BECAUSE . . .'

- Set up for next shot.

productions, the person devising and organizing the project may be operating the camera too!)

This method offers the director considerable flexibility; both when shooting and later when editing. You can select and rearrange the material you have shot, trying out several versions to improve the show's impact. There is none of the feeling of 'instant commitment' which can typify a multi-camera show. But it is slow.

Shooting with a single camera will often involve interruping or repeating the action in order to reposition the camera. The problems of maintaining *continuity* between set-ups, even the way in which shooting conditions can change between takes (i.e. light or weather vary) and similar considerations, are not to be underestimated.

It has been said that 'unlike *multi-camera* production, which is a "juggling act", shooting with a single camera allows you to concentrate on doing one thing at a time; on optimizing each individual shot'. You are free to readjust each camera position, rearrange the subject, change the lighting, alter sound pick-up arrangements, modify the decor, etc., to suit each take. That's great! But shooting can degenerate into a self-indulgent experimental session. It is all too easy to put off problems till tomorrow, with '*We'll sort it out during the edit*' or '*Let's leave it till post-production*'!

When shooting with a single camera you do not have to worry about coordinating several different cameras, each with its different viewpoint. You are relieved of the tensions of continually cueing, guiding, intercutting between cameras. All refinements and supplementary features from background music to video effects are added at a later stage, during the post-production session. The other side of the coin is that when shooting with a single camera, you finish up with a collection of tapes containing a mixture of takes (good, bad, and indifferent; mistakes and all) shot in any order; all needing to be sorted out some time later. So compiling the final tape, including titles, music, effects, etc. can be a lengthy process.

Multi-camera production If you are shooting continuous action with a single camera, and want to change your camera's viewpoint, you have two choices. You can move to a new position while still shooting (i.e. move 'on shot'), or miss some of the action as you reposition the camera at the next set-up. A multi-camera group simply switches from one camera to another; a clear advantage when you are shooting a series of events going on at the same time or spread over a wide area.

Unlike the director on a single-camera shoot who is close to the camera, the director of a multi-camera production is located away from the action; watching a series of picture monitors in a production control room; issuing instructions to the crew over their intercom headsets; and to the floor manager who guides the talent on the director's behalf.

In a *live* multi-camera production most of the inter-shot transitions (cuts, mixes, wipes, etc.) are made on a *production switcher* (*vision mixer*) during the action. Editing techniques are rudimentary. There are no opportunities to correct or improve. However, you do have the great advantage that you can continuously monitor and compare shots. And you do not have continuity problems of the kind that can develop when shooting with a single camera. An experienced multi-camera crew can, after a single rehearsal, produce a polished show that is '*ready to air*' or for 'straight through' videotaping in just a few hours. At the end of the taping period, the show is finished.

Videotaped multi-camera productions may be shot as:

- '*Live-on-tape*' – From beginning to end without a break (e.g. in a talks show).

- *'Scene-by-scene'* – A scene or act at a time, correcting/polishing each in turn.
- *'Shot-by-shot'* – Short action sequences, with inter-camera switching to avoid interrupting (or repeating) the action.

Multi-camera production can degenerate into a shot-grabbing routine; simply intercutting between several camera viewpoints for the sake of variety. But for directors with imagination and the ability to plan ahead and a skilled team it can produce results of the very highest standards.

11.2 Multi-camera variations

When the action cannot be repeated, or events are unpredictable, some directors make use of an *ISO* (isolated) camera. This simply means that while all the cameras are connected to the switcher as before, one of them is also continuously recorded on a separate VCR. This ISO camera takes wide shots of the action (cover shots), or concentrates on watching out for the arrival of the guest for instance, without any fear of missing the important moment. Shots on the ISO tape can be played back during a live show, or edited in where necessary later.

In another multi-camera approach, each camera has its own associated video-recorder (*dedicated VTRs*). Instead of intercutting between cameras with a switcher, shots from their separate videotapes are edited together later during a post-production session. Any voice-over narration, sound effects, video effects, music, etc., are then added.

11.3 What is the aim?

Some directors (and camera operators) imagine that they are using their cameras to show their audience 'things as they are'. They are not. The medium is inherently *selective*.

Even if you simply point your camera at the scene, and leave the rest to your audience, you have, whatever your intentions, made a selective choice on their behalf. *They* have not chosen to look at that particular aspect of the scene; *you* have. How much they see is determined by the type of shot you have shown them, and your camera's viewpoint. They cannot see the rest of the scene.

In fact, a skilled director uses camera and microphone to create an illusion; to give the audience *the impression of reality.* They feel that 'they are there', actually experiencing the event.

Program-making is a *persuasive* art – persuading your audience to look and to listen; persuading them to do something in a particular way; persuading them to buy something, whether it is an idea or a product.

You want not only to arouse their interest, but to sustain it. You want to direct their attention to certain features of your subject, and would prefer that their minds did not wander to others.

You achieve all this by the shots you select, and the way you edit them together; by the way you use sound. Persuasion is not a matter of high budget and elaborate facilities, but of imagination.

You can even take a dull unpromising subject, such as an *empty box*, and influence how your audience feels about it!

Imagine you are sitting in darkness, when up on the screen comes a shot containing nothing more than a flatly lit wooden box in light gray surroundings. How do you think your audience would react?

Intercom instructions

In a multi-camera production, the director gives instructions to the studio crew through their headsets (cameras, sound, etc.). This *intercom* (*talkback*) cannot be overheard by microphones or performers.

Opening shots please	Cameras to provide initial shots in the show (or scene).
Ready 2	Stand-by cue for Cam. 2.
Give me a single (two shot)	Just have person(s) indicated in the shot.
Tighten your shot	Slightly closer shot (slight zoom in).
Go wider	Slightly more distant (slight zoom out).
Lose the hands	Compose shot to omit the hands.
Cut at the hands	Compose shot to just include the hands.
Kill the flowers	Remove them (unwanted, obtrusive).
Lose focus on Joe	Let Joe become defocused.
Stand-by for a rise (or sit)	Talent is about to stand (sit).
Hold the boy	Keep subject in shot as he moves.
Let him go	Allow subject to move out of shot.
Lose him	Recompose or tighten shot to exclude him.
Clear on 2	Cam. 2 can move to next position.
Stand him by	Alert him, ready for a cue.
Cue action/cue Joe	Give hand signal to Joe to begin action.
Hold it	Stop action/performance (to correct error).
Freeze there	Stop movement; hold it quite still (e.g. to check a position).
Back to the top/take it from the top	Begin again at start of scene; repeat the rehearsal.
Pick it up from 20	Recommence rehearsal (or shooting) from Shot 20.
Would they just walk it?	Ask actors to move through their action, without dialogue or performance.
Clear 2's shot	Something/someone is obscuring Cam. 2's shot.
Tighten them up	Move the people closer together.
Give him a mark	Make a floor mark (chalk) to show him a location point.
He should work to 2	He should face Cam. 2.
Stretch him	Tell him to go more slowly (i.e. there is time to spare).
Tell him to pad/keep talking	Tell him to improvize until next item is ready. (Hand signal: thumb and extended fingers touch and part.)
Give him a minute	He has a minute left (hand signal).
Give him a wind/wind him up	Signal him to finish.
Kill him/cut him	He is to stop immediately.
Give him a clear/clear him	We have left him. He is free to move away.

Also general camera guidance such as 'pan left', 'dolly back', 'zoom in'.

On seeing the shot, most us would *assume* that the picture is supposed to have some sort of meaning or purpose. So we start by wondering what it is all about. 'What are we supposed to be looking at? Does the box have some significance that we've missed? Is someone coming on in a minute to explain?'

You have your audience's attention for a moment or two, for they are trying to understand what is going on. If there is a word stenciled on the box, they will probably read that, and then try to puzzle out what it means. They will look and listen, and finally get bored. But all that has probably only taken a few *seconds*!

You cannot rely on the *subject* alone, to hold your audience's interest. How you present it, is all important.

Let us imagine ourselves again in darkness, but now on the screen appears . . . a box, half-lit from behind . . . only part is visible . . . the rest falls away into a silhouette. A low rhythmical beat steadily fills our ears . . . The camera creeps slowly along the floor . . . creeps forward . . . very very slowly . . . pausing . . . then moving onward . . . stopping abruptly . . . then moving on again . . . Slow chords from an organ grow louder . . . and louder. . .

How is your audience going to react to *that*? If you have done it well, they are on the edges of their seats, anxious to find out what is in the box! The same box!

All right, so you cannot use such dramatic techniques in all programs! But it does show how persuasive the medium can be. It shows us how even such a simple situation, with an empty box, can be influenced by techniques.

But it is a reminder too, that the production treatment needs to be *appropriate*. It needs to create an ambience, an atmosphere, that is suitable for the occasion. Whether your program is to have show-biz glitter, or the business-like neutrality of a newscaster's reports, the enthusiastic participation of a kid's show, or the reverential air of a remembrance ceremony, its style of presentation should suit the occasion.

11.4 The camera's role

The camera is an 'eye'; but whose eye? It can be that of an onlooker, watching the action from the best possible position at each moment. This is its *objective* role.

Or you can use your camera in a *subjective* way. Moving around within the scene, the camera represents your own eyes, as you move through a crowd, or push aside undergrowth. The effect can be quite dramatic, especially if people within the scene seem to speak to you directly, through the camera's lens.

11.5 The camera as an observer

This is the way the camera is used in many types of program. It shows us the scene from *various viewpoints*, and we begin to feel a sense of space, as we build up a mental image of a situation – although the camera is only showing us a small section of the scene in each shot. The camera becomes an observer, moving close to see detail, and standing far back to take in the wider view.

We might, for example, watch two people sitting talking. As one speaks, we see a close shot of one. A moment later, the camera switches to show us the other person listening. From time to time, we see them together.

There is nothing *imaginative* about this treatment; but then, it is not intended to work on the audience's emotions. It is intended to show us clearly what is going on, who is there, where they are, what they are doing. It intermixes closer shots of the detail we want to see at a particular moment (people's expressions) with wider shots giving us a more general view of the situation. In fact, to treat a conversation in front of the camera in any other way, by dramatizing its presentation, would normally be quite inappropriate.

11.6 The persuasive camera

If, on the other hand, you are shooting a pop group, shots may be as bizarre and varied as you can make them. You are aiming to excite and to shock, to create great visual variety. There is no room for subtlety. Picture impact, strange effects and rapid changes in viewpoint thrust the music at your audience.

Between this brash display, and the subtle play on the emotions we met earlier (Section 11.3), there is a world of difference. Yet they all demonstrate how you can influence your audience through the way you choose and compose your shots, move the camera, and then edit those shots together.

The high viewpoint looking down on the subject with an air of detachment; the low viewpoint that gives the subject exaggerated importance; the increasing tension as the camera dollies in, and which falls as we move away from the subject, are all typical of the ways in which the camera can affect your audience's responses to what they are seeing.

11.7 Beginning and ending

Part of a program's impact lies in the way it is packaged, how it is introduced, and how you bring it to its end.

At its start, your main aim is to grab the audience's attention, to arouse their interest and to hold it. You can do this in various ways: by shocking them, by intriguing them, by making them feel welcome, by impressing them, and so on.

One of the dreariest ways of introducing any program, is to provide a series of titles in dead silence, giving the name of the program, followed by lists of those appearing in it and those responsible for the production.

Music and attractive graphics can set the scene: jaunty happy music and quirky titles for a comedy; severe regal music and formal titling for a solemn occasion.

Today, titling does not pose too many problems, for apart from 'casual titling' that is finger-drawn in sand, or formed from children's blocks, or chalked on a wall, you can achieve excellent results with rub-on transfer sheets, or even home-computer generated lettering.

At the end of a program, you want your audience to be left with a feeling of completeness: that the program is now concluded; not that the show has petered out, or that someone has forgotten to put on the last reel!

You can achieve this partly by the inflexions in a commentator's voice during concluding words, or by the way a musical background winds up. Generally speaking, it is poor practice to fade out in the middle of a musical passage, or as it is just beginning a new sequence, or to use music that has no apparent conclusion.

Again, you can end your program in several ways:

- gradually winding down to a quiet conclusion,
- with a climax; with a logical ending to a statement,
- with an open question, for the audience to answer,
- with a summary of earlier facts.

And finally of course ... **THE END** ... leaves your audience in no doubt.

11.8 Production methods

Most types of program follow paths that have been trodden in the past. For instance, there is no sparkling new way of interviewing someone; pretty well all feasible methods have been tried at some time or other. But that does not make such programs any less interesting. It does mean though, that you can benefit from what others have discovered.

There are no infallible, all-purpose formulae. But there certainly are approaches that experience has shown to suit particular subjects. In the following sections, you will find hints and reminders that could help you when shooting various regular forms of program.

11.9 There is nothing there!

We become so accustomed to seeing pictures accompanying any subject under the sun, that we can overlook one fundamental paradox. For many situations there is, strictly speaking, *no subject to shoot!* There are no pictures!

You will meet this problem on various occasions:

- Abstract subjects have no direct visuals (philosophical, social, spiritual concepts).
- General non-specific subjects (transport, weather, humanity).
- Imaginary events (fantasy, literature, mythology).
- Historical events – where no authentic illustrations exist.
- Forthcoming events – where the event has not yet happened.
- Where shooting is not possible – prohibited, or the subject is inaccessible.
- Where shooting is impracticable – dangerous, or you cannot get the optimum shots.
- Events now over, that were not photographed at the time.
- Events where the appropriate visuals would prove too costly – would involve travel, or have copyright problems.

So how do you cope with such situations? The least interesting method is to show someone standing outside a building, where the camera was not allowed in to watch a meeting, telling the audience what they would have seen if they had been there.

Newscasts frequently use this approach, for the event has come to an end. The bank robbery, the explosion or the fire are now over, and we can only look at the results.

Another method is to show photo-stills, or artwork of the people or places involved, with explanatory commentary over. And this could be the solution if you were discussing history such as the discovery of America or the burning of Rome. There might be some museum relics available to show, to enliven interest, but they are usually only peripheral to the main subject.

Sometimes you can show substitutes; not a picture of the actual bear that escaped from the circus, but one like it. You cannot show pictures of next month's parade, but you may be able to use shots of last year's fun and frolics.

At times, you may not be able to illustrate the subject directly. Instead, you will have to use visuals that are closely associated with it. For instance, if you do not have photographs or drawings of a composer, you might be able to show shots of his native country (e.g. by exploring projected slides with the camera). At a pinch, you could even zoom in to his birthplace, on a map. Otherwise, you could use atmospheric effects to accompany his music, such as pictures of sunlight rippling on water, wind in trees, waves breaking on the shore, reflections, children at play, or any other associated image that will serve as a visual accompaniment.

'Visual padding' of this kind (sometimes called 'wallpaper shots') is widely used in broadcast programs, in the form of general views of town and countryside, shots of traffic or people moving around.

These shots can:

● serve to fill out scenes that may be running short during a commentary,
● be used as cutaways,
● be used wherever we do not have suitable visual material for one reason or another.

11.10 Shooting objects

If you simply put something down in front of the camera and shoot it, results are often disappointing compared with those you can achieve with a little extra care. So here are a few reminders of how you can give such shots that added quality.

One successful method of arranging background material is to form a continuous crease-free plane from a hanging sheet of seamless paper, draped onto a table-top.

Whether you are shooting a vase of flowers, a sculpted form or a piece of jewelry, try to ensure that it has a suitable background. Plain contrasting tones are best (light against dark, or dark against light), or a contrasting pale colored background (e.g. fawn, light blue or pale green).

Dazzling white backgrounds make the subject itself look darker than normal, and exaggerates the brilliance of its colors. They can overwhelm the subject.

Figure 11.1 Shooting objects
Here are a few 'obvious' points to remember, when presenting an object. But count how often you see them overlooked on air!
1 Avoid clutter.
2 Try to have contrasting background tones.
3 Multi shadows can confuse and distract.
4 Avoid confusing or distracting backgrounds.
5 Do not cut off parts of the object, unless you are showing detail.
6 See that handling does not obscure important detail.
7 Avoid shadowing the object (demonstrator or camera).
8 Do not show an unfamiliar viewpoint, unless you want puzzle pictures.

1. Avoid clutter

2. Have contrasting background tones

3. Multi-shadows can confuse

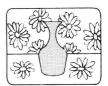
4. Avoid confusing or distracting background

5. Do not cut off parts of subjects

6. Handling can obscure

7. Avoid shadowing the subject

8. Don't show an unfamiliar view of subject

Black backgrounds too need to be used with care, for although they can throw the subject into prominent relief, they may emphasize color, and dark areas around the edges of the subject can vanish into the surroundings. If you increase backlight to prevent this, it can produce an inappropriate glittering halo of light around the subject.

It is not always practicable to increase the illumination of large areas (e.g. a cyc) as it would involve more lamps or extra power. If a background appears too dim, consider reducing the subject/foreground lighting a little and opening up the lens. If the background is too bright, increase the subject lighting and stop down a little.

Strong background colors (e.g. red, yellow, or bright green) are not only very distracting, but they will modify the apparent colors of your subject.

If the subject you are showing is *flat* (e.g. a framed picture), shoot it from a straight-on viewpoint, and tilt the frame down a little to avoid light reflections, camera reflections or a shadow.

If a demonstrator has to put the item in position for the camera, it is often a good idea to have an unobtrusive position-mark on a table, to guide where it should be placed. A nearby monitor can show the camera's shot, to ensure that there are no reflections.

Solid objects are best lit with 'three-point lighting' (key; fill; backlight), or a side light to left and right with some frontal fill-light.

Close shots with a wide-angle lens, will create considerable distortion.

If the depth of field is too limited in a 'detail shot', you probably need to use a smaller *f*-stop; but this requires higher light levels. Instead of trying to increase the *overall* light level, take a separate close-up shot of the item afterwards, under stronger *localized* lighting, and insert this. Otherwise you will have to take a longer shot.

Rather than move the camera in an arc round the object (a difficult move to carry out smoothly), you may find it better to place the object on a turntable (manual or motor driven), which is slowly turned to see it from all directions.

A camera looking down on to an object on a table may not show it particularly successfully. Try putting the object on a small box or block on the table, to raise it, so that the camera can get a better straight-on shot. (Directors sometimes use this idea for seated people, placing their chairs on a raised platform or rostrum, so that the camera has a level viewpoint.)

Try to show objects *individually*, either by displaying them one at a time, or excluding others nearby with a tightly framed shot. If objects are in a group, you may be able to use localized lighting to select an individual item. Otherwise you may have to rely on differential focusing (i.e. a carefully focused zone) to give you a sharp image of your subject while blurring others. At worst, you can use a pointer to concentrate the viewer's attention on a particular object (see Section 6.15).

Shooting people

11.11 A single person

Yes, it *is* possible to shoot a single person badly, so let us go over the basics and see how.

When anyone is speaking straight to the camera, you will not normally want anything larger than a close-up, framed to just below the neck-tie knot.

Figure 11.2 Shooting a single person

Be prepared! (a) When someone is sitting, be ready to follow him if he stands ('rises'), or you will cut his head off! (b) Similarly, be ready for him to sit, if he is standing. Both situations are a reminder that you cannot lock-off the panning head during action.

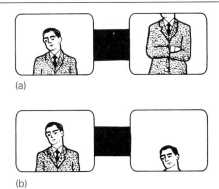

(a)

(b)

Be prepared for him to move

Space restrictions. As shots get tighter (closer), the amount of action they can enclose becomes less. Demonstrators often need to know how much room they have available to work in.

Think twice before using really close shots of a person, because your audience is more likely to start inspecting than listening. They become more aware of the trim of a mustache, a facial defect or teeth. A screen-filling full-face shot is out of place in most everyday productions, although it can be dramatically powerful when used at the right moment.

Unless it is quite unavoidable, do not take close shots of people on a narrow-angle lens (e.g. 10° or less), particularly if their head is angled to the camera, for the flattening 'cardboarding' effect can be most unattractive.

A waist shot (mid shot) will still show a person's expressions clearly, while allowing them a certain amount of movement. If they move around in a tighter shot though, they are likely to move out of the frame.

The more a person wriggles around in a chair, leaning, settling back or waving arms, the wider the shot you will need. You could cut off the gestures deliberately, and let them fall outside the frame, but the resulting shot will look very cramped.

When someone walks around, you will usually find that a waist shot is the closest you can use comfortably, although a full-length shot gives a better impression of the surroundings.

A sustained shot of someone speaking to the camera soon becomes boring, and you can improve the picture by gradually tightening the shot to increase interest, or slowly widening it, to relax the audience's concentration. But don't overdo camera movement on a static person, or the effect becomes fidgety.

You can create visual variety, by *cutting* to different sized shots, but avoid either very slight size-changes or extreme changes. They are distracting. If you make a cut at the end of a thought sequence, preferably at the end of a sentence, it will not disrupt the flow.

You can help to 'motivate the cut' by having the speaker turn at an agreed moment, to be shot from another direction; although this can look mannered if it is done too deliberately. Position cuts of this sort can be useful too, when the speaker has made a mistake and re-started from the break, or cannot remember more than a few sentences at a time. In these circumstances, the cut will hide the intermittent shooting, and result in a smoothly flowing narrative.

Instead of continually showing shots of *a person talking*, try wherever possible to show what they are talking *about*. This not only makes the program more interesting to watch, but it becomes more informative, for it gives the viewer time to examine the subject itself, rather than just hear about it.

If the program is intended to concentrate on the *personality* of the speaker, then use plenty of portraiture shots. But if it is really intended to be showing us how to do something, or how something works, that should decide the sort of shots you mainly use – not continual shots of the cook, but shots showing us the cooking process.

A warning here! Although you can change the size and angle of the speaker's shot while screening a picture of what he/she is talking about, take great care if you cut to a shot of him/her in *another location*. Your audience will be stopped in their tracks, if, for example, a person they last saw in a lounge suit in an office, appears in the next shot on board ship in Bermuda shorts, without some sort of explanation.

11.12 Conventional arrangements

Generally speaking, you will find that shots showing people talking, fall into 'formal', 'informal', or 'grouped' arrangements.

Formal arrangements are the normal format you meet in studio interviews, newscasts, public affairs programs, games shows and similar situations, where people are grouped around (all sitting or standing) in a regular layout.

Informal arrangements include people sitting in their own home, standing in the street, walking, driving or speaking while working. Informal approaches also include *wildtrack interviews*, in which we see pictures of someone busily occupied (sawing wood for instance), and hear them in a non-synchronous audio wild-track of an interview made separately. The audience accepts this convention, without wondering how the talent is speaking without moving their lips!

Arranged groups are mostly found in drama productions, where people are deliberately positioned to form compositional patterns, that direct the eye, and influence our response to the action.

11.13 Effective shots

When you are shooting groups of people (anything from two upwards), your shots should always answer the basic questions: Who is there? Where are they? What do they have to say?

We want to see reactions, and to hear replies. Shots of people just sitting listening quietly without expression have limited value. So effective shooting is a matter of appropriate selection of the right person at the right time.

A regular productional approach is to begin with a group shot showing everyone present . . . cut to the chairperson . . . then cut to close-ups of individuals as they speak . . . with intercut reaction shots. Shots of part of the group are often included, e.g. a person with their partner. But if a shot includes more than three people, details of their expressions may be lost.

Figure 11.3 Following movement

Part 1 *Uneven framing.* 1. Varying framing during movement looks crude and clumsy. 2. As you pan with a moving subject, try to keep it steady in the frame, just behind picture center. The amount of offset increases with the subject's speed.

Part 2 *Direction and effective speed.*

A. Someone moving across the screen quickly passes out of shot.
B. Diagonal moves are more interesting (and take longer).
C. Moves towards (or away from) the camera are sustained longest. But they may take too long (distant walk on a narrow-angle lens).

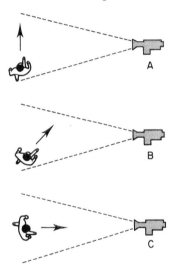

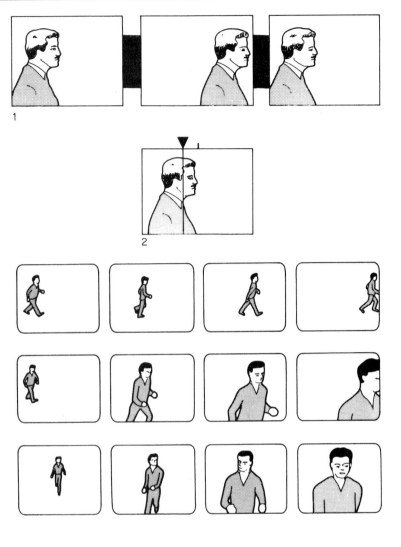

Figure 11.4 Improving viewpoints

Part 1
Widely spaced moves. If two people are some distance apart, you can cut between them, pan between them (A), or shoot the action from a more oblique viewpoint (B).

Intercutting does not interrelate them effectively. Panning from position A can create greater tension, but may cover irrelevant background. The shot from position B can appear more dynamic.

Part 2 *Masking.* When one performer obscures another ('masks them'), move the camera sideways slightly to correct the shot.

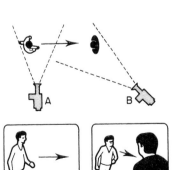

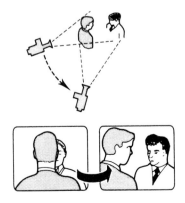

For most purposes, frontal shots (with the person facing the camera), or ¾-frontal shots (looking 45° to either side), are the most effective. In a profile shot (side view), which is the least familiar view of most people, the camera seems to be *scrutinizing* the guest, and the effect is not particularly attractive, although admittedly, it can be dramatic in a strong aggressive interview.

You can use a back view (or ¾-back) of an interviewer, or a member of a group, to form a foreground silhouette on one side of the picture. But take care in case they lean into the frame and mask other people in the shot.

11.14 Concentration

If you are watching someone at work, painting, cooking, quilting or whatever, it is quite natural for the camera to concentrate on *what they are doing* and *how they are doing it*, rather than dwelling on their expressions. Cut away from the center of interest for too long to shots of an interviewer for example and your audience will become impatient, feeling cheated of the real action.

Quite often such cutaway shots are really effective editing devices, introduced so that you can reduce over-lengthy shots of the action. Instead of going on and on and on watching the bread dough being kneaded, you show part of the action with an establishing shot, then introduce a cutaway shot (hopefully of something that is *relevant*) to disguise the fact that you have interrupted and removed part of the action during editing.

When showing a situation where there is a continual feeling of apprehension as to whether the action will succeed (e.g. during a cliff climb), regular intercutting between the action itself and the person's expressions of concentration, will heighten the program's impact.

You will meet occasions when a director shooting an interview, continually includes 'fidget shots' of drumming fingers, hands fiddling with jewelry, straightening a tie, and so on. Although such shots may seem to reveal the guest's unconscious reactions, more often they just distract the audience from what is being said.

If someone is being questioned closely during an interview, you might use a tighter shot than normal. And should the situation become particularly heated, you could even move closer and closer to the 'guest' during questioning. But these are not techniques to be used lightly during a normal, cool, polite interview. In any case, there's always the risk that once you have reached the closest shot, anything after it is an anticlimax!

11.15 Interviews

If you are shooting two people in a continuous interview or discussion with a single camera, treatment is inevitably restricted to some extent. But with a little foresight, your audience will not even realize that you had any problems!

There are two ways of approaching the interview:

● In the first, the camera moves around, changing its viewpoint.
● In the second, the camera remains with the guest throughout.

Interviews are best shot in one continuous take. When restricted to just one camera, you might for example, open with an establishing long shot, showing the participants and where they are. Slowly the camera moves in to a mid shot of the interviewer who is introducing the guest. As he/she turns to face the guest the camera pans slightly and the shot is widened to

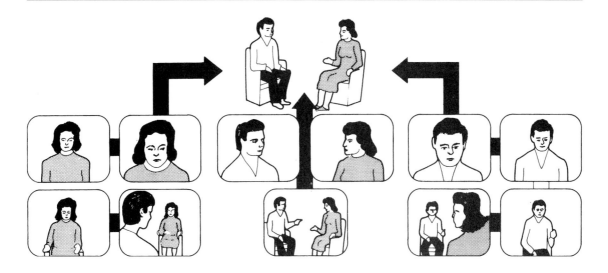

Figure 11.5 Formal interviews
In a formal interview, there are relatively few effective shots.

include them both again. You can then tighten the shot to a single close-up of the guest.

Using a different approach, you could begin with a waist shot of the interviewer . . . slowly pull out (zoom or dolly) to include the guest in a two-shot . . . then gradually pan over and move in at the same time to concentrate on the guest, and exclude the interviewer. As the interview ends, you can simultaneously pull out and pan over to a two-shot . . . finally tightening on the interviewer for his/her closing words. If the interview is quite long, you can vary the guest's shot from time to time by very gradually zooming in and out. Much depends on how interesting, and how animated, the guest proves to be.

Location interviews are often 'one-take' opportunities, in which the camera concentrates on the guest (zooming to vary the shot size). The interviewer, who is unseen, stands near the camera to ask the questions (out of shot, off camera).

Once a *one-camera interview* has concluded it is common practice for the interviewer to tape a series of brief sequences to camera. This avoids disrupting the actual interview or continually panning between the two people as they talk. Speaking directly to camera afterwards, the interviewer introduces the guest(s) to the audience. This sequence may be cut in during editing as a '*to-camera introduction*', or used as a '*voice-over introduction*' which accompanies a long shot of the pair at the start of the interview. The interviewer may then go on to thank the guest, and perhaps make an announcement about the next program in the series. This is attached to the end of the edited tape. Next, a regular procedure is for the interviewer to speak past the camera, as when asking the guest the original questions. (They were probably not heard by the microphone picking up the guest's voice.) Later, these questions will be edited into the interview tape at the appropriate points. Where these questions were scripted or prearranged, this will mean referring to notes or script. Where they were spontaneous, it may involve checking an audio recording or the interview tape itself. In either case it is imperative that these are the *actual questions*, asked with similar *intonation* to those put to the guest!

Many interviews and discussions simply involve straightforward once-through taping. But results can be disappointing. Then it is advisable to do it again, and select the better version, or use parts of each take. Another approach to interviewing is to tape a much longer session than you really need, and extract the highlights to suit the required program length.

This last method overcomes the frustration of finding that the session was just becoming interesting at the point where it was wound up. It copes with guests who take some time to settle down, or who wander from the point or have more to say than there is time for. To provide continuity, and a smooth visual flow in the edited program, questions from the interviewer can be recorded later, to provide cutaways, which are edited in at appropriate points to introduce each topic.

11.16 Editing continuous interviews

A regular method of handling interviews with a single camera is to concentrate the camera on the guest throughout. The interviewer remains out of shot. This treatment is simple, and least likely to distract the guest. But it does leave you with one very long take!

The result is usually a sequence that is far too long for your program slot. It needs 'tightening'. You want to use the most important and interesting passages, discarding any unwanted or irrelevant overmatter.

If you just cut out the parts you require, and join them together, there will be a distracting *jump cut* at the start of each new section, with sudden changes in positions expressions, and shot sizes. Directors often try disguising these cuts with fast mixes or wipes, but the result is seldom satisfactory.

The answer to this dilemma is to take a series of *nod shots* at the end of the interview and to edit them into the main sequence.

The *nod shot* is a familiar feature in all broadcast interviews. It is simply a *silent* reaction shot of the interviewer looking 'with interest', or 'reacting' with occasional head-nods, smiles or concern. The director may also ask the guest to oblige with similar nod shots, to give variety to the editing.

During editing, you use the original interview shot with its soundtrack, and introduce the nod shots wherever necessary, without interrupting the sound.

To be convincing, it is important that the person in the nod shot doesn't speak. If you are taking an over-shoulder shot, make sure that the mouth of the person with their back to the camera cannot be seen moving. Too often they chat to their companion while the nod shot is being taken, with the result that after editing, their mouth movements do not match the sound being heard!

11.17 Shooting groups

Shooting a group effectively with a single camera is a challenge, but still quite practicable. You use the mobile techniques we have just discussed for the interview.

If you possibly can, avoid *hosepiping*, in which the camera continually pans across from one person to another. It looks pretty clumsy, particularly if people are sitting some distance apart, and the camera is panning over meaningless background. If you are shooting with one camera it is usually better to zoom out, to include the new speaker in a wide shot, then perhaps zoom in on him/her.

The exception is when something really dramatic happens (e.g. someone suddenly stands and shouts in opposition). Then you would pan over very rapidly to show the interrupter. However, the disadvantage of a *whip pan*

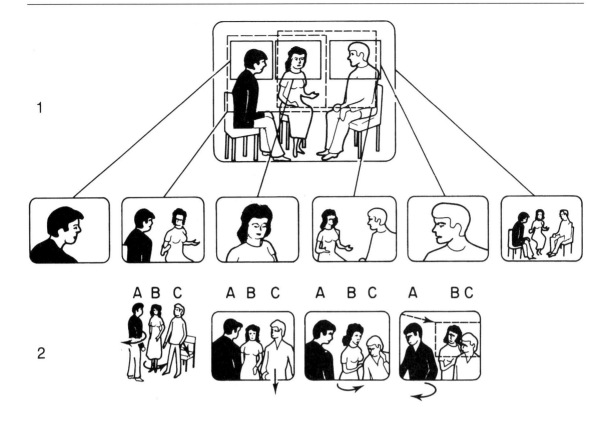

Figure 11.6 Shooting groups

1 *Isolating sections.* You can break a static group into a series of smaller individual shots. Using a single camera, this involves repositioning the camera (or repeated action). With multi-camera shooting, you intercut between viewpoints.

2 *Reforming grouping.* You can introduce 'natural moves' to form new groupings. Here C sits, B turns to him, A turns and exits. The shot tightens on BC. The action has created a series of groupings, and moved attention between the performers.

(zip pan, blur pan) of this kind is that, although it makes a strong visual impact, it is liable to end up with a defocused or badly framed picture that has to be corrected on air.

However, if instead of a whip pan, you had quickly zoomed out from a close-up to a group shot, then immediately zoomed in to a close shot of the interrupter, the out-in maneuver would have looked extremely awkward.

When shooting a group in which people speak at random avoid the temptation to continually arc round and move to new positions, particularly when someone out of shot suddenly starts talking. It is usually less obtrusive to zoom out, and include them in a wide shot.

The trick is to make any camera moves appear as natural as possible. Supposing you were covering a street interview. You might begin with a mid-shot of the interviewer speaking to camera, introducing someone. Then as he/she turns towards them saying: 'Tell me Mr Able, what were the first signs . . .', the camera arcs round on the turn, to shoot Mr Able for the rest of the sequence.

As a general principle, if you can use movement to 'motivate a pan' (i.e. follow something or someone moving past), the result will look much more natural and unobtrusive than simply panning over 'the empty air'.

If you are using two or more cameras to shoot a group, you can prearrange various shots between them. For example, *Camera 1* can take a cover shot (wide shot) of the entire action, and shots of the interviewer or host. *Camera 2* can take opening title cards, and shots of the guest.

Where there are more guests, you can introduce various permutations of singles, pairs, sub-groups and group shots, always being ready to come

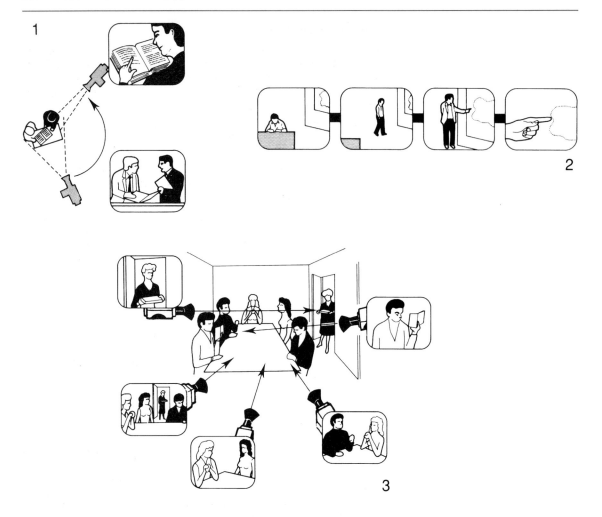

Figure 11.7 The camera explores
Part 1 *The inquisitive camera.*
Although the action itself is static, the camera moves round to examine the subject more closely.

Part 2 *The camera follows.* As the speaker gets up and moves to the map, the camera follows, and goes in to the detail he is pointing at.

Part 3 *The developing (development) shot.* The camera moves around within the scene 'motivated' by the turn of a head, by somebody moving, by the newcomer's entrance ... so that in the end, the audience has seen the situation from many interesting angles, in a continuous shot, without the interruptions of a series of cuts.

back to a cover shot if somebody speaks unexpectedly, when you are in a close single shot on the other camera.

There is, in fact, an important difference between shooting a group who are going to speak in an agreed order, and a group where members speak whenever they wish. In the first case, cameras and microphones can follow along systematically. Where people speak at random, they will be off-mike until the operator with the sound boom has been able to locate them and direct the mike. The camera operator, who has been concentrating on a shot, now has to look around, turn, re-frame and refocus on the new speaker, before the shot can be used. Again, zooming out to a wide shot may save the situation. If you have a group of people, it is often an advantage to have in the front row those you know are going to speak.

During shooting it is best to check that shots are reasonably compatible so that there are no wild jumps in size, or variations in headroom (the space from the top of the head to the upper frame), or changes in camera height. Eye-lines too (i.e. where people appear to be looking) ought to be sufficiently related to suggest that people are talking to each other. If you are not careful when intercutting between various camera positions round a group, they can appear to be looking off camera or at the wrong person.

11.18 Car interviews

Interviews in cars are quite common; but how successful they are will vary between individuals. Some drivers find the nearby camera distracting. Their replies are liable to be perfunctory while concentrating on driving conditions. The audience may find the passing scene more interesting than the interview.

A steady camera is essential, whether the operator is located beside the driver (seated or crouched down) or shooting over the front seats. It can even be clamped to the outside of the car, looking in.

To give the shots variety, or to provide cutaways, you can cheat by reshooting the driver alone or with the interviewer (and no camera in the car!) from another vehicle traveling alongside, or slightly ahead.

Some directors create cutaway shots by showing the passing scene through the car windows, shots in a driving mirror, shots showing a gear change, and so on. But unless these pictures are directly related to the interview (e.g. discussing road safety, the route or driving techniques), they are simply a distraction.

11.19 Walking interviews

Walking interviews do at least get away from the regular seated situation, but don't underestimate their problems. If you just clip personal mikes to the interviewer and guest, or use a communal hand mike, you will have trailing wires – which can be handled perhaps by a sound operator walking alongside but out of shot.

Interviewing techniques

Interviews range from casual *vox pop* street encounters to friendly chats and hard probing interviews.

- Why are you interviewing this person? Is he or she a personality in town? Have they done something unusual? Or seen something unusual? Is an expert explaining something; giving an opinion? Whatever the reason, this will form the basis of your questions and influence how you approach the interview.

- There are circumstances where instead of interviewing people on camera, it is more convenient, or easier, to visit them, and audio record the interview. Their information can then be quoted by a commentator or reporter, or form part of a script.

- Preliminary research on the person always pays off, whether this takes the form of reading their book, biography or newspaper clippings, or asking around.

- Get to know guests before the taping session if possible (hospitality), to put them at ease, to guide them on the form of the interview and to prime them on the mechanics, for example 'Don't bother about the camera . . . If anything goes wrong we can start again . . . I suggest that we just chat as we walk along the path . . .'.

- Avoid going over the whole interview beforehand, for the taped version will lose its freshness. The talent is likely to leave out information during the repeat, or forget sections, thinking that he/she has already covered those points. If that happens, you can always prompt with: 'Earlier, you were telling me . . .'.

- Are there any personal items (e.g. mementos or family album photos) that the guest will want to show during the recording? (You may shoot details later, as cutaway or insert shots.)

- It may be helpful to agree beforehand, whereabouts in the interview you are going to introduce any personal items, maps or photographs.

- Some directors diplomatically ask the guest what they anticipate wearing at the interview, to avoid picture problems with extreme tones (such as white or black velvet), close checks or stripes, vibrant colors or shine (plastic), or noise from personal ornaments. Others dodge the issue, and accept the results anyway.

- Before a taping session, check that chairs are comfortable enough, but will not allow people to swivel around, or lounge back to frustrate good shots. Check the shots with stand-ins, or if necessary with the interviewer and guest, and mark floor positions of chairs (tape or chalk). Similarly note floor positions of cameras.

- If there is a picture monitor nearby, angle it so that the guest cannot see it. Certainly avoid letting the guest see him/herself; it could make the guest nervous (or vain).

- Before taping, have a *voice test* (level test) in which the interviewer and the guest both speak for a few seconds at normal volume, so that the audio channel gain can be adjusted, and prevent 'over- or undermoding'. Do not use interview questions for this purpose, but ask the guest about his or her journey, or a similar neutral subject.

- Develop a fact sheet or background card, noting the points you want to bring up, based on research and conversation. (Don't prepare detailed, written-out questions, which you then read at the guest!)

- Do not have a script yourself, or let the guest work from a script or prompter. Results are so forced and artificial.

For the interviewer, an introduction to the guest may be read from a prompter, as can any statistics or data referred to.

- It is best if questions *appear* to develop from the guest's answers, moving back to prepared topics when possible. Do not simply work through a tick-off list of questions. Quick brief surreptitious glances at your notes are better than your appearing to ignore replies while you read them.

There are regular do's and dont's for interviewers:

- Be punctual for the interview and the preliminary checks: i.e. fitting intercom earpiece, checking voice levels, checking any prompter, shot check (hair, tie, clothing OK?).

- Check which camera is opening the interview. If its tally light goes out, the director has switched to another camera. Simply look down momentarily, then look towards the camera showing the lit tally light.

- Take cues over intercom or from the FM, without any outward sign, and follow them immediately.

- Restrict your hand and arm gestures. If you are going to get up from a chair (rise) or sit, begin the move slowly to enable the camera to follow you smoothly.

- Try to maintain eye contact with your guest as much as possible. It helps them to feel 'involved' rather than interrogated.

Ask specific questions, not general ones. And keep to the point of the interview. If, for example, you are talking to a witness to a fire, his/her opinions about the neighborhood may be relevant or a sidetrack.

Avoid questions which can be answered 'Yes' or 'No'.

Avoid questions with obvious answers, or unrelated questions, or futile questions; e.g. 'Do you think your product is a good one?'

Do use questions beginning: 'Where? When? Why? How? Who? Which? What?'

Use invitations such as: 'Tell me about . . .'; 'Let's talk about . . .'; 'Do you remember, you were telling me about . . .'.

- Ask one question at a time, and wait for replies. Some interviewers get their best responses by simply waiting. The talent feels uneasy at the silence, and says something (often revealing) to break it, so giving the opportunity for further questions.
- Never interrupt interesting replies for the sake of asking prepared questions. And never ignore answers. Even if you only reply: 'I see', or nod, this avoids a feeling of interrogation.
- Do not say too much. (Some interviewers do most of the speaking!)

Use a polite, friendly style, not solemn or over-reacting. Smiles help as long as they appear genuine.

- Persuade guests not to wear dark glasses. They can prevent you from seeing expressions. (You can always point out that the camera exaggerates the sinister effect.)
- If guests smoke continuously, you may find on editing the program that shots appear with and without cigarettes, of varying lengths.

The visual discontinuity can be very obvious.

A less inhibiting method might be to use a shotgun/rifle mike near the camera for sound pick-up, provided its operator has a clear view of the action (i.e. no intervening trees, walls or foliage).

Of course, if you have the facilities, you can provide each speaker with a clip-on mike and miniature transmitter, and pick up their speech at a distance (using two separate receivers and antennas). But there is always the hazard of varying reception difficulties.

Try to arrange a walking interview so that you do not pick up a lot of extraneous noise, such as the crunch of pebbles or gravel underfoot, foliage, wind, traffic or machinery.

If you have real sound pick-up problems, one way out is to shoot a great deal of the action so that the mouth movements are not obvious in the picture (e.g. long shots, rear views), and then lay the speech which has been taped separately (non-sync) over the pictures during editing.

Occasionally, what looks like a 'walking interview' is actually a studio interview, with pictures of the people walking, taken on a carefully angled camera.

During a walking interview, the camera operator has the option of:

- walking backwards (guided by an assistant's hand on a shoulder),
- sitting on a wheeled mounting of some kind, and being pulled in front of the action (in a hospital corridor, it could be a wheelchair),
- locating the camera at an uninterrupted vantage point, and panning with the action,
- walking behind the people, taking a three-quarter back or a rear view.

None of these methods is conducive to steady camerawork for any length of time, especially if the camera is hand or shoulder supported, and the ground is uneven.

The best solution is usually to break up the walk into a series of sections; perhaps letting the speakers walk out of frame at the end of a section. Remember though, if they exit frame left, they must enter the next shot from frame right, so that they appear to be walking in the same direction. Alternatively, you can intercut with a head-on view of them, coming towards the camera.

To avoid any walk becoming unduly long, the speakers can pause at intervals, and still talking, lean on a fence, or sit on a log or stand and look at the landscape, or some other natural activity.

Shooting demonstrations

11.20 Typical demonstrations

A very wide range of video programs can be described as 'demonstrations'. They may involve as little as a single piece of paper (e.g. to show us origami techniques) or illustrate in elaborate detail the intricacies of an industrial process.

General interest programs give a lay audience broad information about a subject, and are usually designed to provide persuasive entertainment, from public relations exercises to propaganda. So you meet this kind of program under such titles as: 'How Maps Are Made', 'Safety in the Home', 'The Beauty of Glass', etc.

Instructional demonstrations, on the other hand, are usually intended to guide the audience *specifically*, and are made for particular markets, such as educational, professional, specialist trades, etc. There are several regular types of instructional programs:

- *How it's made*: showing construction, layout, design features, etc.
- *How it works*: showing technology involved, mechanics, scientific principles, etc.
- *How to prepare/build/construct/assemble, etc.*
- *Maintenance procedures*: showing methods of servicing, trouble-shooting, repairs, etc.
- *Operation*: showing how a system or device is used; operational techniques, applications, etc.
- *Organization*: outlining procedures, administrative methods, etc.
- *Sales*: demonstrating product appeal, marketing, etc.

Comparative demonstration: showing how a subject has evolved, been developed, the varieties available, etc.

Longer demonstration programs are usually made up from a number of separate sub-programs. For example:

- a presenter speaking to camera, outlining the subject's history, principles, etc.,
- a bench demonstration showing construction, design, assembly, etc.,
- a field demonstration, showing equipment in action on the farm, building site, factory, etc.

11.21 Approaches to demonstrations

There are some subjects that you cannot really demonstrate effectively in a video program. Instead, you have to rely on *verbal descriptions* of processes, e.g. perfume making. Other subjects may be only partly

Figure 11.8 Repositioning
Equal distances. If you have a series of things at equal distances from the camera, they can be covered by panning a static camera.

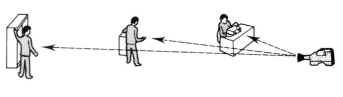

Different sized subjects. When you have subjects of various sizes, put the biggest in the background, and have the demonstrator work towards the smallest, near the camera. This method requires least floor space, and little camera movement.

Moving with the demonstrator. Here the camera zooms out from a close shot, and arcs round to a new viewpoint as the demonstrator walks to the next subject. This dynamic method of presentation requires skilled camerawork (changing focus, smooth arcing and accurate positioning).

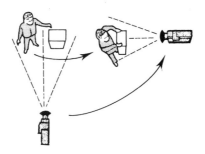

successful, due to the *limitations* of the system, e.g. a demonstration of sound quality.

Arguably, the weakest method of demonstrating anything in a video program is an illustrated talk, showing still photographs, diagrams, maps, etc. However good these may be, the video screen is a place for *action* and you can only introduce very limited movement into such static subjects.

A cookery demonstration, on the other hand, can be extremely effective, for it is full of visual movement and change, a process that develops as we watch – even though the audience cannot smell or taste whether it is as successful as it looks!

The most powerful form of demonstration is where someone speaks to us *directly* through the camera, pointing out each feature of the subject in turn.

The 'documentary format', in which the demonstrator is heard as a 'voice-over', making observations on the pictures, is less personal. But it can be more authoritative; especially if the speaker's visual presence is not particularly impressive on camera for any reason. But the documentary approach is very 'greedy for visuals'. Whereas in the 'direct approach' you can always take shots of the demonstrator speaking to camera, with the 'documentary' method the camera is continually looking at the subject and its surroundings – which may not have enough interest to sustain audience attention.

11.22 Thinking it through

On the face of it, one might assume that any demonstration merely involves showing the item to the camera, and pointing out its features. Some very boring programs get made this way! The secrets of really successful demonstrations are *planning*, *preparation* and *rehearsal*, even for the most familiar subject. In fact, the more familiar it is, the more difficult it can be to make the program interesting, and hold the audience's attention. Too easily, they can assume that they 'know all about that', and daydream instead, looking without seeing and hearing without listening.

A good demonstration program is designed to suit its audience. If it is pitched at too high a level, the uninitiated become bewildered and embarrassed at not being able to grasp the facts. They become confused. They lose their self-confidence. While sorting out what *has been said*, they lose the thread of what *is being said!*

A successful program encourages curiosity and intrigues, leaving the audience with a sense of satisfaction and fulfilment. 'What do you think will happen now?' is much more involving, than: 'When we do this . . . that happens'.

In the panels on pages 237–239 you will find a basic rundown of the points you may need to consider, when preparing a video program of a demonstration. As always, much of it is common sense.

11.23 The problem of time

Demonstrations can take anything from a split second to years to complete. So you often need to stretch or condense time in various ways, to suit the occasion:

- Shoot everything from start to finish. This ensures that your audience misses none of the action, and gets an accurate idea of how long everything takes. Clearly a good approach for relatively brief demonstrations, but quite unsuitable when showing how to paint a portrait or build a house.
- Instead, you can record the action continuously, then edit out the time-consuming, repetitious or boring parts. This can produce a shorter, better-paced program, and ensures that your audience concentrates on the important stages.
- You can arrange the demonstrations in prepared sections. For instance, when showing how to bake a cake, you may first display the ingredients, begin the method of mixing, then place the prepared mixture in an oven (or not, if one is not available). You can then remove (or show) an already cooked cake, and begin to decorate it, finally showing a fully decorated cake.

Not only does this method save a great deal of time but it ensures that the results turn out right at each stage! However, you have to guard against leaving out important information when shortcutting time in this way. For instance, you may inadvertently leave the audience wondering how to tell when the food is fully cooked. Preferably you would both tell them or show them how to test.

● Where a demonstration takes a long time to develop (e.g. a plant growing), the simplest plan is to shoot short sequences at strategic moments (hours, days or weeks apart) and show one after the other. Even photo-stills may be enough for this purpose.

The alternative is an automatic timer that takes a brief shot at regular intervals. When the tape is played back at normal speed, time is compressed, and these *time lapse* sequences show the process highly speeded up. A plant can grow from seed, flower and die in a minute or two. But of course, this method does tie up a camera (and VCR) in its rigidly held position for some time.

● Extremely brief events (showing a bullet breaking glass or how a hummingbird flies) have to be captured with a special high-speed cine camera, or flash still photography.

Sometimes a demonstration program has to be made to a prescribed length, e.g. to fit a scheduled time-slot. You can achieve this by deliberately including material that is interesting but can be trimmed or omitted where necessary. These 'cushions' ('buffers') may be complete mini-items, or just introductory/concluding action, such as gathering the components for the demonstration together, tidying the bench and so on.

If your video program is to be used as part of a live presentation, e.g. in a classroom lecture where a teacher will also be speaking and answering questions, you can design it to be extremely flexible. You can arrange the program as a series of pre-timed self-contained sections, so that the teacher can use just as much as is needed for a particular lesson, without the students feeling that they are being prevented from seeing the entire program.

Preparing a demonstration

The following outline checklist shows the kinds of facts you may need to consider when preparing a video program of a demonstration.

What is the demonstration's purpose?

Is it to show:

● how an item is made?
● how to prepare/build/construct/assemble, etc?
● how it works?
● how to use it?
● how to maintain it?
● development of a process?

Who is it for?

Is it for the general public, for specialist groups or a local group?
At what level is it required: basic, intermediate or advanced?
Is any particular background, qualification, language or group-experience necessary for the audience?

What is the program format?

Is it a single program, or one in a series?
Does it relate to other programs (e.g. continue their discussion or use information explained in those programs)?
Do you need to recap, or remind audience of parts of earlier programs?
Does the program have to cover specified topics?
Is a duration specified for the program?

Research

Do you need to research the subject itself, or find appropriate authorities who can provide information?
Who are they? Are they available as information sources, consultants or performers? (Fees?)
Where is the subject of the program available? (Where do they make it, grow it, use it, etc.?)
Will you need to go to them to shoot the product or the demonstration? (Factory, laboratory, zoo, museum, research center, etc.)
If you are borrowing/hiring items, consider such aspects as availability, time, transport, weight, dimensions, supplies, precautions, insurance, when and how item is to be returned, etc.
Would staff, demonstrator, keeper or guard come with item?

Subject potentials

Does the subject provide inherently interesting visual material?
Can it be prepared in such a way as to appear interesting?
How can you display the particular features or qualities of the subject?
How long does the action of the demonstration take:

- very brief (e.g. firing a gun)?
- a long time to demonstrate completely (e.g. building a house)?
- continuous operation (e.g. a water pump)?

What is the size/scale of the demonstration:

- microscopic?
- small (e.g. a wristwatch)?
- huge (can only shoot it in sections)?
- contained on a table or bench?

Are any precautions necessary during the demonstration? (Fire, flood, fumes, sparks, explosions, brittle, delicate.)
Are any animals being used? (Care, feeding, security.)
Are there problems of over-heating specimens under lights?
Is any special lighting or sound pick-up required (e.g. ultraviolet light to demonstrate rock-fossils)?

Supplementary items/equipment

Is any artwork required (e.g. drawings, photographs, or animated graphics)?
Are any prepared diagrams, graphs or flow-charts needed?
Are any models or analogues needed (e.g. geometric forms or chemical elements models)?
Are any scale replicas, etc., needed (e.g. ship model)?
Are any drawing materials needed (e.g. flip-chart, magnetic board or chalk-board)?
Is any apparatus or equipment needed (e.g. chemical, electrical, tools, etc.)?

Organization

Who will supply/provide/make the above? (Consider available time, transport, costs, fragility, function checks, storage, return, etc.)
Are any electrical supplies needed for apparatus? (Check voltage, consumption, phase, etc.)

Are gas, water or steam needed? Is water drainage needed? (A bucket, siphon, pump, etc.)

Who will operate or show the equipment? (The supplier, a helper or you.)

Who will install, repair or adjust it?

Does it need priming (e.g. chemicals)?

Does it make a mess (e.g. squirt water, foam, etc.)? Is any protective clothing needed (e.g. goggles, gloves, overall)? Should the floor be protected?

Are there any problems in demonstrating at the proposed place (fire risk, noise, wind, weather, etc.)?

Will the item/apparatus need to be assembled at the demonstration site? Is it connected up? It is temperamental?

Does the subject/item need special care?

Are any people needed as part of the demonstration (e.g. as a mock patient)?

Does the process use expendable material (e.g. a supply of paper or chemicals)?

Liabilities

Consider the involvements, relative to: budget, time available, space available, labor, hazards, insurance, transport and facilities.

Alternatives

Consider alternatives that may be: easier, cheaper, quicker, more reliable, more readily available, simpler, less hazardous, etc.

Organizing a demonstration

The nature of the subject

The kind of subject you are demonstrating, and the features you want to bring out, will influence how you use your camera . . . where it concentrates . . . how close the shots are . . . how varied they are. What are these features?

- Is there *action* to watch (e.g. parts moving)?
- Are we watching an *effect*?
- Are we watching an *operator* assembling or forming something (e.g. at a lathe, knitting, planting)?
- Are the items simply *there*, to be explored by the cameras (e.g. works of art)?
- Is it a *continuous* process, or a 'once-only' process? Does it need time to recover?

Does each demonstration need a fresh set-up (e.g. new ingredients)?

- Are there any *hazards* that restrict the shot you can use? Can the camera see the action clearly or will, for example, machine guards need to be removed? Should transparent guards be made (e.g. safety glass sheet) to protect the camera?

Presenting the subject effectively

- Is the subject best seen from certain angles?
- If a process is complex, would a diagram help to emphasize, explain, show features, show what to look out for, or show the stage a process has reached? (Are superimposed subtitles needed?)
- Would it help to intercut between the subject and a diagram. Or should you use a superimposition, or a split screen?
- Wherever possible, have things prepared beforehand (e.g. cut up, weighed), so that the demonstration is primarily an assembly process. (For example, in making a bookshelf, saw and drill the wood and fit it up, then dis-assemble ready for demonstration.)
- Check that equipment/exhibits/models really do work, before the rehearsal period.

Rehearsal

There are several methods of arranging a demonstration for the camera:

1. The demonstrator works while explaining the process direct to the camera.
2. The demonstrator works while explaining to a student standing nearby.
3. The demonstrator works while explaining to the person hosting the program (an experienced interviewer anchor person/chairperson who asks questions on behalf of the audience, e.g. about terms used, methods, problems, etc.).
4. A similar arrangement but here the host continually aids the demonstrator to optimize the demonstration following the director's intercom instructions heard on an earpiece (e.g. advice on adjusting the best positions of items for close-ups; handing articles to the demonstrator, and removing them after use; suggesting questions; speeding/slowing the pace of the presentation).
5. The demonstrator works (mute) while an expert standing nearby explains what is going on.
6. The demonstrator works, while an explanatory written commentary is displayed as subtitles or partial page text.
7. The demonstrator works (mute) to a recorded audio commentary (given by the demonstrator or another).
8. The interviewer works to the expert's instructions and guidance.

Preferably watch a preliminary non-camera rehearsal, so that you can decide on the best viewpoints and shots. You can also guide the demonstrator on how they can show their work best on camera. Give any advice where necessary about handling items (e.g. avoiding light reflections), showing them to camera, position marks, etc., but keep these points to a minimum.

Try to keep items isolated, so that the camera can shoot one at a time.

Preferably have the items/ingredients/specimens at hand, ready to use, in the order in which you are going to demonstrate them, and move progressively, from one item to the next, rather than hop back and forth between them.

Avoid having a lot of items cluttering the demonstration area (e.g. items you've finished with, others to be used later or some there just for the effect). Aim to clear things away as you go through the demonstration. (Have side benches, shelves under the working surface, or an assistant clearing items.) Do not let items accumulate until a recording break, then clear the working area. Otherwise after editing, the clutter will magically disappear on the cut!

Rather than zoom in to detail frequently, edit in insert shots of detail, taken afterwards. But make sure the audience realizes where the detail is located on the subject.

If necessary, have a cue sheet near the camera, to remind the demonstrator of the agreed order of items, but *not* a fully scripted prompter.

Where material is used during a demonstration (paper, ingredients, etc.), have extra at hand for rehearsals and retakes. Have standby spares for items likely to break and abort the experiment.

If parts of a live demonstration are likely to fail, be ready to use:

● a taped section of an earlier successful recording (e.g. rehearsal),
● specimens of a good/correct result (e.g. a cake that *has* risen properly!),
● a photograph of the desired effect,
● a substitute item,
● an explanation of what went wrong, and what the audience *should* have seen.

At the end of a rehearsal, or a take, make sure that equipment is checked over and ready to go, for the next taping – e.g. rewound, reconnected, cleaned off, broken parts replaced, refilled, fresh paper inserted or whatever.

At the end of the demonstration, consider whether any retakes, cutaways or insert shots are needed, before concluding.

Finally, gather demonstration items together and store for dispatch.

Chapter 12

Visual effects

We use an 'effect' to create an illusion . . . which may appear so natural, that the audience accepts it as *real*!

12.1 Using effects

Say 'visual effects', and most people think of impressive spectacle, of lumbering monsters and crumbling cities, raging fires and similar catastrophes. But many everyday 'effects' are quite unobtrusive. They may be decorative or naturalistic, but we use them for entirely *practical* reasons; because they are convenient, safe, save money, and are reliable.

In this chapter we shall look at various methods and mechanisms. Most are quite cheap and simple to apply. Some need extra facilities, but most just require experiment and patience. They will all extend your opportunities.

12.2 Using filters

In Chapter 3 we saw how a filter at the front of the camera lens can modify or control the image. This filter may take the form of a clip-on cap or be slid into a special filter holder. Here is a summary of typical filters regularly used to create visual effects.

- *Neutral density (ND) filter.* A transparent gray-tinted material that cuts down light without changing its color quality. Available in densities ranging from 10% to 1% transmission. Used in strong sunlight to prevent overexposure, or to allow you to use large lens apertures. Also used over light sources or windows to reduce the light intensity.
- *Sky filter.* A graduated neutral density filter, reducing the brightness of the upper part of the picture (sky), while remaining clear below.
- *Diffusion disk.* Overall image diffusion ranging from slight softening, to dense mist and fog effects (*fog filter*). A piece of net, nylons or gauze has a similar effect.
- *Soft spot.* A filter with a clear center, and a progressively diffused surround.
- *Star filter.* Creates a series of radiating light rays around a localized light source (candle, headlight, specular reflection).
- *Polarizing filter.* A filter eliminating reflections and glare from smooth shiny surfaces, such as windows, glassware, water.
- *Multi-facet filter.* Creates multiple images; either around a central subject, or across the frame.

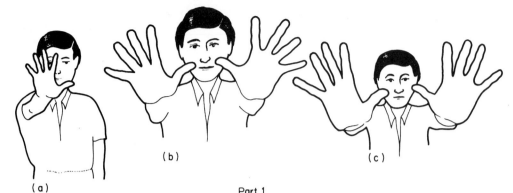

(a) (b) (c)

Part 1

Part 2

Figure 12.1 Deliberately distorting space

Part 1 *Distorting people.* Although you will seldom take big close-ups on a very wide or narrow lens angle, unless you want grotesque distortion, it is easy to forget that even natural body moves (a) can become distorted on wider lens angles (b and c).

Part 2 *Compressing and expanding space.* Wider lens angles appear to emphasize distance (a), while narrow lenses compress it (c).

Part 3 *Fisheye lenses.* Ultra-wide-angle 'fisheye' lenses appear to distort and curve space in a dramatic fashion.

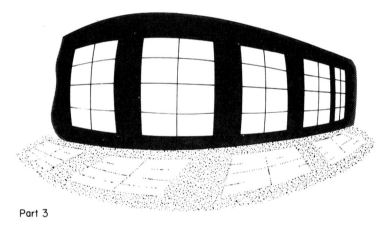

Part 3

12.3 Distorted images

Shoot via a plastic mirror (slightly bent or warped), kitchen foil sheet, through a clear tumbler or bottle, or through decorative glass.

Place a piece of clear plastic or glass over the camera lens and lightly grease or oil the areas you want to distort. You can leave the center untouched to obtain a normal image surrounded by distortion.

Shooting through a tube of kitchen foil, the central image is surrounded by an attractive whorl reflection. A tube of mirror tiles can produce a kaleidoscopic effect.

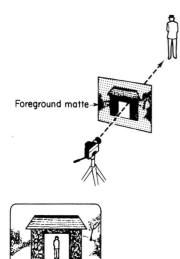

Foreground matte→

Figure 12.2 Foreground matte
The foreground photograph or
drawing has a carefully positioned
hole, through which a distant
subject is visible.

12.4 Mattes

Mattes or masks are simple to make, but can be extremely effective. You
can use them in several ways:

Lens matte. Shooting through a piece of card or a stencil attached to the
lens, you can imitate the view through a telescope, binoculars, or a
keyhole.

Foreground matte (camera matte, gobo). Place a photograph in the
foreground, and cut away an area to show the studio action (e.g. a doorway),
and if you have matched the scale, tones, and colors well, you have a
convincing composite shot. Similarly, you can provide a ceiling for a
setting, or matte out unwanted parts of the shot. To be successful, the shot
must have considerable depth of field.

When you do not want to damage a photograph or painting, you can reflect
it in an angled mirror-plastic sheet in front of the camera, with a cutaway
area for the studio action (similar to the 'Pepper's ghost' set-up; see Figure
12.5).

12.5 Reflections (see Figure 12.3)

Water ripple. The usual method involves shining a spotlight onto pieces of
mirror, in a dish of water. (Metal plates, mirror tiles or kitchen foil can
substitute for mirror.)

Thin metalized plastic sheeting (e.g. survival blanket) resting on the
floor can reflect light, which appears to ripple when the sheet is
disturbed.

Kitchen foil can be cut out into a shape (flying bird, heart or missile), and
stuck to card. Light from a spotlight will reflect in this shape and can be
moved around the background. Flexing the board will alter the reflected
shape.

Light reflected from slightly crumpled kitchen foil will throw interesting
nebulous shapes and patterns onto a plain background. This is particularly
effective behind translucent screens.

Mirror. If you shoot a scene via a mirror, you can apparently:

- position the camera at angles that could otherwise be impracticable (e.g.
  floor, overhead or outside limited openings),
- take the camera farther away from the subject, in confined
  surroundings,
- tilt or cant the camera,
- create a wipe from one situation to another on a single camera. The
  camera shoots the first subject via an angled mirror, which slides aside to
  reveal the second subject.

A mirror image will always be laterally reversed. If this matters, you can
correct it either by using a second mirror (i.e. shoot into a mirror via a
mirror), or by electrically switching the camera's line scan circuits (line
reversal).

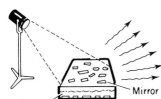

Tray of water

Mirror

Figure 12.3 Water ripple
A spotlight's beam is reflected from
pieces of mirror in a dish of water
to produce convincing water ripples.

12.6 Pepper's ghost

The old theatrical illusion known as 'Pepper's ghost' was originally used to
create transparent ghost effects on the open stage. But it has its application

Figure 12.4 Using mirrors

Part 1 *Confined spaces.* In a confined space, a mirror may make shots possible (although reversed) that would otherwise be impracticable. (Here, shooting into a mirror from a window.)

Part 2 *Inaccessible viewpoints.* When you cannot get a camera and operator into position, a mirror may make a viewpoint possible.

Part 3 *Overhead shot.* A top shot via an overhead mirror may be essential for some table-top demonstrations.

Part 4 *Canted shots.* When you want a canted viewpoint, to suggest instability, horror or madness, a mirror shot may be more convenient than a ground camera.

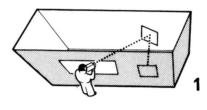
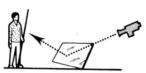
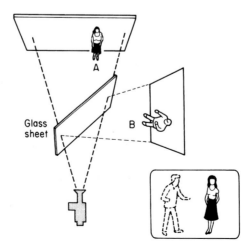

Figure 12.5 Pepper's ghost
A glass sheet reflects a subject, mixing it with the scene in front of the camera. The prominence of the mirrored image of the out-of-shot person (B) depends on the main scene's tones and brightness, and those of the second subject.

in video too, for although it involves only *one camera*, it can achieve some striking effects:

- to provide backgrounds that can be faded in/out and changed in vision,
- to produce transparent superimpositions,
- to light a subject directly along the lens axis, with shadowless illumination.

The principle is extremely simple. The camera shoots through a sheet of clear glass or a semi-transparent mirror (pellicle) held at 45° in front of the lens, and sees both the subject straight ahead, and a reflected image of the background picture (e.g. a large photograph) which is located over to one side.

If you want the background picture to look normal (a 'solid super-imposition'), you will need a black surface behind the subject. Otherwise the reflected background will appear as a ghostly superimposition. If your main subject corresponds with a dark area of the background picture, and the relative scale and brightness of subject and background are reasonably similar, it should not be possible to detect the faking.

The stronger the lighting on the background picture, the bolder it will appear. If you fade out the lighting on the background area, it will vanish and leave you with your subject against a plain black backing.

The background picture can come from a drawing or photograph, or you could use a translucent screen of frosted plastic sheeting with a rear-projected slide.

Because the lens-to-performer distance needs to be similar to the lens-to-background distance, the overall layout for this effect can take up a fair amount of room, even using a wide-angle lens, unless you are working in miniature and using, e.g. model soldiers, or small puppets for the subject.

Superimposition normally requires two cameras with a picture from each. But if you use a Pepper's ghost set-up, you can carry out super-impositions on *one camera*, and that can be an extremely useful facility for a single-camera unit. You could for example, have two photographs: one of a ruined building, and another taken when it was newly built. Place one in front of the camera, and another (printed in mirror image) to be reflected in the plain glass sheet or pellicle, and you can be changing their lighting, fade from one to the other, holding a superimposition if you wish, part way.

12.7 Projected backgrounds

Although you can use commercial pattern projectors (*profile spots*) to project light patterns of all kinds onto backgrounds, a regular slide projector has some very useful applications.

Rear projection. While action is shot in front of a translucent (frosted) screen, you project a slide onto its rear.

You can use this idea to provide a backing outside a window in a studio set, as a display screen during a talk, and even as a complete background for limited shots (close-ups, table-top displays).

Because you do not want light to spill over the screen, washing out its image, the trick is to light *across* the scene as far as possible, and mask off any stray light.

Figure 12.6 Projected backgrounds
Rear projection. A slide projected onto a translucent screen (frosted plastic sheet) provides a background.

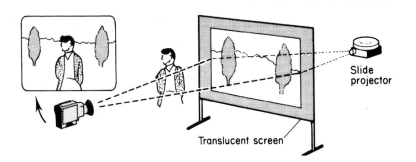

Slide projector

Translucent screen

Front projection. Here you use a hidden or suspended unit to project a slide directly onto a light-toned surface. it is essential to avoid action lighting spilling onto the background.

The brightness of the background image will depend on the projector's lamp-power and lens efficiency, its distance, the slide's density, and the background tones.

Reflex projection. This set-up uses a sort of 'reverse Pepper's ghost' arrangement. A slide of the background scene is projected directly along the lens axis via a half-silvered mirror onto a special screen. The surface of this screen is made up of millions of tiny glass beads, which reflect the background image extremely efficiently, and the camera shooting through the mirror sees both the subject and the screen with its background picture.

Although the projector's image falls on the subject as well as the screen, it is swamped by the subject's lighting, so is not visible on camera. The subject's shadow on the screen is not seen in the picture, provided the projector and camera lens angles are comparable and the system is lined up accurately.

If you cut out a piece of the reflex screen material, to match something in the background picture (e.g. a tree), and stick it on a piece of board, the performer can actually appear to walk *behind* that tree on the slide!

There are disadvantages as always, such as the fact that the camera cannot move during the shot, the light losses through the mirror, and the way light

Figure 12.7 Reflex projection

Part 1 The background scene is projected along the lens axis, via an angled glass sheet, onto a highly directional glass bead screen. The performer's lighting swamps the image falling on him.

Part 2 The camera sees the person in front of the projected background scene.

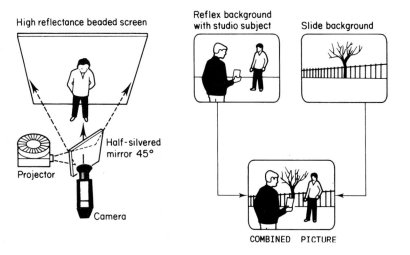

High reflectance beaded screen

Half-silvered mirror 45°

Projector

Camera

Reflex background with studio subject

Slide background

COMBINED PICTURE

tones in the subject (e.g. a white shirt) may reflect in the screen and cause haloes. But these are unimportant, compared with the visual miracles this *single-camera* arrangement can achieve.

12.8 Color medium ('gels')

Colored images. Shooting through carefully selected color media can produce strange color transformations, without totally destroying color values, e.g. 'surprise pink'.

Multi-colored light. Take two sheets of color media (e.g. light blue and yellow), cut a series of holes in both at random, and staple them together. When light shines through them, it will produce color patches of *three* colors (e.g. blue, yellow, green), for a stained glass effect that can be projected onto a plain background.

Angle two differently colored spotlights onto a slightly crumpled kitchen foil sheet. Multi-colored patterns will be reflected.

12.9 Light effects

Beam of light. To produce a beam of light (e.g. shining into a room, from a window), a smoke-filled atmosphere would normally be necessary. To create the effect, either superimpose a graphic of a white on black beam, or shoot through a gauze painted/sprayed with the beam shape.

Distant lights. To suggest distant lights (e.g. of a town, roadway, esplanade or stars), string out white Christmas-tree lights on a black cloth background.

If you pin the center of a string of these lights to a black background, and bring its separate ends towards the camera, this V-shaped string of lights resembles an airfield landing strip at night. The camera takes an over-shoulder shot of a seated person, facing the black background. Raising and lowering the strings of lamps makes the 'aircraft' appear to dive and climb. As the aircraft gets closer, the strings are parted. Add aircraft noises to complete the illusion for brief shots.

High lamps. A PAR lamp fixed to the top of a vertical hand-held pole can be useful:

- when you are shooting in awkward places, and need a high lamp for a short time,
- as a 'swinging keylight', gently swaying from side to side, to suggest a ceiling lantern on board a ship at sea, or a hung light set swinging in a bar brawl.

12.10 Scenic effects

Scrims/gauzes. If you paint on scrim/gauze material, the surface will appear solid when lit from the front, provided you leave areas behind the scrim unlit. If you light the areas behind the scrim instead, surface details almost disappear on camera.

So you can create various mystical, magical effects, simply by light switching (e.g. solid room walls disappear, to reveal whatever is beyond). Both white and black scrim can be used. White can create 'misty' effects and soften off the image. Black can provide 'solid' painted features or decoration, apparently suspended in mid air.

Figure 12.8 Projected shadows
You can cast shadows from a lamp
on the ground, using branches,
wire, grilles, metal-foil stencils, etc.

Tree branches. Tree branches a few feet long, with or without leaves, can be pressed into service for a number of purposes.

- Near the camera, they appear as undergrowth or small growing trees (nailed vertically to wooden floor supports or pushed into the ground).
- Waved gently in front of a yellow-orange lamp on the floor, a small branch can simulate firelight-flicker. (Alternatively, use a stick with close strips of hanging rag.)
- Supported in front of a lamp, a branch can produce dappled light, to suggest sunlight through leaves, or mysterious shadows in a night scene.
- Do the same thing with *colored light*, and an attractive decorative effect results. Try several lamps, using different colors. (Alternatively, use sheets of kitchen foil with a pattern of holes cut in them, to dapple the light.)
- Placed in front of a lamp lighting a translucent screen from the rear (hung, or on the floor), a tree branch will cast decorative shadows.

Chapter 13

Electronic effects

13.1 Effects can extend horizons

Many of the video effects we see regularly on our TV screens are used for their sheer pizzazz – to create an exciting visual impact. Pictures unfold, break up into fragments, rotate, transform in intriguing ways . . . But for the small production unit with limited resources, electronic effects can play a far more important role. They provide a way of building up *totally realistic illusions* quickly, and at low cost, that would not otherwise be quite impracticable. With a little time, patience, and imagination, you can create outstanding results!

Seeing is believing? A whole range of video trickery is just the result of carefully controlled switching processes. Not particularly interesting? Well, let's look at an example of how useful even the simplest effects can be.

We have two pictures:

A woman standing in front of Camera 1.

A videotape showing a street scene.

- We use a *special effects generator* (*SEG*) to apply a simple *box wipe* (Figure 13.1) to Camera 1's shot.
- This blanks off most of its shot, leaving the woman standing in a small rectangle within a black screen.
- The SEG inserts the videotaped scene into the blank surrounding, combining the two shots.

Here we have the *mechanics*. But what does your audience see?

They are watching a street scene showing a woman standing in a house doorway. We know that in reality she is there in front of the studio camera, within the masked area generated by the *SEG*. We know that the videotaped street scene is a stock shot from our tape library. But for them, the effect is totally convincing! Yet all we have done is to combine two different images with a basic video trick.

13.2 Opportunities for improvement

There are two diverse approaches to picture making. The first simply sets up equipment to manufacturers' standards, and leaves matters at that. The alternative is to continually adjust the equipment in order to create the most effective results.

The difference between these approaches is most obvious in the case of program sound. We can just record the 'straight' sound from the microphone and use it in that form as the program soundtrack. Or by making slight changes adding a little reverberation perhaps, or adjusting equalization we may produce sound that has a much more convincing, more realistic character. The choice is ours.

Similarly, by making subtle changes to a picture, we can often transform it from a very ordinary shot to a more eye-catching, more appealing, or more appropriate entity. Our impressions of 'picture quality' are very subjective. It is surprising how often we prefer a picture that looks just a little 'warmer' or has slightly exaggerated contrast when compared with the original scene.

Many larger studios, continually monitor picture quality, and make adjustments:

- to give better visual continuity between shots (e.g. as camera angles vary),
- to compensate for changing conditions (e.g. varying lighting intensities),
- to adjust picture quality for artistic reasons; e.g. enhance a lighting effect, or create a particular atmosphere.

These variations of *lens aperture, black level (lift, sit), video gain, color balance, gamma*, are made on the *camera control unit (CCU), remote control unit (RCU)*, or a *vision control desk*.

For smaller production units, various supplementary units are available to achieve these effects, such as: *image enhancers*, *video effects units*, *desktop video software*.

13.3 Adjusting picture quality

You can alter picture quality in a number of ways; for a particular shot, or perhaps for an entire scene:

Sharpness	By *lens filters*; by defocusing the *lens*; or by picture channel adjustment.
Brightness	Adjusting the *lens aperture*; and/or *video gain*.
Tonal range and contrast	Adjusting the *gamma*. (Higher gamma settings produce a coarser, exaggerated contrast; while lower settings result in thin reduced tonal contrasts.) Lowering the picture's *black level* moves all picture tones down towards black and crushes the lowest tones. Raising the *black level* lifts all picture tones, but does not reveal more detail in blackest tones.
Color intensity	Increased *saturation* emphasizes strength of color. Reduced saturation (diluting with white) gives a more pastel effect.

Color fidelity

To simulate firelight or moonlight, or make a picture 'warmer' or 'cooler', shooting with 'wrong' *color temperature* compensation may suffice. Otherwise color balance can be changed by adjusting the video gain, black level or gamma of the separate red, green, or blue color channels.

13.4 Electronic effects sources

There are various ways in which you can create electronic effects:

- A *special effects generator (SEG)* – This is often incorporated into the switcher unit. It produces a variety of mask patterns which allow you to selectively insert sections of one picture into another and create a range of wipe patterns.
- *Luminance keying* – An automatic switching device that is activated by a specified tone (usually black or white) in the master shot.
- *Chroma key* (chromakey) – A facility that relies on a color backing (usually blue) to activate automatic switching and insert a subject into a background scene.
- *Computer software* – A variety of computer software programs are available which further extend opportunities for video trickery. To enable a PC to be used with a video system, intermediate equipment is necessary. (An encoder converts the PC's digital data into an NTSC (PAL) signal. A genlock unit allows computer-generated images to be mixed with video.)

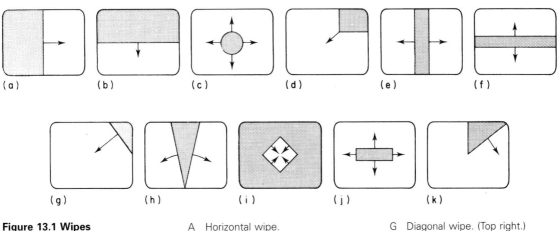

(a)   (b)   (c)   (d)   (e)   (f)

(g)   (h)   (i)   (j)   (k)

Figure 13.1 Wipes
There are hundreds of wipe patterns.

Here are a few of the commonest.

A   Horizontal wipe.
B   Downwards vertical wipe.
C   Iris or circular wipe. (Out or in; expanding or contracting.)
D   Corner wipe – top right. (When static, this provides a corner insert.)
E   Barndoors/line-bar/horizontal split-wipe. (Expanding or converging.)
F   Vertical split wipe/field wipe. (Wipes in or out.)

G   Diagonal wipe. (Top right.)
H   Fan wipe. (In or out.)
I   Diamond wipe-in.
J   Box wipe-out.
K   Rotary/clock wipe.

13.5 Matting or keying

The easiest way to understand matting processes is to regard them as cutting a hole in one picture and inserting an exactly corresponding area from another picture. Within the area covered by the matte the SEG switches from the main picture channel to a second picture source. The edges of this insert may be sharply defined (*hard-edged*) or diffused (*soft-edged*) so that they blend unobtrusively into the composite.

Depending on the electronic effects device you use, and the effect you are aiming at, the switching action may be triggered by either of two different methods:

- *'External keying' ('separate key')*. This specially prepared matte or mask may be created *automatically* (as in the SEG) or *manually* using a suitable cut-out card, painted or inked shape, or a stenciled shape from a computer graphic. This matte may have a geometrical or an irregular shape.
- *'Internal keying' ('self keying')*. Here the system is triggered by a selected *tone* (*luminance keying*), or a particular color (*chrominance keying*) appearing in the master picture.

13.6 Using mattes

We use mattes for several different purposes:

- To *insert* all or part of a second image (pictorial or titling) into the main picture.
- To *prevent* a particular area in the main picture from being affected by changes we are making.
- To allow us to *'overlap'* one image (or part of it) onto another.
- To change the *appearance* of a selected area.

Although the matte usually becomes an integral part of the new composite picture, it is sometimes used at an interim stage when developing an effect, then removed (*garbage matte*).

13.7 The special effects generator (SEG)

Of course, you don't have to know how equipment works to use it effectively. But understanding its basics does help you to anticipate opportunities and problems. So let's take a closer look at the SEG's potentials.

As you know, television pictures are built up using a line-by-line scanning process that is similar to the way we read a book. The image is traced along a series of parallel paths – scanning left to right . . . from the top of the screen . . . to the bottom in a regularly repeated rhythm. (More about that in the next chapter.)

The *special effects generator (SEG)* is an ingenious automatic switching device that continually flips between two different picture sources. By varying the rate of this inter-camera switching you can produce various 'stencil effects' on the screen in which sections of one picture are inserted into another. (There are some typical examples in Figure 13.1.)

The SEG does this by generating a selection of waveforms (i.e. varying voltages) which activate the inter-switching. The shape and the frequency of the waveform we select controls the pattern it produces. If this switching waveform is constant, the pattern on the screen appears stationary.

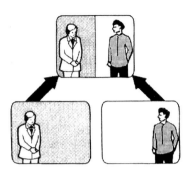

Figure 13.2 Split screen
A horizontal wipe, which has been stopped mid-way to show halves of two separate pictures.

Gradually alter it in any way, and the pattern will move and/or change shape. All these effects are quite independent of the *pictures* involved. This idea will be clearer if we look at some regular examples.

Split screens Let's take two shots from Cameras 1 and 2. Both cameras' pictures are fed to the SEG unit while we watch its output. As the scanning process starts, the SEG switches to Camera 1's picture. But at the instant scanning has reached half-way across the screen, the SEG flips to Camera 2's picture instead for the rest of that scanning line. (At the end of each scanned line it switches back to Camera 1's output.) It goes on interswitching in this way for every line of the picture. The result? On the screen we have the left half of the Camera 1's shot and the right half of Camera 2's shot. In other words, a *50:50 horizontal split screen*. This used to be a favorite way of showing both ends of a telephone conversation on the screen at the same time.

Horizontal wipe If we set the SEG to switch before scanning reaches the midway point of each line the left section of Camera 1's picture will now be correspondingly *narrower* in the combined shot compared with Camera 2's. Switch a little *later* and the reverse happens. So by changing the moment of switching we can alter the relative widths of the two sections.

The special effect generator usually has a *variable control* which does exactly that. It may be controlled manually or automated with an *auto-wipe* button, but in either case the result is a *horizontal wipe* across the screen as one shot progressively displaces another.

Vertical split screen Choose a *'vertical split'* setting and we see Camera 1's picture forming in the normal way . . . until scanning reaches half-way down the screen. Then the SEG system's switches over instantly to Camera 2's shot as the lower half of the screen is scanned. The resulting effect shows the upper part of Camera 1's picture and the lower part of Camera 2's shot – a *vertical split screen*. Adjust the moment at which it switches, and you have a *vertical wipe* upwards or downwards.

Inserts/Insets By combining forms of vertical and horizontal splits, the SEG can provide a small square or rectangular screen anywhere within the main shot – a useful way of displaying a *detail shot* within the main picture, for example where one's interest is divided between the broader view (e.g. a shot of a full orchestra) and localized action (e.g. concentrating on a soloist).

13.8 SEG adjustments

Although the effects are always geometrical, the special effects generator may provide a useful range of adjustments:

- *Size* – Creating an expanding or contracting pattern.
- *Shape* – A circle can become an ellipse; a square becomes a rectangle.
- *Frame position* – Placing the pattern anywhere in the frame. Holding it there as a *fixed insert* (*inset*).
- *Pattern movement* – Moving the pattern around vertically, horizontally, diagonally.
- *Speed* – Setting the speed at which the pattern changes, using a fader lever or *auto-wipe* button.
- *Symmetry* – Adjusting the pattern's symmetry.
- *Edges* – Adjusting the edges of the pattern so that they are clearly defined (*hard-edged*) or diffused (*soft-edged*).
- *Border* – Placing a white, black or colored border round a pattern insert.
- *Weave or ripple* – Causing the pattern to move rhythmically from side to side.
- *Spotlight* – Picking out detail with a light-toned spotlight pointer.

13.9 Luminance keying

In a system using *luminance keying* (*luminance matting*), wherever a black area appears in the master shot a corresponding section of a second picture will replace it. (Although black is usually chosen as the *keying tone*, you can select either *black* or *white* to trigger luminance keying in both monochrome and color systems.) At first sight, not particularly exciting perhaps. But let's experiment:

- Place a yellow card with bold black lettering in front of Camera 1, which is connected to the effects generator. This will both provide a picture and trigger the switching process. Camera 2, which is also fed into the equipment, is shooting a *red* card, used to provide the inserted effect. The cameras' outputs combine in the composite, and we see a yellow screen with *red* lettering.
- Replace the red card with a spotted surface and you will have spotted lettering.
- By choosing a range of materials for Camera 2's shot you can produce titling that appears to be cut out of brick, cloth, wood, pebbles, rock, grass...
- There is no end to the kinds of subjects you choose for your second picture source. Shoot *billowing smoke, a water spray, flames*, to provide the inserted effect, and this same titling will become strangely transformed with a nebulous texture!

But luminance keying is not restricted to titling effects. Even with this apparently simple facility there are opportunities for the unusual!

- Use the silhouetted shape of a dancer to trigger the system, and insert defocused glittering, water reflections of colored lights ... within the moving shape.
- With the map of an island attached to a black background ... we can insert a videotaped aerial view of moving seas around it.
- Taking a still photograph of trees in winter, standing out as black silhouettes against a white sky ... we can transform the tree outlines into golden tracery. The sky can be shaded to suggest an impending storm, a glorious sunset, or filled with mysterious shapes...

The chroma key process

13.10 What is chroma key?

Chroma key techniques have endless potentials. Yet they are based on a very simple principle. Wherever a chosen *keying color* (usually blue) appears in the *main* or *master shot* the system switches automatically to a second source (the *background*); and exactly replaces that blue area with the corresponding section from the second picture instead – rather like fitting a piece into a jigsaw puzzle.

When chroma key techniques were first used it was not unusual to see all manner of strange effects, from ragging around the edges of inserted subjects to curious, unexpected breakthrough. Some of these anomalies were due to equipment limitations, but many were the result of the inexperience (or impatience) of those using the system. Today many of chroma key's technical problems have been overcome, and people are becoming increasingly aware of its applications.

Basic chroma key techniques have the major disadvantage that the camera needs to hold an immobile shot; unable to pan, tilt, zoom, or move, for this

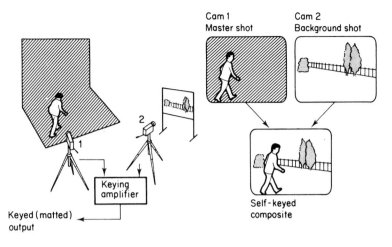

Cam 1
Master shot

Cam 2
Background shot

Keying amplifier

Keyed (matted) output

Self-keyed composite

Figure 13.3 Chroma key
The subject is set up in front of a blue background. Wherever this *keying hue* appears in the master camera's shot, the system switches to a separate *background picture* instead. In the combined result, the subject appears in front of the background scene.

Subjects within the *master shot* must not contain or reflect the keying hue, or there will be spurious breakthrough of the background scene. The background shot may include any colors.

would immediately destroy the realism. Currently a number of costly technical solutions are emerging that promise to overcome this limitation and allow the camera free movement. Explored under the general term ***virtual reality***, this complex technology is at present only available to major studios. But as we shall see, there are ways of working round this situation, and even simpler chroma key systems can be extremely effective.

13.11 What can chroma key do?

You can use chrominance keying in a number of quite different applications. Here are some typical examples:

- *Inserting people* – Inserting a person or object in the studio into a selected background picture.
- *Display panel* – Inserting text or a picture into a 'screen' in the setting.
- *'Magic paint'* – To create a 'magic paint' illusion.
- *Camera mattes* – To mask off part of a camera's shot.
- *Transformation* – To transform part of a camera's shot.
- *Abstract effects* – To create abstract effects.

13.12 Inserting people

This is probably the most exciting and the most practical use of *chroma key*. Whether you are shooting the action in a small room or an equipped studio, you can conjure the illusion that the person in front of a camera is located, for example in a real room, a castle, standing in a field, out on the seashore, or in a town square . . . at the press of a button. To be really convincing, this needs some care of course, but we shall be looking at techniques step by step.

Chroma key backing

Figure 13.4 Background insertion
If a general-purpose chroma key backing is used, any kind of background can be inserted behind the subject, including plain tone (gray), flat color, patterns, drapes, photo-slides, videotaped or 'live' shots.

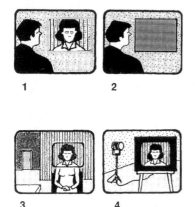

Figure 13.5 Display panel

1 A person appears to be watching a wall screen, which is displaying text, graphics, etc., or showing videotape, film, or a guest.

2 In fact, they are facing a blue wall panel in the wall of the setting. (They are watching the subject on a nearby picture monitor.)

3 When isolating a subject/person from a wider 'background' shot you need to position them in the frame, to correspond with the display screen in the master shot.

4 You can use a picture monitor's shot as the inserted subject, but its picture quality will deteriorate.

Figure 13.6 Window backing
Just a blue flat or hung cloth is needed to insert an exterior scene 'beyond' a window.

It all begins with a plain color surface (usually blue) behind the subject. This may be formed from a continuous run of stretched cloth (e.g. a cyclorama) or scenic flats set edge-to-edge. The important thing is that we present the camera with an even-toned shadowless surface. Bright blue (e.g. cobalt blue) is normally chosen for the keying color, for that hue is least likely to be found in typical subjects. (Other keying colors such as green or red can work equally well, provided they do not appear in the main (master) shot; but blue has generally proved to be a 'safe' hue.) You do need to take care that there are no surfaces (or reflections) of this color in the master shot – or instead of the speaker's blue tie you are likely to find part of the background street scene 'behind him' breaking through and appearing in its place!

13.13 Display panel

You will find this simple chroma key device used in many kinds of program, from lectures to elections, demonstrations to children's stories, fashion shows to cookery...

Yet all it needs is a blue rectangle painted on the wall, or a temporarily attached blue panel which can be removed when necessary. Because this panel can be of any size, it offers a very economical method of providing an impressive giant display screen in a shot.

● As a '*picture monitor*': You can display titling, graphics, film, maps, videotape shots, etc. keyed in from a video source – an idea that is used regularly in many newscasts.
● As a '*window*': A large display panel can be used to create the illusion of a window in any setting. Display a photo-slide shot of the 'exterior view on a freestanding blue panel or on a flat or cloth outside a scenic window unit.
● As an '*extension*' of the setting: Even a small setting can be made to seem large if you use a chroma key flat strategically placed beyond an arch or outside a doorway to suggest extensive surroundings.

13.14 'Magic paint'

There are many intriguing variants of this technique:

● As an artist standing at an easel in the master shot paints on a blank canvas the picture of a *live* dog appears.
● A photograph of a town shows how it was a century ago. As an architect paints over the photograph it changes to show how the town looks today.
● As a child tears an illustration from a book its character comes to life to remonstrate.
● A photograph of a garden in winter. A hand comes into shot and peels it off the page ... to reveal the same garden transformed in spring.

Simple! We *paint* in the blue keying color or *remove a top surface* to reveal a blue area beneath, which keys in another camera's shot.

13.15 Camera mattes

The usual application for a *camera matte* is to hide unwanted parts of a scene and/or insert another image in their place in the composite picture. A camera matte consists of a vertical *chroma key* surface supported on a frame in front of the camera. This is usually made from blue card which has been

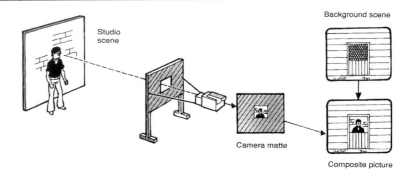

Figure 13.7 Camera matte
Here the camera shoots a blue matte board. The scene beyond is visible through a central hole, which can be of any shape. The background scene appears in the blue matted area. Particularly useful for longer shots, the matte masks off most of the surroundings, and carefully restricts the action area. It avoids the need for large areas of blue backing when using chroma key techniques; invaluable when space shot limited. To give good overall clipping, all blue keying surfaces should be evenly lit and free from shadows.

cut away to leave selected parts of the studio scene visible. Alternatively, you can use a sheet of clear plastic or glass, covered with patches of blue paint (or stuck-on blue sheet) where subjects from another shot are to be introduced.

Masking Where suspended lights are visible at the top of a shot they are not only distracting but in many situations will be quite inappropriate (e.g. a setting of a house interior). These lamps can be masked off with a camera matte and a neutrally toned area or a picture of a room ceiling inserted.

Substitution You might want to use a shot of an exterior from a photo-slide, film, or videotape . . . but find that this shot includes obtrusive features that you would prefer to avoid (e.g. buildings, advertising, a nearby highway, etc.). By using localized masking (e.g. a patch of blue paint on a glass sheet) you can insert something more appropriate in place of the offending item.

Addition You can add a new feature to the original scene. Two performers on an empty stage . . . but mask off the lower part of a shot, and insert a rear view of a group of people. Now they appear to have an audience!

Creating an environment If you cut a hole in a camera matte you can combine the action in front of the camera with an inserted picture. Let us suppose that although space is restricted, you want to show a couple dancing in a large empty ballroom. With care, you can use a camera matte and a photo-slide to do exactly that. Where you want the dancers to appear, cut a rectangular hole in the matte. Then you can treat the effect in either of two ways:

● A photograph of a ballroom fills the chroma keyed area. The dancers are visible through the cutout. (However, in this example it might be obvious that the floor in the photograph does not match the studio floor seen beneath the dancers' feet.)
● If necessary you can remedy this situation by arranging for the dancers to work in chroma key colored surroundings; e.g. blue cyclorama and a blue floor covering. Then there need be no discernible differences in the combined picture.

When setting up any special effects you always need to bear in mind any inherent limitations. Have you spotted a potential hazard in this example? What happens if the dancers move outside the limits of the matte? They will be cut off or even disappear! So you take care to let them know the floor area within which they must work.

13.16 Transformation

Many of us have discovered strange and 'magical' effects quite accidentally through '*I wonder what happens if . . .*' experiments. Put a picture of a seascape through the chroma key system and the blue summer sky becomes transformed into a lowering storm, dawn, a strangely menacing spectacle . . . Use green as the keying color and shots of the countryside take on a mystical quality according to the inserted tones or hues you use.

13.17 Abstract effects

The visual opportunities here are endless. Dress a dancer in a shiny black costume which reflects blue light at random, and insert anything from newsprint to dancing flames in the blue reflections.

Staging with chroma key

13.18 Taking care

Chroma key techniques offer video production extra dimensions. Fundamentally, it is a surprisingly simple process. All you need in front of the camera is a plain flat background with a dull finish in the keying color. It may be formed from a stretched cloth, hung 'background paper', a side-by-side run of scenic flats, even a painted wall. Whether this background is itself colored or a white surface illuminated with blue light is of little importance.

- *How large does this background need to be?* This will vary with the kind of action and the widest shot you anticipate using. For close shots of articles on a tabletop a vertical chroma key card as little as a meter (yard) wide may be sufficient. So much depends on the type of production and the way in which it is to be presented. An interview in a couple of chairs requires only a modest set-up. But if you are hoping to provide a chroma key background for a marching band the requirements are somewhat more demanding.
- *Space is very restricted, but you want to convey the impression that the action is taking place in spacious surroundings* Set up the camera (wide lens-angle to emphasize space). Use a camera matte with a cutout which will cover the maximum action area (Section 13.15). Check that the action keeps within the space covered through the cutout. Ensure that the picture for the chroma key insert is reasonably proportioned to the main subject.

  OR

  Set up a chroma key background behind the action. Check the camera's shot of the action area. Position chroma key colored flats (wings) near the camera, at the left and right edges of the shot, to mask off where it overshoots the keying background and reveals the studio walls.
- *Is it necessary to color the floor in the chroma key color?* Where the camera is working below head height and the floor is mainly hidden behind foreground objects (e.g. desk, table) the studio floor may be quite

A

Closer shot

Longer shot

Background

B   Composite picture

Figure 13.8 Close and long shots
(A) In closer shots, or where the visible floor is appropriate for the composite shot, a simple chroma key backing is all that is needed. (B) But where the ground shown in the background scene is quite different, the keying color must be extended by a blue floor cloth or painting.

satisfactory. If the studio floor is prominent and incompatible with the chroma keyed scene (e.g. which may show grass or water!) the illusion will obviously fail and a key-colored floor will become essential. The floor covering may be cloth, scenic paper, paint, temporary colored floor panels, etc.

13.19 Background selection

Even the simplest production needs an *appropriate* background of some kind behind the action. But what is *appropriate*? So much depends on the type of subject, the purpose and direction of the program. You may need a *specific* location, a *type* of location, a particular *atmosphere*, or an entirely *neutral non-associative* background. When shooting on location, with interviews in offices, workplaces, homes, you will usually have to accept what you find – although you may be able to shoot selectively or to change things around to some extent.

When shooting at your base – which may be anywhere from a studio to a hall, a classroom to a room in your home – *chroma key* allows you considerable flexibility. Set up stretched blue cloth behind the action (on portable frames if necessary), and introduce chroma key backgrounds to suit each situation. Many of the programs made by smaller production units involve *talks*, *interviews*, and *demonstrations*. These are often staged most effectively against a neutral background. You can provide this simply and economically by using shots of textural materials such as cloth, timber, canvas, earth, sand, leather, carpeting as background patterns. Treated photographs of such materials (e.g. defocused, edge-lit, colorized) have proved remarkably successful as 'stock backgrounds' for regular usage.

Scenery is expensive to construct, and poses storage problems. But a selection of basic *modular units* can be a very successful way of building up an all-purpose facility. Combined with a chroma key set-up, you can ring the changes in many ways at minimum cost. (See Section 6.5).

13.20 Coping with problems

Initially, the list that follows may look formidable. But you will find that checks and adjustments quickly become routine.

● *Are there problems if the chroma key background is uneven (wrinkles, folds, creases), patchy, varying brightness or color, different textures?* In a word – YES! When setting up the chroma key background avoid shadows or unevenness in the keying surface, for this is likely to cause irregular keying and tearing around edges. Some chroma key systems are more critical than others, depending on design. But it is advisable to check out these points. With care, even the simplest equipment generally provides good results if you do so.

● *Is spurious triggering avoidable?* Some systems are easier to adjust than others. The main operational control for a chroma key system adjusts the *clipping level*. You normally adjust it until you are seeing firm clean edges around inserted subjects. If the clipping levels are set too low, the subject you are inserting will show severe edge ragging around its borders. Set it too high, and parts of the inserted subject are likely to disappear. The *background picture* can contain any colors and shades and be sharp or soft focused.

The colors and surfaces of the main shot in front of the master camera can be quite critical. If the studio scene includes blue-colored surfaces, or reflects blue light, or blue light falls onto the subject, or the brightness of the blue keying surface varies considerably, you may well have clipping problems.

● **Will there be difficulties in matching the relative proportions of the subject and the inserted background?** Strictly speaking, you want the studio shot to accurately match the background in all respects: perspective, scale, lighting, color values, etc. In practice there can be remarkable differences, and your audience will not notice! A lot depends on your subjects, the background scene, and the amount of action involved. In most cases, if someone is sitting at a desk in the foreground we willingly accept the composite version. But if they are going to get up and move away from the studio camera . . . and as they move away into the distance, they appear to grow larger, even an uncritical viewer is likely to notice that there's something wrong! Obviously, scenes that contain many clues to perspective and scale, such as rooms, need particular attention; whereas open-air scenes of the countryside or seascapes are usually uncritical.

It is advisable to save time by checking chroma key shots before camera rehearsal begins. The only parameters you can adjust are your camera's lens angle, and/or your camera's distance from the person in the studio. (You can seldom do anything about the background picture you are using, except to alter its size.) Ideally, the studio camera's height and lens angle should match those of the camera shooting the background shot. But in the real world you do not have this information, and in any case, it is seldom really critical.

You can achieve a reasonable match with a certain amount of trial and error:

● Display the *background picture* on a monitor. In most photographs you can make a shrewd guess at the heights of various features in the scene – such as doorways. Look out for such items, in the foreground and the distance in the *background scene*.
● At these points on the monitor picture *draw vertical lines* approximating to a person's height with a dry marker or wax pencil. Ideally you want at least two trial '*height markers*' in the background picture which represent this typical height at different distances.
● Now chroma key a person into this *background scene* (adjusting the clipping level) with the *master camera's* zoom lens set to a 'normal' angle. Position them so that they coincide with the nearest '*height-marker*' in the composite. Adjust the camera distance so that they are about the same height. Next have the person move away from the camera until they appear level with the far marker. If the perspective is reasonably correct they will approximate to marker heights in both positions.
● If they walk away and appear shorter at the distant '*height-marker*' you need to zoom in a little and dolly back slightly to compensate. If the reverse happens, and they look unusually tall at the distant marker, zoom out a little, and dolly in. In practice this maneuver only takes a moment or two. If you are now overshooting the blue area in the studio, use a camera matte to mask off the overshoot (shoot-off) or use a wipe pattern to clip off unwanted areas.

What sort of incongruities can develop?

Working with chroma key for the first time can be a process of discovery! Various strange and unexpected effects can arise. We have covered most of them here, but with experience, you will quickly come to recognize, anticipate, and correct them during rehearsal as a matter of course:

- It is inadvisable to readjust the camera or zoom lens once you have them correctly lined up for a shot. During recording, everything normally remains locked-off.
- If you should want to alter the *shot size* during a sequence it is often practicable to stop the action and readjust the zoom lens angle provided you can alter the size of the background scene *correspondingly*. It is normally important to keep their relative proportions right; unless the background is plain or featureless. Where the background comes from a photograph shot by a second camera you zoom *both* cameras by a similar amount to readjust the combined image.

If you zoom in on the master camera alone *during the take*, all subjects in the master shot will grow correspondingly larger (rather than get nearer). A great effect for the right occasion but daunting at other times. *Zooming out* makes them grow smaller.

If you *dolly (track) in* the inserted subjects will apparently grow in size, depending on their actual distance from the master camera.

Dolly back and again, the effect is most noticeable in subjects closest to the camera.

Tilting up causes subjects to slide down the frame. *Tilt down*, and they fly upwards. (Again, a useful trick in the right place.)

Pan left and all subjects slide right; and vice versa.

- Check that a person walking away from the camera does not appear to rise or fall in the composite. (This can happen if the *studio camera's height* is very different from the *background picture's viewpoint*.)
- Check that everyone's feet in the master shot are in positions that are compatible with the background shot. Otherwise they can appear to 'walk in mid-air', or stand 'half-way up a wall' or 'balance on furniture'! Tilt or pan the master camera a little when finalizing the shot to correct errors or reposition anyone in front of the camera as necessary.
- You may see blue fringes developing around the borders of keyed-in subjects, particularly where they have less well-defined edges. This can be caused by system limitations, blue spill light, or optical flares. Adding 'compensatory' yellow back-light or introducing soft-edge keying are arguable palliatives.
- One of the main limitations of regular chroma key systems is that when subjects cast shadows these do not appear in the composite picture. Any shadows falling onto the keying surface are normally removed during insertion. At times this can look odd. Ironically, real-life shadows falling onto keying surfaces may make it difficult to adjust clipping levels. Where the ground in the background scene is dark, or very broken up, the absence of shadows can pass unnoticed. It is most obvious on very light-toned floors. There are solutions to these shadow problems but they involve more sophisticated equipment.*
- Simpler chroma key systems have troubles when inserting *finer detail* (e.g. hair, fur, feathers, lace) or unsharp subjects such as smoke, steam, or glass. Edges become blue-fringed or break up, due to indecisive switching action. More complex circuitry is necessary (e.g. *linear keying*) to insert such subjects without these side-effects.

Are these various limitations really important in practice?

The true answer is that for many years broadcasters used basic chroma key systems with generally satisfactory results. As systems developed, and allied devices such as *Ultimattte* became available, limitations became fewer. For smaller production units, working round these problems is a small price to pay considering their advantages.

*You will find more details in *Television Production* (13th edn) by Gerald Millerson.

13.21 Compatibility

There should be a reasonably close match between the general appearance of the foreground subjects and the background; although even quite marked differences are often overlooked:

Lighting	The light's apparent intensity, color temperature, quality (hard or soft), and direction should be an acceptable match.
Tonal values	Whether they are high or low key; have high or low contrast.
Color quality	The general feeling of warm or cool tones; intense or desaturated (pastel) color values.
Style	Associative qualities (e.g. period, location, time of day).

- Take care to avoid background photographs that include 'frozen' moving subjects such as street scenes with people and traffic, seascapes with breaking waves, aircraft in flight . . .

- As a routine, always check '*scale*' and '*proportions*'. You can inadvertently create 'giants' and tiny beings.
- When the *depth of field* in the master shot is very limited, parts of the inserted subject matter will be *very defocused*. If you combine this foreground shot with a pin-sharp background scene, the resulting soft-focused zone in the composite can look very strange. The only remedy is to defocus the background picture slightly.

13.22 Practical chroma key staging

Let's look at some further features of everyday staging for chroma key systems.

How does someone standing in the master shot manage to relate to the background scene?

- You can have someone in the studio appear to sit, climb, walk on surfaces in the background by painting matching items in the keying color (blue) and arranging these in the studio in positions that correspond to those features in the background picture.
- If someone in front of the camera is to move '*behind*' a feature in the *background* scene (e.g. a wall), you place a corresponding blue surface in the studio. Otherwise they will always be seen moving '*in front of*' anything in the background scene. Other methods are possible, including those involving using a silhouette camera matte, corresponding to the item in the background scene.
- If you are using totally blue surroundings (walls and floor) in the master shot, and little furniture or other 'landmarks', it can be almost impossible for talent to relate to the background scene. How do they know where they stand? How can they '*walk over to the door*' – that they cannot see – in the background shot? And how can they look in a specific direction (correct *eye lines*) during performance?

To indicate where someone should stand, tape blue disks (e.g. 1 ft (30 cm) across) on the floor as location points. These can have identifying letters or numbers. These disks will be easy for the talent to see yet invisible on camera. Otherwise, performers have to relate to furniture and scenery in the master shot. Where it is important for someone to look in a certain direction at '*something in the background picture*' hang a colored light in the eye line direction that they can use to focus on.

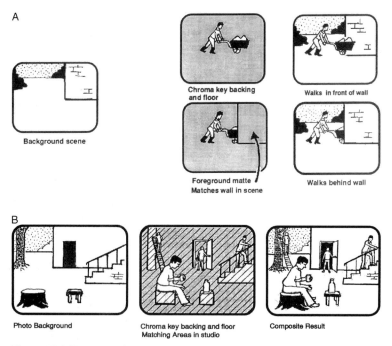

A

Background scene

Chroma key backing
and floor

Walks in front of wall

Foreground matte
Matches wall in scene

Walks behind wall

B

Photo Background

Chroma key backing and floor
Matching Areas in studio

Composite Result

Figure 13.9 Foreground mattes
(A) Anyone in the master shot who moves in front of the chroma key backing will normally appear *in front of* anything in the background scene. If a surface painted in the keying color is positioned to correspond with an item in the background scene, they will appear to pass *behind* it. Where a blue flat coincides with the wall, the person moves 'behind' it.
(B) Position suitable items painted in the keying color in the master shot (in this example, a couple of blue blocks, a blue column, blue steps), and people can apparently sit, lean, climb, or put objects on features in the background scene!

13.23 Shot-by-shot production

The action in any scene strongly influences how we shoot it. But how does the chroma key camera's immobility inhibit us when shooting action? Let's take a look at typical situations in everyday production.

Static performance   We see someone sitting in a chair, reclining on a couch, standing looking out of a window . . . alone, or reacting to another person. No problems there.

Local action   We see people move around within a 'held shot'. The camera remains stationary, and they have free movement within the area taken in by the master shot:

- You can use your camera as an observer; overseeing the action while the talent goes about its business. They may be actors in a drama, a person working at a craft, or musicians playing. In each situation they perform and we observe through the camera.
- You can arrange for the talent to *work to the camera*: e.g. talking directly to the audience through the camera . . . coming closer to show us a particular item . . . Create 'reasons' for them to move around in order to create visual variety:

For instance, we see a lecturer in an impressive library (chroma keyed background slide) sitting on the edge of a desk, telling us about a moment in history (in mid-shot). He or she stands and walks over to a bookshelf in the background (it becomes a long shot), selects a map from a nearby table, and then walks forward, up to the camera to show us a detail in a close shot. The camera has not moved (it cannot!) and the 'imposing library' just consists of a desk and a small table with a blue backdrop. But the situation is interesting to watch.

And remember, if you want a closer view of the subject, you may zoom in on the master camera provided the background picture is also enlarged. We see from these examples that a static camera does not mean static shots.

Widespread action What do you do if the action moves outside the area taken in by the camera? Normally, you would have the choices of

Moving the camera to follow the action, or
Panning after the subject, or
Cutting to a new viewpoint on another camera.

Your master camera is immobile, but you can create an impression of movement and change by varying its viewpoint and/or the size of the shot.

Where it's necessary for someone to move away from the foreground acting area you would normally let them walk out of the shot, and during editing, cut to a new camera set-up. You can do this in several ways:

- **Change the background scene** Switch to another background picture showing the library from a different viewpoint. If necessary change or rearrange any furniture. Position the talent; check the shot; continue videotaping and cue the action to restart.

  Where an alternative background picture is not available it is surprising how often you can use *the same shot* horizontally reversed or even different parts of the same background photograph to suggest a change in the surroundings without the audience being aware of the trick!
- **Use a common landmark** During an action sequence you may want to cut from a shot with one background to a shot with another view. If you do just that you may leave the audience disorientated; wondering where they are on switching to the second viewpoint. The solution is to introduce a fairly prominent feature that is common to both shots. If, for instance, there are some prominent drapes (on a portable frame) on the left of the original library shot, and they can be seen again in the subsequent shot, these will help to orientate the audience and connect the two viewpoints.

13.24 What is 'virtual reality'?

We have been exploring the characteristics of regular chroma key systems and seen something of the opportunities and limitations. Undoubtedly the major problem lies in the fact that we cannot move the master camera or zoom. Otherwise we see size changes, side-slips, vertical hops, and varying perspective. To overcome these restrictions, ingenious equipment has been developed that gives the chroma key camera unrestricted freedom to move and look around. What these various systems do with varying success, is to transmit precise information about the camera's floor position, height, shooting angle (head tilt) and lens setting to a computer, which selects appropriately from the background scene.

Normally, if a regular chroma key camera pans, the inserted subjects slide to one side while the background picture remains stationary. When the *'virtual reality'* camera pans around, the viewer sees *corresponding changes in the background scene*, which now appears to move to the side as it would in real life.

As with regular chroma key systems, the background scene may derive from a video camera shooting a photographic display, a three-dimensional model, or a computer-generated graphic.

We have been looking at various points one needs to consider when staging a chroma key presentation. Most of these still apply to 'virtual reality' processes too if the inserted foreground and the background are to blend together unobtrusively.

13.25 Further video effects

There seems to be no end to the methods you can use to control and manipulate the picture image! Some are little more than a passing fashion or an eye-catching gimmick, others provide a useful productional device.

Many video cameras and VCRs now incorporate gizmos that produce changes in the image. As well as more 'ordinary' changes that alter picture tones and color, soften details, etc., there are the various *image enhancers*, *video effects units*, *digitizers*, *computer programs* and whatever, which offer all kinds of 'video magic'. Here is a brief list of typical opportunities:

- *Freeze frame.* Stopping movement in the picture, and holding a still frame. (Held for too long, you can wear and stretch the tape.)
- *Frame grabbing.* A sequence in which a series of single frames are frozen at regular intervals during the action. (From every 2 secs. to almost instantaneous).
- *Strobe.* A similar effect, displaying action as a series of still images flashed onto the screen at a variable rate.
- *Reverse action.* Running the action in reverse.
- *Fast or slow motion.* Running the action at a faster or slower speed than normal.
- *Picture in picture.* A miniature picture inserted into the main shot. By copying and re-inserting, a pattern of up to 81 frames can be created on the screen!
- *Mosaic.* The picture is reduced to a pattern of small single-colored squares of adjustable size.
- *Posterizing.* Reduces tonal gradation to a few coarse steps.
- *Mirror.* Flipping the picture from left to right, or providing a symmetrical split screen.
- *Time lapse.* Still frames shot at regular intervals. When played back at normal speed, the effect is of greatly speeded-up motion.
- *Digitizer.* A frame is grabbed, then treated in various ways (redrawn, colors/texture changed, etc.).

The versatile PC

- *Titling.* As a character generator, providing titling/subtitling of all kinds in various fonts. Lettering can form on screen, scroll, collapse, rotate, etc.

You can key titling into live or recorded video, or combine it with computer-generated graphics, plain color backgrounds. etc.

- *Graphics.* You can devise illustrations ranging from charts, graphs, tables, diagrams, to 'watercolor' effects, posters, textured drawings, cartoon, logos, etc.
- *Three-dimensional images.* You can create photo-realistic images of three-dimensional subjects.
- *Paintbox.* A video still or a photo shot can be treated in many ways: e.g. color, texture, etc., can be added, removed, altered, details can be strengthened or redrawn. New features can be inserted, and defects such as color bleeding removed.

- *Animations.* A series of still images can be shown in succession, to create animated effects; e.g. cartoons, moving logos.
- *Picture transition effects.* Pictures can be shifted around, obliterated by straight geometrical wipes, decorative curtain wipes, etc. Areas can be 'flown in/out'.
- *Inserts.* You can take a complete picture (or part of it) and insert it within a shot; e.g. as a 'wall display screen'. You can present a series of different shots (stills or moving) side-by-side.
- *Chroma keying.* A subject in front of a blue background, can be overlaid into another shot.
- *Music.* Musical soundtracks of all kinds can be generated, using synthesized or digital audio sampled sounds.
- *Sound effects.* You can use effects to simulate or replace natural sounds; to create background noises (e.g. for outer space shots). Even artificial speech is available!
- *Synchronized sound.* Digital sound can be synchronized with animated action.
- *Prompter.* You can provide a moving script for performers/newscasters to read while looking at the camera.
- *Edit decision lists.* Here you check through shots, select which you want to keep, and note their in and out times. This log can be used either as a *guide* to later editing ('off-line editing'), or to actually *drive* the equipment in an editing suite; picking out the chosen shots and joining them in order. Advance preparation considerably reduces costly editing suite time.
- *Storyboarding.* A production planning aid, in which you arrange how you are going to break down action into a series of separate shots.
- *Scriptwriting aids.* Software aided script layout (e.g. two-column display).
- *General organization.* Software programs for creating forms, labels, order sheets, logs, etc.

Desktop video

13.26 Extending facilities

As the speed and storage capacity of personal computers (PCs) grew, ingenious systems developed in the audiovisual field to do jobs that previously required costly dedicated equipment. 'Desktop video' equipment has had a growing success for it is able to integrate video, audio, text and graphics seamlessly in remarkably adaptable processes. Desktop video systems cover a spread of designs, from regular PCs using special software to multi-task workstations. The quality and performance of this equipment suits users ranging from enthusiastic hobbyists to those working to precise broadcast standards. Many organizations making video productions on a modest budget now have a spread of facilities previously beyond their hopes.

13.27 Desktop video formats

In a typical desktop video system, the monitor screen displays may include:

1 Small viewing screens   2 Illustrations of controls   3 Indicators
         4 Information boxes   5 Selection icons

1 **Small viewing screens** These show the output or main channel picture and one or more preview channels. Small horizontal strip displays showing the soundtrack(s) set against a time scale.

2 **Controls** Instead of actual switches, faders, push buttons, rotating knobs, etc. these are displayed by symbols which can be 'operated' at the computer keyboard (e.g. by mouse or keys).

3 **Indicators** These take the form of graphics which change as 'controls' are operated and are in the form of numbered windows, pointers on scales, bar graphs, etc.

4 **Information boxes** Displaying menus, lists, messages, instructions, dialogue, timing, etc.

5 **Selection icons** Small 'push button' symbols used to call up various processes and procedures.

13.28 Operation

Like regular computers, *desktop video systems* are digital. All pictures, sound, text are stored and manipulated in digital form and stored as data on a hard disk or solid-state devices. These ingenious systems do have their drawbacks. In many applications, the picture monitor screen becomes overcrowded with pictures, controls, indicators ... This can make the selection and one-handed adjustment of controls awkward as you operate a mouse, roll-ball/track-ball, or touch-screen.

Many operations are simple and rapid. Unlike video tape, where editing involves continual shuttling to and fro to select sections, data recorded on the hard disk can be tracked down virtually instantaneously in any order. This facilitates rapid, non-destructive *non-linear editing*. You can quickly cut-and-paste material and rearrange alternative treatments.

However, some processes can be quite time consuming if you need to correct or revise a step. Others, which are quite simple when handling real controls, may become more laborious (e.g. increasing/decreasing several faders simultaneously) or even impracticable (e.g. fading one channel up while fading another down).

On a *multi-task station* it may not be possible to leave one operation partly developed and move on to another (e.g. from a '*graphics mode*' to a '*video effect mode*').

13.29 Memory limitations

As always, a great deal can depend on the design of individual equipment and on what you are seeking to do. (Even dedicated professional equipment has its quirks!) All pictures involve a great deal of data, so insufficient memory can be a real limitation at times. (A minute of regular *NTSC* 4 by 3 aspect ratio picture can take up to 10 Mb of hard disk space.) So it may not be practicable to display full-screen high-quality pictures. Instead, PC-based systems usually have to rely on displays in which pictures are demonstrated with low resolutions, or restricted duration, drop frames, show action at reduced speed, lower color reproduction.

For many checking purposes high-quality pictures are not essential. Remember they are only intended for identification purposes and will be of optimum quality in the final videotape. Low picture quality is quite adequate for many jobs, such as identifying frames during editing, or for a *multi-frame index* screen showing the contents of a slide library.

13.30 Broadcast quality

To accommodate the stringent technical parameters of broadcast-quality video you may need special-purpose hardware and software. Various anomalies between computer and broadcast systems can result in unwanted effects such as:

- Flicker on fine horizontal detail, where a horizontal line in the computer picture is so thin that it only appears in one TV line; causing flicker to occur as scanning switches between odd and even fields.
- Jagged diagonals or curves ('jaggies', 'staircase'). Aliasing in computer images causes this effect, due to low sampling rates.
- Detail that is visible on the computer monitor may not be shown on the TV screen.
- There may be 'glitches' (visual disturbances), jumps, or bumps that are not acceptable for broadcast use.
- Color from computers may be too highly saturated (too pure), so that it appears dazzling and artificial in the video picture. It is advisable, for instance, to avoid strong reds for they are likely to bleed over into nearby areas.
- The aspect ratio (picture shape) of computer displays vary. Few accurately match the 4 by 3 broadcast standard, so there may be a loss of edge information, or spurious edge borders.
- Look out for woolly edges, chroma noise, or poor color harmony that are not evident in the computer picture.

Chapter 14

Video basics

How it works.

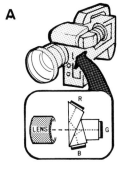

A

Figure 14.1 How video works
(*continued overleaf*)
A. Just behind the camera lens a *prism block* with color filters (dichroics), is used to produce three images, corresponding to the red, green and blue in the scene.

Attached to these prisms are three *CCD light sensors*. A pattern of charges builds up on their tiny elements, corresponding to the light and shade in their color images.

B

B. The pattern of charges on each CCD is read out in a regular series of lines, to produce a *video signal*. Thanks to *synchronizing pulses* the three CCDs are scanned exactly in step (synchronous).

14.1 Technical details

By now it is obvious that you don't need to understand technical design features, to produce good pictures and audio. But you will meet situations where a general idea of what is going on, will smooth away problems; e.g. when interconnecting equipment. So let's take a look at the underlying principles.

14.2 Producing video

It all begins with the *lens system* which focuses the image of the scene onto the light-sensitive surface of a *charge couple device*, or '*CCD*'. (This solid-state device within the camera head has replaced the *camera tube* used in earlier TV/video cameras.)

A CCD is typically $\frac{1}{3}$ in. (9 mm), $\frac{1}{2}$ in. (12.5 mm), $\frac{2}{3}$ in. (18 mm) across, and includes hundreds of thousands of tiny independent cells (*pixels*; *elements*). Each cell develops an electrical charge according to the strength of the light falling upon it. The result is an overall pattern of electrical charges on the CCD that corresponds to the light and shade in the lens image.

To produce the *video signal*, scanning circuits continually read across this charge pattern in a series of parallel paths or 'lines' (525 or 625). The fluctuating voltage produced, corresponds to the strength of each cell in turn.

This basically, is how the monochrome ('black and white') video camera generates its pictures.

14.3 Reproducing the picture

Several types of screen are used to display the video signal's picture. The commonest are the *picture tube* and the *LCD* (*liquid crystal diode*) screen. Most TV receivers, picture monitors and professional TV/video cameras have picture tubes, but LCD screens of various sizes are increasingly used; particularly on portable TV receivers, picture monitors, computers, consumer cameras.

Figure 14.1 (*continued*)

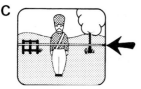

C. If we look at a single line as the system reads across the picture...

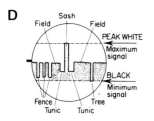

D. ... we see how the strength of the video signal fluctuates with the tones at each moment of the scan.

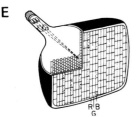

E. The TV receiver is fed simultaneously with the three different video signals – red, green, blue.

The screen of the *picture tube* in the TV receiver or monitor, has a pattern of three different phosphors on its inner surface. Streams of electrons are controlled by the RGB video signals. As they scan across their respective sets of phosphors, these glow red, green, or blue, and build up a color picture.

Figure 14.2 The video signal
The video signal is a varying voltage, corresponding to light and shade in the image. While the scanning system *retraces* at the end of each *line* and *field*, *sync pulses* are inserted to ensure that the entire system scans in step.

A brief *color burst* reference signal (subcarrier frequency) ensures color accuracy.

In the picture tube, a beam of electrons scans across the screen, causing its phosphor-coated surface to glow. If we use the video signal to continually adjust the strength of this scanning beam as it sweeps across the screen, it will 'draw' a light pattern on the phosphor. When the video is strongest (corresponding to a white surface in the original scene) the screen will glow brightly at that point. Where there is little light reflected from the scene the screen will appear much darker.

In the LCD screen the density of each element of the screen varies with the strength of the video as the picture is scanned.

14.4 How we see color

Our eyes contain selective 'cones' which detect color by analysing the visible spectrum into three primary color regions – red to orange, green to yellow, and blue to violet.

Most colored surfaces reflect a color mixture of red, green, and blue light in varying proportions. So, for instance, the various shades of 'green' we see in foliage are actually color mixtures reflecting quite a wide spread of the visible spectrum. Even yellow, can be reproduced by adding suitable proportions of red and green light!

14.5 How the camera sees color

The color video camera too, relies on this *additive color mixing* process.

Any light-sensor (CCD or camera tube) can only respond to the *intensity* of light. It cannot directly distinguish *color*. However, by placing red, green, and blue color filters over three light-sensors we can analyse the scene into its separate color components. If a subject appears to have similar proportions of all three primaries we see this mixture as *white*.

In the color video camera the lens' image of the scene passes through a special prism, which splits it into three identical versions. Three CCD sensors with their respective red, green, and blue color filters provide three *video signals* corresponding to the light and shade of these colors in the scene.

14.6 The color picture

Look through a magnifier at the scene of your TV set or picture monitor and you will see that it has a tiny pattern of three separate sets of phosphors. These glow red, green, or blue as the scanning beam passes over them. The brightness of each point corresponds with the video strength at that moment. Our eyes cannot distinguish these individual phosphor points, but instead, blend their images to form a natural-colored picture.

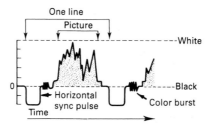

14.7 Practical cameras

While larger professional video cameras use a three or four CCD format other camera designs are often simplified in order to provide a more compact unit, and reduce cost.

For example, instead of three separate chips, a segmented multi-color filter may be placed over a single sensor. Although picture detail is reduced, results are quite satisfactory for many purposes.

There are a number of variations too, in the types of CCD used, and their resolution.

So how do such technical details concern the video maker? Well, they will affect picture clarity (particularly under low-intensity lighting). While, for example, top-quality cameras can resolve as many as 700 vertical black and white stripes across the picture width, simpler cameras may only manage to reproduce half that number. (Then finer detail will be blurred however carefully you focus.) Color fidelity is less accurate or consistent in simpler designs, and there is a greater possibility of disturbing picture defects (e.g. vertical smear, background patterning). In the best video cameras these are negligible.

As you will see, these issues can become important where pictures are copied several times over during editing or creating special effects.

14.8 Scanning

Let's look more closely at the scanning process we met earlier. The scanning circuits read off the CCD charge pattern 60 times a second.

To reduce picture flicker, the odd lines are actually read first, then the even lines. These odd and even *fields* are *interlaced* to form a complete TV picture or *frame*. So the entire picture scanning process using 525 lines takes place in 1/30 of a second. (In a 625-line system, there are 50 frames or pictures a second; 312½ lines in each field.)

Broadcast television has always used this *interlaced scanning* process for it has certain technical advantages. But there are drawbacks too. So when computer technology developed, a different, more straightforward *sequential* method of scanning was used instead in which all picture lines are read out one after the other to build up the total image. (There are arguments for applying this to television/video picture generation, but that remains for the future.) We are not concerned here with such technical niceties, but we do need to realize that TV uses *interlaced scanning*, and computer systems use *sequential scanning* – a technical distinction that has to be accommodated when integrating the two media.

Another matter that is currently in a state of flux is the shape or *aspect ratio* of the television screen. Having been standardized for decades as a *4 by 3* shape (four horizontal units for three vertical units), there is a newly emerging TV standard of *16 by 9* aspect ratio which can directly influence how you compose pictures and arrange action (see Chapter 3).

14.9 Sync pulses

To reproduce the TV picture accurately, in full color, without tearing, break-up, or picture roll it is essential for the scanning process in the TV receiver or picture monitor to be exactly in step with scanning in the camera. So regular synchronizing pulses ('sync pulses') are combined with the video. These pulses need to pass through the system accurately, to provide stable pictures.

There are two forms of sync pulses:

- those that keep the horizontal or line scanning in synchronism (line syncs),

  and

- those that time the vertical scanning rate (frame syncs).

The video information together with its sync pulses (including an additional 'color burst' signal which stabilizes color accuracy) is called the *composite video*.

14.10 Color video

Although it is possible to transmit color from camera to screen in the form of three separate color components – red, green and blue video signals – there are technical disadvantages.

When the American NTSC color TV system was developed its designers had to ensure that color transmissions could also be received on black and white receivers. This required some ingenious engineering tricks – which are also used in derived PAL and SECAM color systems.

Picture information was coded into:

luminance (Y) conveying picture brightness, and the scenic tones;

and

chrominance (C) which conveys color in the scene.

The chrominance component is quite complex, for it has two features: the 'I' signal (red minus luminance) and the 'Q' signal (blue minus luminance) – in PAL systems, called U and V.

Decoding circuits in the color picture-monitor or receiver recover the original RGB components from these signals.

14.11 Transmitting the signal

A regular method of sending a color video signal along a single cable is used in most domestic video recorders. Here the composite video signal. together with its accompanying audio signal, are fed to a small device called a 'modulator'. This produces a modulated radio frequency (RF) which is fed to the antenna (aerial) socket of a TV receiver.

14.12 Forms of video signal

Summarizing then, the video signal can be distributed in several different forms. Each has its advantages. The particular kind used, will affect interconnections between equipment.

- As separate red, green, blue video signals (RGB); perhaps with separate sync pulses.
- As a combined composite video signal (total video plus syncs).
- Video can also be distributed as two separate signals: *luminance* (*Y*) and coded color or *chrominance* (*C*). A 'signal converter' can be used to convert a Y/C signal into separate R G B signals.
- As a modulated radio frequency signal. (A convenient one-wire method of distributing picture and sound, but with a slight deterioration in picture quality.)

14.13 Program sound

The audio accompanying the picture is handled as a single separate circuit (two in the case of stereo sound), routed quite independently of the video circuits. Where an RF modulator unit is used however, the audio channel can be fed into this in addition to the composite video, to provide a signal suitable for the antenna (aerial) socket of a TV receiver.

14.14 Reproduced quality

How much detail can the system reproduce? That will depend on the type of equipment used, and its design refinements. For example, a conventional TV receiver may typically be able to reproduce up to 320 vertical black and white stripes; while a more advanced design can resolve over 560 lines.

A typical VHS recorder can resolve around 250 lines (3.2 MHz), while a Super VHS video recorder can resolve over 400 lines (5.13 MHz).

Audio too, will depend on system parameters. The highest and lowest ends of the audio scale ('top', 'bass') are limited on many receivers and VCR systems, distortion reducing clarity and overall fidelity. For others, audio quality is comparable with that from compact disc systems.

14.15 Units

You will find two approaches to equipment design:

● That in which all circuit functions are incorporated within the same unit.
● Systems in which a series of separate sub-units are interconnected.

While, for instance, a broadcast studio will have separate precision units generating the synchronizing (sync) signals, which are fed to all cameras, switchers, video recorders, etc., a portable video camera has to be entirely self-contained.

In the box on pages 274–278 you will see an outline of typical video and audio units used in a video/television system.

14.16 Monitors and receivers

Although both *TV receivers* and *picture monitors* are widely used in video production, they have important differences.

TV receivers. These are designed to display off-air pictures of broadcast programs, with their accompanying sound. For technical and economic reasons, picture and sound quality are a compromise; although the performance of top-grade receivers can be extremely good.

If a camera system or videotape recorder includes a *modulator* unit, (which converts its video into a modulated RF carrier), its output can be plugged into the regular *antenna (aerial)* socket, of the TV receiver. But there is inevitably a certain amount of picture deterioration.

Many modern receivers have a choice of inputs. A *video input* socket allows the direct video signal from a camera or VCR to be fed to the receiver for improved performance (better detail, less noise). For higher picture quality there are separate *RGB* inputs, and/or *Y/C (luminance/chrominance)* video inputs.

Picture monitors. Specially designed to provide accurate, stable picture quality, their circuit sophistication is reflected in their higher cost. Picture monitors do not include circuitry to receive off-air pictures. Instead, they are fed directly by cable, with a video signal – in encoded form, with picture plus sync pulses, as separate red–green–blue picture components, and/or in Y/C form.

Program sound is reproduced through a separate audio system.

Termination. A resistance introduced into the video input of a monitor or other equipment to match it to its connecting cable and avoid signal reflections, distortions or losses. Where a series of monitors are *looped through*, only one termination is required at the end of the chain.

Video equipment

A wide range of equipment is used in the video chain. You can clarify its purpose broadly as:

Supplementary (e.g. switcher),

Compensatory (e.g. TBC),

Effects (e.g. SEG).

Some units combine more than one function (e.g. a switcher that incorporates effects).

Computer technology

Computer technology is essentially digital. It conveys and stores information (data) through sequences of pulses. Regular *television*, on the other hand, is mainly an *analogue* process in which digital equipment is increasingly used. Digital and analogue systems are incompatible unless intermediate equipment is introduced for *analogue/digital (A/D)* or *digital/analogue (D/A)* conversion.

Supplementary equipment

Switcher (vision mixer). Equipment allowing the outputs from various video sources (cameras, video recorders, telecine (film channel), character generator, etc.) to be inter-switched, faded, mixed.

Sync pulse generator (SPG). This provides

- the *horizontal and vertical drive pulses* that initiate the scanning process,
- the *blanking pulses* that suppress the scanning read-off as it moves on to the next line or frame,
- the *sync pulses* at the end of each line and each field,
- the *color burst* which provides a reference signal to stabilize color fidelity when encoding color information with the luminance information (color sync; color subcarrier).

  Sometimes single 'black burst' signal is generated. This incorporates blanking, syncs, and black level video. This 'black-burst' signal is used as a synchronizing source, and equipment is genlocked onto it.

Distribution amplifier (DA). An amplifier used to isolate and distribute video signals.

Camera control unit (CCU). In multi-camera set-ups, each camera head is cable-linked to a *camera control unit (CCU)*, where most of the circuitry providing power, scanning, sync signals, etc. is centralized. The CCU has all the camera's main electronic adjustments, affecting picture quality (exposure, black level, gain, etc.). All cameras' CCUs are grouped together, and controlled by a video operator or 'shader', or extended to a central video control panel. Similarly, a BSU (base-station unit) or CPU (camera processing unit) controls digital cameras.

Multiplexer. Device with a movable mirror, enabling one camera to see several different picture sources (slide projector, film projector (telecine), filmstrip, captions).

Patch panel/jack field/jack strip. Rows of sockets to which the inputs and outputs of various video units are permanently wired. Units may be interconnected connected with a series of plugged cables (patch cords).

Routing switcher. A unit enabling various video (and audio) sources to be interconnected by pressing appropriate buttons.

Compensatory/corrective equipment

Genlock. All equipment in a video system needs to work from exactly the same synchronizing pulses. Otherwise when shots are inter-switched (cut) or combined (i.e. mix, wipe, insets and other effects) there will be picture disturbances such as frame roll, displacement, etc. To avoid this, the sync pulses from one of the video sources (e.g. a remote camera) are used to synchronize *all* units via a genlock unit, so that they scan in unison. Similarly, a computer, character generator, slide scanner must be fed with communal syncs.

Genlock systems may generate either a standard NTSC (PAL, SECAM) signal over a single conductor (combined Y and C), or separate Y and C signals (e.g. for S-VHS, Hi8, ED-BETA sources).

Processing amplifier (Proc-amp)/stabilizing amplifier. Corrects errors that develop in the video signal from any source. Because the proc-amp can correct signals from unstable VCRs, it is invaluable when copying tapes. It can reshape, reinsert, or separate sync pulses from the composite signal (i.e. video plus syncs), and may also correct color errors.

Image enhancer. The enhancer can improve apparent picture detail, crispening edge sharpness of vertical (perhaps horizontal) edges.

However, it cannot compensate for poor resolution or soft focus, or show detail that does not already exist. Over-correction leads to an artificial 'cartoon' effect, with emphasized outlines and increased graininess. The enhancer can subjectively improve picture quality when copying tapes, reducing detail loss effects.

Advanced image enhancers can also remove color fringing around outlines, correct any color displacement, reduce video noise ('snow'), suppress 'ringing' at edges, regenerate syncs, etc.

A *pre-enhancer* between the camera and the VCR can boost detail (higher frequencies) before recording, so improving apparent definition.

Image processors can improve or modify picture quality, by adjusting color saturation, hue, tonal contrast, white/black levels, picture strength (brightness), detail enhancement. And improve matching in color quality between shots, correct color balance, etc.

Time base corrector (TBC). Circuitry used to insert accurate sync pulses when the incoming sync pulses are lost or distorted. The TBC removes jitter on VCR playback, correcting color and sync errors.

A TBC that includes a *frame store synchronizer* can lock up an unsynchronized video source to your system's sync pulses. If the picture is momentarily interrupted (e.g. shooting on location) it will insert an image of the previous frame during the break. Many TBC units today include *proc amps* (above). Again, over-correction can lead to greater picture noise, degraded grays/blacks, color deterioration.

Color corrector. Circuitry that allows you to correct a chosen color, with minimum effect on others. It adjusts the gain (amplification), black level, gamma (tonal contrast) of the separate red, green, blue channels.

Standards converter. Electronic equipment that enables program material originating from one TV system (e.g. *NTSC*) to be converted into a form that can be used by a different TV system (e.g. *PAL* or *SECAM*).

Effects equipment

Special effects generator (SEG). A unit for creating various wipe patterns, keying effects, mattes, etc.

Character generator (CG). A system for providing electronically generated titling of various sizes and forms. As well as letters, numbers, and symbols, the CG may include facilities for creating graphics (logos, maps, charts).

Image enhancer (see above). May also be used for video effects: e.g. reduce color to black and white; create negative images; change selected colors (e.g. red car to green!); tint the picture overall (sepia for old photos, blue for 'moonlight'); dilute (wash out) color; emphasize color; adjust brightness and/ or contrast.

Digitizer. An encoder unit used to translate a regular analogue video signal into digital form e.g. for treatment in a *computer* system. You can hold (grab) individual video frames, and modify/adjust/redraw them; e.g. to create graphics, cartoons, animations.

Conversely, a digital/analogue encoder is needed to convert digital signal (from a computer) into NTSC (PAL, or SECAM) form.

Video effects unit. Various designs allow you to *freeze frame*; strobe (grab stills at 0.2–2 s intervals); *mosaic* (break pictures into small squares); *posterize* (reduce tonal gradation to a few steps); *superimpose* (intermixing effects); add *shadowing* and *edging* to titling; *alter colors* of titling/ background; *fade* video, titles, or background.

Superimposer. A unit enabling the output of a computer (e.g. providing titling, statistics) to be mixed with the composite video signal (NTSC, PAL) from a camera.

Video test equipment

Picture monitors

There are disadvantages in setting up a monitor so that edges of the picture are lost beyond the screen mask ('over-scanning'). A mike or lights on the edge of the shot may go uncorrected. Synchronizing faults may not be visible.

Underscanning (reducing picture size) so that the entire picture area is visible (no edge cut-off) immediately reveals a bad signal (instability, jitters).

A *pulse-cross monitor* can be switched to displace the picture, and display the edge and bottom of the TV picture in the middle of the screen. With increased brightness, you can detect any synchronizing faults, and check VCR replay (tape tension, tracking). Using a special converter box, a regular monitor can be used in this way.

Waveform monitor

This is an oscilloscope displaying a fluctuating line, which traces the variations of the video signal, the sync pulses, etc. You can select and examine individual picture lines. It has several uses, including: checking for exposure errors, ensuring that the video does not exceed the system's limits (i.e. so that light tones do not crush out or clip off to white; shadows do not merge to black); checking accuracy of sync pulses.

Color bar generator

A test signal comprising a series of vertical bars of standard colors (white, yellow, cyan (blue-green), green, magenta (red-purple), red, blue, black). It is usually generated electronically, although a color chart can be used.

Vectorscope

An oscilloscope used for checking the color accuracy of all parts of the system (cameras, switcher, VCR, etc.). Wrong adjustments can totally wreck color quality! White and black should be neutral, producing a central blob on the screen. When a *color bars* test signal is displayed, a series of e.g. six bright dots appear around the screen – ideally within small engraved boxes.

If the 'chroma gain'/'chroma level' (color strength) is too low, a test color will fall outside its box, closer to the screen's center. Nearer the screen's edge, it is too high. If the dots are clockwise or anticlockwise of their boxes, the 'subcarrier phase' or 'burst phase' (hue) may need adjustment. If some dots appear normal but others are displaced, check white balance and/or color temperature, otherwise the 'encoder level' may be wrong. If in doubt, don't! Ideally, the color responses of all cameras should match. Color bars are recorded at the start of each videotape, to check color accuracy.

Test signal generator/pattern generator

Various signals and patterns can be generated electronically, to check and adjust the system's resolution (definition), tonal gradation and contrast (gamma), tonal limits (black level, white level/clipper), color bars, circles crosshatch, staircase, split field.

Audio equipment

Audio equipment too can be considered as

Supplementary (e.g. mixer),

Compensatory (e.g. EQ),

Effects (e.g. echo).

Again, some units have more than one function.

Supplementary equipment

Pre-amplifier. An amplifier used to adjust the strength of audio from one or more audio sources to a standard level (intensity). It may include source switching, basic filtering.

Power amplifier. A unit used to amplify the output of the pre-amplifier, and deliver power to drive a loudspeaker unit. A *cross-over filter network* is often used to subdivide the amplifier's output to drive speakers covering sections of the audio spectrum (tweeter, mid-range, woofer).

Patch panel/jackfield/jack strip. Rows of sockets to which the inputs and outputs of various audio units are permanently wired. Units may be interconnected with a series of plugged cables (patch cords).

Audio mixer. A unit or sound desk used to select, control and intermix all audio sources. It may include filter circuits, reverberation control, etc.

Sound control

Audio filters. Audio filters may be used to reduce background noises (traffic, air-conditioners, wind), or compensate for boomy surroundings. They can take several forms.

Slope filters (*RSA – response selection amplifiers*), which accentuate/reduce the strength of either end of the audible scale (adjust top/treble, bass).

High or low pass filters, which cut off lower or higher audio (bass cut; top cut).

Graphic equalizer (*shaping filter*), which has a series of slider controls, allowing selected parts of the audio spectrum to be boosted or reduced.

Notch filter (*parametric amplifier*), filter producing a very steep peak or dip in a selected part of the audio spectrum; e.g. to suppress unavoidable hum, whistle, rumble, etc.

Presence circuits, which boost/cut around 2–6 kHz, to improve clarity, audio separation, bring a sound source 'forward' from others, improve sibilants.

Noise reduction. Circuitry for reducing unwanted noise from tape, disc and other background sounds. This can be done by *noise gate circuits* (suppressing quiet sounds), *compressor/expander circuits* (reducing then restoring the dynamic range), pre-emphasis/de-emphasis boosting higher notes during recording, and reducing them during reproduction (e.g. Dolby systems). A *dynamic noise reducer* simply reduces treble during quieter periods.

Limiter. A device for preventing loud audio from exceeding the system's upper limit (so causing overload distortion), by progressively reducing circuit amplification for louder sounds.

Effects equipment

As well as using audio filtering for effects (e.g. imitating telephone conversations), sound can be manipulated in various ways.

Compressor/expander. Deliberately used to reduce or emphasize the audio dynamic range (i.e. the difference between the quietest and loudest sounds).

Reverberation. Device for increasing or adjusting the amount of reverberation accompanying a sound. Systems include spring delay, echo room, digital methods.

14.17 The digital world

In an *analogue* audio system a fluctuating electrical voltage follows all the air vibrations impinging on the microphone. We've only to consider the complexity of the single audio waveform representing the combined sounds from an orchestra or a choir to appreciate the task! (In the phonograph record, the needle attempts to trace and reproduce this complex waveform!) Any inaccuracies in the process we experience as *distortions* of some kind.

In a *video analogue* system the strength of the video signal corresponds with light, shade, detail in the original picture.

As technology advanced, *digital techniques* developed which convey information in quite a different way. Instead of attempting to follow each intricate fluctuation of the analogue waveform, a digital system measures the waveform's strength at regular intervals, using an *analogue/digital (A/D) converter*.

These figures are stored as a simple *binary code*, in which a constant voltage is switched on and off in a prescribed pattern. This switching is represented as a series of *0's* and *1's*. So, for example, *10* is transcribed into **00001010**. To restore this data to its original analogue form, it is fed into a *digital/analogue (D/A) converter*.

Although this method may at first appear cumbersome, it has many practical advantages:

- All types of information can be conveyed and stored by digital systems, including text, graphics, music, speech, pictures (still or moving).
- Data is easily stored, using computer techniques.
- It is a very robust accurate method, that is not easily distorted.
- Errors can be detected and corrected relatively easily.

● Because all information is represented by a sequence of numbers, if we deliberately alter individual pieces of data, the resulting effect changes.
 – So, for instance, by varying a number that represents the sharpness, tonal value or hue we can alter that particular feature whether it occurs in a graphic, an illustration, titling, text, or a photograph.
 – In a digitally stored piece of music we may be able to change pitch, loudness, duration, etc.
 – In some text or titling, we can similarly alter the font or lettering size, or other attributes simply by renumbering data.
● Digital information is easily selected, edited, reversed, duplicated, modified in various ways. Whether we are isolating a single tree from a picture, a musical phrase, words in a speech, they can be treated or transformed. The opportunities are endless.
● Data in digital form can be compressed in order to take up less storage space and subsequently restored to its original form.

Digital techniques are transforming video/television program making; not only in the greatly improved quality of sound and picture they offer but also in the additional productional opportunities that are becoming available. But in the end, it is the effectiveness with which the medium is used that really matters. If a comedian stands in front of the camera, and the picture is superb, the sound impeccable, but the performance is poor . . . technology and techniques amount to little.

Figure 14.3 Digital quantizing
Where a source such as a microphone produces a continuous fluctuating signal output, an *analogue system* tries to follow every variation. Any inaccuracies in the system's performance result in distortion to some extent.

A *digital system* adopts a different approach, and samples the strength (amplitude) of the original analogue signal at regular intervals. Each measurement is then stored in a *binary code* form – a series of on/off switching instructions for a single voltage. This form is less likely to become distorted, and can be adjusted/manipulated in various ways.

To restore the signal to its original analogue form (e.g. to operate a loudspeaker), this data is converted by a *digital/analogue converter* unit.

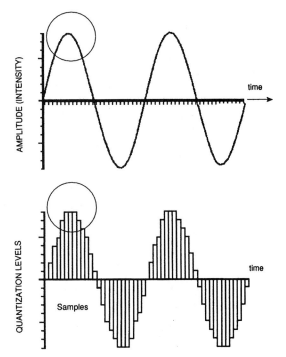

Appendix A

Battery care

If your power supplies fail during shooting, you could find yourself with a lot of expensive equipment . . . that does *nothing*!

Types of power

For most of us, electrical power is just another everyday utility. It's embarrassing, even catastrophic, when things go wrong and that supply fails. Yet quite often, if we understand the fundamentals, these problems need never arise. So it's worth taking a few minutes looking at the basics of power supply. The emergency you avoid may be your own!

Utility supplies

Because there are no *internationally* agreed standards for power distribution we find that public utilities electricity supplies (mains supplies) vary between countries and sometimes between regions. Typically we find AC supplies of 100, 110, 120, 127, 200, 210, 220, 230 or 240 volts, and frequencies of 50 or 60 Hz.

Equipment

All electrical equipment is designed to be used with a particular form of electrical supply. It may be *AC* (*alternating current*) or *DC* (*direct current*).

- *AC* supplies are easily transformed into a *DC* form that may be of higher or lower voltage than the original *AC* supply.
- A *DC* supply is less readily converted to an *AC* form. There are several different standards for connectors and cables.

Some equipment can be powered from either internal or external batteries, or from an AC utility supply. Most portable video equipment uses *rechargeable batteries*; although by using a special adaptor, you can power it from AC household supplies instead:

- *Batteries* have the advantage that they allow maximum portability for equipment. But the output of a battery falls in use and it is susceptible to damage.

- *Household supplies* provide a *constant* output, as an adaptor converts the *AC* to the lower-voltage *DC* that the video equipment requires. But this type of supply necessarily involves trailing supply cables.

Electrical basics

Equipment is designed for a specified *supply voltage*. During operation, current flows in the circuits, which may range from as little as a few *milliamperes* (*mA*) to several *amps/amperes* (*A*) overall. The power consumed in the process (rated in *watts*) is calculated by multiplying the voltage by the *amps*.

Fuses are fitted to equipment to avoid electrical damage if a fault condition should cause excess current to flow. (The thin wire or foil in the fuse melts, breaking the circuit.) To calculate the maximum acceptable *current* flow, for a particular fuse rating, divide the equipment's *power rating* (*watts*) by the figure for the *supply voltage*. For the maximum acceptable power, multiply the *current* by the *voltage*.

Battery basics

What we generally refer to as a *battery* is usually made up of a number of identical individual *cells* joined together. When linked to an electrical circuit, the chemicals in these cells react, causing an electric current to flow. This chemical action progressively falls off until the supply is insufficient for the equipment to continue to function effectively. Or as we say, the battery is *exhausted*.

The primary cell The voltage at the terminals of an individual cell depends on the types of constituent chemicals used. The amount of power it can deliver relates to its volume. A typical '*dry cell*' or '*primary cell*' used in most flashlights, for example, has a maximum voltage of 1.5 volts.

To provide a battery with a higher overall voltage, a number of these cells are wired in series, i.e. the **+ve** (red) of one cell to the **–ve** (black) of the next cell.

To increase the capacity of a group of cells (i.e. so that they last longer) all their **+ve** poles are wired together, and separately, all their **–ve** poles are wired together.

The secondary cell Widely used for power applications ranging from automobile batteries to portable power tools, the secondary cell again generates current through chemical action. But in this case, this chemical process can be reversed. By passing an electric current through the battery during a *recharging* process, these chemicals can be converted into their original form, ready to deliver power again when required; although the time taken to replenish is considerably longer than the time for which it delivers current in use.

Batteries and equipment The batteries fitted to video equipment, may be carried in several ways:

- Internal ('on-board') battery, fitted within the equipment.
- Battery belt; a series of batteries carried in a waist-belt.
- Snap-on battery-pack; clips to rear of camera.
- Shoulder sling bag; used to power a lamp (e.g. 80–100 W) in a mounting-shoe on top of the camera, or hand-held. May power the VCR.
- Trolley-pack; a wheeled cart/trolley carrying a VCR, monitor and high-capacity battery.
- Car battery; supply run from automobile's engine battery (using cigar-lighter outlet).

Several battery supply voltages are used currently for video equipment, from 10.5 to 17 volts. A 14.4 standard is now specified by all major manufacturers to eliminate previous problems with 12 volt standards.

In selecting the type of battery to be fitted to equipment the manufacturer has to take several factors into account:

- The available space in the housing.
- The terminal voltage required.
- How long will the battery hold this charge when it is left unused or partially used (*shelf life*)?
- How much current can it deliver in use (gradually or suddenly), i.e. its *capacity*?
- How long will it supply this current before needing to be recharged?
- Will its terminal voltage return to the original value (*full voltage*)?
- How many times can it be recharged successfully?

That is why it is important for replacement batteries to match the recommended originals.

Using batteries

When you are moving around, or working away from household supplies, batteries are an essential power source; and provided they are cared for, they can be used and re-charged many times. But mishandle them or use them incorrectly, and their performance deteriorates and their useful life shortens.

Your video system draws power directly it is switched on. Remember, supplies are needed for the camera (its viewfinder, power zoom, video light), for the VCR (when recording, replaying, rewinding), and any separate equipment (monitor, audio recorder, hand-held lamp).

Apart from the actual shooting/recording time, the equipment will be using power while you are adjusting it, checking shots, rehearsing action, testing lights, and so on; and a surprising amount of time can pass doing these things. (A *film camera*, on the other hand, only uses power while it is running.) Thus a battery might only last for a single cassette when shooting and rehearsing, whereas it might last for several cassettes when shooting a news event continuously.

You can conserve battery power by switching units off until they are needed (e.g. monitor), and switching the camera and VCR to 'standby' (warm-up) when possible, ready to switch-on and use. On some cameras, 'auto-switch-off' saves the power when the unit has not been used for several minutes.

Table A.1 Typical video camera battery capacities (minimum)

Consumption for 12–14 volt portable camera	1–1.5 hour overall capacity	2 hour overall capacity
10–14 watts	1.2 Ah NiCad	2 Ah NiCad
15–25 watts	2 Ah NiCad	4 Ah NiCad
25–35 watts	4 Ah NiCad	4 Ah NiCad
35–50 watts	4 Ah NiCad	8 Ah NiCad
		12 Ah silver-zinc

Cell capacity

How long a fully charged battery will provide current before its voltage falls, and it needs recharging is indicated by its rating in *ampere-hours* (Ah). Knowing this figure, you could say theoretically, that a 2 Ah battery will supply a current of 2 A for a camera for 1 hour (i.e. Ah divided by amperes).

In an ideal world one should be able to deduce that if, instead, you use that same battery for a lamp drawing 8 amps, it should last about $\frac{2}{8} = \frac{1}{4}$ hour or 15 minutes. Unfortunately, batteries do not always behave as simply as that, and it may only last 10 or 11 minutes.

If a fairly high current is drawn from a lead–acid battery its effective capacity falls, i.e. it does not last as long as you might expect from a battery of that Ah rating, before needing recharging. The *NiCad* cell's output capacity, though, is more constant.

This is a point to bear in mind when you are supplying several pieces of equipment from the same battery, especially when using high consumption battery-operated lamps.

Not only will the battery's capacity be reduced if it is asked to supply a heavy load, but the supply voltage will fall (voltage drop), and may in fact become too low to operate the camera and the VCR.

So you can use a relatively larger high-rated battery, that lasts longer and permits heavier currents to be drawn; or a similar compact lower capacity one, sufficient for short-period working, that is more frequently replaced with fresh standby batteries. So for instance, a 2 Ah 'in-board' battery within a camera may last about an hour, while a power belt 4–7 Ah could give 2–3.5 hours' use.

Types of cell

Lead–acid cell

There are several versions of this type of battery, from those fitted to automobiles (containing a sulfuric acid electrolyte in liquid form, which may periodically require 'topping up' or be accidentally spilt), to totally sealed types with the electrolyte in jelly form.

This is the cheapest and toughest, but the bulkiest and heaviest cell. It is tolerant of brief short-circuits and extreme working temperatures.

It has a minimum 2 volts per cell (which falls to 1.65 volts minimum). Typical capacities for lead–acid cells are 2–30 Ah. (Car batteries are up to e.g. 100 Ah.)

Lead–acid batteries should not be left in a discharged state but fully charged before storage to avoid internal '*sulfating (sulphating)*'.

Nickel–cadmium (NiCad) cell

The popular *NiCad* or nickel cadmium cell (1.2 volts per cell), is smaller, rugged, long-lived and easy to charge, but more costly. Its voltage falls at higher temperatures.

It has a maximum of 1.2 volts per cell (which falls to 1.1 volts minimum). It should not be discharged at over 20 times its capacity, nor recharged at over one-tenth of its capacity, i.e. $\frac{1}{2}$ amp for a 5 Ah battery.

Nickel hydride (NiMH) cell

More expensive than the NiCad type of battery, this has a 20% higher energy density for its size, and suffers much less from memory effect. Its improved life can provide up to 40 more run times than the NiCad, permitting as many as 500 charge to discharge cycles. However, it does lose its charge rather quickly; falling by as much as 10% in 24 hours. It can be recharged without being fully discharged, and recharging can take as little as 1.5 hours.

Lithium cell (Lithium ion, Li-Ion)

Even more efficient, and lacking memory effect, this type does tend to self-discharge when stored for a while. The terminal voltage falls even when not in use. However, lithium cells maintain a constant voltage for longer, and are better in extreme hot or cold conditions than other types of cell. (Currently mainly used in laptop computers.)

Battery care

Look after your batteries, and you will find them a reliable effective power-source. Although they are quite robust, it pays to handle them carefully, for mechanical shock, blows, dropping, or excessive flexing of connections (especially inter-wired cells in power-belts) can cause unexpected breakdown.

Many batteries are ruined by the way they are used. Take care when fitting or charging a battery to avoid connecting it the wrong way round (reversed polarity).

Measure a battery's voltage while it is working ('on-load'), not when you have removed it from the equipment, for then it is liable to give you a higher, more optimistic reading, than it should. A fitted indicator on the camera will usually show you the 'state of charge'.

Avoid storing batteries in extreme temperatures, e.g. leaving batteries in a car in the sun, or out in temperatures below freezing. NiCad batteries retain their charge well in cool storage, losing it rapidly in hot surroundings.

If you are storing NiCad batteries, temperatures of around 68° to –22°F (20° to –30°C) are preferred. Much higher temperatures tend to reduce the life of the battery to half or even a quarter of normal.

Their working efficiency varies with temperature. Best at around 65–75°F (18–22°C), the cell's output falls over 120°F (50°C), or under –40°F (–40°C).

In cold weather, some camera operators shoot with their NiCad battery-belt worn underneath a jacket, to keep it warmer.

Lead–acid batteries can work effectively in temperatures as low as –40°F or up to 150°F (66°C).

The battery's voltage remains reasonably constant in use, falling rapidly when nearing the end of its capacity. It is good practice to carry around several fully charged standby batteries, and you should replace the one in use when its volts are down to the official minimum: 1.6 volts per cell for lead–acid, 1.1 volts per cell for NiCad.

Do not discharge a battery below 1 volt per cell. And certainly never *completely exhaust* a battery ('flat', deep discharge), for example by leaving the equipment switched on and forgetting it. A new battery can be ruined that way.

Do not leave discharged cells around for long periods (i.e. cells below full voltage), but recharge them as soon as possible. (However, see the comments on 'memory' in the next section.) If a NiCad cell falls too low, it can actually go into reversed polarity, and when the battery is charged next, the faulty cell will appear satisfactory, but lose its charge quickly, and this can result in the entire belt being permanently damaged.

As batteries age, they tend to *discharge themselves* to a noticeable extent when left, and in the worst cases you could find that, after a few days, a fully charged battery has very little charge left in it. If in fact some cells in a battery are faulty, any attempt to charge the battery may destroy the remaining good ones, which become overcharged.

A battery can only be recharged/discharged a limited number of times ('its 'cycle-life') before its rated capacity falls. If you find a battery's voltage falling quite quickly in use, it could indicate that it is coming to the end of its useful life, especially if during charging, it also seems to be taking less time than normal to reach full charge from a completely discharged state.

The cycle-life for a NiCad battery is typically several hundred cycles, much better than that of a lead–acid type.

If you leave a *charged* NiCad battery for a long time without discharging it, internal crystals may form, which can cause high self-discharge or even a dangerous internal short circuit.

Battery charging

A battery charger should always be appropriate for this job. For example, don't use a 'lead–acid' charger for NiCad or silver–zinc cells. They require different charging voltages and rates.

While a lead–acid battery is generally charged from a *constant voltage* source, a NiCad battery requires *constant current* when charging.

There have been notable developments in charger design. Because only a totally drained NiCad battery will fully recharge for maximum performance, it should either be used until it is *exhausted (flat)* or recharged with equipment that includes a proper *battery discharger unit* which will drain the battery to e.g. 0.9 volts per cell, before recharging. Alternatively, the charger system may apply a series of brief *discharge pulses* to the battery while charging it; a trick which encourages the recombination of gases which were formed during quick charging. Used regularly, this *burp* or *reverse-load charging* technique can add as much as 15% to the life of the Nicad battery. Other designs regulate the process by monitoring the battery's *temperature* while recharging; but this is said to '*cook*' the battery. '*Smart chargers*' adjust the charge to suit the batteries' condition and capacity.

A battery should be recharged at the correct rate for its type, using an appropriate type of charger unit. Normally, a lead–acid battery will take about 15 hours at 2.4 volts per cell to charge fully from a discharged condition. A NiCad cell requires around 12–16 hours, depending on the charge-rate (current); about $\frac{1}{8}$ or $\frac{1}{10}$ of its Ah capacity rating. In practice it is best not to continue once charging is complete.

The exception to these charging rates is the 20–60 minutes taken when using special *fast-charger units* with suitable Nicad batteries.

Fast recharging sounds like a great boon to the busy camera operator. But unless it is carried out correctly, it can put quite a strain on the battery, particularly if it is not in top condition, or the ambient temperature is unusually high or low.

NiCad batteries should really only be fast-charged at normal room temperature (65°–75°F) (18–23°C). At temperatures under about 60°F (15°C), or above 100–110°F (38°C) damage is inevitable. Many feel that it is safer to carry more batteries, and that a slow overnight charge is preferable.

Avoid *cycling*, i.e. taking a battery from a fully charged to a fully discharged state, for this will reduce its storage capacity. There is the danger that individual cells of the battery will not return to the same maximum voltage (imbalance), and the poorest cell will reduce the battery's overall performance. A battery-belt or pack can never be better than its poorest cell. So never mix new and old cells.

Unlike lead–acid batteries, NiCad cells can develop a 'memory' condition (depressed voltage) if you give the battery an overlengthy 'trickle charge' (low charging current for a long period), or if the battery has been frequently overcharged, and then left around partially discharged.

If you continually use a battery for a short period (say half an hour), then recharge it fully, you may find that this battery regularly starts to drop after half an hour, instead of giving its full capacity.

A battery that has developed a 'memory' appears normal after full charge, but will not deliver the full running time in use. You can cure this condition by deliberately discharging the battery to one volt per cell (measured *off-load*, i.e. disconnected), and recharging it for 20 hours at about 77°F (25°C), repeating the process several times.

It is generally recommended that freshly charged cells should be allowed to stand for some time to stabilize before using them. Take care when using a freshly charged battery for a portable lamp that it does not burn out ('blow') its bulb (typically 30 volts, 150, 250 or 350 watts).

Appendix B

Useful data

Power consumption

This table shows how much current (in amperes) is drawn by equipment, so that you can avoid overloading supplies. Check the supply voltage. Then add up the consumption of individual units in watts, to find the total current being consumed. (All figures are proportional: e.g. 150 W = 100 W + 50 W.)

	12 V	110 V	120 V	220 V	240 V
50 W	4.2	0.46	0.42	0.23	0.21
100 W	8.4	0.91	0.83	0.45	0.42
200 W	17.0	1.82	1.67	0.91	0.83
300 W	25.0	2.7	2.5	1.36	1.25
375 W	31.25	3.4	3.2	1.7	1.6
500 W	41.66	4.6	4.2	2.3	2.1
800 W	–	7.33	6.66	3.64	3.33
1000 W	–	9.1	8.33	4.55	4.2
1250 W	–	11.4	10.4	5.7	5.2
2000 W	–	18.2	16.7	9.1	8.33
3000 W	–	27.3	25.0	13.6	12.5
4000 W	–	36.4	35.4	18.2	17.0
5000 W	–	45.0	42.0	23.0	21.0

Typical light levels

1 foot candle (fc) = 10.764 lux; 1 lux = 0.0929 fc. For most purposes you can approximate 1 fc = 10 lux.

Light source	Foot candles	Lux
Bright sun	5000–10 000	50 000–100 000
Hazy sun	2500–5000	25 000–50 000
Bright, cloudy	1000–25 000	10 000–25 000
Dull cloudy	200–1000	2000–10 000
Very dull	10–200	100–2000
Sunset	0.1–10	1–100
Full moon	0.001–0.01	0.01–0.1
Television studio	100–200	1000–2000
Office	20–30	200–300
Living room	5–20	50–200
Corridors	5–10	50–100
Good street lighting	1–2	10–20
Candlelight (20 cm away)	1.5	15

Lensless spot		Flood	(fc/lux)	Spot	(fc/lux)	ft/m
250 W		90°	32/350	45°	140/1500	10/3
600 W		90°	74/800	45°	223/2400	10/3
800 W		90°	37/400	45°	130/1400	16/5
2000 W		75°	93/1000	35°	370/4000	16/5
Six-light (PAR) floodlight bank						
6 × 650 W			140/1500		74/800	33/10

Typical color temperatures (in kelvins)

Standard candle	1930 K
Household tungsten lamps (25–250 W)	2600–2900 K
Studio tungsten lamp (500–1000 W)	3000 K
Studio tungsten lamp (2000 W)	3275 K
Studio tungsten lamp (5 kW, 10 kW)	3380 K
'Quartz' (tungsten-halogen) lamps	3200–3400 K
Photoflood	3400 K
Fluorescent lamps	3000–6500 K
Sunrise, sunset	2000–3000 K
1 hour after sunrise	3500 K
Sunless daylight	4500–4800 K
Midday sun	5000–5400 K
Overcast sky	6800–7500 K
Hazy sky	8000–9000 K
Clear blue north sky	10 000–20 000 K

Lens angle

When we refer to lens angle we mean the *horizontal* coverage (angle of view). Its *vertical* angle, which determines the height taken in by the shot, is three-quarters of this value. Thus a 40° lens has a vertical coverage of 30°.

The angle covered by a lens depends on its focal length, and the camera's light sensor (CCD) image size.

Here are the approximate focal lengths (in millimeters) needed to provide typical lens angles, with different size light sensors:

Typical lens angles

Lens angle	5°	10°	15°	20°	25°	30°	35°	40°	45°	50°	55°	60°	
2/3 in. CCD	101	50	33.5	25	20	16.5	14	12	11	9.5	8.5	8	Focal length (mm)
1/2 in. CCD	73	37	24	18	14.5	12	10	9	8	7	6	5.5	Focal length (mm)

From these figures you can see how by referring to the lens angle rather than the focal length we have a stable standard against which to judge shots. Quoting the focal length can be misleading, for the same lens will produce different shots with various camera sensor sizes. Another advantage is that you can draw a lens angle on any scale plan, and see exactly what the shot opportunities and problems will be, when planning.

To see the maximum detail available in a TV picture, we should ideally sit at around four to six times the picture height away from the screen. At this distance, the picture width covers an angle of about 28–20° to the eye. If the camera lens covers a similar angle, the perspective will appear natural in the shot. So a lens shot of about 28–20° is termed *normal*.

A lens covering much less than 20° is called a *narrow angle* (long focus) lens. One covering over about 30° is called a *wide* angle lens.

Available shots on a normal 25° lens

	BCU	CU	Chest	Waist	Knees	Full length
Meters	1.0	1.25	1.75	2.0	4	+6.0
Feet	3.3	4	5.7	6.5	13	+20

Typical lens coverage

Angle (°)	Width at 3 m	Width at 10 ft
5	0.26 m	10 in.
10	0.53 m	1 ft 9 in.
15	0.79 m	2 ft 7 in.
20	1.06 m	3 ft 6 in.
25	1.33 m	4 ft 5 in.
30	1.61 m	5 ft 5 in.
35	1.89 m	6 ft 4 in.
40	2.18 m	7 ft 4 in.
45	2.49 m	8 ft 4 in.
50	2.80 m	9 ft 4 in.
55	3.46 m	11 ft 7 in.

Shot heights

Level shot:	Standing person	4–5 ft (1.2–1.8 m)
	Sitting person	3.5 ft (1.1 m)
Low level shot:	Ground level to	3 ft (1 m)
Very low angle shot:	50–60° upwards	
Low angle shot:	20–40° upwards	
High angle shot:	20–40° downwards	
Very high angle shot:	50–60° downwards	
Top shot, overhead shot:	Straight downwards ±5°	

Hyperfocal distance

When a lens is focused at its *hyperfocal distance* (*H*), the scene is sharp from about half this distance, to the farthest distance (infinity). Any action within this distance range will appear in focus.

You can calculate the hyperfocal distance in meters from:

$$\frac{(\text{focal length in cm})^2 \times 100}{\text{lens stop No.} \times 0.05}$$

or the hyperfocal distance in feet from:

$$\frac{\text{(focal length in inches)}^2}{\text{lens stop No.} \times 0.002}$$

Aspect ratio

Because the screen has a rectangular 4×3 shape, graphics need to be roughly of this aspect ratio, if information round the edges is not to be lost.

Horizontal size (in. or cm)	10	15		20	25		30	35		40	45		50
Vertical size (in. or cm)		7.5	11.25	15	18.75	22.5	26.25	30	33.75	37.5

Audio tape formats

Reel-to-reel tape
Tape width: $\frac{1}{4}$ in. (6.35 mm)
Spool diameters:
3 in. (75 mm) with 175 ft of tape; 4 in. (100 mm) with 300 ft;
5 in. (125 mm) with 600 ft; $5\frac{3}{4}$ in. (145 mm) with 900 ft;
7 in. (175 mm) with 1200 ft; NAB $10\frac{1}{2}$ in. (265 mm) with 2400 ft.

Tape speeds per second:
$^{15}\!/_{16}$ in. (2.35 cm); $1\frac{7}{8}$ in. (4.75 cm);
$3\frac{3}{4}$ in. (9.5 cm); $7\frac{1}{2}$ in. (19 cm); 15 in. (38 cm).

Running time:
1200 ft = 32 min at $7\frac{1}{2}$ in. (19 cm) per second.
1 min = 38 ft (11.6 m);
30 min = 1125 ft (342 m). Other lengths and speeds in this ratio for standard tape.

For other tape thicknesses, multiply duration by:
long = $\times 1.5$; double play = $\times 2$; triple play = $\times 3$;
quad play = $\times 4$.

Cassette
Tape width: 3.5 mm. Speed 4.75 cm/s ($1\frac{7}{8}$ in.).
Cassette maximum durations:
30, 60 90, 120 min (turning cassette over at the end of first side).

Appendix C

Camera set-up graph

The graph shows how much any lens sees at various distances. (The *height* of the area seen is $\frac{3}{4}$ of the width.)

1 *How far away does the camera have to be, to get a certain type of shot?* Select type of shot you want on vertical scale . . . then down to the *distance scale.*
2 *What lens angle is needed for a certain type of shot*? Trace a line across graph from the shot you want (vertical scale) . . . draw another line, up from camera's distance on the bottom *scale*. Where they cross, shows the best *lens angle.*
3 *What type of shots will I get from here?* Draw a line up from the *distance scale*, to the *lens angle*(s) you have available (max and min zoom angles). Then across left, to the *shot* scale.
4 *How much will the camera see from here*? As 3, but read the scene *width/ height scales.*
5 You can get the *same shot size* at different distances by altering lens angle. Trace a line right from the shot needed (e.g. CU) and note the distance at which it cuts various lens angles.
6 *To make a subject fill a certain proportion of screen width* (e.g. $\frac{1}{3}$: Measure the subject width; multiply this by 3 for $\frac{1}{3}$ width (4 for $\frac{1}{4}$, etc.). Look up this screen width on the left vertical *width scale*. Trace across to the *lens angle used*, then down to the *distance* needed. The subject will now fill $\frac{1}{3}$ screen width.

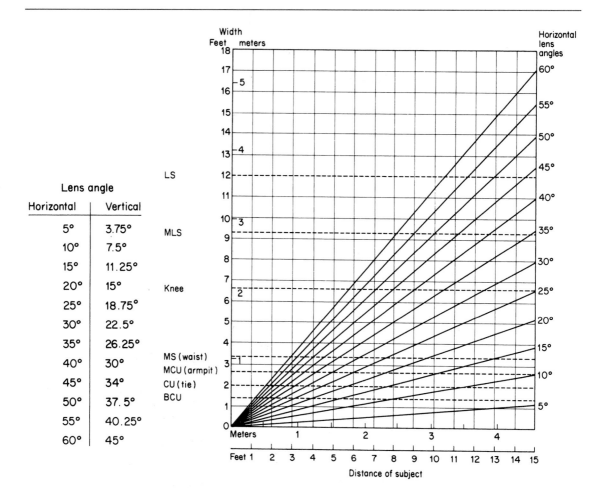

Lens angle	
Horizontal	Vertical
5°	3.75°
10°	7.5°
15°	11.25°
20°	15°
25°	18.75°
30°	22.5°
35°	26.25°
40°	30°
45°	34°
50°	37.5°
55°	40.25°
60°	45°

Index

⨍ Focal Press

www.focalpress.com

Join Focal Press on-line

As a member you will enjoy the following benefits:

an email bulletin with **information on new books**

a regular **Focal Press Newsletter**:

- o featuring a selection of new titles
- o keeps you informed of **special offers, discounts and freebies**
- o alerts you to **Focal Press news and events** such as author signings and seminars

complete access to **free content** and reference material on the focalpress site, such as the focalXtra articles and commentary from our authors

a **Sneak Preview** of selected titles (sample chapters) *before* they publish

a chance to have your say on our **discussion boards** and **review books** for other Focal readers

Focal Club Members are invited to give us feedback on our products and services. Email: worldmarketing@focalpress.com – we want to hear your views!

Membership is FREE. To join, visit our website and register. If you require any further information regarding the on-line club please contact:

Emma Hales, Marketing Manager
Email: emma.hales@repp.co.uk
Tel: +44 (0) 1865 314556
Fax: +44 (0)1865 315472
Address: Focal Press, Linacre House,
Jordan Hill, Oxford, UK, OX2 8DP

Catalogue

For information on all Focal Press titles, our full catalogue is available online at www.focalpress.com and all titles can be purchased here via secure online ordering, or contact us for a free printed version:

USA
Email: christine.degon@bhusa.com

Europe and rest of world
Email: jo.coleman@repp.co.uk
Tel: +44 (0)1865 314220

Potential authors

If you have an idea for a book, please get in touch:

USA
Lilly Roberts, Editorial Assistant
Email: lilly.roberts@bhusa.com
Tel: +1 781 904 2639
Fax: +1 781 904 2640

Europe and rest of world
Christina Donaldson, Editorial Assistant
Email: christina.donaldson@repp.co.uk
Tel: +44 (0)1865 314027
Fax: +44 (0)1865 314572

Great Meetings!

HOW TO FACILITATE LIKE A PRO

BY DEE KELSEY AND PAM PLUMB

HANSON PARK PRESS · SECOND PRINTING

Published by Hanson Park Press
P.O. Box 3883, Portland, Maine, 04104-3883.

Cover and page design by Jennifer Ellis.
Illustrations in chapters 6 and 11 by Kippy Rudy.

First printing May 1997
Second printing May 1999
Manufactured in the United States

ISBN 0-9658354-0-5

ACKNOWLEDGMENTS

THE WRITING OF *GREAT MEETINGS!* HAS BEEN AN EVOLUTIONARY PROCESS BORN OF A combination of the practice and training of facilitation. Many people have helped along the way to make it possible. Our collaboration over many years with the University of Southern Maine's Center for Continuing Education encouraged us to begin writing down the information we were using in our facilitation training. In particular, we are grateful for the support of Joanne Spear, Susan Sinclair Nevins and all the staff at CCE. In addition, we thank our many students who have added insights, additional tools and even editorial comments which have become part of this book.

Our many clients over the years have given us the opportunity to practice, gain experience and learn what works (and what doesn't!) in a wide variety of situations. Their feedback and encouragement in our work have been invaluable in building our experience and our approach to facilitation.

We thank all of the organizations and individuals who have given us training, coaching and feedback over the years and who have been generous in sharing their materials — and reviewing ours.

When we moved from copying our material for handouts to publishing a book, the leap took us well beyond our realm of knowledge. We are grateful to Jennifer Ellis, our editor and designer. With patience and flexibility, she has turned vague concepts into reality and brought our text alive with her skillful design work. We also thank our illustrator, Kippy Rudy, who from the early years of training manuals has made our graphics examples more professional and fun.

Finally, none of this would have been possible without great patience and support from those who had to live with us on the home front while we were buried in writing and panicked over deadlines. We asked a lot of a five-year-old and hard working husband. To Emily Kelsey and to Peter Plumb, bless you both.

TABLE OF CONTENTS

INTRODUCTION

GREAT MEETINGS! IS DESIGNED TO PROVIDE A PRACTICAL GUIDE FOR PEOPLE WHO ARE interested in making their steady stream of meetings more productive, creative, effective and fun. This book is not a scholarly dissertation, but a "how to" book built from years of practical experience. It is based on the belief that groups of people can generate better decisions than any one of us might come up with alone. The members of a group will provide different insights, bring unique experiences and expertise to bear on the problem and feed on each others' ideas to build a synergy, a whole which is greater than the mere mathematical sum of the parts.

It isn't easy to work as a group. Meetings take planning and preparation to be successful. Agendas need to be designed carefully to meet the needs of the situation. Managing a meeting takes a host of facilitation skills and a full bag of process tools. This book is designed to help you understand the various preparation and design steps that will assist you in planning effective meetings and to give you a wide variety of facilitation tools and techniques for managing meetings well.

WHAT'S IN THE BOOK?

CHAPTER ONE: FACILITATION: WHAT'S IT ALL ABOUT? clarifies what facilitation is, distinguishing it from meeting organization, process design, process coaching, organizational development consulting and group therapy. You will find a description of the facilitator's role and a discussion of the different roles that you may be called on to play simultaneously in a meeting. In addition, we outline the attitudes and characteristics that we feel are critical to effective facilitation.

CHAPTER TWO: KNOWING YOUR GROUP focuses on group dynamics. It is not a thorough study of this complex subject, but an overview of how groups work and develop. Its purpose is to build your awareness of the complexities of groups as you plan for and facilitate meetings. The chapter covers factors in group dynamics, stages of group development, behaviors and roles that affect the functioning of groups, and overt and covert group issues.

CHAPTER THREE: GETTING A GOOD START guides you through the steps of preparing for a meeting. It outlines how to assess the purpose and desired outcomes of the meeting and how to gather relevant background information. The chapter concludes with a detailed meeting preparation checklist.

CHAPTER FOUR: DESIGNING A GREAT MEETING gives you guidance in effective meeting design, with ideas for how to handle the logistics of a meeting and what to accomplish during each stage of the meeting itself.

CHAPTER FIVE: UNDERSTANDING PROBLEM SOLVING offers a format for approaching problem solving. We then discuss each step of the problem solving process and suggest helpful tools to use in each of those steps.

CHAPTER SIX: TOOLS FOR PROBLEM SOLVING provides a broad selection of tools to use in problem solving. Each tool's description will let you know when the tool is most helpful and how to use it.

CHAPTER SEVEN: MAXIMIZING THE GROUP'S POTENTIAL outlines a number of process techniques to help your group work at its highest potential. It includes warm up techniques for group forming, methods for generating discussion and techniques for keeping groups on track.

CHAPTER EIGHT: PROMOTING POSITIVE COMMUNICATION deals with the communications skills which are critical both to your effectiveness as a facilitator and to the participants' ability to have a successful meeting. This discussion includes establishing a good communication environment, listening skills, "I" messages, different types of questioning, and ways to reframe language.

CHAPTER NINE: MANAGING CONFLICT IN GROUPS addresses conflict in groups. It begins with an explanation of the sources of conflict, and then offers methods for intervening in group conflicts, addressing interpersonal conflicts that arise in group settings and ways to prevent unnecessary, energy-draining conflicts.

CHAPTER TEN: INTERVENTIONS discusses methods for intervening in challenging group situations or with difficult individual behaviors. We offer a method for analyzing the nature of the problem and choosing the appropriate approach for intervening. Included are case studies to demonstrate this process in action.

CHAPTER ELEVEN: INTEGRATING GRAPHICS INTO YOUR MEETINGS introduces you to the basics of using graphics to enhance your facilitation and gives you some ideas on how to employ graphic methods to help organize a group's thinking. It includes a number of graphic symbols and formats to add to your tool kit.

CHAPTER TWELVE: REFLECTING ON THE ART OF FACILITATION gives you an opportunity to look at personal issues that affect your ability as a facilitator. It invites you to reflect on what is likely to get in your way of being successful and what you can do to stay as grounded and effective as possible. There is a discussion of how to define success for yourself as a facilitator. And finally, it raises some critical ethical questions that relate to facilitation.

HOW CAN YOU USE THIS BOOK?

There are several ways you can use this book. You can read it from cover to cover, gain a new understanding about how to prepare and facilitate effective meetings and then put it away. We hope, however, that you will keep the book handy and use it as a regular reference. When you have a meeting coming up, you can use the preparation checklist to remind yourself to ask all the necessary questions before you start to design the meeting. You can use the agenda planning model to help outline your agenda or check the problem solving graphic to work out where your group is in its process. Once you have planned your agenda and picked the appropriate tools, you can copy the tool and take it with you to the meeting. You might want to copy your back up tool ideas as well. If you hit a stumbling block in a group, you can turn to the book for some ideas on how to get moving again. Our hope is that your book will become dog-eared from frequent use.

> We hope your book will become dog-eared from use

Great Meetings! is also designed to be useful for those of you just starting out in facilitation as well as those who are already experienced and are looking for new insights and tools of the trade. Hopefully, each of you will take from the book the level of information you need.

The facilitation material in *Great Meetings!* is generic in the sense that it is not designed for just one venue, such as corporate teams, non-profit boards or public meetings. Regardless of the arena in which you are using your facilitation skills, the basic tenets of the material should serve you well. Every situation has its own special needs and you will have to take those needs into account each time you plan and facilitate a meeting.

Because of the breadth of applications for *Great Meetings!*, when we use the word "client" we intend it to be understood very broadly as whoever is asking you to facilitate: yourself, your supervisor, a co-worker or a paying client. Also, on the subject of language, we use the terms extrovert and introvert as defined in the Myers Briggs Personality Type Indicators, meaning that an extrovert is likely to process ideas by talking them through while an introvert is likely to process ideas internally first. We also struggled with how to use personal pronouns in this book in regard to gender. We have no intention to have you picture facilitators as the sole province of either men or women, but find using he/she everywhere to be tiresome. Our solution is to alternate gender pronouns by chapter.

CREDITING SOURCES

The field of facilitation has been growing rapidly. Tools and techniques have been traded around over and over again, growing and changing with various evolutions along the way and often obscuring the actual originator of the technique. Where we know the originator, we have acknowledged that ownership, but in most instances we simply don't know who it is. We always welcome information from our readers which will help us identify the original sources and will add these credits in future editions.

The book has a variety of tool descriptions which can be copied and used repeatedly. Please feel free to do so. But we ask that you acknowledge the source and use integrity in distinguishing between copying small sections and expropriating the whole book.

We welcome any suggestions you have for improving our book. Please send your suggestions, comments or book orders to Hanson Park Press, P.O. Box 3883, Portland, ME 04104-3883. You can also contact us by e-mail at hppress@aol.com, or call us toll free at 1-888-767-6338.

CHAPTER ONE

FACILITATION: WHAT'S IT ALL ABOUT?

FACILITATION IS THE PROCESS OF HELPING A GROUP COMPLETE A TASK, SOLVE A PROBLEM or come to agreement to the mutual satisfaction of the participants. Successful facilitation takes preparation and planning, a constructive attitude, certain skills and behaviors, and a collection of process tools.

If you were to look at a continuum from a meeting planner to a therapist, the facilitator would fall somewhere in the middle. As a facilitator you are doing much more than just setting up the logistics of a meeting. You are making assessments about the needs of the group, providing consultant advice on the best design for the meeting and the best tools and techniques for accomplishing the tasks. You are being very attentive to the needs of the group as a whole and individuals within the group. Your role, however, is focused on the group's needs to accomplish its task. You are not the organizational development specialist called in to diagnose organizational problems and recommend changes. Nor are you the therapist for the group or any of its members. Your job is to support your group to get its task accomplished.

THE PLACE OF FACILITATION IN A SPECTRUM OF GROUP ACTIVITIES

Groups have different kinds of support and service needs. It is important to understand the distinction between these needs so that you can assess whether you are the right person for the job, both in terms of your interest and your skills. The chart below outlines some of the services groups require, the role and body of knowledge required to provide that service. In this book, our focus is only on facilitation. The more complex roles require additional training and expertise.

SERVICE	ROLE	EXPERTISE
Meeting Organizer	• Schedule and organize the logistics of a meeting	• Need for space, schedules, equipment, refreshments, room set-up
Facilitator	• Prepare and facilitate a meeting	• Assessment, meeting design, process tools, facilitative behaviors and skills, group dynamics, conflict management, graphics, communication skills
Complex Process Designer	• Design steps in a multiple meeting process involving a variety of stakeholders	• Same as Facilitator, plus information gathering, stakeholder analysis
Process Coach	• Observe a group and give feedback regarding their process	• Understanding of interpersonal and group dynamics, meeting design management
Organizational Development Coach	• Diagnose, analyze, intervene, give feedback on organizational systems	• Dynamics of systems, facilitation coach, process coach
Group Therapist	• Guide personal growth and understanding in the context of a group	• Therapeutic technique, intrapersonal and interpersonal dynamics

The facilitator impacts and guides the process but does not give input on the content of a meeting — that comes from the participants. The facilitator's job is to serve the group, not to dominate it. One measure of good facilitation is that the group members feel they've done their work themselves. The facilitator's role is different from that of many other consultants in that her job is to give process advice, rather than content advice.

THE FACILITATOR'S JOB DESCRIPTION:

- plans and designs the meeting process, in partnership with the client
- helps everyone get acquainted and feel welcome
- clarifies the purpose of the meeting, the desired outcomes, the process to be used and the roles of each person
- works with the group to establish and get buy-in to the ground rules
- draws out opinions and encourages full participation from all members
- clarifies communication between people
- helps keep the group focused and on track
- protects participants from attack
- provides a safe place for creative ideas
- listens intently
- handles difficult situations and behaviors
- names conflict when it arises and guides those involved through a negotiation of their differences
- adapts the process as necessary to help the group move forward
- makes process suggestions
- encourages the group with affirmation and appreciation
- monitors meeting pace
- summarizes progress of the meeting at key points
- guides the group in coming to conclusions, agreements, clarity
- maintains neutrality, reflecting content and process back to the group
- serves the whole group rather than individuals, and the process over content

FACILITATIVE ATTITUDES

The following are attitudes that will support facilitators in doing quality facilitation work. They are simple to understand, but for many of us will require a life time of practice to adopt fully.

> What
> would serve
> the group best
> right now?

SERVANT OF THE GROUP AND ITS PROCESS: The facilitator's role is to serve, which means putting aside one's ego and need to control individuals or solutions. Process, prevention and intervention decisions are always prefaced by asking yourself, "What would serve the group best right now?"

RESPECT AND COMPASSION: The facilitator is best able to serve the group if she can truly feel respect and compassion for the individuals within the group as well as the group as a whole. This is not the same as personal fondness. It means respecting intentions, always listening for understanding out of a belief that everyone has something to offer which is worth understanding, and having compassion for the challenge of working in groups as well as the problem at hand.

POSITIVE: It is important to trust that groups can work and to encourage the group — especially when it gets bogged down. Always be constructive in your own comments and attitude.

FLEXIBLE: Have a deep tool kit of process techniques and be willing to change processes if necessary. Be a process advocate and educator, but also be willing to let go of a process if it doesn't work and try something else.

NON-DEFENSIVE: When someone in the group attacks or challenges you, don't argue back. Stay centered and focus on their concerns. Defending yourself just adds a complicating dynamic to an already complicated situation and focuses attention on you rather than the issue at hand. Often anger directed toward you is displaced anger or frustration about the group.

NEUTRAL: When you are a pure facilitator, leave your own opinions on the subject behind. It is the group's issue and they must define it and solve it in their own way. Even if you have a brilliant solution for them, if it isn't theirs, they won't own it, believe in it or be willing to implement it. Being neutral does not mean being passive; it means remaining non-judgmental and out of the group's content. Be an advocate for good process, not for content.

FACILITATOR'S SKILL KIT

There are many skills that a facilitator needs, skills that are built over a lifetime of working with groups and can be developed whenever you are in a meeting, whether facilitating or not. Here are some of those skills needed:

GROUP DEVELOPMENT SKILLS: A facilitator should have an awareness of group development and group dynamics. There are many factors here to be aware of, including the group's history, size of the group, formality or informality, task or social orientation, stage of group development, etc.

MEETING MANAGEMENT SKILLS: Because the facilitator wants to ensure a successful meeting, she will need to work with the leader and group to make sure the meeting mechanics are set up in a way that supports them. While the content of the agenda is up to the group, the facilitator should insist upon an agenda that is realistic for the time allotted and that matches the expectations of the group as a whole. The facilitator should also help the group assign general time limits for each item on the agenda and to clarify the specific desired outcomes of the meeting. A rule of thumb in terms of time is

> Take what you think is realistic, and cut the work back by one-third

to take what you think is realistic and cut the work back by one-third — you can use this formula until you develop a sixth sense of what a group can accomplish in a given amount of time. The facilitator should also help the group establish ground rules that will define desired behavior (confidentiality, respect for difference, etc.), agreed-upon procedures (decision-making methods, starting and ending on time, etc.) and the limits of the content to be covered (what will and will not be discussed).

PROBLEM-SOLVING SKILLS: Facilitators are most commonly brought in when a group is at some stage of the problem-solving process. The group may need to define a problem, analyze the problem and envision a goal, generate options for its resolution, narrow those options, pick the best course of action, develop an implementation or evaluate the success of the implementation. One of the most common problems groups have is confusion over what point they are at in terms of the problem-solving process. Groups can find themselves picking a course of action before they have established a careful definition of the problem, or narrowing down options when they mean to be brainstorming options. Therefore, it is critical that the facilitator understand the problem-solving process thoroughly and be clear about what each step accomplishes.

PROCESS SKILLS: In addition to understanding the process, facilitators need a variety of methods to help the group move through each stage of the process. Since the facilitator is responsible for guiding the process of the meeting, she needs to know a variety of ways to ensure a good process. In the process tool kit, there should be tools for promoting group inclusion, generating group discussion, gathering opinions, helping the group stay on track, managing conflict and dealing with "difficult" behaviors (self-oriented behaviors that do not serve the group). The facilitator should also understand the different needs of introverts and extroverts in a group setting and be able to provide processes that address those different needs.

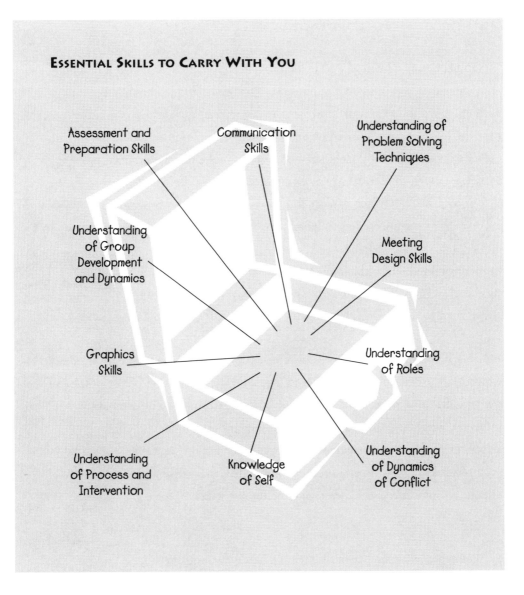

ESSENTIAL SKILLS TO CARRY WITH YOU

Assessment and Preparation Skills

Communication Skills

Understanding of Problem Solving Techniques

Understanding of Group Development and Dynamics

Meeting Design Skills

Graphics Skills

Understanding of Roles

Understanding of Process and Intervention

Knowledge of Self

Understanding of Dynamics of Conflict

The above graphic illustrates the various skills an effective facilitator must have available at all times. Every situation in which you facilitate will be unique, and you will need a full set of skills to draw on. Gaining expertise in these areas is an on-going, life long process.

Qualities of an Effective Facilitator

Someone once painted a physical portrait of a facilitator that is a helpful reminder of the qualities an effective facilitator must have. The image is a person with BIG EARS to listen both to what is being said and what is between the words, to hear the foundation of consensus being built even before the group can hear it; CLEAR EYES to read body language and other visual clues the group is offering; a SMALL MOUTH to keep her opinions about the content to herself (if a pure facilitator);

 a STRONG HEART to have concern that each person be treated with respect, and to have compassion for the challenge of people working together; and finally, LARGE FEET to keep  firmly grounded when challenged, when one person is trying to sway the group or the group is getting ahead of itself and needs to be brought back on track.

An effective facilitator has to have respect for the group members as adults, expecting the best in participants and fostering the expression of the best by modeling and affirming positive behavior. Facilitators also have to be assertive, be able to intervene when necessary to protect group members from attack, to name a conflict when it has emerged, or to bring the group back on focus. A calm presence, flexibility, creativity and a sense of humor will make everyone, including yourself, have a more satisfying time.

> Be mindful of your strengths, weaknesses and "hot buttons"

Being a quality facilitator also means being continually mindful of your strengths, weaknesses and "hot buttons" that affect your facilitation.

CLARIFYING YOUR ROLE AS A FACILITATOR

At the outset of a meeting it is extremely important that all involved be clear about their roles. The group members should know what is expected of them, as should the chair or leader of the group. As the designated facilitator, it is possible to play one or more of the following roles.

PURE FACILITATOR: This means you are serving the group by guiding the process of the meetings: helping with the flow of discussion, working to get full participation, keeping the group moving towards its goal, etc. While you should have general familiarity with the content of the meeting (be "content literate"), you do not have to be a content expert and you will not be contributing to the content of the meeting.

FACILITATOR/EXPERT: If you have a content expertise, you may be asked to both facilitate a group and offer your advice about the content the group is considering. For example, if you are a marketing specialist and are facilitating a group which needs to make decisions about marketing a new product, you might be asked to give your opinion about what marketing strategy will work best. However, in the role of facilitator/expert, you don't have a stake in the outcome of the group's work.

FACILITATOR/LEADER OR FACILITATOR/MEMBER: This dual role implies that you have a stake in the product of the group as well as the process of the group—you care about what the group accomplishes as well as how it accomplishes it. As leader or member you will want to be able to give your opinion during the meeting. As the facilitator you will want to insure that a high quality process is followed. Beware: It is challenging to play the dual role well!

RECORDER OR SCRIBE: As the recorder or scribe you are responsible for writing down any output of the group onto flip charts. In other words, you are creating a visual group memory. This requires excellent listening and summarizing skills, as well as a good graphics ability. Some groups assume that the person playing this role is also responsible for getting the materials typed and mailed out. Clarify explicitly who is expected to handle this task.

TIME KEEPER: The time keeper is responsible for keeping an eye on the clock and the time limits agreed upon for each item on the agenda.

BREAK MONITOR: When the group seems to need a break or has agreed to stretch at certain intervals, the break monitor's role is to announce that it's time for a stretch.

Sometime before the meeting gets underway, you should discuss with the group the role you intend to play and check for their agreement. Some of the above roles can (even should!) be given away to the group, both to make your job easier and to get the group members more involved in the ownership of the meeting.

BALANCING THE DUAL ROLES OF FACILITATOR AND GROUP LEADER/MEMBER

Much of what is available in the literature of facilitation describes the role of a "pure" facilitator — a person with no stake in the outcome of a group's decision making who is present to guide the process. However, we are often called on to be facilitators for groups which we also lead or participate in. It is tricky to balance the roles of facilitator and leader or member, because a participant often has a vested interest in the product of the meeting and thus can have a tendency to use process to move the group to her desired outcome. Below are some guidelines to follow if you are called on to play these dual roles.

1. Define clearly to the group what roles you will be playing. Name explicitly the roles you will be playing in this particular meeting. For example: "Today I am going to facilitate this meeting — that is, keep us on track with the

agenda and suggest some ways we might go about making a decision. As a member of this unit, I also want a chance to add my opinions to the group discussion. I will let you know when I am switching roles."

2. Notify the group when you are switching roles. For example: "Could someone else facilitate for awhile? I'd like to step out of my role as facilitator and give my opinion about this topic." Then, "Thanks for facilitating, Becky, I can move back into that role now."

3. Be sure the group understands what authority it has and what authority the leader has in the decision making process. At the outset discuss where the leader will intervene in the decision making process. Is she seeking advice or a decision from the group? What will happen to the group's input? Discussing this up front will keep the group from feeling that the rules changed midstream.

> Be sure the group understands what authority it has in the decision making process

4. Be careful not to use your role as facilitator to manipulate the product outcome. A danger of playing dual roles is that you unconsciously (or consciously) can choose a process that will lead to the outcome you desire.

5. Make sure to get agreement for the agenda from the group, encourage participation from everyone present (not just those who agree with you), check the accuracy of your summaries, and use an agreed-upon decision making method. Ask the group to help you in facilitating in a fair and balanced way, and to tell you when you are not.

6. Keep open the option of bringing in an outside facilitator. If you or other group members have strong opinions about the outcome of a particular discussion, or strong feelings about some of the participants, give yourself permission to bring in an outside facilitator. This will free you up to put your energy on the content of the meeting.

CHAPTER TWO

KNOWING YOUR GROUP

BOOKS HAVE BEEN WRITTEN ON THE SUBJECTS OF GROUP DYNAMICS, GROUP DEVELOP-
ment and group process. In this chapter we are not trying to reproduce such in
depth work. Rather our goal is to focus on the group dynamics and group development issues which you will want to consider as you design and implement processes
for facilitation.

GROUP DYNAMICS

Any time a group of people comes together to work there are dynamics at play.
External forces (norms, organizational culture, etc.), the history of the group, sub-
groupings and individual members, membership within the group, group norms, the
size of the group and informal and formal leadership within the group are just some
of those dynamics. You should know enough about the group to facilitate effectively. It's the "enough" that's the tricky part. If your only role is facilitator of a simple
process, don't worry about knowing everything about past history and group

dynamics. Just make sure you know about any major "events" in the history of the group — positive or negative — that may impact this facilitation. Too much knowledge may even work against your effectiveness. Your role is to serve the group now and to guide and model effective process.

On the following pages are some of the factors in group dynamics and possible implications and interventions for facilitation. This list can be used along with the meeting preparation checklist in *Chapter Three: Getting a Good Start.*

FACTORS IN GROUP DYNAMICS	POSSIBLE IMPLICATIONS AND/OR INTERVENTIONS FOR FACILITATION
EXTERNAL FORCES: Norms, expectations, assumptions, culture of, or scrutiny by the larger organization, the public, etc.	• Acknowledge and discuss impact on the group. • May affect ground rules.
HISTORY: Of the group or task	• Acknowledge it. • If the history needs to be overcome, structure activities that will help the group move forward.
Of individuals	• Ignore unless it brings value to or interferes with the group. • Acknowledge impact (positive or negative) of past leaders and members. • Get agreement that people will leave "baggage" behind.
GROUP NORMS:	• Norms in a group are often unspoken. Establishing ground rules encourages discussion about which norms are desired.

FACTORS IN GROUP DYNAMICS	POSSIBLE IMPLICATIONS AND/OR INTERVENTIONS FOR FACILITATION
<u>MEMBERSHIP</u>: Old/new members	• Integrate new members into the group. Acknowledge contribution of old members.
Willingness to be members	• Determine what resistant members need to participate fully.
Changing membership	• Establish ground rules re: staying fully informed, revisiting decisions, etc.
Sub-groupings	• Acknowledge them. • Encourage dialogue between groups. • Use exercises that mix groups.
<u>SIZE OF GROUP</u>:	• Smaller groups can often be facilitated informally. Larger groups need more formal procedures. • Often people monitor their own behavior more responsibly in a small group than in a large one. • Be honest with yourself about your own comfort and skill level with small vs. large groups.
<u>LEADERSHIP</u>: Formal/informal	• Acknowledge and clarify the role of the formal leader. • Actively involve informal leaders; however, don't let them take the meeting in an inappropriate direction.

FACTORS IN GROUP DYNAMICS	POSSIBLE IMPLICATIONS AND/OR INTERVENTIONS FOR FACILITATION
OTHER FACTORS:	
Voluntary versus mandated participation	• Acknowledge; ask what members need to participate fully.
Volunteer versus paid work	• Surface and address expectations volunteers may have regarding compensation (recognition, develop new skills, friendships, etc.)
Longevity in workplace, gender, age, individual agendas, power relations	• Listen for ways these factors may impact effectiveness of group. • Address when factors impact the group's work or cohesion.

GROUP DEVELOPMENT

All groups go through stages of development. The amount of time and intensity of each stage will depend on the group, its dynamics, its task and the amount of time it has. Groups develop in a variety of ways. Some go straight through, while others skip stages and need to come back to them later. It is possible for a group to get stuck in one stage — particularly storming — and never progress. However, with good facilitation, you can mirror back to the group where the group seems stuck, and help them move forward.

As external and internal factors cause change in the group and/or its task (new members join and old leave; crisis or change of direction in the organization, etc.), the group is likely to revisit earlier stages of development.

In his article, "Developmental Sequence in Small Groups" (Psychological Bulletin 63, vi 1965), Bruce Tuckman proposes his four stage model for group development: forming, storming, norming and performing.

FORMING: This characterizes the time when a group is first coming together, or when new members are joining the group. Some have referred to this as the "ritual sniffing" phase. Group members are concerned about inclusion: whether and how they belong and how safe it is to be part of this group. Therefore, this stage is characterized by politeness, low conflict and superficial disclosure. The group often looks to the facilitator or leader for strong direction.

FACILITATOR'S TASK: The task of the facilitator in this stage is to assess what work needs to be done in the group around forming and then to structure an appropriate opening so that people can feel safe, legitimized, valued and have a sanctioned way to "sniff" one another, as needed. Forming can be accomplished through:

- introductions and orientation
- reviewing the "road map" (desired outcomes and agenda)
- warm up activities
- inviting expressions of expectations
- establishing ground rules
- agreeing upon decision-making methods

WHEN THE FACILITATOR IS NEW TO AN EXISTING GROUP: An interesting twist to the forming stage occurs when the facilitator is new to an intact group. In this instance, you need to draw the group back to the forming stage just long enough to get to know you and be assured that you are safe enough to include in the group. Beware doing too much forming for your sake (long introductions of each person); you may lose the group. You will have done some of this work, of course, prior to the start of the first meeting by meeting group members, learning about their history, culture, in-jokes, etc.

 **STORMING:** Storming is the stage where members are concerned about control, power and influence. It often manifests through disagreements about process, emotional responses to task demands, and challenges to the facilitator or leader.

<u>FACILITATOR'S TASK</u>: The task of the facilitator in this stage is to assess and name the specific storming issues of the group, and guide and model good conflict resolution process. This can be accomplished by:

- first and foremost, remembering you are not the target
- serving as a mirror to the group
- separating the problem from the person
- acknowledging, then dealing with or deferring concerns (See *Chapter Ten: Interventions* for a detailed discussion of this.)
- enforcing the ground rules
- being assertive in your role as process expert

Note: Not every conflict is an indication of storming. Healthy conflict over content and process can occur at every stage of group development. (See *Chapter Nine: Managing Conflict* for a detailed discussion.)

NORMING: Norming is the stage in which group members move toward interdependence. Individually, group members are focused on building caring and a sense of belonging in the group.

<u>FACILITATOR'S TASK</u>: The task of the facilitator is to support the group in their high functioning by:

- mirroring back and recording norms that are emerging
- affirming the group's cohesiveness and the work it has taken to get there
- affirming the positive value of expressing differences
- guiding the group through collaborative negotiation
- providing opportunities for the group to enjoy its connectedness

PERFORMING: Performing is the stage where the group is working collaboratively and is highly productive. To an outsider, the group might appear to be only task focused, but the strong underpinnings of trust, respect, shared norms and overarching goals are in place.

FACILITATOR'S TASK: The task of the facilitator at this stage is to:

- offer effective processes for getting the task accomplished
- format the work in a way that is useful to the group
- affirm the good work of the group
- stay out of the way when not needed

BEHAVIORS AND ROLES THAT AFFECT THE FUNCTIONING OF GROUPS

Behaviors in groups can be categorized by whether they: 1. help accomplish the group task (task-oriented); 2. help maintain good relationships among members (socially-oriented); or 3. hinder the group by expressing individual needs or goals unrelated to the group's purposes (self-oriented).

As a facilitator, it is important to know what behaviors to support and encourage in groups. You want to encourage the expression of both task- and social-related roles, and to maintain a balance of the two as necessary. Of course, you want to discourage self-oriented behaviors as much as possible, and intervene if they are distracting or draining the group.

We each behave in a way that reflects our personality and needs, but, from the group's point of view, the most valuable behaviors are those that fulfill a need of the group for getting the job done or for sustaining satisfying relationships. If you were to videotape a group, you would notice that one person might take on several different roles during the course of the meeting, or that at different times several people might play the same role. It's not that these roles are assigned, but as a group develops, individuals fill the roles needed to make a group work. Each group is unique in how it fills the roles, and an individual who plays a certain role in one group may play an entirely different role in another setting.

Sometimes individuals unintentionally acquire a "monopoly" on a role. The group will be less effective if capable members are prevented from taking needed roles or from switching roles from time to time. As facilitator, you can serve as a mirror to the group, noting when this is happening and offering suggestions for how to be more fluid with roles. The following chart describes these behaviors.

GROUP-ORIENTED BEHAVIORS

TASK-ORIENTED BEHAVIORS
Any behavior that promotes the accomplishment of the task:

- initiates ideas
- seeks or provides information
- summarizes data
- clarifies problems
- questions assumptions
- tests decision making readiness

RELATIONSHIP-ORIENTED BEHAVIORS
Any behavior that promotes group cohesion:

- checks on feeling level of group
- offers encouragement
- promotes inclusion
- resolves conflicts
- is friendly
- gives positive feedback

SELF-ORIENTED BEHAVIORS

Any behavior that diverts the energy of the group, damages group cohesion or group effectiveness:

- arrives late or leaves early
- dampens energy of group
- interprets others' remarks
- holds side conversations
- withholds needed information

- dominates air time
- puts down efforts of others
- "yes, but" s ideas
- ignores group process
- refuses to participate

OVERT AND COVERT GROUP ISSUES

A final concept that may be useful in your role of facilitator is the iceberg of group dynamics, developed by W. Brendan Reddy. It is a good reminder that hidden beneath the tip of the iceberg of the group's task are levels of overt and covert group issues, as well as values, beliefs and assumptions and unconscious issues that impact the group. An important rule of thumb is don't take the group deeper than it needs to go to accomplish its task. And never take a group to a deeper level than you have the time or ability to handle. Facilitation is not therapy.

CHAPTER THREE

GETTING A GOOD START

THE KEY TO GREAT MEETINGS IS PREPARATION. YOU WILL NEED TO ALLOW A SIGNIFICANT amount of time for preparing: assessing the needs of the group; understanding the purpose of the meeting; determining your role and that of others; agreeing who is in charge of which logistical details; deciding how to structure the agenda; and which tools to use.

Whether you are planning your own meeting, responding to a request from a supervisor or discussing a possible job with a client, it is necessary to go through a preliminary assessment process. Assessment means asking a series of probing questions to be sure you understand what needs to be done to plan a successful meeting. It will mean checking on the purpose of the meeting, the relevant background information, the desired outcomes of the meeting, the people who need to attend, the nature of the group and any internal issues.

MEETING PURPOSE

The first step is to be clear about the purpose of the meeting in order to determine if a meeting is, in fact, the best way to accomplish the desired purpose. Appropriate purposes for a meeting might be to:

- share information
- get information
- clarify information
- understand different points of view

- resolve a problem
- identify a vision
- establish goals and priorities
- make decisions

In order to determine whether a meeting is the best way to accomplish the purpose, ask yourself these questions:

- Is interactive communication necessary?

- Do you want a variety of ideas and opinions leading to agreement?

- Do you need group ownership of a problem and its solution?

- Do you want to create a sense of group commitment to an idea, goal or project?

If you answer "yes" to any of these questions, a meeting will probably be useful. If you can't say "yes" to any of these, then you might want to consider some alternatives. Nothing makes people grumpier than making time for a meeting when they could have gotten the information or the result in a more efficient or flexible way. If you don't need to bring people together, try another technique, such as a memo, a consultation with another person, individual or conference telephone calls, a training program or a social gathering.

WHAT IS THE PURPOSE OF THE MEETING? Once you have determined that the purpose is best met by holding a meeting, you will need to work with your client to define the specific purpose for the meeting.

IS THE PURPOSE CLEAR? Check with yourself or with the person asking you to facilitate. Is the purpose clear? Is it understood and agreed upon by all? Does your own re-examination or your active listening lead you to believe that there is a secondary purpose beyond the presenting one? If so, articulate it and check it out with the client. Restate or reframe the purpose until there is clarity and agreement on a purpose statement. A purpose statement should explain why the group is meeting or why the project is being undertaken, and there may be more than one reason.

> A purpose statement should explain why the group is meeting

EXAMPLES:
- to build a stronger sense of involvement in the team
- to develop a work plan for the next quarter
- to explain the new benefits system and respond to questions and concerns

DESIRED OUTCOMES

The desired outcomes define the hoped-for end products of a meeting. What does the client want as a result from the meeting: a solution; a decision; a recommendation; a list of ideas; a better understanding of an issue or situation? What does the client want to walk away with at the end of the meeting? Often it takes several variations on this same question to get a clear response from the person who has asked you to facilitate. Clarity on this point can make all the difference between a successful and a disappointing meeting.

1. A clear desired outcome statement is a product, not a process. It is helpful to check for nouns in your desired outcomes instead of verbs, or to ask yourself, "Will I know if I've accomplished it?"

   EXAMPLES:
   - a short list of ways to improve the communication between our depart-

ments, rather than *developing ideas for improving communications.*

- 1-3 recommendations on how to ease the parking problem, rather than *working on the parking problem.*

> A clear desired outcome statement defines a clear, measurable goal

2. A clear desired outcome statement defines a clear, measurable goal for the meeting, such as lists, time lines, a problem statement, etc. Goals such as increased understanding, satisfaction and better attitudes are not measurable and therefore are not very useful desired outcomes.

EXAMPLES:
- a list of key elements in our vision for a new service offering
- a list of services which could be coordinated between two departments
- agreement on the responsibilities of a team leader

3. A clear desired outcome statement sets realistic goals for the given time frame of a meeting. You might want to have a detailed strategic plan as an outcome, but that is not realistic in a three hour meeting. You need to pick a smaller, more manageable outcome. You could establish a number of steps in a longer process and develop desired outcomes for each step along the way, as well as the desired outcome of the total process.

EXAMPLES:
- a recommendation to the department head for the space needs of the department for the next 24 months *(an outcome for the whole process)*
- a definition of the space problems *(an outcome for a single meeting)*
- a time schedule for accomplishing the work *(an outcome for a single meeting)*

4. A clear desired outcome statement focuses on the format rather than the specific content of the outcome of the meeting. A desired outcome statement should say "final approval of a department budget," rather than "final approval of a $1.5 million department budget."

EXAMPLES:

- a list of 1-3 recommended solutions to the problem
- a time line for the steps in the department's computer conversion

5. A clear desired outcome statement stays open to the group's process, creativity and needs. If the desired outcome statement says "a list of 12 recommendations," more than twelve ideas may be stifled and fewer than twelve ideas may feel like failure. The desired outcome should say "a list of recommendations," or use words which give you some wiggle room, such as short, long or a range.

    EXAMPLES:

    - a short list of recommendations for reducing the number of back orders
    - a list of 2-5 alternatives for a new meeting room location for the department

It is important to understand that a desired outcome can change during the meeting. Because of new information or timing, it may no longer be appropriate. For example, part way through a meeting, the group may realize that it isn't ready to develop a time line for a new project (its original desired outcome), but instead needs to define the root problem. A desired outcome also serves the group as a way of keeping the group on track if the group starts to wander off the subject. For example, if the group starts discussing something tangential to the original desired outcome, the facilitator can help the group refocus by restating the desired outcome and asking if the tangent is necessary to reaching that outcome. The time spent understanding and clearly articulating the desired outcomes is a critical part of the preparation for a successful meeting.

> The time spent understanding and articulating the desired outcomes is a critical part of preparing for a successful meeting

RELEVANT BACKGROUND INFORMATION

Below are a number of critical questions to ask in order to familiarize yourself with the history of the group and with all the details which may make a difference in the meeting. The answers to these questions will help you assess what will be needed for the meeting to be successful.

1. What is the history or background affecting the group and this meeting?

    - What is the organizational context within which this group works?
    - Is the group coming together for the first time?
    - Does it have a history of conflict?
    - Are there preexisting subgroups?
    - Is there a need to build team spirit or overcome negative history?
    - Are there any special characteristics of the group?
    - What has occurred which might affect how this group works together?
    - Has the group had other facilitators?

2. Would it be helpful to talk with a wider group of people before planning the meeting? If you encounter any of the following situations, then interviews or meetings with additional people might be helpful.

    - Different opinions about the purpose of the meeting
    - A history of conflict and factions where it would be helpful to hear different points of view
    - Gathering information in advance to save time at the meeting

3. Who needs to be at the meeting?

    - those who have special information or opinions to contribute
    - those who have official responsibility for the matter
    - those whose approval may be needed in decision-making
    - those who are expected to carry out the decisions

4. What is the time frame within which the work needs to be accomplished?

   - Is this meeting part of a larger project or series of meetings?
   - Is the project on the fast track and timing critical?
   - What amount of time is needed to get the job done well?
   - Is the time allotted realistic and workable?
   - Can everyone commit the time and agree on a convenient time?

5. Who is taking which roles?

   - What is your role?
   - What is the role of the "leader"?
   - Who will record?
   - Who is responsible for minutes?
   - Who is responsible for the logistics of the meeting? (room reservation, equipment, refreshments, etc.)

6. Background Information

   - What background information does the group need in order to discuss the issue cogently and to make a decision?
   - Who will gather the information?
   - Who will circulate it in advance? Participants can't read, absorb and make decisions on lengthy documents in one meeting.

7. Compensation

   - Do you need to discuss with your supervisor the time you are spending facilitating? Do you need acknowledgment for its purpose and value, release from other responsibilities and/or compensatory time?
   - Are you charging by the hour, day or a flat sum?
   - Does compensation include preparation time and expenses?

MEETING PREPARATION CHECKLIST

PRELIMINARY DISCUSSION

- ☐ What is the purpose of the meeting?

- ☐ Is a meeting the best way to accomplish the purpose?

- ☐ What are the desired outcomes of the meeting?

- ☐ What is the history of the situation?

- ☐ What is the history and makeup of the group?

- ☐ What is the actual or proposed size of the group? If you have concerns about the size or makeup of the group, raise them.

- ☐ Who are the stakeholders?

- ☐ What is the "real" problem, or situation?

- ☐ What aspects of the work might present difficult situations that you should be aware of?

- ☐ In what time frame does the client propose that the work be done?

- ☐ Are there any issues about you as the facilitator that need to be discussed:

    - ☐ Are you perceived as neutral by all involved?

    - ☐ History with any of the members of the group?

    - ☐ Level of your content literacy?

    - ☐ Past experience with this kind of group, project, meeting?

MEETING PREPARATION CHECKLIST, CONTINUED

FINALIZING THE PLANS

- ❑ Develop a clearly stated, mutually agreed-upon purpose statement

- ❑ Develop a clearly stated, mutually agreed-upon desired outcome(s)

- ❑ What exactly are you agreeing to do in your role of facilitator?

- ❑ Who is the client?

- ❑ Who will be the recorder?

- ❑ Who will be responsible for getting out the minutes and group memory?

- ❑ Who will be responsible for the logistics of the meeting (room reservations, equipment, refreshments, etc.)?

- ❑ What background information is needed and who will supply it?

- ❑ Can you and the rest of the group commit the time and find agreed-upon times to meet?

- ❑ What are the lines of communication within and among the group, its leadership, stakeholders and the facilitator?

- ❑ How will communication with the media be handled?

- ❑ What time do you have available to spend on the project?

- ❑ Compensation, if applicable, and what that compensation includes.

CHAPTER FOUR

DESIGNING A GREAT MEETING

WHILE EACH MEETING DESIGN WILL BE DIFFERENT, TAILORED TO THE NEEDS OF THE SPE-cific group, there are certain key elements which are important to consider as you build that unique design.

Each meeting will need an opening to launch the session and set the stage for the work to be done, the body of the meeting, which may include one discreet task or several steps, as well as closure so that participants leave with a clear understanding of what has been accomplished and what will happen next.

> Each meeting needs an opening, body of the meeting and closure

These elements may be designed differently for different groups, but you need to include all three elements in each meeting. Often a single meeting is part of a longer, larger project. The whole project design will need to reflect these key elements, as will each individual session.

OPENING

The opening, whether very brief or quite extensive, should build a solid foundation from which the group can work on its task. It should help the participants understand clearly what the task is, why they are doing it and what the hoped for outcome of the meeting is. It should establish how the participants will work with one another and build a conducive environment for doing productive work together.

1. CLARITY ON MEETING PURPOSE, OUTCOMES AND AGENDA: The opening should include a review of the purpose and desired outcomes of the meeting. Working from a flip chart, handout or overhead so that everyone can see the information at the same time, review these pieces, checking for understanding and agreement. If your preparation has been thorough, there are not likely to be any big surprises or deviations from what you have prepared. But it is possible that a participant may need clarification or may suggest that something be changed. Like the announcement on the airplane, "Welcome to flight number 245 to Cleveland," it is important that everyone in the meeting be headed toward the same destination.

> Everyone should be headed toward the same destination

Similarly, it is important to review the agenda so that everyone understands the time frame, as well as when different subjects will be addressed. Again, you need to check for understanding and agreement. For a longer discussion on developing purpose statements and desired outcomes, see *Chapter Three: Getting a Good Start.*

2. ESTABLISHING GROUND RULES: Groups determine the parameters of appropriate behavior by setting ground rules. Some groups may have pre-existing ground rules that can simply be referenced. Others may have such difficulty working together that setting ground rules may take a great deal of time. The concept of ground rules is based on the belief that everyone involved in a meeting should

be treated equally and fairly. Ground rules explicitly spell out behavior and procedures that people normally consider fair but sometimes abandon in the dynamic interaction of a group. The process of establishing ground rules provides a sanctioned opportunity to discuss what constitutes "good behavior," which may help a contentious group let go of some behavior which has been getting in its way.

The best way to get buy-in is to have the group define its own ground rules for the meeting. If you feel that the group has overlooked an area which should be addressed, such as confidentiality, ask them to consider it and decide how they would like to handle it. As facilitator, you can ask for ground rules that you know you will need for yourself. Be sure to check for agreement, asking if everyone is willing to live by the ground rules. During the meeting, the group can enforce its own rules and you can refer to them as necessary. Ground rules can also be added along the way as needed.

It is best to write out the ground rules, especially for a group that will be meeting on an on-going basis. Then, at the beginning of each meeting, the list of ground rules can be unfurled and available for everyone to review. The time spent establishing ground rules usually pays off handsomely by both keeping the group on track and maintaining good relations.

As a facilitator, ground rules are valuable because they transfer much of the responsibility for enforcement of correct behavior, procedure and structure to the group. You can stand by the flip chart and point to the ground rule, reminding the group of its agreement, rather than confront the behavior in the group.

In their book, <u>Managing Public Disputes</u> (Jossey-Bass, San Francisco, 1988) Susan L. Carpenter and W.J. D. Kennedy describe three types of ground rules: behavioral, procedural and substantive.

<u>Behavioral:</u> Behavioral ground rules cover the group's norms for behavior. Some examples of behavioral ground rules are:

- We will treat each other with respect.
- We will not use language that stereotypes others.
- It's okay to disagree.

<u>Procedural:</u> Procedural ground rules include any guidelines for how the meeting will proceed. Examples of procedural ground rules are:

- Only one person talks at a time.
- When one of us leaves the room, the discussion stops (or will continue).
- When one of us misses a meeting, it is her responsibility to get filled in.
- Meetings will begin on time and end on time.

<u>Substantive:</u> Substantive ground rules describe what content will be covered during the meeting. Examples of substantive ground rules are:

- We will only discuss issues over which we have direct control.
- We will discuss the manufacturing center as a whole, but not individual departments within it.

SAMPLE GROUND RULES TO CONSIDER

- No side conversations
- Share the floor
- No interruptions
- Encourage everyone to participate
- Debate ideas not individuals
- Level of confidentiality: complete confidentiality, no attributions
- No evaluation during brainstorming

- Stay on the subject
- Be constructive
- Begin and end on time
- Arrive on time, stay to the end
- Consistent attendance from one meeting to the next
- Substitutes are (or are not) acceptable

HINTS FOR ESTABLISHING GROUND RULES

Groups are often resistant to establishing ground rules, either because of the time it takes or because they feel it is childish to define good behavior. A sense of humor, a declaration that you, as facilitator, need the ground rules, and a promise to keep the process of generating ground rules "crisp" usually is enough to engage the group.

IN GENERATING GROUND RULES WE USE THIS PROCESS:

1. Ask for suggestions for ground rules. All ideas are welcome.
   Example: A group member says, "I want everyone to be polite."
2. Define the suggestion in terms of behavior. Asking "what would it look like if..." helps.
   Example: The facilitator says, "John, what would it look like to you if everyone were being polite?"
   John: "No one would interrupt anyone and there would be no personal attacks."
   Facilitator: "So you are proposing two ground rules; no interruptions and no personal attacks? "
3. Check with yourself to see if the ground rules really serve the group. If not, explain your concern to the group and offer an alternative
4. Check for consensus on the ground rule.
5. Write it up on the flip chart.
6. After the ground rules are written, confirm that everyone can abide by them.

3. CLARITY ABOUT ROLES: It is important to clarify your role as facilitator. Are you a neutral facilitator or will you be a participant as well? What is the role of the group leader, an equal participant or the ultimate decision maker? Participants need to be clear about their expected role. Following are sample role definitions:

SAMPLE ROLE DEFINITIONS

FACILITATOR: I am your facilitator for this meeting. I have helped to design the agenda and will be leading you through the process. I will not contribute any ideas on the content of the meeting. It is my job to make it easier for you to arrive at your own agreements.

LEADER: I have called this meeting today for us to decide on a solution for the parking problems. I have asked Mary to facilitate and would like someone to volunteer to record. (Or, I will be facilitating myself and contributing my ideas from time to time.) I will be participating with the group. I would like this group to arrive at consensus on how to solve this problem. If that is not possible, I will make the decision personally, based on the ideas raised in the group.

RECORDER: I will be recording and will try to capture your ideas on the board. If I miss anything or haven't gotten it quite right, please let me know so that I can correct it. I will (or will not) ask for time to participate and add my own ideas.

PARTICIPANTS: Our role as participants is to contribute, generate the content, listen carefully, share concerns and ideas candidly, act constructively, and make commitments.

4. <u>ESTABLISHING DECISION MAKING METHODS</u>: There are many ways that groups can make decisions and it is important that the group be clear in advance which method or combination of methods it wants to use. Some decision making techniques are:

- Majority voting
- Voting with two-thirds, three-quarters or higher percentage required
- Deferring to a subgroup
- Consensus with a back up
- Consensus without a back up

It is also important to be clear about the group's role in the overall scheme of decision making. Are they being asked to give recommendations, or to make a decision themselves? If the group believes that it is empowered to make a final decision and finds out later that it was only a recommendation, the members will feel deceived. Refer to *Chapter Five: Understanding Problem Solving* for a more detailed description of decision making.

5. <u>BASKET (PARKING LOT)</u>: This useful tool (which has many names — basket, bin, parking lot) provides a place for ideas that are off the subject of the agenda. Title a flip chart page "Basket" (or whatever name you are using) and post it throughout the meeting. It allows the group to acknowledge and save ideas without getting sidetracked by them. It also helps reduce the repetition of the one track mind participant by having her issue up on the chart with a promise to deal with it eventually. The group must be committed to return to the basket by the end of the meeting to decide when and how those issues will be handled. The basket should not be used as a trash can!

6. <u>GROUP FORMING</u>: There are several aspects of group forming, ranging from the simplest gestures which set a constructive tone to significant efforts at team building. Using the information gathered during your early preparation, you need to decide what kind of group forming would be useful for your meeting.

Remember that doing work in groups is hard and demands some level of trust and ability to work together. Consider the following three levels of group building to see what is needed for your agenda. Then, refer to *Chapter Seven: Maximizing Your Group's Potential*, for details on group building techniques.

Setting the Tone: The facilitator sets the tone for the meeting from the moment participants walk through the door. By greeting people cheerfully and introducing yourself, welcoming them, indicating that you are glad they came, and thanking them for their participation, you are setting a positive, constructive tone from the start.

Introductions: The nature of the group, how long it has been working together, and the nature of the problem it is working on will determine what kind of introductions and warm-up exercises are most appropriate.

Team Building: If there is a low level of trust or little common ground among the participants, there may be a need to plan some team building or trust building work into the opening of the meeting before the group gets to the more difficult work or decision making.

BODY OF THE MEETING

The central part of the meeting is the task that needs to be accomplished by the group. There may be more than one task, depending on the desired outcomes for the meeting. To build the agenda for the body of the meeting, work directly from your desired outcomes and decide for each one what process steps need to be taken to arrive at the desired outcome.

For example, if the desired outcome is a list of roles and duties for the new executive director, look at what the group needs to do to complete a list that will serve them well. Do they need information about the roles of the previous director, or about another position they are using for bench marking? Do they need information on typical executive directors in order to get started? Or do they need to break loose from old formats and think outside the box? Each of those circumstances would require a different process approach. Is the group large or small? The size could determine which technique you use for generating ideas. See *Chapters Six and Seven* for a more detailed description of tools and techniques.

The task of most meetings falls under the heading of problem solving. The subject of problem solving has a chapter all its own, *Chapter Five: Understanding Problem Solving*, because it is so important to understand the sequence of activities in problem solving, from problem identification to analyzing the problem to envisioning the goal to generating and deciding on the solutions.

CLOSURE

Just as a meeting needs clarity in the beginning, it needs clarity at the end. Participants need to leave the meeting with a clear, common understanding of what has been accomplished, what has been agreed upon, what needs to happen next and who is assigned to do what and when. In addition, it is valuable to evaluate the meeting, so that the next meeting can be improved and the group can congratulate itself on what went well. Lastly, at the conclusion of some meetings or projects there needs to be personal closure.

1. <u>GROUP AGREEMENTS:</u> Reiterate and even make a separate list of the things which the group has agreed upon in the course of the meeting. Agreed that:

    -   the problem is...
    -   the causes are...
    -   the most reasonable solutions are...

2. <u>NEXT STEPS:</u> In order to ensure follow through, it is important that there are clear assignments to which everyone agrees. The following chart helps to make the follow through clear.

<u>What</u>	<u>Who</u>	<u>Date</u>
type and circulate minutes	John	4/25

3. <u>MEETING EVALUATION:</u> At the very end of the meeting it is useful to take five minutes for a meeting evaluation to ask what went well and what should be changed or improved upon next time. The suggestions can run from needing a break or refreshments, to comments on the space, to the need for more participation. This provides valuable information to help improve each subsequent meeting. A simple chart showing the positives and what to change will do.

4. <u>PERSONAL CLOSURE:</u> When a group has completed a challenging piece of work or is disbanding, participants will have formed a special bond or learned to work with each other in a new way and the participants need a way to have personal closure, acknowledging and thanking one another or saying good bye.

MEETING LOCATION AND FACILITIES

The details of where the meeting is held or how the room is equipped may seem minor, but they can have an impact on the success of your meeting. A room which is the wrong size, uncomfortable or ill-equipped will make it harder for the group to be productive.

<u>LOCATION</u>

- Neutral: Meetings that are part of resolving disputes may need to be held on neutral territory so that neither party or group feels at a disadvantage.
- Convenient: Meetings take enough time without adding travel time.
- Separate: Meetings are more productive if they are away from the interrup-

tions of traffic, phone calls, other people stopping in with messages and questions, etc.

FACILITIES: Some factors to consider:

- right size
- appropriate break out space for small groups, if necessary
- handicapped accessibility or other special needs
- comfortable lighting
- appropriate collection of chairs and tables (preferably movable ones)
- plenty of wall space for hanging flip chart paper
- necessary equipment: flip charts, tape, markers, black board, overhead projector, handouts, etc.

AGENDA PLANNING

The facilitator's personal agenda will be highly detailed, providing all the notes you will need for yourself. The agenda for the group will be less detailed, leaving out much of the "how," but should be sent out in advance, posted for the meeting and reviewed at the opening of the meeting with the group. On the following page is an example of an agenda planning sheet.

SAMPLE AGENDA

Time	Activity	Method	Leader
9:00 – 2 min each x12 people =24 min	Introductions	Name, affiliation, why you agreed to serve on the Commission	Facilitator
9:30 – 10 min	Desired Outcomes	Review, check for agenda clarity	Facilitator
9:40 – 20 min	Ground Rules	Generate ground rules from the group, be sure to check confidentiality and substitutions	Facilitator
	Decision Making	Discuss options, select one	
10:00 – 15 min	Commission's Charge and Responsibilities	Report	Chairman
15 min	Questions		Chairman
10:30 – 15 min	Vision work	Opening visualization Use hot air balloon	Facilitator
10:45 – 15 min	Break		
11:00 – 45 min	Brainstorming	Divide into small groups	Facilitator
11:45 – 30 min	Reconvene	Post small group work mill around to read	
12:15 – 1 hr	Lunch		

CHAPTER FIVE

UNDERSTANDING PROBLEM SOLVING

THERE ARE MANY DIFFERENT KINDS OF MEETINGS — MEETINGS TO GENERATE A VISION, to reconcile disputing parties, to develop a plan, and so on. Most of these meetings fall into the category of solving a problem. We use the term "problem solving process" quite loosely. By it we are really talking about a process of making change. That change may be from a good situation to a better one, from a bad situation to an acceptable one, from a current situation to a different future, or something else in between.

Generally speaking, there are three components to change: 1. analysis of the problem, which includes defining the problem precisely and analyzing the context of the problem (physical, economic, emotional climate, etc.), its possible sources, etc.; 2. envisioning the ideal, which involves developing an image of the desired future state; and 3. decision-making, which includes generating options, narrowing alternatives, selecting the best option, implementing that choice and developing an evaluation procedure.

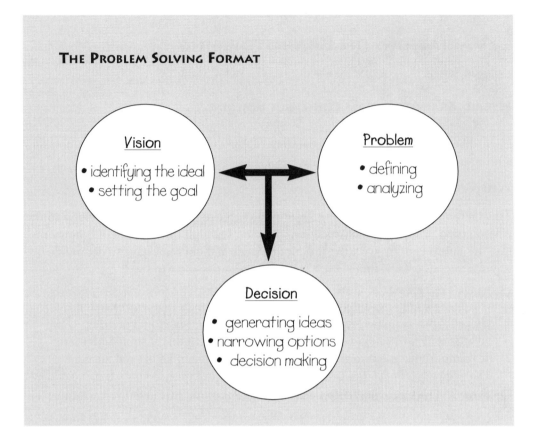

THE PROBLEM SOLVING FORMAT

Vision
- identifying the ideal
- setting the goal

Problem
- defining
- analyzing

Decision
- generating ideas
- narrowing options
- decision making

In several steps of the problem solving process, such as defining the problem, setting the goal or agreeing on a solution, you will want to open up the field of creative ideas, narrow those ideas down to the ideas which make the most sense for the group, and close by coming to a decision. Like all other aspects of facilitation, the problem solving process in practice is not linear. Depending on the desired outcome of the meeting, or of a part of the meeting, the group may choose to start at different places in the process. For instance, you may begin a process by visioning the ideal and later return to the problem specifics. There is, however, one critical tenet of problem solving: You can't generate a viable solution if you haven't agreed on the nature of the problem.

> You can't generate a solution if you haven't agreed on the problem

CONDITIONS FOR SUCCESSFUL PROBLEM SOLVING

1. JOINT ACKNOWLEDGMENT OF NEED FOR PROBLEM SOLVING: There has to be agreement that there is a problem or a situation that needs to be changed.

2. TIME: Those involved must be willing to commit sufficient time to the problem solving process. Occasionally it can be a short process, but more commonly it takes time.

3. COMMITMENT TO STAYING WITH THE PROCESS: Problem solving can have tedious moments. People must be willing to stay committed for the long haul.

4. FOCUS ON THE PROBLEM: Particularly in a highly conflictual situation, people need to remain focused on the problem, rather than the people.

 ### HINTS FOR PICKING THE RIGHT TOOL

Every facilitator needs a set of tools and techniques in order to be able to suggest processes for groups to use when problem solving. Different problem solving tools are needed for different situations. In selecting the correct tool, you need to answer two questions.

1. Where is the group in the problem solving process? You should be able to suggest the appropriate tool for moving the group along in its process.

2. What other factors are influencing the group right now? Some things to be aware of are: size of the group; stage of group development (i.e., forming, storming, norming or performing); energy of the group; introvert/extrovert mix in the group; group's ability to use the tool; power dynamics in the group; and whether the topic is highly conflictual.

THE STAGES OF PROBLEM SOLVING

Below you will find comments on each stage of the problem solving process and tools that can be used effectively in that stage. Tools preceded by the wrench icon are described in detail in *Chapter Six: Tools for Problem Solving*, where they are organized alphabetically. This is not an exhaustive list. Use whatever tools work for you and your group.

1. DEFINING AND ANALYZING THE PROBLEM

One of the most important steps in the problem solving process is to get a clear, measurable definition of the problem. An unclear problem statement will almost always bog down the process and lead to a mediocre result.

Participants in a group may have very different ideas about what the problem really is. Therefore, it is important to get everyone's ideas on the table through some form of idea generation. As much as possible, build a shared definition of the problem, rather than defining it strictly as one person's or one side's problem.

When it comes to defining the problem, insist that people provide specific descriptions or examples. If someone says, "The problem is the way this town is run," ask for specific ways in which they see a problem with town management. Language that is vague or carries value judgments is impossible to work with in the problem solving process. Terms such as good or bad, loud or quiet, efficient or inefficient are all subjective terms that need concrete definition.

If the stated problems appear to be more of a cause than the real problem, push for deeper levels by asking why it's a problem. For example: Quentin says, "The problem is flextime." As facilitator, you ask, "Why is that a problem?" Quentin answers, "Because there are not enough people here at 8:00 to answer the phones." "Why is that a problem?" "It means we aren't serving our customers."

"Why is that a problem?" "It means we are potentially damaging the viability of our business." The challenge in this process is to know when you have reached an appropriate level of problem. If you continue to ask why is that a problem, you may find yourself in larger realms than you are able to affect.

Another way to look at problem definition, when there is not an obvious presenting problem, is to do a definition of the current situation asking questions such as:

- What do you like about the current situation and want to save?
- What would you like to change?
- What are the strengths and weaknesses of the current organization?
- What external threats are there to the organization?
- What opportunities are out there?

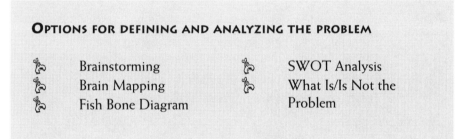

OPTIONS FOR DEFINING AND ANALYZING THE PROBLEM

🐾	Brainstorming	🐾	SWOT Analysis
🐾	Brain Mapping	🐾	What Is/Is Not the
🐾	Fish Bone Diagram		Problem

🐾 *Refer to Chapter Six for a description of tool.*

2. VISIONING THE IDEAL GOAL OR PREFERRED FUTURE STATE

Visioning is the process of identifying the ideal state of a situation. In its early stages, the vision may be a broad view of the ideal state. For example, if a group is focused on improving the local high school, the vision may describe "students excited about learning, well-paid teachers, state-of-the-art facilities and no drop outs."

However, in order to turn the vision into an attainable goal, the group needs to develop a clear statement of the desired result. By the time a vision is translated into a goal, it should be put in a time context and be described in measurable terms so that you can tell whether or not you have actually achieved the goal. It should also be positive and inspiring, something which the group is excited about accomplishing.

> If a group is discouraged or divided, try visioning as a motivator

There may also be multiple goals, but generally not more than five. The ideal goal should make statements about the future, not action steps about how to get there. For example, "By 1997 the drop out rate from Morris High School will be below 7%, teachers' salaries will be at least 5% above the state average and a new multipurpose building will be built.

If a group is discouraged or divided, it can be useful to begin with the vision step as a motivator and a way to find common ground before working on a problem definition.

OPTIONS FOR VISIONING THE IDEAL

🐎 Create a Poster 🐎 Picture the Future
🐎 Go Wishing 🐎 Visualization
🐎 Newspaper Article

🐎 *Refer to Chapter Six for a description of tool.*

3. <u>INFORMATION GATHERING</u>

The group may need to collect outside information from others in the organization, from stakeholder groups, from technical experts, or through background research before clearly identifying the problem, or before generating ideas or evaluating options. The group should agree what information is needed, how it will be gathered and who is responsible. The needed information could be a simple set of figures or an elaborate series of focus groups, surveys and public meetings. In contentious situations, agreeing on the source of the information can be a significant first step. Having neutral, mutually acceptable data is important in a dispute.

OPTIONS FOR INFORMATION GATHERING

- Ask an expert
- Conduct a survey
- Interviews by phone or in person

- Meetings of constituent groups
- Public meetings
- Identify how others are solving the problem

4. GENERATING IDEAS

This is an expansive phase of the problem solving process and you want to encourage groups to consider all possible options. To have a successful option generating session, you need to guide the group away from two situations: any attempt to critique ideas; and prematurely settling on one option.

The idea is to generate as many creative ideas as possible. Encourage people to look beyond the obvious, to be silly or outrageous — but above all to be creative. To do this requires a safe place where the participants know they won't be rejected for a wacky idea. Don't permit any evaluation during brainstorming or react yourself in a negative or dismissive way to any ideas. It's equally important not to react in an enthusiastic way to one idea or another. Use your enthusiasm to praise the process. For example, "You are coming up with a great list. There are lots of creative ideas here!"

OPTIONS FOR GENERATING IDEAS

🦒 Brainstorming   🦒 Brain Mapping
(and variations)   🦒 Sticky Note Technique

🦒 *Refer to Chapter Six for a description of tool.*

5. CLARIFYING, EVALUATING AND NARROWING OPTIONS

After options have been generated, the next step is to check for understanding of the ideas. Make sure everyone is clear about what is meant by each statement on the list; the narrowing process will be faulty if group members are carrying different notions of what statements mean. Remember: if you are unclear, there is a good chance that someone in the group is also unclear, so ask and encourage questions at this stage.

> For many, evaluating and narrowing are the most challenging aspects of problem solving

For many facilitators, the next steps of evaluating and narrowing are the most challenging aspects of problem solving. In brainstorming, you were careful to steer the group away from evaluative comments. Now it is time for the group to look at the list critically. Invite the group to comment on the ideas they have generated. Ask for any observations or concerns they may have about the ideas generated. Listen carefully and be ready to follow up on concerns expressed.

Once the group has concluded its comments and concerns have been resolved (often easier said than done!) you must now select the right tool for evaluating and narrowing options. It is important that you and the group be clear about what kind of evaluating and narrowing is needed.

The following questions will help you choose which decision making tools to use:

- Do you need to prioritize the list?
- Do you need to compare options to a set of criteria?
- Do you need to decide yes or no to an idea?
- Do you want to combine compatible ideas or eliminate unworkable ones?

The chart below offers guidance about when to use which tools:

NARROWING AND DECISION MAKING TOOLS

Narrowing of Ideas	Consolidation of Ideas into Groups	List in Order of Priority	Yes – No Decision
🐾 Multi-Vote 🐾 Option Comparison Grid 🐾 Nominal Group Technique	🐾 Affinity Groups 🐾 Loop & Group • Summary Sheet	🐾 Multi-Vote 🐾 Nominal Group Technique 🐾 Paired Comparisons	• Vote-Majority Super Majority 🐾 Pro/Con Sheet 🐾 Option Comparison Grid • Thorough discussion followed by vote

🐾 *Refer to Chapter Six for a description of tool.*

Note: In every type of decision making, it is a good idea to conclude by looking for consensus, summarizing the results for the group, and checking for agreement.

6. MAKING THE FINAL DECISION

Now it's time to make a final decision. At this stage, the facilitator can help the group by summarizing the results of the evaluating and narrowing process and developing a clear statement of the decision it needs to make. For example, "You have sorted through a number of options for software packages to purchase for the high school. After comparing the six choices to your criteria, the Zoom 2000 package best meets the criteria." Before you finish, do one last check for clarity, "Are you ready to make a final decision? Is there any further discussion you want to have before we check for consensus?"

At the beginning of the meeting, the group will have agreed which decision making method to use. Following is a more in depth discussion about decision making methods.

> It is important for group members to share a common meaning for consensus

CONSENSUS: Increasingly, many work groups choose consensus as their decision making method. The advantage is that when a group reaches consensus, everyone "buys in" to the decision. The major disadvantage is that consensus can take a great deal of time.

It is important for group members to share a common meaning for consensus and to have agreement about what to do if they do not reach consensus. If the group decides to use consensus, it needs to:

1. discuss and adopt an agreed-upon meaning for consensus; and

2. decide whether it will use "pure" consensus, with no alternative method for decision making, or "modified" consensus, with a fall-back method (such as voting or executive decision) in place. Both can work; what is critical is that the group be clear about which method it is using before it begins a decision making process. It is also useful to define precisely the circumstances under which the fall-back method will be used (the

time limit is reached, for minor decisions, etc.). Where a hierarchical fall-back process is in place, it is important for the person in charge to convey clearly when the group has control of the decision making and at what point she will have the final word.

SENSE OF THE MEETING: The facilitator, leader or a group member may choose to state the sense of the meeting. This is a summary of what that person understands and feels the decision of the group to be. Sense of the meeting honors the group as an entity that is more than the sum of its individual members. Thus there may not be unanimity of agreement coming from every individual, yet the decision is clear for the group. Any time someone speaks her sense of the meeting, it must be checked out and agreed to by the group.

> Sense of the meeting honors the group as an entity that is more than the sum of its individual members

VOTING: Voting is a commonly used decision making method. The advantages of voting are that it is quick and gives a decisive result. A disadvantage is that the results leave winners and losers, and losers may not support the decision with as much enthusiasm as the winners. When a group chooses voting as its decision making method, it should be clear which of the following it is choosing to use:

Simple Majority: The decision is made by choosing a solution which is acceptable to more than half the entire group, with each person having equal power (one person, one vote).

Super Majority: The decision is made by choosing a solution which is acceptable to more than 2/3 or 3/4 of the entire group, with each person having equal power (one person, one vote).

Majority - Minority Opinion - Majority: The decision is made by holding a straw vote. If the result is less than unanimous, the "minority" are asked to explain why they are voting against the issue. Then a final binding vote is held.

OPTIONS FOR DECISION MAKING

🐾 Levels of Consensus

🐾 Multi-voting

🐾 Nominal Group Technique

🐾 Option Comparison Grid

🐾 Paired Comparisons

• Voting (majority, 2/3, 3/4)

• Majority vote - minority opinion - majority vote

• Sense of the Meeting

🐾 *Refer to Chapter Six for a description of tool.*

CHAPTER SIX

Tools for Problem Solving

THE BASIC TOOLS THAT SHOULD SEE YOU THROUGH the phases of problem solving are described in this chapter. This collection is not intended to be an encyclopedia of all the tools available. Every day we discover or invent new ones — and so will you. In the Reading and Resources section at the end of the book are some suggestions for additional reading which will describe more tools.

The tools are listed alphabetically. Each one starts on its own page in order to make it easier to copy them. Each tool includes a brief description, an indication of when it is useful, and, where appropriate, a list of pros and cons. There is an explanation of how to use the tool and, finally, an example. If you want to review all the tools that we suggest for a particular step in the problem solving process, refer to the lists under each step in *Chapter Five: Understanding Problem Solving*.

AFFINITY GROUPS

This tool helps order ideas which are developed through sticky note brainstorming. It enables the group to decide how the ideas should be organized.

WHEN IT IS USEFUL:

- to generate a lot of ideas and then group them in themes or categories
- for a large group in which you want everyone to participate
- to move fairly quickly with no debating
- to provide an opportunity to get up and move around

PROS AND CONS:

- everyone has a chance to move things around
- whole new orders can arise
- it can move along pretty rapidly
- people do not have a chance to explain the reasons for their moves

HOW TO USE IT:

1. Have each participant put his ideas on sticky notes or separate pieces of paper and stick them on the wall using thumbtacks, masking tape, adhesive paper, etc.
2. When all the ideas are on the wall, invite the group members to reorder the ideas into affinity groups without talking. Each member is free to move any idea and the process continues in silence until no one wants to make any further moves.
3. Invite the group to discuss their choices and check for agreement.

EXAMPLE:

Your group wants to identify ways to improve inter-departmental communications. Each person puts on the wall as many ideas as he has from "start a newsletter" to "hold monthly department meetings." Members then read all the ideas and begin silently to group them. A group of ideas around newsletters and written communications emerges. Another forms around physical rearrangement, and another around meetings. One person may create a grouping that others don't agree with, and the ideas get moved again. When everyone is either comfortable with the results or runs out of steam, the group sits down and discusses what it has created.

BRAINSTORMING

Brainstorming is a process for generating a list of ideas about a topic. It is sometimes called popcorn brainstorming because anyone can speak up at anytime until all the ideas are out.

WHEN IT IS USEFUL:

Brainstorming is appropriate any time a group needs to come up with a list of ideas. Coming up with lists can be part of any step of the problem-solving process. Here are some examples of when brainstorming could be used:
- to generate a list of problems or potential problems
- to generate a list of causes of problems
- to generate topics for data collection
- to generate a list of suggestions for what the ideal would look like
- to generate a list of potential solutions
- to generate a list of next steps

HOW TO USE IT:

1. Have enough space to accommodate lots of ideas. You can use flip chart, butcher paper, chalk board, white board or self-stick sheets.
2. Review the rules of brainstorming with the group. If the concept is unfamiliar to the group, post the rules on a sheet of paper.

RULES FOR BRAINSTORMING:
- Express whatever comes to your mind. Don't monitor, censor, or hold back responses. The more ideas, the better. No idea is too far out.
- Do not evaluate your ideas or anybody else's ideas. Do not make positive evaluations, negative comments or non-verbal agreement or disagreement. It is especially important for the facilitator and recorder to refrain from giving any indication of evaluation.
- Do not discuss the ideas as they come up. Discussion will interfere with the generation of creative possibilities. Ask only clarifying questions about brainstorming items.
- Repetition of ideas is okay. Write down each idea, even if it sounds repetitious. There is no value in having a narrowed-down list at this point and people can feel rejected if their ideas aren't written down.

BRAINSTORMING, CONTINUED

- Piggy-backing on someone else's ideas should be encouraged. This is often the building block of workable solutions.
- Silence is normal in brainstorming. When it seems as though people have run out of ideas, restate the topic of brainstorming and then ask, "Anything else?" Wait 10 seconds or so; often after a period of silence there is a burst of creativity.

3. Record all ideas that participants offer, being careful to model the above rules.
4. After you have finished brainstorming, ask the group to review each item for clarity and completeness.

HINTS FOR BRAINSTORMING

- Review the rules for brainstorming every time you use this method.

- Set a time limit for brainstorming and stick to it.

- Get people away from the table: have them sit in a circle of chairs around the easel or even on the floor in order to break out of customary ways of thinking.

- Affirm humor, laughter and anything creative.

- Summarize an idea and then check with the person to make sure you have understood correctly what he was saying.

- Be assertive in stopping any judgmental comments. Remind the evaluating person gently that right now the group is generating ideas, not evaluating them.

VARIATIONS ON BRAINSTORMING

HYBRID BRAINSTORMING/ CONSENSUS BUILDING

Hybrid Brainstorming/Consensus Building is a process that combines brainstorming with narrowing and decision making.

WHEN IT IS USEFUL:

This method is useful for creating ground rules. Since the ground rules belong to the whole group, everyone needs to agree to them. Through this method of brainstorming, the group ends up with the product it needs and does not have to do any further narrowing or selecting.

HOW TO USE IT:

1. As each idea is suggested, the facilitator gets consensus from the group. The item is only written on the list after everyone agrees that it should be there.
2. It is important to reinforce and encourage the value of all offered ideas.

ONE-AT-A-TIME BRAINSTORMING

One-at-a-time brainstorming is a variation on brainstorming that provides individual thinking time. It encourages participation by getting everyone involved.

WHEN IT IS USEFUL:

One-at-a-time brainstorming is a valuable method for groups with introverted members who are usually more comfortable developing ideas internally prior to speaking, or for groups with members who tend to dominate discussions.

HOW TO USE IT:

1. Each person, working individually, makes a list of ideas.
2. Ask each person in the group to read out one item on her list.
3. After one or two rounds of collecting ideas from individuals, open it up to regular brainstorming until all ideas have been shared. Opening it up keeps the process from becoming too tedious.
4. After all ideas have been shared, invite the group to add anything else it has thought of as the list was being created.

VARIATIONS ON BRAINSTORMING, CONTINUED

STICKY NOTE BRAINSTORMING

In this brainstorming variation, group members write their brainstormed ideas on sticky notes, and then place the notes on a wall for everyone to see. The ideas are then grouped by topic or theme, providing a visual picture of which ideas are most often mentioned by the group.

WHEN IT IS USEFUL:

This is good method for energizing the group. It's particularly useful as a way to brainstorm with a large group or a group whose members are hesitant to speak up.

HOW TO USE IT:

1. Give each person markers and several large sticky notes or cards (the larger the better). Ask participants to put one idea on each card. If you are seeking contrasting ideas, such as what works and what doesn't, provide different colored cards or stickies. Remind the group to write clearly and boldly so the ideas can be read from a distance.
2. Ask participants to stick their cards on the wall. You can ask participants to read one another's' cards and group them according to similar ideas, or you can group them yourself. The former provides for more involvement; however it requires that people are clear about what they are supposed to be grouping.

SUBGROUP BRAINSTORMING

Subgroup brainstorming divides the whole group into smaller groups. The task of each small group is to generate a list of ideas to be shared with the whole group. Working in smaller groups gives participants more opportunity to participate and can be more comfortable for some.

WHEN IT IS USEFUL:

Subgroup brainstorming gives everyone air time in a short amount of time. It's also a valuable way to get input from those who don't speak easily in a large group, or from those who don't wish to be personally associated with certain ideas.

VARIATIONS ON BRAINSTORMING, CONTINUED

HOW TO USE IT:

1. Divide a large group into subgroups of 2-4 participants. Give a time limit and ask each subgroup to choose a recorder/reporter.
2. Each group generates a list of ideas.
3. Ask each reporter to read out one idea.
4. After one or two rounds of collecting ideas from reporters, open it up to a regular brainstorming session until all ideas have been shared.
5. After all ideas have been shared, invite the group to add anything else it has thought of as the list was being created.

SUBSET BRAINSTORMING

Here the facilitator invites brainstorming ideas from different perspectives: frivolous, serious, boring, funny, etc. This kind of "thinking outside the box" helps groups get their creative juices flowing.

WHEN IT IS USEFUL:

Subset brainstorming is useful when a group needs to be creative, when it's stuck on very serious solutions or is just bored with regular brainstorming. Sometimes unusual ideas can turn out to be more practical than they might seem at first.

HOW TO USE IT:

1. Encourage the group to generate ideas "outside the box" of sensible ideas. Remind them that putting out an idea is different from thinking it is necessarily good or workable.
2. As the group is brainstorming, challenge them with subsets for brainstorming (e.g. practical solutions, boring solutions, improbable solutions, illegal solutions, funny solutions, etc.). You might say something like, "Those were great practical solutions, now how about all the illegal solutions you can think of."
3. Follow the steps for regular brainstorming.

VARIATIONS ON BRAINSTORMING, CONTINUED

WARM-UP BRAINSTORMING

Warm-up brainstorming uses a topic that is non-task related to warm up the group.

WHEN IT IS USEFUL:

This tool helps a group loosen up and demonstrates the creative solutions possible in brainstorming. It can be especially useful when a group is taking itself too seriously.

HOW TO USE IT:

1. Show any object (soda bottle, lint brush, comb, etc.) and ask the group to brainstorm all possible uses. Or give the group an imaginary situation and ask them to brainstorm all possible solutions. For example, "You're in Mexico on vacation and your wallet and airplane ticket have been stolen. How are you going to get home?"
2. Follow the steps for brainstorming.

BRAIN MAPPING

Brain mapping is a graphic way to display the analysis of different parts of a problem or issue. The main problem or issue is placed in a central circle and the causes of the problem are represented as separate spokes or circles attached to the central circle. There can be more detail attached to any of the causes with additional spokes or circles.

WHEN IT IS USEFUL:

- helps to break down a problem, showing the causes and the subsets of those causes in relationship to one another
- is useful to analyze an issue whether you are looking for the causes or trying to understand all the parts of an issue
- can also be used to break out the pieces of a task or the steps in reaching an outcome or goal
- can be used to follow the consequences of an action and analyze whether there might be unintended consequences

PROS AND CONS:

- good graphic display
- promotes clarity
- sense of order to thinking
- stimulates thinking for thorough analysis
- can result in too much detail
- can get sidetracked on debates over placement
- needs to be rewritten to be useful

HOW TO USE IT:

FOR ANALYZING A PROBLEM OR BRAINSTORMING:
1. At the center of your paper, draw a circle with the problem written in the middle.
2. Draw spokes out from the center on which you write the causes of the problem.
3. As participants further define each cause, add the ideas on spokes attached to the cause spokes.

BRAIN MAPPING, CONTINUED

EXAMPLE:

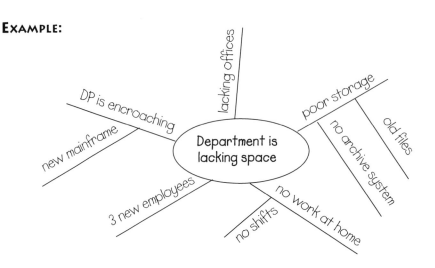

FOR THE CONSEQUENCES OF AN ACTION:
1. Write the action in the center circle.
2. Put the consequences of that action in circles attached to the central circle.
3. As those consequences have further consequences, attach more circles.

EXAMPLE:

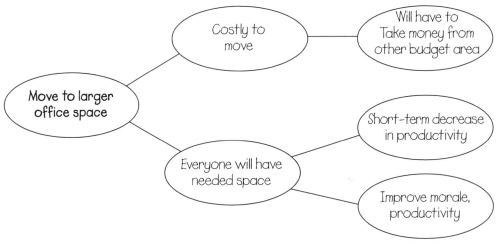

FORCE FIELD ANALYSIS

Force Field Analysis is a tool for assessing the forces that can affect a possible change. It is a tool generally used during the narrowing phase of problem solving..

WHEN IT IS USEFUL:

This tool is particularly useful when a group wants to articulate, analyze and influence the factors that push the group towards, and restrain them from making, a particular change.

HOW TO USE IT:

1. Create a chart as shown in the example.
2. At the top of the chart, write a clear statement of the specific action or behavior you want to affect. Use language that frames the change positively rather than negatively.
3. Brainstorm the specific factors (personal, situational, organizational, etc.) that could work toward reaching this desired outcome and write them on the chart. Then, brainstorm the specific factors that could work against reaching this desired outcome and write them on the chart. Remember to assess the situation from the perspective of all stakeholders.
4. Examine each list to see which items stand out as critical factors for and against this change. It is possible that the data you have just generated will give you your decision. If it doesn't, continue on to steps 5 and 6.
5. Circle 2-3 driving forces you can increase the strength of, and 2-3 restraining forces that you can minimize the impact of.
6. List some steps you can take to increase the strength or decrease the impact of each driving or restraining force you have circled.

FORCE FIELD ANALYSIS, CONTINUED

EXAMPLE:

Statement: We want to increase resolution of conflicts at the worker level.

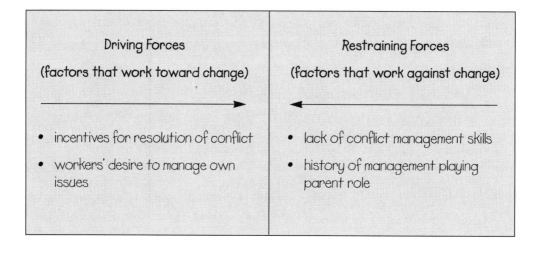

Driving Forces

(factors that work toward change)

→

- incentives for resolution of conflict
- workers' desire to manage own issues

Restraining Forces

(factors that work against change)

←

- lack of conflict management skills
- history of management playing parent role

GIVE ME A WISH

This tool provides a method for encouraging a group to frame the situation positively and focus on the way they want things to be. By asking the participants to use phrases such as "I wish," you encourage them to state what they would like to see rather than being bogged down in problems.

WHEN IT IS USEFUL:

- if a group is stuck on complaining about what is wrong and needs help getting focused more positively
- to spur creativity or fresh thinking

PROS AND CONS:

- can change the focus of a group which is bogged down
- can build a positive attitude and more constructive approach
- may seem disconnected from reality for some participants

HOW TO USE IT:

Ask people to generate options by phrasing statements that begin with either "I wish," "I wonder how to" or "what if."

EXAMPLE:

"I wish we could do something about the lighting in here."
"I wonder how to improve participation in the United Way."
"What if we were to rearrange the desks in here?"

LEVELS OF CONSENSUS

Levels of Consensus is a decision making method which streamlines the consensus process.

WHEN IT IS USEFUL:

Consensus-based groups often "talk an issue to death" as they struggle for unity. This tool provides a format for checking consensus without all the long speeches and discussions that give consensus a bad name. This method shortens the time consensus can take and gives everyone a voice, without compromising the careful listening, reflection, respect and trust that must accompany the use of consensus.

HOW TO USE IT:

1. After the group has had sufficient time for discussion about a particular topic, ask all group members to hold up fingers indicating where they are on the consensus scale (see the Levels of Consensus on the following page). If a quick scan of the room indicates all ones and twos, then the group can quickly see that consensus has been reached. If there are several people indicating threes and fours, or if there is even one five or six, further discussion will be needed to reach unity.

2. No matter what the poll indicates, it is a good idea to ask if there is need for further comments or discussion.

3. It is extremely important to remember that when even one person is not in unity with the decision, the group needs to take the time to hear and consider what the person has to say. If that person is still not in consensus with the group, then the group needs to decide whether the decision making will be carried over to a later time to give more time for reflection, research, etc.; whether they will continue discussion until they are able to find an acceptable solution; or whether they will use their fall-back decision making method.

LEVELS OF CONSENSUS, CONTINUED

THE LEVELS OF CONSENSUS:

1. I can say an unqualified "yes" to the decision. I am satisfied that the decision is an expression of the wisdom of the group.
2. I find the decision perfectly acceptable.
3. I can live with the decision; I'm not especially enthusiastic about it.
4. I do not fully agree with the decision and need to register my view about why. However, I do not choose to block the decision. I am willing to support the decision because I trust the wisdom of the group.
5. I do not agree with the decision and feel the need to stand in the way of this decision being accepted.
6. I feel that we have no clear sense of unity in the group. We need to do more work before consensus can be reached.

VARIATIONS ON LEVELS OF CONSENSUS

STOPLIGHT CARDS

Stoplight Cards uses red, yellow and green cards, rather than thumbs, to indicate agreement, hesitation or disagreement with the decision being proposed.

HOW TO USE IT:

1. Distribute red, green and yellow index cards or sheets of paper to each participant.
2. When a decision is being proposed, ask group members to indicate with the appropriate card how they feel about the decision:
   - Green means agreement with the decision.
   - Yellow means some hesitation or caution about the decision, or it can be defined as "I can live with it."
   - Red means disagreement or "no go" with the decision.
3. As with Levels of Consensus, indication of hesitation or disagreement calls for further discussion.

THUMBS UP

Thumbs up is a pared down version of the six finger method. It is simpler; the disadvantage is that you lose the gradations that Levels of Consensus offers.

HOW TO USE IT:

1. Ask group members to indicate with their thumbs how they feel about the proposed decision:
   - Thumb up means agreement with the decision.
   - Thumb straight across means some hesitation or caution about the decision, or it can be defined as "I can live with it."
   - Thumb down means disagreement or "no go" with the decision.
2. As with levels of consensus, indication of hesitation or disagreement calls for further discussion.

LOOP AND GROUP

This is a technique for helping a group to consolidate ideas after a brainstorming session by grouping similar items. By circling in a common color items that are similar or belong to a common theme, you can visually link common ideas and reduce the number of items under consideration.

WHEN IT IS USEFUL:

- helps to bring order to a random collection of ideas
- can start the narrowing process

HOW TO USE IT:

1. Use questions to the group to solicit their opinions on what belongs together or, if it would help the group, reflect what you see as similarities. Some questions that you might ask are: Are some of these items really the same issue? Are some of these items part of a single larger issue? What would you call that larger topic? What is the title? Are there any items which do not belong on the list of this topic?
2. Circle or underline the ideas belonging to one group using the same color marker.
3. Using a different color, circle the ideas that belong to another group.
4. If the original list, with its multi-colored circles, is getting hard to read, you may want to create a new list of the titles of the new, larger topic areas.

EXAMPLE:

Your group has generated twenty different ideas on how to improve the parking situation at your work place. You ask if any of the ideas are similar or belong in the same category. The group decides that four of the ideas have to do with ways to reorganize the parking spaces in the parking lot. You circle those four ideas with a purple pen. Next someone suggests that several of the ideas are really alternatives to driving your own car to work. The group agrees and you circle those ideas in green. You continue in this way until the list is organized into a number of manageable areas. If the original sheets with the 20 ideas is now hard to read, or the titles of the new groupings are not clear, make a new sheet with the titles of the topic areas and identify the color of the topic's "loops".

MULTIVOTING

Multivoting is a process for narrowing down a larger list of items and indicating a group's interest or priority in each item.

WHEN IT IS USEFUL:

Multivoting is appropriate when a list needs to be narrowed down, as long as it is acceptable that some items may drop off completely. It is especially useful when a group wants to get a "quick read" on its priorities. Multivoting is not appropriate when the group needs to consider carefully each item on a list and/or when it needs to incorporate each idea into a final recommendation. Multivoting should not be used as a way to avoid conflict or circumvent an important, but perhaps difficult, discussion.

HOW TO USE IT:

1. Make sure there is clarity about the meaning of each item on the list. Where there is agreement to do so, combine like ideas.
2. Everyone gets the same number of votes. Members can cast votes by making marks on the flip chart, by a show of hands or secret ballot. A benefit of marking the flip chart is that people can get up and move around, which often raises the energy level in the group.
3. Clearly describe the method for vote distribution. There are two common ways for individuals to distribute their votes. One way is to agree that no item on the list can get more than one vote from one person. For example, if group members each have 5 votes, they would vote on 5 different items. The second way is to agree that an individual can distribute his votes however he chooses, putting all votes on one item, or distributing them in any other way among multiple items. If each group member had 5 votes, he could put all 5 votes on one item, one vote on 5 different items, etc.
4. Once the votes are tallied, be clear about what happens to all the items on the list. Don't assume that those items that received fewer votes should be cast aside. Sometimes the group will want to save them, or include them in a report.
5. The N/3 (N over 3) method is a good way to determine how many votes group members should get. N equals the number of items on the list; divide that number by 3.

NEWSPAPER ARTICLE

Asking the group to write a newspaper or magazine article about their organization as they hope to be reported in the future is a way of capturing the group's concepts of the desired future and building a belief in how it could be.

WHEN IT IS USEFUL:

- to establish a vision of the future
- to build a belief in the possible and generate enthusiasm
- to provide inspiration and/or summary for a group

HOW TO USE IT:

1. Ask the group members to picture themselves and their organization two years in the future. The organization is running well. What would they hope to see reported in the newspaper about them or what would Time Magazine be saying about them.

2. Let them brainstorm a list of ideas or comments that they would want to have in the article. Look for agreement on the key ideas. Then, have the group work on a headline for the article, using small groups to come up with ideas. Generate agreement around one or two headlines.

3. If you are in a process that includes a subsequent meeting, ask for some volunteers to actually write an article based on the group's ideas and then bring it back to the group at the next meeting..

EXAMPLE:

You are working with an organization which has been having difficulty with its public image. Bickering among Board members and difficulties with the previous director has created negative feelings in the community. The group wants to develop a plan to improve the working relationships within the Board and with the staff, and to improve the organization's public image. They are having trouble imagining the way they want the relationships to be. You ask them to picture themselves two years in the future in a smoothly running organization. A reporter from the local paper has done a feature article on them. What does the article say? What are the key ideas that it conveys? What

NEWSPAPER ARTICLE, CONTINUED

activities does it report on? What kind of vocabulary does she use to describe the organization and its activities? What does she say about the Board meeting that she attends? Ask them to work in pairs or small groups to generate ideas. Collect the ideas and look for agreement on key themes, ideas and vocabulary. Next, ask the group to work in their pairs or small groups again to come up with a great headline for the article based on the ideas that the group just agreed to. Again, bring the ideas together and look for agreement on one or two headlines, or a new one encompassing several of the ideas. If your group will be meeting again, ask for 2-3 volunteers to actually write up the article, to be shared with the group next time.

NOMINAL GROUP TECHNIQUE

Nominal Group Technique is a narrowing down and decision making method that allows for input by all group members while minimizing group debate.

WHEN IT IS USEFUL:

This tool is particularly useful when the group wants to avoid getting into debates or power struggles or when the decision involves strong differences in values.

HOW TO USE IT:

1. Each person individually decides his order of preference for the options given. Each option is ranked (first choice is 1, second choice is 2, etc.)
2. For each option, the facilitator asks for comments on why that was or was not a choice. There is no discussion; everyone has chance to speak.
3. Group members have a chance to reconsider their order of preference based on the comments given.
4. The facilitator records each person's order of preference on a prepared flip chart.
5. Scores are tallied for each option.
6. Whichever option gets the least number of points is chosen.
7. As with any decision making method, the group should look at the results and check that they make sense and are in line with the group's goals, resources, etc.

EXAMPLE:

	Option A	Option B	Option C
Henry	2	1	3
Ian	2	3	1
Emily	1	3	2
Mercedes	1	2	3
Total	6	9	9

OPTION COMPARISON GRID

The Option Comparison Grid is a narrowing and decision making technique for comparing options against a set of criteria.

WHEN IT IS USEFUL:

This tool is used when multiple options need to be measured against a set of criteria in order to decide on the best option. Some examples of comparisons are: candidates for a job, different brands of a product, types of awards, etc.

HOW TO USE IT:

1. Develop a set of criteria that the final choice must meet. Because options that don't meet these criteria will be tossed out, make sure that these criteria are critical.
2. Develop a second set of criteria that would add value to this option.
3. List the options across the top of the chart.
4. Compare each option to each "must" criteria.
5. If an option does not meet a "must" criteria, toss it out. There is no need to continue the comparison for that option.
6. Compare each option that has met all the "must" criteria to the "add value" criteria. Write in any relevant comments.
7. After comparing all the options, assess which one best meets your set of criteria.
8. As always in a decision making process, ask if the final result makes sense. If some group members express hesitations about the choice, probe that discomfort to see if some criteria have been missed or over or under valued.

OPTION COMPARISON GRID, CONTINUED

EXAMPLE:

Hire New Marketing Director

"Must" Criteria	Candidate A	Candidate B	Candidate C
1. 5+ yrs. dept. management	yes	yes	yes
2. MBA degree	yes	yes	no
3. Budget management	yes	yes	yes
4. Windows 95	yes	yes	yes
Added Value Criteria			
1. PR experience	yes	no	n/a
2. Media buying experience	no	yes	n/a
3. Knowledge of industry	yes	no	n/a
4. Team leadership	yes	yes	n/a
Comments:	• Brother of CEO • Knows PR • Strong team leadership	• Seems like a a good fit • Knows media • Can't start for 6 mos.	• Has relevant industry experience • High salary requirements

Overall, which meets criteria best?   Candidate A

PAIRED COMPARISONS

Based on a group decision making process (ISM) developed by John Warfield and written about and utilized by Carl Moore and Roberta Miller, Paired Comparisons is a method of establishing a prioritized list through a thorough debate of the items. It is done by discussing and then voting on whether one item is a higher priority than another until you have established the relative importance of all the items.

WHEN IT IS USEFUL:

- to create a thoroughly debated prioritized list
- to prioritize items which are not easily related to one another (apples and oranges, road repairs and rose gardens)
- to help a group make "politically" difficult decisions
- to determine the highest priorities for funding when the budget is limited

PROS AND CONS:

- individuals have an opportunity to argue for what is important to them
- all the items are thoroughly debated
- can provide order to a messy problem of prioritizing options
- takes time to debate each pair
- hard to do with a long list of options
- the items being prioritized need to be clearly defined and agreed upon

HOW TO USE IT:

1. Make sure the items to be prioritized are clear and that the list is not too long.
2. Try to anticipate how much debate there is likely to be. How contentious is the subject matter? How significant is the impact of the result on the people in the room? How complex are the issues? Set your time frame accordingly.
3. In advance, make a placard for each item to be prioritized which is large enough to be readable by the entire group. The placards will need to be moved during the process, so have tape, adhesive paper and other necessary equipment handy.
4. Create an area on the wall for the pair of items under discussion. Write "is a higher priority than" in the middle and leave space above and below for placards.
5. Begin by comparing item A and B. Place the placard for item A over the phrase "is a higher priority than" and the placard for item B below. It now reads "Item A is a higher priority than item B."

PAIRED COMPARISONS, CONTINUED

6. Ask if the participants agree or disagree with the statement and why. Allow a thorough debate and when the group is ready, call for a simple vote. Is item A a higher priority than item B? Everyone must vote one way or the other. If the vote is yes, then place A over B on the priority ladder.

7. Now introduce item C. Is C a higher priority than B? (Move the B placard back to the comparison side for the discussion.) Again, encourage a discussion and call for a vote. If the vote is yes, then C belongs higher than B in the priority ladder. Now you need to know if C is a higher priority than A, so you set up that comparison and repeat the process of discussion and voting. If the vote is yes, then C moves above A on the ladder.

8. Continue to introduce new items starting in the middle of the priority ladder, repeating the process of discussion and voting. If it is a lower priority than the item it is compared with, then move to the next item down the ladder for your next comparison. If it is a higher priority, then move to the next item up the ladder. Continue until all the items have been introduced and found their resting places. The result is a completely prioritized list.

EXAMPLE:

You have three requests for capital expenditures for your department: a new carpet ($4000); a telephone and voice mail upgrade ($10,000); and two new computer stations ($12,000). You need to prioritize these capital requests to see where the limited money should go. Set up your placards on the wall and begin the comparisons:

First Round:	Second Round:	Third Round:
(A) carpet is a higher priority than (B) telephone. Discussion, vote – no.	(C) computer is a higher priority than (B) telephone. Discussion, vote – no.	(C) computer is a higher priority than (A) carpet. Discussion, vote – yes.
Priority Ladder	Priority Ladder	Priority Ladder
(B) telephone (A) carpet	(B) telephone (C) computer (A) carpet	(B) telephone (C) computer (A) carpet

PICTURE THE FUTURE

Picture the future is a graphic way of capturing the group's concepts of the future and a sense of movement toward that goal by using a drawing and symbolic representations of ideas.

WHEN IT IS USEFUL:

- to establish a vision of the future, a path to get there and a view of the present
- to create a graphic display of ideas
- to sketch the larger concepts and ideas
- to provide inspiration and/or summary for a group

PROS AND CONS:

- can provide clarity, excitement and summary
- some people are more likely to grasp a visual presentation of the material
- does not provide a detailed plan

HOW TO USE IT:

1. Attach a large, preferably horizontal piece of paper to the wall. Print the label "Present" on the left side and "Ideal" or "Future" on the right.
2. Ask your group to describe the characteristics of each. Capture those ideas graphically on the appropriate areas of the paper. Draw mountains in between and a road wending its way over the mountains and into the future. Indicate what mountains must be climbed to reach the future. You can add signposts next to the road to indicate steps that must be taken along the way.

EXAMPLE:

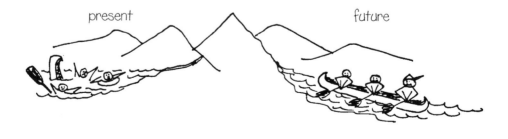

SWOT ANALYSIS

SWOT (Strengths, Weaknesses, Opportunities and Threats) analysis is a tool for analyzing the current situation both internally (strengths and weaknesses) and externally (opportunities and threats). It provides helpful baseline information for a group that wants to vision the future or analyze a problem.

WHEN IT IS USEFUL:

This tool is used as part of a planning process to help a group determine where it stands and what it might need to work on in order to get to where it wants to go.

HOW TO USE IT:

1. For strengths, ask the group to look at those activities which it does very well, at the skills of the group or of individuals within the group, at valuable experience, at the depth of its work force or the quality of its leadership. List their ideas on flip chart paper. It is important that enough safety and openness has been created in the process so that responses are candid.
2. For weaknesses, ask the group to consider and list the same wide range of possibilities. Again, candor is important. Some agreement on the items raised is helpful, but this is usually a step in a longer planning process, not an end in itself.
3. Ask the group to identify opportunities — the external factors which could be used to the benefit of the group. They could be in the form of funding sources, marketing possibilities, disarray in the competition, a favorable political climate or public awareness. These are events or circumstances over which the group has no control, but which will help the group go where it wants to go.
4. Ask the group to identify and list the threats — those negative possibilities that are waiting in ambush to trip the group up, or the storm clouds on the horizon that might necessitate changing course or shortening sail.
5. You can use any form of generating ideas (see Brainstorming) and identifying some group agreement (see Decision Making).

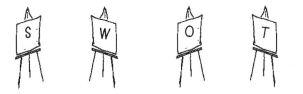

VISUALIZATION

A visualization is a technique to help the participants paint a picture in their minds.

WHEN IT IS USEFUL:

This tool is particularly useful in getting people to identify what they would like to see in the future. It gives participants a chance to "see" the details, which then help them articulate their vision of the way they want things to be

PROS AND CONS:

- very open way to collect ideas
- helps people focus on the future or the intangible
- generates quite varied ideas which can make summarizing a challenge
- for some the "close your eyes and imagine" approach may feel uncomfortable

HOW TO USE IT:

1. Create a scene for the group (often of an ideal or changed scenario) by leading the group through a visualization where they have the ability to see from the vantage point of a hot air balloon or some imaginary point. If it is important to consider particular facets of the organization's future, ask participants to do so.
2. Ask people to notice what they see, hear and feel.
3. Give participants a moment to make notes about what they have seen.
4. If the group is large (more than 8), break up into small groups. This will give individuals a chance to talk and generate more ideas in less time.
5. Pull the whole group together and gather the ideas. Look for areas of agreement and areas of differences that need to be worked out.

EXAMPLE:

Ask participants to close their eyes and imagine with you. "It is now the year 2002 and your organization is functioning beautifully, just the way you would like it to be. You have special powers to view your organization. You can fly to any height and can see the town or the whole state in a glance. You also have x-ray vision and enhanced hearing. What do you see, hear and feel? Whom is the organization serving? What is the structure of the organization? What kind of facilities is it operating in? What is the tenor of the conversation around the water cooler?" You can highlight whatever is important for the group to focus on.

WHAT IS/ISN'T THE PROBLEM

What is/isn't the problem is a problem definition method for narrowing the focus onto the true problem or issue.

WHEN IT IS USEFUL:

This tool is useful when a group is having trouble sorting out what the precise problem is.

HOW TO USE IT:

1. Define the overall problem area. For example: The lack of quality play equipment in the neighborhood playground.
2. Make one list that indicates what is the problem and a second list of what is not the problem.
3. It is best to put both lists up at the same time — either using two sheets of flip chart paper or two sections of a white board or chalk board. Then you can record whatever ideas people come up with.

EXAMPLE:

What Is the Problem	What Isn't the Problem
• lack of federal, state or municipal funds for purchase of equipment	• the willingness of the city director of playgrounds to accept suggestions for improvement
• lack of city personnel to maintain the equipment	• lack of families that use the playground
• low priority of this playground relative to other playgrounds in the city	• individuals in the neighborhood who are willing to give their time and energy to upgrade the park

CHAPTER SEVEN

MAXIMIZING YOUR GROUP'S POTENTIAL

EVERY GROUP HAS ENORMOUS POTENTIAL TO BE CREATIVE AND ACCOMPLISH GOOD work. Helping groups to maximize their potential is one of the purposes of facilitation.

Some groups are like white water rapids, spilling over with exciting, somewhat chaotic energy and momentum. In such a group, your challenge as facilitator will be to provide processes to channel the group's energy to its best use. Other groups are like a still pond, quiet with little outward activity. For such a group, your work will be to get the waters stirred up a bit — using warm-up activities to generate energy and encouraging the participation needed for a group to identify important issues, clarify its goals, problem solve and make decisions. And still other groups are like a meandering river, winding here and there on its destination to the sea. Here your facilitation work will be to help keep the group on track so it doesn't use its energy in needless digressions.

In this chapter, we offer several suggestions for warm up activities, encouraging participation, keeping groups on track, and getting them back on track when needed. Some of the concepts in this chapter necessarily overlap with the previous chapter, *Chapter Six: Tools for Problem Solving*. There we described problem solving tools to fit various types and sizes of groups. If you don't find what you need here, check Chapter Six.

ENCOURAGING PARTICIPATION FROM START TO FINISH

People participate in groups when they have something to say, feel safe in expressing their ideas and opinions and are given opportunities for participation. Simple as that is to say, every facilitator knows there are many factors which influence group participation. For a fuller discussion of group dynamics see *Chapter Two: Knowing Your Group*.

GUIDELINES FOR MAXIMIZING PARTICIPATION

1. Begin by being participative in your planning: build desired outcome statements and an agenda with your client prior to the meeting.

2. Make meetings belong to everyone by giving away jobs: have participants bring refreshments, set up the room, keep time, record information, etc.

3. Give immediate positive feedback on participation. Acknowledge the value of all behaviors that serve the group, whether task or social behaviors.

4. Allow people time to think. Some people process information and questions more slowly than others. Where appropriate, ask people to write their ideas first and then discuss. *See Variations on Brainstorming in Chapter Six.*

5. Don't allow personal attacks to go without a response. Make sure that a distinction is made between the people involved in a problem and the problem itself.

6. Before the next meeting, or at a break, talk to individuals who aren't participating, and invite their participation. Try to identify an area of expertise or special perspective they bring that is crucial to the group.

7. If the group has some participants who dominate, establish a ground rule that everyone speaks once before anyone speaks a second time, or some similar rule that enables equal participation.

8. Separate the generation of ideas from the assignment of responsibilities. Just because Jennifer proposed a solution to the problem doesn't necessarily mean she should be the one to implement it.

> Separate the generation of ideas from the assignment of responsibilities

9. If the group as a whole is silent and various techniques don't increase participation, ask the group for its understanding of why there is no participation. Is it time of day, lack of understanding, fear of having to do more work? If this question fails to get a response, there is a good chance that something (mistrust, anger, fear) is present in the group to such a degree that no one will risk sharing in a group setting. One-on-one conversations might reveal the problem.

10. Remember that silence does not equal non-participation. A participant may be waiting to speak until she has a real contribution to make.

WARM-UP EXERCISES

There are a variety of exercises that help group members to get to know one another, break the ice, restore energy after lunch or illustrate a point. On the following pages we have described a few. The bibliography also offers suggestions for additional reading that will provide you with even more warm-up exercises.

EVERYONE WHO HAS EVER...

WHEN IT IS USEFUL:

- as an energizer
- as a way to help a group know more about its members
- groups from 8-40

HOW TO USE IT:

1. You will need a bean bag (Frisbee or other object which can serve as a base on the ground) for each person in the group.
2. This exercise is a second cousin to the musical chairs game you played as a child. Assemble the group standing in a circle. Give each person a "base" to put on the ground by her spot. You stand in the middle of the circle without a base.
3. Explain that whoever is in the center needs to think of something interesting, mundane, unusual she may have done in her life. The person in the center gives the instruction: "Everyone who has ever milked a cow change places." Everyone who has milked a cow (and is willing to admit to it) must change to a different base while the person in the center is also trying to find a base. The result will be that someone different will be left without a base and will become the person in the center.
4. The process begins again. The person in the center can choose any activity as long as she has actually done it herself.
5. The game can go on until everyone has been trapped in the middle or until you run out of time.

Note: In this, as in all introduction exercises, it is important to structure the exercise so that you respect the individual's right to control what and how much is disclosed.

GALLERY WALK

WHEN IT IS USEFUL:

- in group forming
- in groups from 8-20

HOW TO USE IT:

1. You will need a piece of flip chart paper for each participant and water color pens.
2. Ask the participants to draw an image or series of images which create a picture of who they are and what is most important to them. Reinforce that this is not an exercise about artistic talent, just an effort to use images to introduce themselves to one another. Do one for yourself quickly as an example for them showing trees and mountains for your interest in hiking, stick figures for the members of your family, books for your pleasure in reading novels and so on.
3. Give the group 5-10 minutes to work on their drawings. If you have the wall space to hang them up, ask the group to do so. Then walk around the gallery asking each person to introduce herself through her picture.

Note: In this, as in all introduction exercises, it is important to structure the exercise so that you respect the individual's right to control what and how much is disclosed.

NAME JUGGLE

WHEN IT IS USEFUL:

- early in group forming
- group size 6-25
- as an energizer after lunch
- to illustrate a point about how many balls everyone has in the air at once

HOW TO USE IT:

1. You will need a collection of tennis balls, bean bags or stuffed animals (anything small and soft that you can throw around), preferably as many objects as you have people.
2. Assemble the group standing in a circle. If the participants are wearing name

tags, have them put the tags on their backs or out of sight. Start with one of your throwable objects. Explain that participants are going to throw it around the group from one member to another until all participants have had a chance to catch and throw it once.

3. Each participant must call out the name of person to whom they are going to throw the ball before they throw it. The receiver must then thank the thrower by name.

4. In the first round, it helps to ask each participant to raise her hand after she has caught and thrown the ball to indicate that she has already had a turn.

5. Remind the participants to remember from whom they received the ball and to whom they threw it, because they will need to repeat that sequence. Try the first round. Make sure everyone has a turn, no one has it twice, everyone remembered to call out the name of the receiver and to thank the thrower by name.

6. Once the group has the system down, begin steadily introducing more balls into the system until the group has nearly as many objects in the air as there are people. It will be noisy and a little crazy, but if you set a tone of calm, steady attention the others will follow. Finally, you stop adding new objects and the last ones make their way around.

ORGANIZE BY BIRTHDAYS

WHEN IT IS USEFUL:

*   as an energizer after lunch
*   to help groups who are working on leadership or problem solving questions
*   in a group of any size

HOW TO USE IT:

1. Explain to the group that their assignment is to organize themselves by their birthdays. Give them no further instructions. You are intentionally giving them an ambiguous assignment. Birthday could be interpreted to mean year of birth, month or day of birth, or other variations. What you are actually asking them to do is to figure out how they want to define it and then implement that order.

2. Your job is to observe their process, looking for how leadership emerges, what roles different members of the group play, what processes they use, and so on. Debrief by asking them to reflect on their own process and, where helpful, sharing your observations.

PERSONAL ATTRIBUTE

WHEN IT IS USEFUL:

- to help a group get to know one another better
- as an energizer
- any size group

HOW TO USE IT:

1. You will need index cards or similar paper and a basket to collect the cards.
2. Ask everyone to write something about themselves that people are unlikely to know on a card. For example: I'm a certified underwater diver. I grew up in east Africa. I write poetry on the side, etc.
3. Then collect the cards in a basket.
4. Each participant draws a card from the basket and has to locate the person who wrote the card.
5. Participants sit down when they have found their person and have also been found.
6. After everyone is sitting, go around and read the information from the cards.

SOMETHING IN COMMON

WHEN IT IS USEFUL:

- early in group forming
- in groups where people know each other superficially
- in groups with conflicts

HOW TO USE IT:

1. Ask the group to break into pairs. Give the pairs 1-2 minutes to find something that they have in common which is not obvious. That they both wear glasses, have black hair or are women doesn't count; it must be something which requires discussion to find out. At the end of the time, sample a few of the results.
2. Then ask the pairs to join up with another pair to make a group of four. Give the groups 2-4 minutes to find something that all four have in common. Again, sample a few of the results.
3. If your group is large enough and you have time, try again in groups of eight.

Note: In this, as in all introduction exercises, it is important to structure the exercise so that you respect the individual's right to control what and how much is disclosed.

SORTING BY OPPOSITES

WHEN IT IS USEFUL:

- to help a group learn more about one another
- as an energizer

HOW TO USE IT:

1. Ask the group to sort itself based on a series of opposites which you pose to them. For example: Everyone who is a democrat run (or walk) to this corner of the room and everyone who is a republican run (or walk) to that corner of the room. Everyone who lives in the city to this corner. Everyone who lives in the suburbs or the country to that corner. Everyone with brown or hazel eyes and everyone with blue or green eyes, etc.
2. Controversial and topical divisions can be introduced into the exercise, allowing participants to acknowledge disagreements.

THREE BALLS

WHEN IT IS USEFUL:

- as an energizer after lunch
- in a group that is working on problem solving
- in a group where you want to emphasis thinking outside of the box
- in groups size 8-40

HOW TO USE IT:

1. You will need three balls or bean bags and a watch with a second hand.
2. Assemble the group standing in a circle. Explain that you are going to throw a ball or bean bag to a participant, who will then throw it on to another, until everyone in the group has had a turn. It helps if the participants raise their hands after they have had a turn so that the others can see who hasn't had a turn.
3. Remind the group that they are to be gentle in throwing and that they need to remember their sequence, since you will ask them to repeat that sequence each time they throw the ball around the group. Start the first round to get the sequence established.
4. Now tell them that you are going to add two more balls after the first one and

these must also be passed around the same sequence. Give it a trial run with the three balls, starting one after the other.

5. Now tell the group that you are going to time them to see how quickly they can accomplish the task. Remind them that everyone must handle each ball and that it must go in the established sequence. Start counting the time when you throw the first ball and stop when all three are back to you again. Tell them how long it took.

6. Ask if the group can cut the time in half. Start the process again. The group may ask you if they can move closer together or change places. The only rules that you have for them is that everyone must handle each ball and that it must go in the established sequence. If they need time to talk among themselves that is fine. Eventually they will be ready to try again. Time them again.

7. Now ask them if they can cut the time in half again. This will definitely generate some group discussion. They may choose some significant restructuring of how they are doing it. Everything is acceptable as long as everyone handles each ball and it goes in the established sequence.

8. Finally they will be down to a few seconds and you can call it off. Ask the group what its presumptions were about the "rules" in the beginning and what it took to reduce the times. It requires letting go of assumptions about the order they stand in, where they stand, what "touching" or "handling" the ball means.

THREE QUESTIONS IN PAIRS

WHEN IT IS USEFUL:

* in group forming
* as an energizer
* in any size group

HOW TO USE IT:

1. Ask the group to stand up and find a partner. If you have an uneven number there will be a trio.

2. Next explain that each pair has one minute to tell one another every living thing in their households from significant other, to plants and mold in the refrigerator. Keep it light and brief.

3. When the minute is up, ask them to change partners. This time ask them a question which is somewhat related to their work at hand and give them 2-4 minutes. For example, if they are nervous about the planning process they're working on ask them, "What is the most exciting, positive possibility that you think

the future holds for the organization?" They then have 1-2 minutes each to tell their partner their idea. Remember that this is just a short warm up exercise so keep the questions to something that can be answered quickly.

4. Ask the group to change partners again and ask them another question with some relevance to their work, again giving them 2-4 minutes. After you have finished, ask the groups to briefly report some of the ideas.

Note: In this, as in all introduction exercises, it is important to structure the exercise so that you respect the individual's right to control what and how much is disclosed.

THREE TRUTHS AND A LIE

WHEN IT IS USEFUL:

- in group forming when group members are ready to learn a little more about one another
- as an energizer
- in a group size 8-20

HOW TO USE IT:

1. You will need index cards or similar paper and pins.
2. Give each participant an index card or 3x5 piece of paper. Ask each person to write three things about themselves on the card in print large enough for others to read easily. Two of the things should be true, one should be false. Ask them to pin the card on like a name tag.
3. Now ask the group to circulate, pairing up with people to try to guess which one on the other person's list is not true. Ask them to continue circulating until they have seen every member of the group. Remember with an uneven number of people there will always be a trio.

Note: Here again, it is important to structure the exercise so that you respect participants' right to control what and how much they disclose.

METHODS FOR GENERATING DISCUSSION

Depending on the size and type of the group, the time of day, the stage of group development, different methods of generating discussion will be appropriate. It's good to have a spare method or two in your hip pocket in case the one you have chosen first doesn't invoke the depth of discussion needed.

DISCUSSION BY CATEGORIES OF PARTICIPANTS

HOW TO USE IT:

If there is a reason to do so, call on people by categories, e.g. employees with more/less than than five years with the company; supervisors or team leaders; union/non-union; men/women. Sometimes it helps these categories of participants to meet first to think through their perspective.

PROS AND CONS:

- It may draw out particular perspectives that would otherwise not have emerged.
- If there are different "power" levels present, it may encourage those who perceive themselves to have less power to speak out.
- It can create or reinforce divisions.
- People can feel put on the spot.

PRE-DISCUSSION QUIET TIME

HOW TO USE IT:

Give participants a few minutes to write down some thoughts about the topic, and then ask for their contributions.

PROS AND CONS:

- It gives each person thinking time, which is especially appreciated by introverts.
- It can make for a more thoughtful discussion.
- Some people — including the facilitator — may be uncomfortable with silence.
- It may quiet the energy of the group in a way that jumping right into the discussion wouldn't have.

QUAKER DIALOGUE

HOW TO USE IT:

Quaker Dialogue is a discussion method that promotes equal participation and careful listening. This method of discussion is useful when equality of participation is important or when group members need to listen to one another more attentively.

1. Explain the process and rules for Quaker dialogue: Anyone is free to pass; and no one comments on another's contribution until everyone has had a chance to speak. It might be a good idea to put a time limit on each person's speaking if you think long windedness could be a problem.
2. Go around the room offering each person the opportunity to give her thoughts on a subject without being interrupted or questioned.
3. Before opening the floor to questions and discussion, check with the people who passed during the first round to see if they want to speak.

PROS AND CONS:

- Each person is given an equal voice.
- When the members of the group don't seem to be listening to one another, this method encourages better listening.
- When individuals aren't participating, this gives them a way to get involved.
- A sense of the group often evolves from the collective comments of individuals.
- The process can get bogged down, especially with a large group, and thus drain energy.
- Some people are uncomfortable being in the spotlight.

SMALL GROUP DISCUSSION

HOW TO USE IT:

The whole group is divided into sub-groups. Each small group can address the same question or be given different questions. Often, each group appoints a "reporter" to relay the key points of its discussion to the whole group. A variation is that each sub-group comes up with a list of responses to the question and each group reads one item from its list before any group shares a second item.

Remember: the smaller the group the higher the percentage of participation you can expect. For example, in a two person group, 100% participation is almost guaranteed. In a five person group, participation may be considerably less.

PROS AND CONS:

- Usually the comfort level is higher in a small group, which leads to greater participation.
- This method gives everyone the opportunity to speak.
- The sound of people speaking in the room can energize everyone.
- The facilitator or leader can't be sure that the groups are on track.
- Self-oriented behaviors such as dominating or complaining can negatively affect the sub-group and are harder to confront in a small group.
- Groups complete their tasks at different rates.
- Reporting back can take a long time and can be tedious. To increase attentiveness, encourage reporters to give the highlights of the sub-group's discussion, not to read back everything the group developed.

WHOLE GROUP DISCUSSION

HOW TO USE IT:

The group is asked a question or given a problem to which anyone may respond. Generally it works better to ask an open-ended question (e.g., how could this problem be solved?), which invites longer responses rather than closed-ended questions (e.g., is this problem solvable?) which only require a yes or no answer.

PROS AND CONS:

- When the members of a group are engaged in the topic, this method of discussion is lively. Energy is created and a good product can result.
- The smaller the group, the more likely that everyone who wants to will participate.
- If members of the group don't participate voluntarily, or if some members dominate while others are silent, the energy of the group can be sapped.
- Because of time limitations, everyone may not have the opportunity to speak.

KEEPING GROUPS ON TRACK

> Being on track means the group is progressing toward its agreed-upon goal; it doesn't mean that every minute has to be regimented

Being on track in a group means that the group is progressing toward its agreed-upon goal. This doesn't mean that every minute of the meeting has to be regimented; there should be enough latitude for creative brainstorms and humor as well as the group's social needs.

There are several steps a group can take to ensure they are in agreement about the direction of their meeting:

1. Establish and get agreement on a clear agenda that has realistic time limits. Put the agenda on a flip chart or white board where everyone can see it.

2. Establish ground rules about discussions that aren't relevant to the agenda, additional agenda items that may crop up during the meeting and anything else that might take the group away from its task. Use the "parking lot" to capture these ideas.

3. Establish roles such as time keeper, break monitor, process attendant, etc.

WHEN THE GROUP IS OFF THE TRACK

The first step to helping a group get back on track is to analyze why they have gone off-track in the first place. The following questions investigate the major reasons groups get off-track.

1. Is the goal of the meeting clear? "If you don't know where you are going you're liable to end up somewhere else." — Robert Mager

2. Are the steps to reaching that goal clear? For example, do all group members understand the problem-solving process? See *Chapter Five: Understanding Problem Solving* for details.

3. Is the group avoiding a particular issue?

4. Is the group resisting the leader of the group, subtly wanting to undermine the leader or the meeting by sabotaging the agenda?

5. Are individuals within the group being undisciplined (or unconscious) about attending to the group's needs over their individual needs? Are people more focused on getting attention, story telling, etc. than on accomplishing the task?

GETTING BACK ON TRACK

Obviously, getting the group back on track will depend on your analysis of the situation. Here are some suggestions:

1. Physically point out on the flip chart agenda where the group is in terms of the agenda. Remind the group why it needs to be where it is. For example: "George, it sounds like you've made up your mind about how to resolve this problem. However, the group agreed to spend thirty minutes generating options. Please hold your solution until we get to that on the agenda; then we can take the time to hear your thinking in more detail." Such an intervention affirms the participant and also puts the group back to the appropriate place on the agenda.

2. If someone seems to be wandering off track, ask the person to relate her point to the topic at hand. For example, "Harriet, I'm not sure I see the connection between last year's sales goals and the company's environmental policies (the topic of the meeting). Could you explain the linkage for us?"

3. Ask the group if a particular diversion is helpful in moving toward goal. For example: "We didn't make time on the agenda to talk about the impact of a good environmental policy on company profitability; do you think it would be helpful to talk about that now? If so, what section of the agenda shall we take the time from?"

4. Name what you are perceiving. For example: "We've been trying to start this discussion for ten minutes without much progress. I get a sense that people are reluctant to talk about a downsizing policy? Am I right?" Or, more generally: "It seems like we're having a tough time sticking to the agenda. What's going on?"

CHAPTER EIGHT

PROMOTING POSITIVE COMMUNICATION

EVERYTHING THAT GOES ON IN A MEETING INVOLVES COMMUNICATION: LISTENING, expressing opinions, reporting information, questioning, decision making. The facilitator is the group's model, teacher and monitor of quality communication. It's easy to see then that communication is the bedrock skill for an effective facilitator.

SETTING THE TONE

First, a facilitator needs to create an atmosphere in which good communication can happen. Here are some ways to set the appropriate tone.

HAVE THE ROOM READY: Make sure the room is ready to go when participants arrive, or enlist the help of early arrivals. Include the following items:

- flip chart paper and markers
- chairs and/or tables arranged to encourage collaboration
- name tags or name "tents" ready to be filled in
- agendas, handouts, etc. ready to go

Having the room prepared gives the message that you know what you are doing and are taking the meeting seriously.

BE THERE TO GREET MEETING MEMBERS: When appropriate, make a personal connection with each person. This connection will give you information about who the participants are and will give them a chance to get to know you.

CREATE AND BE SENSITIVE TO THE TONE OF THE MEETING: Create a positive tone for the group at every opportunity: be sincere, upbeat and human. Pay attention to the mood of people as they arrive; you're likely to get helpful information regarding the attitudes of group members. For example, if you hear lots of grumbling about having to attend this meeting, mumbling about a waste of time, you will want to address that issue when the whole group is assembled. Say something like, "I heard some comments as you all were coming in that made me think that the time spent here needs to be very productive. How can we make sure that happens?" If people are arriving in a jovial mood, don't be too serious or formal. Conversely, if people are very tense and quiet, don't be flip. Your behavior will convey the message that you are paying attention to the nature of the group.

LISTENING SKILLS

There are two types of listening — non-verbal and verbal. Non-verbal listening involves using eye contact, body position, encouraging expressions and silence to convey your attentiveness and interest in what a person is saying. Verbal, or reflective, listening refers to the service you provide in reflecting back what the speaker has said and clarifying your understanding of what he meant. Most often you will use and encourage both ways of listening. It's important to remember that listening does not involve agreeing or disagreeing, giving your opinion (either verbally or non-verbally) or adding your story.

Note: We have moved away from the once-common terminology of "active" and "passive" listening, because our experience is that all facilitative listening requires active engagement.

NON-VERBAL LISTENING SKILLS

As implied by the title, non-verbal listening means the listener is not speaking back to the talker. Some of the components of a facilitator's non-verbal listening are:

GOOD EYE CONTACT: Generally speaking, maintain eye contact 70-80% of the time. However, it's important to remember that different cultures have different rules about eye contact. In some cultures, direct prolonged eye contact is considered disrespectful. Be sensitive to whom you are listening.

BODY POSITIONING: If you have been standing, sitting on the edge of a table or in a chair will convey a sense of equality. A relaxed posture is usually most effective. Avoid folding your arms across your chest — this is sometimes perceived as a defensive or "closed" body posture. Instead, place your arms comfortably on the armrest of the chair or rest them in your lap.

FACIAL EXPRESSIONS: Nodding and facial expressions have great impact on the person who is speaking. If you are uncertain about the impact of your facial expression, or receive feedback that you look irritated, bored, happy, etc. when you are not meaning to convey those feelings, you may want to watch yourself on videotape or practice in front of a mirror so that your intent is mirrored on your face.

ENCOURAGING EXPRESSIONS: These run the gamut from door openers such as, "Say more about that," "I'd like to hear…" to encouraging grunts such as, "Oh?!" "Ummm..." "Really?" "Ah...Of course" and so forth. These are to let the person know you are listening without breaking the flow of conversation.

SILENCE: Silence is an important component of facilitation. People often need time to frame what they want to say before speaking. A comfortable silence will often encourage the speaker to talk. As a facilitator, don't fear the "void" of silence.

VERBAL (REFLECTIVE) LISTENING SKILLS

Being a mirror is an important skill for the facilitator. Reflective listening is the process of reflecting back what an individual or the group has said in order to confirm your understanding and to allow them to hear what they have said.

Depending on the situation, you may choose to reflect back the literal content of the message, your perception of the meaning behind the content and/or the feeling expressed behind the content. Or you may need to ask a question for clarification. For example, Hallie says, "I'm tired of this whole process." You might reflect that back in several ways: "Hallie, you sound frustrated with the way this decision making process is going." Or, "Hallie, do you think this decision making process is taking too long?" Or, "Hallie, are you suggesting we take a break?"

HINTS FOR REFLECTIVE LISTENING

FEELINGS: Try to identify the feeling without either overstating or understating it. Don't worry too much, though, because if you miscalculate the intensity of the feeling, the speaker will almost always correct you. Remember to keep your own feelings out of your statement.

SUMMARIZE: At the end of a lengthy explanation or discourse, it is often helpful for the facilitator to "sum up" the gist of what the speaker has just said. Doing this helps everyone focus on what has just been said and promotes clear communication.

<u>TO SUM UP, REMEMBER</u>:

1. Paraphrase (not parrot) your understanding of the communication, including facts, and, when appropriate, feelings.

2. Hold back your opinions, reactions and evaluations of what the speaker has said. Remember you are a mirror for the group.

3. Listening is a very powerful tool. A good listener can help the speaker gain greater understanding of himself and even assist the individual or group in problem solving.

"YOU" AND "I" MESSAGES

"You" statements are door slammers; they shut off communication because they often leave the receiver of the message feeling threatened and defensive. This type of message places blame and increases tension, anxiety and guilt. "You" messages remove the ownership for behavior from the person speaking. They are ineffective because they label the receiver instead of describing the thoughts or feelings of the speaker; they put the receiver on the defensive; and they build distrust.

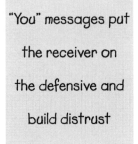

"You" messages put the receiver on the defensive and build distrust

Common "you" messages include the following:

*   Orders and commands: "Stop doing that!" " Get on with the agenda."
*   Blaming and name-calling: "You're acting like a jerk!" "You're driving me crazy!"
*   Threats: "If you continue pushing this idea, you will force me to withdraw from the committee."
*   Statements that give solutions but do not explain them: "You should forget about that idea."

> "I" messages promote positive communication and foster effective interpersonal relationships

"I" messages promote positive communication, which in turn fosters effective interpersonal relationships. They promote ownership by the speaker of his needs, wants, and feelings, rather than a projection onto the listener. As a facilitator, you want to do everything possible to steer people away from you messages and toward "I" messages. Model "I" messages whenever possible. Below are some examples:

- "I need a stretch break right now," rather than, "Anybody need a break?"
- "I'm frustrated by the lack of information," rather than, "Your committee did a lousy job of collecting information."
- "I am furious that the council didn't fund this project," rather than, "You all deserve to be recalled."

If you, as facilitator, are not hearing "I" messages, you can restate what is said or ask a question. For example, if someone says, "Your committee did a lousy job of collecting information," you might restate it: " Luis, you're pretty frustrated at not having the information the group needs here." Then remind people that it's helpful to the group to use "I" messages.

"I" messages are effective because:

- They place responsibility with the sender of the message. They reduce the other person's defensiveness and resistance to further communication.
- They provide information about the other person's behavior without evaluating it.
- They promote open, adult-to-adult communication.
- They build trust, create empathy, and facilitate understanding between sender and receiver and the whole group.

THE ART OF EFFECTIVE QUESTIONING

Asking questions so that you get useful, constructive answers is an art that is mastered through experience. It's important to know your own assumptions, values, and biases, so that they don't become obstacles to effective questioning, either through the words you choose or as reflected in tone or body language. In this section, we will consider four types of useful questions, and one type to avoid.

> Know your own assumptions, values and biases so they don't become obstacles to effective questioning

DIRECT QUESTIONS: Direct questions seek specific information. For example:

- When did the budget shortfall become evident?
- Is that your understanding of the problem?

If overused, however, direct questions may make individuals or groups feel they are being interrogated. Also, closed-ended questions, requiring only a yes or no answer, tend to shut down a discussion.

OPEN-ENDED QUESTIONS: Open-ended questions stimulate discussion and give more information about the issues to be addressed. For example:

- What are the problems that concern you?
- What is the background to this situation?
- You referred to an incident in the park. Could you say more about that?
- What would be the best possible outcome for you in this situation?

CLARIFYING QUESTIONS: Clarifying questions clarify the listener's or speaker's perceptions:

- I'm not sure I'm with you; do you mean....?
- Let me see if I understand you, you...?

- What's the difference between what's happening now and what you'd like to see happening...?

- First I heard you say you supported the idea; now I think you're saying you don't. Can you clarify your position for me?

PEEL THE ONION QUESTIONS: Peel-the-onion questions facilitate a deeper understanding of the feelings involved in a situation or discussion. The turning point in a tough discussion often comes when the parties start to tell each other how they feel. For example:

- You say you're frightened that an AIDS hospice might be located in your neighborhood. Can you say more about that? What frightens you?

 LEADING QUESTIONS: Caution! Leading questions attempt to align the speaker with the questioner, by using such phrases as:

- Don't you think....?
- Wouldn't you rather ....?
- You don't really think that's going to work...?

Such questions should be phrased more directly. For example:

- I think ending the meeting is a good idea. Do you agree?
- I think ending the meeting is a good idea. I hope you agree.
- I'd like to end the meeting now. Is that okay with you?

REFRAMING LANGUAGE

In an attempt to encourage participants to understand one another's points of view, facilitators can help by restating judgmental or blaming language used by participants into more neutral language. By reframing the problem to focus on the issues and removing judgmental statements, you can enhance the ability of group members to hear each other. For example:

> *By reframing the problem, you can enhance the ability of group members to hear each other*

GROUP MEMBER: "I put in hours of extra time doing what should have been Melissa's work. I can't believe she couldn't even show me the courtesy of a simple thank you."

FACILITATOR: "You worked hard to help Melissa out and are upset about her apparent lack of appreciation. What would be helpful for you now?"

Refocusing language is also appropriate when someone asks you a question which implies agreement. For example:

GROUP MEMBER: "Wouldn't you be mad if somebody said they were coming prepared to the meeting and then didn't?"

FACILITATOR: "Since I'm facilitating, I'll leave my opinion out of it. However, it seems as if it's creating a problem for you that those materials aren't here."

CHAPTER NINE

MANAGING CONFLICT IN GROUPS

CONFLICT IS A NORMAL, NATURAL PART OF HUMAN INTERACTION AND SOONER OR LATER it is part of virtually every group's experience. It is important to recognize that conflict has the potential to be very healthy for the group. Conflict, when acknowledged and dealt with in a positive manner, can clarify differences, increase the creativity of the group and build a strong team. On the other hand, if left untended, it can be damaging to the productivity and coherence of the group.

We define conflict as a problem that evokes strong feelings. A problem is a puzzle to be solved; a conflict is often a struggle for power and control. Understanding conflict and guiding a group in addressing conflict — rather than eliminating it — should be your goal as facilitator. Here are a few thoughts on conflict to keep in mind as we talk about managing conflict in groups.

> A problem is a puzzle to be solved; a conflict is often a struggle for power and control

SOURCES OF CONFLICT

Often, we jump the gun by trying to solve a conflict before we have identified its roots. In order to deal with it satisfactorily, it's important to understand what caused it in the first place.

Knowing the sources of a conflict will help you, as facilitator, name the conflict for the group and choose a strategy for working with that conflict. There is great power in saying to a group, "I am hearing that you have very different priorities for how to spend this money," or "You are naming different needs that have brought you to serve on this board."

Most complex conflicts will have their sources in several or all of the following categories:

MISCOMMUNICATION/MISINFORMATION: Miscommunication includes such dynamics as lack of information, inaccurate or assumed information, misunderstood information, inaccurate encoding or decoding of communication, and differing analyses of information. Examples of miscommunication in groups are: withholding of information; individual or group misunderstanding the communications of another individual or group; or different interpretations of the same data.

REAL OR PERCEIVED DIFFERENCES IN NEEDS AND PRIORITIES: Here we are referring to tangible needs such as competing demands for fiscal, material or time resources, as well as different priorities and methods for accomplishing tasks. This category also includes psychological needs, such as the need for security, competence, social acceptance or creativity. Examples of differences in needs include: different ideas about how to spend money; competing needs for access to a computer; differences between one group member's need for consistency and another's need for creative self-expression; or internal conflict within one's self between the need to be liked and to be competent.

<u>REAL OR PERCEIVED DIFFERENCES IN VALUES, PERCEPTIONS, BELIEFS, ATTITUDES AND CULTURE</u>: This is a broad and extremely important category that includes the totality of culture, personality, belief systems, etc. that form the lens through which we perceive and make meaning of the world. Examples of such differences include: attitudes about appropriate behavior within an organization; views about gender roles and capabilities, work ethics, etc.

<u>STRUCTURAL CONDITIONS</u>: Here we refer to situations where structures, whether physical, organizational or legal, are at the root of the conflict. This could include: lack of a clear task definition; unclear or missing descriptions of the role of members; physical distance between parts of organization; or regulations (terms of a labor management contract, ordinances, etc.).

 HINTS ON IDENTIFYING A VALUES CONFLICT

The words "should" or "ought to" will give you a clue to a values conflict. For example, if someone says, "He ought to know not to be late for this meeting," the speaker is describing her value system about lateness.

The greatest "heat" comes from values conflicts, because most people experience the clash of values and perceptions viscerally, as personal attacks rather than as interesting differences.

INTERVENING IN GROUP CONFLICTS

To respond to conflict effectively, facilitators need a variety of skills and strategies, many of which are described below or in *Chapter Seven: Promoting Positive Communication*, and *Chapter Ten: Interventions*.

> Conflict can be valuable as a way to clarify points of view

In every group it is important to acknowledge the value of conflict. Discuss with your group the fact that conflict can be valuable as a way to clarify points of view and to develop more creative products or services. You also want to affirm the value of — and right to — different opinions. It is natural that there are different opinions in a group.

When there is conflict in a group, it is important to be aware of it and then assess what steps to take. The following intervention process can be used, whether the conflict is within the entire group, among two or more members, or between you and group members. Note: This process is similar to the one described in *Chapter Ten: Interventions*.

STEP I: READ THE GROUP: Conflict may be indicated by lack of eye contact, distancing body language, leaden silence, a shift in behavior from actively participating to withdrawing, attacks, tension, not listening, sarcasm or accusations.

STEP II: DECIDE WHETHER THE CONFLICT IS IMPACTING THE GROUP: There may be a minor disagreement between two people that has surfaced but doesn't affect the group's performance. While you may decide to let this type of conflict go, generally speaking, conflicts should be identified and addressed.

STEP III: NAME IT: Mirror what you see for the group, being careful not to blame the group. For example, "The group was having a lively discussion until Bill made the comment about the budget. Then everyone got quiet. I wonder if there is some concern about the information Bill gave?"

STEP IV: CHECK YOUR PERCEPTION WITH THE GROUP: Ask the group, "Do I have it right?"

STEP V: MAKE OR ASK FOR RECOMMENDATIONS TO ADDRESS THE SITUATION: What you do will depend on the type of conflict. Here are some possible interventions:

- Acknowledge the value of conflict. Discuss the value of conflict as a way to clarify points of view and to develop more creative products/services and stronger organizations.

- Name the source of the conflict as you see it. Miscommunication, differences in needs or priorities, difference in values or beliefs and or structural conflict. Often it is an "elephant in the living room" that no one has dared acknowledge.

- Focus on outcomes and behavior, not values. In the case of a values conflict, help the group focus on the actual behavior or result they want, rather than on trying to change the conflicting values. While some might think everyone "should" dedicate their lives to the organization's fund raiser, the desired outcomes might be that the work gets done, that the needed money is raised and no one feels burned out afterwards.

- Use your ground rules. Refer to any ground rules that are relevant to the conflict. Examples of ground rules that support healthy conflict management include: one person speak at a time; attack the problem, not the person; people are encouraged to speak their truth; use "I messages" when giving opinions.

- Look for common ground. Help the group discover where it does share common ground as well as where there are differences. Examples of common ground: joint desire for a good working relationship; importance of the company turning a profit; serving customers; protecting children, etc.

- Affirm the value of and right to different opinions. Discuss that different opinions are natural in a group. Make sure the group separates the difference of opinions from personal attacks on the person holding the opinions.

- Name the area of disagreement precisely. Make sure you are focusing on the right problem or conflict. You may be surprised how many problems go away simply by a more careful definition. For example, instead of, "John and Lynn, you seem to disagree about flextime," say "John and Lynn, you seem to disagree about whether flextime is possible in the personnel department during first shift."

- Grab hold of an agreement and build on it. Listen for areas where people agree or suggest common ground and point it out to the group. For example, "I heard both Maria and Jeff say they were ready to work with the finance team. Who else is willing to do that?"

- Use the Aikido principle of moving with, rather than against, energy. Notice where an individual's energy or the group's energy is flowing and then move with it, rather than resist it. Reflective listening is one powerful way to do this.

- Take a break. When deadlocked, sometimes groups will benefit from a short change of scenery or a stretch. The mood can change dramatically after a break.

- Negotiate or mediate. Use the collaborative process described on the following page as a guide when there is conflict between group members or between you and a group member.

USING THE COLLABORATIVE CONFLICT RESOLUTION PROCESS IN GROUPS

The collaborative conflict resolution process involves these steps:

ADDRESSING CONFLICT: Determining whether to address the conflict in a group setting or privately with the individuals involved requires some analysis.

- Does the problem belong to the whole group? If so, address it with the whole group.
- Is the problem affecting the whole group? If so, name the problem to the group and ask the individuals involved whether they wish to address the conflict here or by themselves.

NAMING THE CONFLICT: If it is appropriate, name the conflict as you see it in tentative terms. For example, "Jake and Kate, you seem to have different views on this subject. I think it might be useful to take time to understand those different opinions." Or if the whole group is involved in expressing different opinions, you might say, "Everyone seems to have some strong opinions about flextime. Let's take time to make sure everyone has a chance to speak."

NEGOTIATING THE CONFLICT: If you need to guide two or more people through a negotiation process, use the following steps:

1. Explain to the group the process you'll be going through. You might even write the steps on a flip chart or easel.

2. Establish or reiterate the group's ground rules about each person having the opportunity to speak without interruption and making no personal attacks (i.e. focus on the problem, not the person).

3. Ask one person at a time to explain her view. "Jane, why don't you tell us your views about flextime." After she finishes, "Lynn, tell us your viewpoint."

4. Summarize, or ask the group to summarize, each person's major points. If appropriate, ask the group to add additional views.

5. After every party to the conflict has spoken, summarize the issues that exist, "After listening to everyone speak, I hear the issues as being that flextime should be fair to each person, that it should not interfere with serving our customers, and that we need to rotate coverage. Did anyone hear any other issues?" Of course, you can also ask the group to summarize the issues for you.

6. If appropriate, take one issue at a time and work with it until you have a group agreement. Then take up the other issues, one at a time, until all have been discussed. An often-successful tactic is to start with the issue that will be easiest to resolve, so the group can get a sense of its ability to resolve an issue. Then the group can build on its success.

Start with the issue that will be easiest to resolve so the group can build on its success

7. Summarize whatever agreement the group has made regarding the issues, including follow-up.

8. Mirror back to the group the good work it has just done.

ENCOURAGING OPEN DISCUSSION

Encouraging open discussion is a tool for building understanding and reducing the heightened emotions around differing opinions which often block listening. One of the challenges when there is a conflict is how to move from a "crossed-arm" position to open discussion. Following is an easy-to-use method when there is a difference of opinion between two people, adapted from training work done by the National Coalition Building Institute.

PROCESS FOR BUILDING UNDERSTANDING BETWEEN TWO PEOPLE

<u>STEP I:</u>   Person A states her opinion without interruption.

<u>STEP II:</u>   Person B restates what he has heard person A say, without adding anything.

<u>STEP III:</u>   B asks A questions to encourage her to explain why she has that particular opinion.

<u>STEP IV:</u>   Switch roles. B states his opinion without interruption.

<u>STEP V:</u>   A restates what she has heard person B say, without adding anything.

<u>STEP VI:</u>   A asks B questions to encourage him to explain why he has that particular opinion.

<u>STEP VII:</u>   Begin interactive discussion around the topic.

Note: Prior to the discussion, you may want to establish ground rules such as: let one person finish before another starts talking; challenge ideas, don't attack the person, etc.

ADDRESSING PERSONAL CONFLICTS IN A GROUP SETTING

Even conflict between two people can substantially disrupt a meeting. When you believe such a conflict is disruptive, it is important to address it. If the conflict seems to be just between two people, you might suggest the above process or ask if others in the group have concerns about the same topic. If the people involved don't feel it is appropriate to air their differences in front of the group, you might suggest that they agree to discuss it with each other before the next meeting and in the meantime agree to refrain from any jibes at one another. Or, as always, you can turn it over to the group to ask how they want to handle it.

Be aware that many individuals and groups are uncomfortable with conflict and will want to ignore or minimize it. If that happens, offer a "process education moment" reminding the group that the conflict has the potential to interfere with the efficiency and effectiveness of the group, and that there are positive ways to manage it.

PREVENTING UNNECESSARY CONFLICTS

> Unnecessary conflicts use up the time and energy of the group without producing a positive result

It is important to remember that much of the conflict in meetings is needed and healthy. As facilitator, you want to save people's energy for those conflicts by being skillful in preventing the unnecessary ones. Unnecessary conflicts are those conflicts which only serve to use up the time and energy of the group without producing a positive result. Examples of unnecessary conflicts are:

- Someone not bringing pertinent materials to a meeting. A phone call or e-mail asking that person to remember the materials would have prevented an unnecessary waste of people's time.

- An enthusiastic individual dominating the conversation because a ground rule was not established about equal participation.

- Group members being unsure what the role of their supervisor will be in the final decision making. A discussion at the start of the meeting about the extent of the group's decision making authority would clarify this.

Generally speaking, you can prevent such conflicts by doing a thorough job of assessment and preparation, and working with the group to be very clear about roles, responsibilities, ground rules, expected outcomes and decision making methods. The material in *Chapter Three: Getting a Good Start* and *Chapter Four: Designing a Great Meeting* provides detailed advice about preventing unnecessary conflicts.

How do you tell the difference between an unnecessary and a necessary conflict? If you have identified a conflict as being one that can be prevented and yet the group continues to give evidence of a conflict, you may need to help the group deal with a deeper issue. Look for unexpected reactions to what you think is a completed discussion.

For example, you and the group spend time discussing who has the final decision making authority in the group. The supervisor, Amanda, says, "I will go along with whatever the group decides about a vacation policy." You paraphrase, "so whatever the group thinks will work the best, Amanda agrees to implement." As you say that, you see one person rolling his eyes and another pulling her chair back from the table and looking out the window. Oops, looks like the group has just hit an iceberg! At this point a skillful facilitator would assess that there is some issue here to be probed...a necessary conflict to be addressed, possibly about the trustworthiness of Amanda's promise. Time for an intervention. See *Chapter Ten: Interventions*.

CHAPTER TEN

INTERVENTIONS: WHEN TO STEP IN

EVEN WHEN YOU HAVE DONE AN EXCELLENT JOB OF ASSESSING, CONTRACTING AND SETting up the meeting, you will undoubtedly need to intervene in the group's process at times.

An intervention is an action by the facilitator to bring about some change in the meeting process. Interventions can be extremely subtle or can be obvious to all. For example, shifting your gaze away from a talkative member toward someone who hasn't spoken may be all that is needed to equalize participation. On the other hand, you may need to say, "I notice that many people in the room haven't spoken. How about if we hear some new voices on this question?"

The goal of intervention is to keep the meeting positive, productive, safe and on task. Therefore, the facilitator needs to alter an unproductive situation in such a way that the group is maintained and, to the fullest extent possible, so that the individuals have their dignity intact and remain viable members of the group. It is also important to sort out what is distracting for you personally and what is affecting the group. For example, gum chewing may be irritating to you, but the group may not be disturbed at all. Unless the behavior keeps you from doing your job, it is not an appropriate place for an intervention.

METHODS FOR INTERVENING

Disruptions to a meeting's progress can come from two sources: (1) Group situations — for example, the group is tired, confused, off track, uncomfortable, dealing inappropriately with a conflict, needs a new process approach, etc.; and (2) Individual behaviors of group members — for example, individuals who dominate air time, attack other group members or the facilitator, refuse to participate, etc.

INTERVENING IN GROUP SITUATIONS

Here we are referring to those difficult, distracting or debilitating situations which prevent most or all of the group from accomplishing its task. The general method for intervening in a group situation is as follows.

STEP I — READ THE GROUP: Pay attention to changes in the group's energy or focus. When a usually enthusiastic group becomes silent or everyone is suddenly leaving to go to the bathroom, you are being given a message!

STEP II — CHECK WITH YOURSELF: Check to assess whether this is your issue or really a group issue. What are you feeling? Confused, tense, angry, frustrated? Where is your energy level? Is your reading of the group coming from something particular to you or is it an accurate reading of the group? The purpose of checking in with yourself is to keep from projecting personal issues onto the group. If you are exhausted from being up all night with a sick baby or are feeling lost and frustrated because of technical language the group is using, you can ask for help. However, it is helpful to know it's your problem, not the group's.

STEP III — NAME WHAT YOU ARE PERCEIVING: Mirror to the group the problematic behavior you are seeing. Use descriptive, not blaming terms.

STEP IV — CHECK YOUR PERCEPTION: Ask the group if your interpretation of the behavior is accurate.

STEP V — MAKE A RECOMMENDATION: Since you are the process expert, you should offer a suggestion for how to solve the problem, rather than ask the group what to do. If the group disagrees with your idea, or has a different suggestion, by all means go with what works for the group.

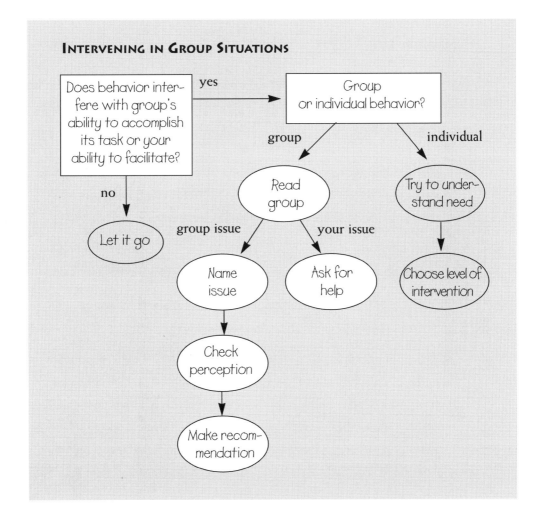

INTERVENING IN GROUP SITUATIONS

Does behavior interfere with group's ability to accomplish its task or your ability to facilitate?

yes — Group or individual behavior?

no — Let it go

group — Read group

individual — Try to understand need

group issue — Name issue

your issue — Ask for help

Choose level of intervention

Name issue → Check perception → Make recommendation

Case Studies

On the following pages are three examples of group situations and possible ways to intervene. These are offered to illustrate the use of the above steps; they are not meant to be the definitive way of intervening. Please remember that there is no "cook book" method for intervention in a particular situation. Your style, the group's dynamics and its stage of development will all affect the type of intervention you choose.

Case One: The Overwhelmed Board

SITUATION: A group of ten board members has been working hard for a day and a half on a strategic plan. It is after lunch on the second and last day of this board retreat.

STEP I — READ THE GROUP: You see people looking glazed, making no eye contact with you; several people are doodling. There doesn't seem to be much energy in the room.

STEP II — CHECK WITH YOURSELF: You are a little tired but feel the work is going well and that you've been doing a good job as facilitator.

STEP III — NAME WHAT YOU ARE PERCEIVING: "I'm noticing some drooping eye lids and people's attention being elsewhere."

STEP IV — CHECK YOUR PERCEPTION: "I'm wondering if people are tired and unsure how to accomplish the rest of this task in just a few more hours?" In the discussion that follows, there is group consensus that they are feeling overwhelmed by how much work it takes to develop a strategic plan. It is clear that they won't be done by 4:00 this afternoon.

Step V — Make a recommendation: "I'd like to suggest that we stop right now and look at the big picture — identify what you've accomplished so far and what is left to be done. Then we could develop a time line for accomplishing the remainder of the plan. How does that sound?"

Case Two: Recovering From a Dramatic Incident

Situation: An education task force that has been meeting over a period of six months is an hour into its monthly meeting when one of the members starts crying. She apologizes for disrupting the meeting, and tells the others that she just learned this morning that her brother has inoperable cancer.

Step I — Read the group: You see people are frozen. Your sense of the group is that this new piece of information has surprised and saddened the group, making it unable to focus on the work at hand. A couple of people say, "Oh, I am so sorry," but otherwise there is silence. People are looking to you, apparently for guidance.

Step II — Check with yourself: You are shocked and knocked off center by what has just happened.

Step III — Name what you are perceiving: "I think we are all stunned. Mary, what sad news."

Step IV — Check your perception: In this case, you probably would want to check your perception non-verbally, making eye contact with group members, looking for nods, etc.

STEP V — MAKE A RECOMMENDATION: "I'd like to suggest we take a brief break." At this point you would go to Mary and ask her if she would rather leave the meeting, take a few minutes as the group reconvenes to talk about her brother, or just continue the meeting. When the group reconvenes, let them know Mary's choice. Then acknowledge that it's hard to get refocused after such news. Ask if anyone needs to say anything before you continue, and when the group is ready, proceed with the agenda.

CASE THREE: THE OVERHEATED PUBLIC MEETING

SITUATION: A public meeting is being held about the future of the city's biggest park. Fifty people have come out to express their opinions. Despite ground rules, the tone of the meeting is getting louder and more contentious by the minute.

STEP I — READ THE GROUP: You hear voices getting louder and louder. Speakers have started to interrupt one another. There are a lot of hands waving and people verbally expressing agreement or disagreement with a speaker.

STEP II — CHECK WITH YOURSELF: You are worried that the meeting may get out of hand. You know you have trouble with overt expression of conflict. You want to be careful not to squelch healthy conflict, but you want to establish some order.

STEP III — NAME WHAT YOU ARE PERCEIVING: Standing to get people's attention you say, "Several people are talking at once. People are not honoring the ground rules."

STEP IV — CHECK YOUR PERCEPTION: "I think I'm right in saying that many of you feel very strongly about this issue and want your views heard."

STEP V — MAKE A RECOMMENDATION: "First, I'd like to review the ground rules and ask that you recommit yourself to them. Second, I'd like to suggest a way to proceed so that all voices get heard. It seems that we have four major groups: the neighbors of the park; those concerned about plant and animal life in the park; those who are involved in events held in the park; and those who use the park frequently. Have I missed any major groups? (If so, add them). I'd like to suggest that we take 20 minutes and have each group come up with a list of its top five concerns and appoint one person to explain your list to the rest of us. We'll then hear from each group and end this meeting with a half hour of discussion. Does anyone have an objection to that plan?"

INTERVENING IN INDIVIDUAL NON-PRODUCTIVE BEHAVIORS

By using the intervention model, you have already decided that the situation calls for intervention and is centered around an individual.

STEP I: Assess what the behavior is and what the person's underlying need might be that gives rise to that behavior. This doesn't mean that you have to be a psychiatrist. Remember that behaviors stem from needs, and the needs may be different from person to person. If you can address the underlying needs of the person, you may be able to gain his productive participation in the group.

STEP II: Decide what kind of intervention to make. Remember that interventions range from subtle to very obvious. Always begin with the minimum intervention necessary to succeed, increasing the level of intervention only as required. Your goal is to balance empathy and understanding for the individual with the needs of the group. If the two become irreconcilable, ultimately the primary goal is to serve the group.

LEVELS OF INTERVENTION WITH INTERACTIVE DIFFICULT BEHAVIORS

LEVEL ONE:

A. Ignoring the difficult behavior, treat the person's core idea as a legitimate concern, using whatever summarizing or reframing is necessary. If it is on target for the group's current work, integrate it into their work by recording it in the appropriate place or opening discussion on it. If it is off the subject, use the basket or parking lot to put off discussion to a later time. Often, validating a person's idea will reduce or eliminate disruptive behavior.

B. Approach the behavior obliquely by stating the problem in terms of your own need. For example, "I'm having trouble hearing the person speaking; it would really help me if only one person talks at a time."

C. If a ground rule exists regarding side conversations, another alternative is to point to the list of ground rules to remind the group. Without naming or directly interacting with the person with the difficult behavior, he will most likely get the message.

D. Naming the behavior in general, rather than pinning it on one person, can be effective. For example, "I'm seeing eyes rolling. Help me out — what does that mean?" If you do not get a response, you might offer your own theory on the behavior. For example, "I'm wondering if there is some concern about the amount of time this process is taking."

LEVEL TWO: If the behavior continues, name it. For example, "Joe, that is the second time you have raised that concern." Check that you understand the concern: "As I wrote on the flip chart, you are afraid you will have to work overtime. Does that express your concern accurately? Is there anything you want to add?"

LEVEL THREE: If the behavior continues, speak to the person privately during a break or between sessions. In a friendly tone, indicate what the behavior is and what effect it is having on the group. Ask for the person's cooperation in changing the behavior.

LEVEL FOUR: As a last resort, if the behavior is extremely disruptive and continues, confront the person publicly. If necessary, ask the person to leave if he can't stop the behavior. This level is very rarely used because it is counterproductive both for your relationship with the person and for the cohesiveness of the group.

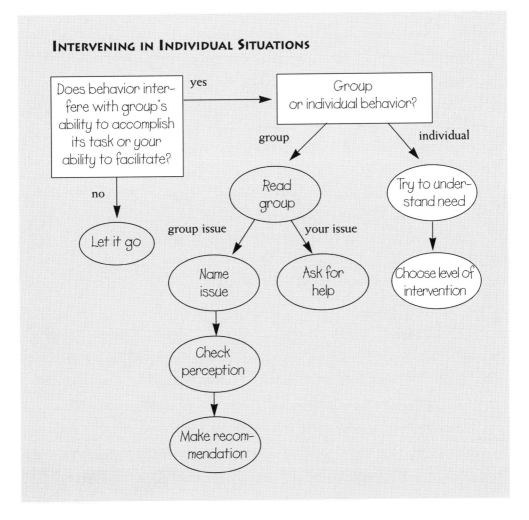

INTERVENING IN INDIVIDUAL SITUATIONS

CASE STUDIES

On the following pages are three examples of interventions with individuals. As before, these are offered to illustrate the use of the above steps; they are not meant to be the definitive way of intervening.

CASE ONE: UNDERCURRENTS OF HOSTILITY BETWEEN GROUP MEMBERS

SITUATION: You are facilitating a Quality Action Team meeting. There are undercurrents of hostility between Andrea and Jake. Jake rolls his eyes and sighs quietly whenever Andrea speaks. Andrea starts playing with paper clips whenever Jake speaks. You learned in your assessment that Andrea arranged to have Jake transferred from her area a couple of years ago because of personality problems. Prior to the meeting you asked each of them if they thought they could work together on this QAT and they both said yes.

STEP I: Assess what the behavior is and what the person's underlying need might be that gives rise to that behavior. The hostility from Jake's and Andrea's nervous behavior indicate that past conflicts have not been resolved.

STEP II: Decide what kind of intervention to make. Because you are unclear about how the group is being affected, you wait until the break to ask Andrea and Jake to speak with you. You decide to move to a Level Two intervention and describe the behavior you are seeing from each of them. Tell them that they need to resolve the tension between them if they are going to be contributing members of this QAT. You help them make a plan for resolving the tension. Then you ask that, for the remainder of this meeting, they stop their non-productive behaviors.

CASE TWO: THE PARTICIPANT WHO ATTACKS THE FACILITATOR

SITUATION: You are facilitating a workshop session on visioning for the VPs at the local hospital. At the beginning of the meeting, Dr. Hanes asked you what your credentials were for doing this work. She also asked if you had ever worked with hospitals before. You explained your training and experience and took the opportunity to explain the role of facilitator as process, not content, expert. About an hour into the meeting, after you have suggested using the hot air balloon visioning exercise, Dr. Hanes says to you, "You don't have a clue about the reality of hospitals." And then looking at the other VPs, she says: "I question the value of continuing with this consultant."

STEP I: Assess what the behavior is and what the person's underlying need might be that gives rise to that behavior. Dr. Hanes is attacking your credibility and trying to get the other VPs to agree with her. You suspect that she is uncomfortable with the visioning process and is looking for a way to end her discomfort.

STEP II: Decide what kind of intervention to make. You decide to use the Level One, Option D — treat it as a group concern. You say, "I hear some concern about my ability to facilitate this process. It is important that you have confidence in my ability. I'd like to hear any concerns you may have." After getting agreement from the group that you, in fact, are qualified to be their facilitator, you might need to call a break so that you can center yourself and get the meeting back on track. After the break, you talk about the challenge of and possible discomfort in visioning. You conduct a quick process check on the group's comfort level with what has gone on so far.

Case Three: The Nay-Sayer

SITUATION: You are facilitating a volunteer group which has been asked by the mayor to come up with innovative uses for a no-longer needed school building. One person, Geri, has started "yes-butting" other's ideas.

STEP I: Assess what the behavior is and what the person's underlying need might be that gives rise to that behavior. Geri is giving a reason why each idea won't work. You wonder if she is doubtful that the committee's results will be used.

STEP II: You decide to intervene on Level One, Option A: "Geri, you seem to feel that most of the ideas mentioned so far won't work. I'd be interested in hearing what innovations you think will work." If Geri gives some ideas, treat them respectfully and then suggest a ground rule that in the brainstorming phase, all ideas are welcomed. If Geri says that she thinks no one will listen to the committee's ideas, poll the rest of the group for their concerns in this area and then develop a plan for making sure their ideas are considered by the appropriate authorities. That plan may need to be in place before the group can brainstorm with enthusiasm. If the group does not share the concern, ask Geri what she needs in order to continue to participate.

CHAPTER ELEVEN

INTEGRATING GRAPHICS INTO YOUR MEETINGS

GRAPHICS REFERS TO THE VISUAL PRESENTATION OF THE WORK GIVEN TO THE GROUP OR developed by the group while you are working with them. It is your visual way of communicating, capturing their ideas, organizing their thinking, promoting clarity and understanding, summarizing thinking, capturing a record and even setting a tone for the meeting.

For example, when you begin the meeting, you have prepared in advance the desired outcomes and agenda on large sheets. The way in which you prepare those sheets will affect the clarity with which the information is understood, the sense of how organized or prepared you are, and the tone of the meeting.

Similarly, as you are recording information for the group and helping the group find its own understanding of issues, the use of graphics can promote clarity and understanding, add humor and organize thinking. It is important to be able to write clearly and to capture each person's idea, but using graphics reaches much further to showing concepts in a tangible way, to connecting ideas, to showing flow or direction of actions. Graphics can serve your group in a variety of ways.

WHY USE GRAPHICS?

The following list is adapted from work by Geoff Ball. Using graphics can:

- help group build a shared collective view and common language
- add visual stimulation to auditory input
- reduce complex notions to relatively simple images
- show patterns of interaction and relationships
- allow people to extend their short-term memories and provide an ongoing group memory
- prevent groups from getting fixated on just one idea

DIFFERENT WAYS OF LEARNING

People learn and take in information in different ways: visually, auditorily and kinesthetically. To accommodate these needs and make sure that everyone in a group is understanding clearly, you need not only to vary your facilitation methods but also to consider a variety of approaches to presenting information visually. For some, the narrative information on a list is the clearest, most understandable information. They need to see it written down. Others may not be able to visualize from the narrative text the relationship of one activity to another, or one level of the organization to another. They may require a graphic presentation of those relationships to be able to see it. Therefore, you will want to have a number of tools at your finger tips to find the ways which help all the members of your group understand the issue at hand. Keep in mind that it may require more than one technique to reach everyone.

> Find ways to help all the members of your group understand the issue at hand

The nature of the group will also impact the type of graphic techniques which will be most effective. Some groups need a lot of graphic symbols to reinforce the narrative ideas on the sheet: light bulbs for new ideas or realizations; groups of little figures to underscore teams of people working together, etc. It brings the ideas to life for them. Other groups might find the symbols silly or distracting. One group might need the familiar organization of an agenda set up like a matrix with times and tasks listed in order. Others might prefer a flow chart showing the movement from one section of the agenda to another. As always, the secret is to discover the techniques which serve your group most effectively.

> The secret is to discover the techniques which serve your group most effectively

FACILITATOR'S SUPPLIES

Depending on the nature of your facilitation project you may need only a few supplies or a whole bag full. You may arrange for someone else to provide the basic supplies, but it is always better to be over prepared than to find yourself without something that you need. The following list will give you an idea of the basic equipment.

PAPER

Flip Chart Paper: There are different qualities of paper. You will need to choose the one you prefer, balancing quality and price. The paper can be plain, 1" ruled or 1" grids. Check the backing card board if your stand does not have a solid back to write against. Some card board backs are sturdier than others.

Self-Stick Paper: These flip chart size sheets have adhesive across the top and can be attached to a surface, removed, then reattached. It saves on masking tape, but is tricky to roll up at the end of the meeting.

Dry Erase Sheets: There are erasable, reusable, dry erase sheets which attach to a surface via static electricity. They come in 20" x 30" and 27" x 34". You need to use dry erase markers.

Butcher Paper: This sturdy white paper comes in a variety of widths up to 30" in large rolls. You will need a paper cutter or a pocket knife to cut off the sheets. It is stronger than standard flip chart paper or newsprint and allows you to select any length you want.

Newsprint: You will need to call your local newspaper for availability of the end rolls of newsprint. When available, it is generally free. The paper quality is not great, but for situations where you need a lot of paper, the price is right. The cores need to be returned.

MARKERS: It is important to know the difference between permanent, water based and dry erase markers. For flip chart paper, look for water based (water color) markers. You will want a large supply with a variety of colors. Permanent markers will go through the paper onto the next sheet or the wall, so it's a good idea to avoid them. For white boards, which are often found in meeting rooms, you will need dry erase markers. For overhead projector transparencies you will need pens which are designed for that purpose.

SCISSORS OR POCKET KNIFE: You may need to cut sheets of paper, so scissors or a pocket knife can be a useful addition to your bag of supplies.

CHALK: For working on blackboards — still available in some meeting rooms — you will want to have white and colored chalk.

TAPE: You need high quality masking tape. Cheap tape will not hold or will rip off the roll which can be quite frustrating.

SELF-STICK NOTES: The large size sticky notes are useful for variations on brainstorming.

 STARS AND DOTS: These sticky dots can be used for multivoting or at other times when you want to highlight items.

EXTRA PENS AND PAPER: Sometimes it is helpful to have extra pens and paper for participants to use in exercises, small group work or for taking notes.

NAME TAGS: Even if the participants know one another, name tags will help you to learn their names and to address participants personally.

BALLS, BEAN BAGS OR OTHER TOYS: A number of the warm-up exercises call for various toys such as balls and bean bags.

STANDS: If you are carrying your own stand from job to job it needs to be portable yet sturdy. If you are looking for one which will live more permanently in a meeting room, you might want a heavier model with a solid back. Beware of plastic parts; they tend to break and are not easily replaceable.

THE BASICS OF RECORDING:

1. Title your pages. This helps everyone be clearer about the topic being addressed.

2. Number your pages. When it comes time to type up the group memory, you will be grateful for those numbers as you work to keep the pages of a long meeting in order.

3. Leave room in the margins and plenty of space in general. This allows you to add material later and makes for a cleaner-looking page.

4. Print, don't use script.

5. Vary the print size to EMPHASIZE an idea, but always print large enough and legibly enough to read. Experiment to find out if your writing is more legible in capital letters or small letters.

6. Separate, highlight and emphasize ideas and words with bullets, asterix, boxes, etc.

7. Use dark colored markers (black, blue, dark green, brown, purple) as the primary colors for text so everyone can see what is written. Lighter shades can be hard to read.

8. Use red, orange, pink, and other light colors for underlining, starring items, etc. Use yellow for highlighting only.

9. Alternate colors for different items — either line by line, or for different questions. It makes the pieces of information distinguishable from one another. People can then refer to the "green sheet" or the "blue statement."

10. Number or letter items — this gives people a shorthand way to refer to information: "I think #4 and #6 are saying the same thing."

11. Create a "group memory" by taping completed flip chart sheets in the order they're created to the wall so people can follow the development of information and refer back to previous discussions. Keep everything you have recorded visible to the group. This is also helpful to people who arrive after a meeting has begun. They can "read the walls" to catch up.

12. A rule of thumb is: letters should be one inch high for every ten to fifteen feet away people are from the writing.

13. Use drawings and symbols. Keep images simple: stick figures, arrows, circles, can convey a lot.

14. Give yourself permission to misspell.

15. Don't try to put too many images or words on one page — people tend to shut down when given an overload of information.

USING GRAPHICS TO ORGANIZE THINKING

One of the most important uses of graphics is to help organize the thinking of the group by showing the relationship among ideas, statistics, activities, actions or responsibilities. The graphic possibilities can vary from a pie chart which shows the segments of a budget to a twenty foot long process plan outlining all the meetings and activities for a two year project. Below are a number of formats for displaying information and organizing ideas. This is by no means a complete list, but it does illustrate a variety of possibilities.

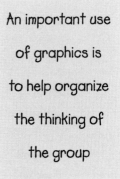

An important use of graphics is to help organize the thinking of the group

ORGANIZATION CHART: An organization chart is among the most familiar and shows the reporting relationships within an organization. It can show succinctly who reports to whom, how many people are within a certain department or how hierarchical or horizontal the organization is.

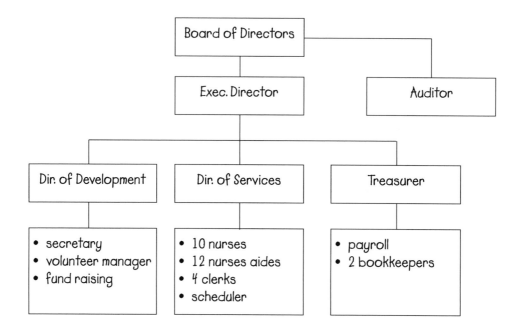

PIE CHART: A pie chart helps to show pieces of numerical information in relationship to one another and as a percentage of a whole, whether that is very specific information like the amount of the budget spent in certain areas, or more general like the percentage of the director's time spent in certain activities.

SOCIOGRAM: A sociogram depicts relationships within a group. It can represent subgroups whose members are very close, new members who are still isolated, and the levels of power. For example, the following group graphic shows a work team of eight people. There are three men who form one noticeable clique. One of them is the director of the department. Three other members have been on the team for some time and tend to stick together. One person doesn't seem to be a member of a group but is informally a leader. The eighth person is new and is still an outsider.

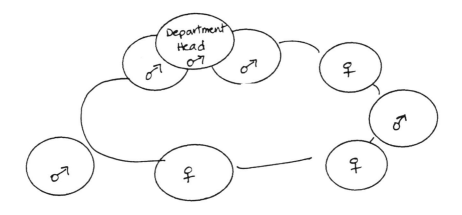

POSTER: A poster is like a billboard, condensing an idea into a visual image. It encourages people to convey the essence of something clearly, in a way that will reach other people. You can use it to do future visions, picture gallery introductions (*see Gallery Walk in Chapter Seven: Maximizing the Group's Potential*) or as a way to sum up the key learning at the end of a session.

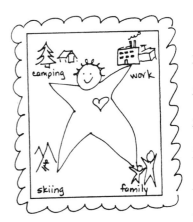

BRAIN MAPPING: Brain mapping is a graphic way to display the complex ramifications of an action, or the extended subsets of an issue as they branch out from the central issue, problem or question. See Brain Mapping in *Chapter Six: Tools for Problem Solving.*

Implications of Layoffs

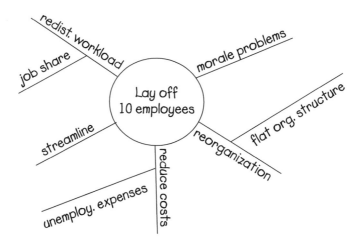

VISION MAP: A vision map is an inspiring way to show where you are, and the path leading to where you want to go. Or the map can simply show the desired future, moving from the most detailed and tangible to the most intangible aspects of the desired future.

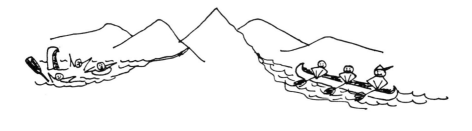

FLOW CHART: A flow chart shows movement and direction. It is a useful way to show the steps in a process, whether a production line, an agenda, or the steps in getting a book published. A process design is a form of flow chart.

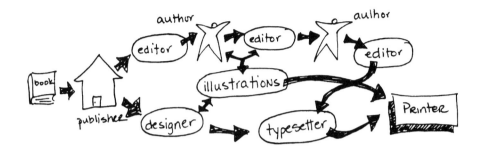

SYMBOLS AND IMAGERY: Sometimes lists of words, no matter how colorful or graphically well arranged, are just not enough to make a concept real or to effectively communicate the feeling around the idea or issue. For clarity, emotion, emphasis or humor, it can be useful to liven up your flip charts with symbols or images which convey a message or an idea. A symbol can add a level of emotion to a concept that the printed word can seldom evoke. For example, to write "team work" on the list of key elements in your company vision does not evoke the same response as the graphic at right:

There are endless graphic possibilities, limited only by your imagination and the tolerance of your group. It does not require artistic talent to master a few basic shapes and forms. Stick figures, houses made of boxes and triangles, suns with big spokes of light, all the things you drew and loved as a child will do just fine. The goal is to suggest a feeling or an idea in a short lived record of a meeting, not to create museum quality art works.

Below are a few samples. Take time to practice drawing simple graphics so you have a ready reservoir when you are facilitating. Doodle away!

People

Groups   Partners

Expressions

sunshine   idea   t.v. media   research

board of directors   community   government

arrow   bridge   breakthrough

CHAPTER TWELVE

REFLECTIONS ON THE ART OF FACILITATION

IN THE FIRST ELEVEN CHAPTERS OF *GREAT MEETINGS!* WE HAVE GUIDED YOU THROUGH the practical aspects of facilitation. We trust that, by now, you share with us the view that facilitation is an art; and like any art form, can manifest in countless ways, but is best executed with polished technical skills. Because you, the facilitator, are the instrument, the medium through which the group accomplishes its goals, we want to end by reflecting on some essential questions that every skillful, ethical facilitator should consider — and return to regularly.

KNOWING YOUR OWN ISSUES

Everyone has issues of his own, issues which are triggered by certain situations, particular vocabulary, types of people, or specific behaviors. Your reaction may be anger, defensiveness, withdrawal or acute discomfort. You may be reduced to tears or to the powerlessness of a child. It is not our purpose here to diagnose why these reactions arise or to resolve them. However, it is important to recognize their existence and to understand how they can affect you when you are facilitating. If you are thrown off base by a behavior which triggers one of your issues, you will have a hard time staying neutral toward that person, focusing your concentration on the task of the group or even maintaining your composure.

For example, if an older man in the group challenges your handling of the meeting and uses the same derisive phrase that your father often used and this is a lingering issue for you, it is likely to provoke a strong reaction. The reaction may be angry defensiveness or may be a complete erosion of your self confidence, but either way it will greatly diminish your ability to serve the group.

The first step in maintaining your effectiveness in these circumstances is to identify in advance what your particular issues are likely to be and, thereby, be prepared for them. Take the time to make a list of the situations, behaviors, personality types and/or vocabulary which provoke strong reactions in you. Make your own assessment of why that might be.

> Recognition goes a long way to diffusing the intensity of your reaction

Think of comments that you can make to yourself to regain your balance or to disassociate the immediate situation from the source of your emotional reaction. Be able to say to yourself, "Oh, I'm having a reaction to the word 'chick' because that's how boys used to make fun of me in high school. But this isn't high school, and I'm feeling fine about myself." Recognition goes a long way to diffusing the intensity of your reaction.

The purpose in this discussion is not to provide a source of personal therapy, but simply to help you serve the group you are facilitating as effectively as possible by not letting your issues knock you off track.

STAYING GROUNDED

The first part of staying grounded is to recognize and anticipate your own issues. But there are other things which can distract or disorient you while you are facilitating. It could be an angry attack directed at you or someone else in the group. It could be that you've made a mistake in choosing the process tool so that the group is bogged down — and so are you. You could simply be tired or lost yourself. Anything which affects your concentration on the group will require that you reground yourself. There are several methods you can use, depending on the nature of what is breaking your concentration.

TAKE A BREATH: Just taking a few seconds to breathe deeply will give you time to regroup. This is particularly useful when a sudden outburst or event has occurred. It gives you time to find your center or to think before you respond.

PLANT YOUR FEET: By spreading your feet a little ways apart and putting your weight evenly over them, you will literally and figuratively regain your balance when something has knocked you over.

ASK A QUESTION: If a rambling or off track comment has broken your train of thought, ask for clarification. "I'm confused. Where are you going with that thought?" Or, "I've lost track of where we are. How does your suggestion tie in?"

TAKE A BREAK: You may need a minute to reconsider the process you are using, to regain your composure or to recharge your energy. It will be time well spent if it helps you work more productively or find a better approach to the situation.

TALK TO YOURSELF (SILENTLY!): Identifying for yourself what is happening will help you let go of it. "I'm getting nervous because the woman in the blue shirt looks just like my fifth grade teacher who terrorized me. But she is really completely different and actually smiles very pleasantly."

Finding Your Own Definition of Success

Ask yourself if you helped the group do everything it could to generate a product which worked for them

How do you measure success when you are facilitating for a group? The purpose of using facilitation skills in designing and facilitating a meeting is to help the group to achieve the most useful or effective product that it is capable of generating. It would be a mistake to evaluate the success of your facilitation efforts by trying to decide whether or not the group's product was "good" or by taking responsibility for the content of the group's work. Instead, ask yourself if you helped the group do everything it could to generate a product which worked for them or if you helped the group work better together.

The content of the decision, solution or plan created by your group is their responsibility. You may have your own thoughts on the quality of the content or on whether or not the solution is the best one, but you are not in charge of the content. If you are comfortable that you have provided the group every opportunity to look at the question cogently, have given them opportunities to generate as many creative options as possible, have used techniques to make the group as productive as possible, have designed a logical, sound process, then you have been successful with that group.

Ethical Considerations: Knowing When to Say No

The work we do in facilitation has the potential to deeply impact the lives of those with whom we work. Therefore, we believe it is of great importance to do our work with integrity. When you consider taking a facilitation assignment, there may be occasions when, for the good of the group or to take care of yourself, the best thing you can do is say no. The following questions provide guidance in considering ethical and personal reasons for declining facilitation opportunities:

1. WHAT IS THE POSSIBLE HARM THIS FACILITATION COULD CAUSE? Does the potential reward outweigh the potential risk of harm to my client or to myself? There are situations in which a facilitated meeting will cause more harm than good. Issues may be exposed that the group is not ready to deal with. Management may already have decided not to follow through on a group's recommendations. Topics are being discussed in the wrong forum. An alert and ethical facilitator will raise these concerns during preparation for facilitation. If you believe that facilitation is not what is needed, you need to let your client know your views. Even if you aren't skilled in knowing what should be done, trust that quiver in your stomach that this isn't a situation for facilitation.

2. WHAT ARE THE LIMITS OF MY ABILITY? Do I have the skill to facilitate this situation effectively? Whether it is lack of knowledge about the subject area (remember content literacy, not content expertise is what you need), concern for the level of conflict in a group, or the size of the group, each of us needs to know and acknowledge our areas of strengths and weaknesses in facilitation. A facilitator should never make it harder for a group to function or accomplish its task.

3. DOES ANYTHING I AM BEING ASKED TO DO COMPROMISE MY VALUES OR BELIEFS? If the task of the group runs counter to your values or beliefs, then you should discuss that concern with your client and, if necessary, decline the invitation to facilitate. If the participants are being coerced into attending, or if the meeting is a thinly veiled attempt for someone to put forward his own agenda, consider disassociating yourself from the project. Saying no to such a project will maintain your own credibility and untarnished reputation as a person who supports healthy group process.

4. IS NEUTRALITY AN ISSUE? There are several aspects of neutrality to consider. The first is your own ability to be neutral. If you can't be neutral because

you have strong feelings about the content of the facilitation; if the facilitation involves people with such close personal ties to you that it would distort your handling of the matter; or if you have such a strong personal response to someone in the project that you don't think you can treat him objectively, the ethical response will be to turn down the facilitation opportunity. The second aspect is others' perception of your neutrality. Although you may feel confident that you can be neutral in your facilitation, others may not see you as neutral. Such a perception could come from past work you have done, the church you attend, your physical appearance or any other of a number of sources. Nonetheless, the groups' perception is their reality. Therefore you either need to put to rest their concerns about your neutrality or decline the facilitation.

> Preparation takes time, and without it you will have difficulty serving the group well

5. <u>Do I have adequate time to prepare for and facilitate this meeting?</u> Time is another issue which may prompt you to say no. One of the great risks is to fill your calendar with meetings which you have agreed to facilitate, whether for hire or within your organization, and find that you have forgotten to schedule any time for the necessary preparation, planning and design work. Preparation takes time, and without it you will have difficulty serving the group well. If you can't find the time to do the preparation work, you need to seriously consider saying no to some of the facilitation requests.

The bottom line in good facilitation is serving your group well. Knowing yourself, your gifts and your limits, will help you to choose those situations where you can be most effective and to serve well.

"You, as a...consultant, are in a position of power, simply by virtue of your role. You need to be sensitive to the fact that people will have different expectations of you than of anyone else in the consulting situation. You are responsible for yourself and the effectiveness of your own helping behavior; you are not directly responsible for the behavior or learning of others. Motivation and caring are critical final determinants of ethical behavior: a good rule might be that if you cannot say 'no' to a proposal, you should not say 'yes.' In the end, a decision based on your sincere concern for people is likely to be an ethical decision."

J.W. Pfeiffer and J. E. Jones "Ethical Considerations in Consulting,"
1977 Annual Handbook for Group Facilitators, University Associates.

CONCLUSION

Facilitation is an art, not a predictable, mathematical science, nor a formula to be memorized and repeated. It is an art that we continue to perfect and improve throughout a lifetime. Hopefully, this text has given you many helpful suggestions, useful tools and frameworks for understanding the art of facilitation. Practicing, gaining experience, trying new ideas and observing other people at work are the steps which will enrich your practical skills. Every time you work with a group you will learn something new that will impact the way you deal with the next group.

Our enthusiasm for sharing these practical suggestions for effective facilitation is based on our profound belief that bringing people together will result in a better, more thoroughly considered decision than any one of us could make on our own.

Good process design and facilitation is what helps groups to succeed at the hard work of making those decisions. It enhances the quality of the result and the satisfaction of the people involved.

Most of all, remember that meetings do not have to be boring, frustrating and ineffectual. With your various skills, tools and techniques, your big ears for listening and big heart for compassion, your watercolor pens and flip charts, you can bring excitement, creativity and success to your meetings!

READING & RESOURCES

- Adams, James L., <u>Conceptual Blockbusting: A Guide to Better Ideas</u>, W.W. Norton and Co., New York, NY, 1979.

- Avery, Michel, et. al, <u>Building United Judgment: A Handbook for Consensus Decision Making</u>, The Center for Conflict Resolution, 731 State Street, Madison, WI 53703, 1981.

- Auvine, Brian, et al, <u>A Manual for Group Facilitators</u>, Center for Conflict Resolution, 731 State Street, Madison, WI 53703, 1978.

- Bradford, Leland, <u>Making Meetings Work: A Guide for Leaders and Group Members</u>, University Associates, San Diego, CA, 1976.

- Doyle, Michael and David Straus, <u>How to Make Meetings Work</u>, The Berkeley Publishing Group, 200 Madison, Ave., New York, NY 10016, 1976.

- Heron, John, <u>Group Facilitation: Theories and Models for Practice</u>, Nichols Publishing Co., East Brunswick, NJ, 1993, 908-297-2862.

- Kaner, Sam, et al, <u>Facilitator's Guide to Participatory Decision-Making</u>, New Society Publishers, Philadelphia, PA, 1996.

- Kayser, Thomas, <u>Mining Group Gold: How to Cash in on the Collaborative Brain Power of a Group</u>, Irwin Professional Publishing, Burr Ridge, IL, 1995, 1-800-634-3961.

- Kearny, Lynn, <u>The Facilitator's Toolkit</u>, HRD Press, Amherst, MA, 1995, 1-800-822-2801.

- Napier, Rodney and Matti Gershenfeld, <u>Making Groups Work: a Guide for Group Leaders</u>, Houghton Mifflin Co., Boston, MA, 1983.

- Pfeiffer, William, John E. Jones, Leonard Goodstein, <u>The Human Resource Development Annual Set (Annuals for Group Facilitators 1975-1995)</u>, Pfeiffer and Co., 2780 Circleport Drive, Erlanger, KY 41018, 1-800-274-4434.

- Rohnke, Karl, <u>The Bottomless Bag Again</u>, Second Edition, Kendall/Hunt Publishing Company, 4050 Westmark Drive, Dubuque, Iowa 52002, 1994.

- Schindler-Rainman, Eva and Lippitt, Ronald, <u>Taking Your Meetings Out of The Doldrums</u>, University Associates, La Jolla, CA, 1975.

- Schwartz, Roger M., <u>The Skilled Facilitator: Practical Wisdom for Developing Effective Groups</u>, Jossey Bass, San Francisco, CA, 1994.

- Sibbet, David, <u>I See What You Mean - Visual Tools for Working Together</u>, <u>Pocket Pics - Difficult Concepts and Fundamentals of Graphic Language</u>, all available from Graphic Guides, Inc., 832 Folsom Street #810, San Francisco, CA, 1-800-494-7683.

- Tuckman, Bruce, "Developmental Sequence in Small Groups", Psychological Bulletin 63, vi 1965.

ABOUT THE AUTHORS

DEE KELSEY has been facilitating groups since her Girl Scout days. In the 1970s, she turned her early interests into more formal work both as a trainer and personnel representative at Hewlett Packard and as a mediator for the city of Palo Alto, California. Since 1985, as principal of Dee Kelsey and Associates, Portland, Maine, Dee has provided organizational development, facilitation, process consultation, mediation, and training services to hundreds of clients ranging from small work groups to large corporations. She is the proud mother of Emily, who offers daily lessons about negotiation, facilitation and love.

PAM PLUMB discovered during her years as a City Councilor and Mayor that managing meetings and conflict management were her true calling. Since leaving local politics, she has created Pamela Plumb & Associates which serves a wide range of non-profit, business and government organizations with process design, facilitation, training, conflict management and organizational development. She lives and sails in Maine with her husband Peter and tracks the lives of her grown children from one end of the globe to the other.

Dee and Pam have in recent years enjoyed collaborating on a variety of projects. Together, they created the Certificate Program in Facilitation for the Center for Continuing Education at the University of Southern Maine in 1993 and have taught the course ever since. They have developed several other courses including three training programs for the Governing Skills Program of the Maine Municipal Association and customized facilitation trainings for various businesses and organizations. They have even found the rigorous process of writing and rewriting *Great Meetings!* together to be a pleasure.